# THE IMPERIAL RUSSIAN NAVY

FRED T JANE

[*Photo by favour of H.I.H. The Grand Duke Alexander of Russia.*

THE BATTLESHIP ROSTISLAV.

(*The Grand Duke Alexander is at present Captain of this ship.*) [*Frontispiece.*

# THE IMPERIAL RUSSIAN NAVY

FRED T JANE

CONWAY
MARITIME PRESS

First published 1899
This impression, reprinted from the fully revised 1904 edition, published 1983 by Conway Maritime Press Ltd, 24 Bride Lane, Fleet Street, London EC4Y 8DR

ISBN 085177 295 1

Printed and bound in the United Kingdom by
The Thetford Press Ltd, Norfolk

TO

MONSEIGNEUR HIS IMPERIAL HIGHNESS

GRAND DUKE ALEXANDER MIHAILOVITCH

OF RUSSIA

CAPTAIN, IMPERIAL RUSSIAN NAVY

TO WHOSE KINDNESS IT IS DUE THAT

I AM ENABLED TO DESCRIBE MUCH OF

WHAT IS SET DOWN IN THESE PAGES

CONCERNING A NAVY

OF WHICH INCREASED KNOWLEDGE HAS

LED TO INCREASED ADMIRATION

# PREFACE TO SECOND EDITION

IN preparing for the Press the new edition of this book, which events in the Far East have called for, I have, so far as possible, retained the descriptions of my visits to Kronstadt and other Russian dockyards as they first appeared. The same applies to various other impressions; for though I would not bind myself to adhere to them too absolutely now, they appear to me to have greater value *qua* impressions on the spot than as opinions.

So far as possible, therefore, I have only laboured to bring the book completely up to date as regards *matériel* and *personnel*, deleting in the former matter that, owing to changes in design and so forth, is no longer applicable.

Perhaps the most important new subject matter is that dealing with the *personnel* as it is at the present day. It is the result of careful observation on board several of the most modern Russian warships since this book first appeared. Most of the old text on this question I have left as it stood, because left thus it is a more valuable index to the increase Russia has made in efficiency.

When this book first appeared, several things in

it were criticised. My spelling of Russian names was one. I have not, however, thought it worth while to effect many changes here—the subject is one in which much latitude is taken by all. As a point of minor interest I may mention that part of the seeming inaccurate spelling is due to the curious fact that it is, or was, fashionable in Russia to give a slightly English twist to pronunciation. Thus Peresvet quite correctly is *Peresviert*; but naval fashion decrees that the ship shall be pronounced *Peresvēēt*. Similar instances exist in all navies; in the British, for example, no one would pronounce "Sanspareil" as it would be done in France or in ordinary shore life. And though *Ingliski*, as I have written it, is totally incorrect, I have preserved it as it reproduces the sound to my mind better than when rendered with an "A" and the more grammatical terminal.

One much criticised statement in the first edition was that I "could not ascertain exactly to whom Galernii Island Yard belonged." *Qui s'excuse, s'accuse.* I ought to have left it at that and not gone on to explain why! However, I am still in the dark on this point; for it still appears to remain a "private yard owned by the State."

The British, and perhaps also the American, view of Russia to-day is that of a country whose political assurances are not worth the paper on which they are written. Therein lies the real crux of the Far Eastern problem, and there must it always lie.

With the making of the Anglo-Japanese Alliance, the first step of the great coming struggle between the Anglo-Saxon and the Slav has been irrevocably taken ; for good or evil we must now see it through. When this book first appeared Russia was a potential ally—she is now the enemy in all but the letter. Pleas for an Anglo-Russian Alliance made in the first edition are now, therefore, out of date. Still I have left them substantially as they stood : for though we have taken one road it may not be amiss to see the other in the light in which the Russians would have had us see it. But as the Anglo-Slav conflict was perhaps ever inevitable, it may well be that we have taken the wiser course in making no attempts to delay that inevitable.

It is not the province of this book to discuss the matter at length. But the situation gives an added interest to all that pertains to the Russian fleet and the great developments that during the last ten years have characterised it—not only in ships and men, but in efficiency. During the last year or two this progress has been more especially marked. And chiefly it is due to that Grand Duke to whom five years ago I dedicated this book—the Hasdrubal of Russia, perhaps. He it is who is at the head of the movement that aims at making Russia the premier power of the world. With her immense bulk and her enormous armies, it may well be in the womb of the future that Russia will overrun all the continents. Between her and full realisation stand the fleets of the island empires, Britain, Japan, and perhaps the United States, for it is hardly possible that America will always be able to pursue an outside, unmolested course. To beat those fleets is one of Russia's distant ideals. To demonstrate how she is diligently, and to a great extent without attracting much attention, working towards that ideal is the primary object of this book.

F. T. J.

*January*, 1904.

## PREFACE TO FIRST EDITION

THE object of this book is to give as fully as possible the essential history of the Russian Navy in the past, a full and detailed account of the Navy as it is, and, finally, to include all those side questions which, though not directly naval matters, are yet intimately connected with the Russian sea service.

Here and there critical readers may discover gaps, or at least a difference in perspective to what they may be inclined to look for after a course of reading about the British or American Navy. As this book claims to be fully complete, it is due to myself, and possibly to the reader also, to make some specific references to these gaps here. In particular I might draw attention to the almost total absence of "budget" and monetary statistics. These are purposely minimised; the reason being that such figures are well-nigh valueless, in some ways worse than valueless. For not only does the cost of production differ in every country, so that comparisons of sums of money mean next to nothing, but the cost of warship construction also varies from year to year. A million spent to-day has no relation to half a million spent some years ago. It may be double; it may equally well be half. Ships to-day need many things that they did not require ten, or even five, years ago, and statistics of expenditure upon war material are useful to no one except financial politicians. Consequently expenditure is a good deal shelved in this book.

Another point is that though *matériel* is most fully and amply dealt with, I have laid the greater stress upon the *personnel.* Here again a practical reason is at the bottom of the matter. It is a saying in the British Navy that "one ship which has been a year or so in commission is worth three of her sisters just mobilised." Broadly speaking this is true, and it is an instance of how much more important than the ship are the men on board of her.

For the rest, the order of arrangement followed is that which appeared most logical—a so far as possible strictly chronological one.

As everyone has his own rendering of Russian spelling, and as of many ships several widely different spellings are in existence, the more popular forms of spelling are here and there adopted. As a general rule, however, the correct more or less phonetic spelling suitable for the English language is also introduced.

The name Ksenia—Xenia, or Zenia—is a case in point, the first being a Russian spelling, the last an English adaption. When possible the phonetic sound is indicated by the use of accents over the vowels in order to avoid an ugly appearance. Rŏssīa and Sĕvastôpol are names in point.

The matter is not one of supreme importance, and

is only drawn attention to because in a number of cases the usual English pronunciation bears no relation at all to the Russian one. When such a simple name as Rossia is spelt in English (as it occasionally is) "Rossija," and recklessly pronounced "Rossyjar," one may well acquit the Russian officer who told an Englishman that they had no such ship in their Navy.

The substance of the chapter on Anglo-Russian relations, though some definite alterations have since been made, appeared serially in the *Daily Chronicle*, and most of the sections relating to Dockyards were published in the course of a series of articles in the *Engineer*. To the proprietors and editors of these newspapers I desire to tender my thanks. I am also indebted to the *Engineer* for the loan of certain blocks. Most of the plans and two or three of the illustrations of vessels are taken from *The Jane Naval War Game*, or from *All the World's Fighting Ships* by courtesy of the publishers, Messrs. Sampson Low, Marston, & Co.

I owe it chiefly to the great kindness of His Imperial Highness Captain the Grand Duke Alexander Mihailovitch of Russia that I am in a position to write at all this book about the Navy of a great nation.

I am also deeply indebted to Herr C. G. Björkman of Stockholm for his kind and untiring assistance, by means of which I have secured the interesting historical matter in the Appendix. Others to whom I chiefly owe thanks are Mr. C. de Grave Sells; Messrs. Yarrow (for the excellent photograph of the Sokol);

Mr. John Sampson of Messrs. Maudslay, Sons, & Field; Messrs. Hawthorn Leslie; Mr. Soper of Messrs. Humphrys & Tennant; Mrs. Kinsman; and several British and Russian naval officers. For assistance in sifting matter for the early historical chapter I owe much to my brother, Mr. L. Cecil Jane.

Much is written in England and America about the secrecy with which the Russians shroud their dockyards and ships. It may be so; but my own experience did not tally with the legend; indeed, everything was the direct antithesis, nor were any restrictions of any sort laid upon me as to what I might afterwards write concerning this particular piece of globe-trotting. Much that is in this book is certainly not Russophile; in the historical chapters it may perhaps seem distinctly the reverse—no curtain is discreetly drawn over Russian blunders and defeats. To these things, indeed, I would rather draw attention; for if a lesson lies anywhere it lies in the history of how Russia has ever marched to victory through blunders and disaster. Almost invariably she has won by sheer "pegging" against heavy odds; in the end, either with the peace or after it she has secured her object. England has in the past been more often with her than against her. She may be both many times yet, though the truest interests of both countries lie in the former.

F. T. J.

*December*, 1899.

# CONTENTS


| | | PAGE |
|---|---|---|
| | PREFACE | 9 |
| I. | THE GERM OF THE RUSSIAN NAVY, 865–1613 | 23 |
| II. | 1613–1645 | 40 |
| III. | THE BIRTH OF THE RUSSIAN NAVY, 1645–1725 | 44 |
| IV. | 1725–1762 | 71 |
| V. | THE RUSSIAN NAVY UNDER EKATERINA II. | 77 |
| VI. | PAUL, 1796–1801 | 110 |
| VII. | ALEXANDER I., 1801–1825 | 118 |
| VIII. | NAVARINO AND THE CRIMEAN WAR, 1825–1855 | 127 |
| IX. | THE EARLIER IRONCLADS, 1855–1877 | 151 |
| X. | NAVAL HISTORY OF THE TURCO-RUSSIAN WAR | 180 |
| XI. | 1878–1885 | 202 |
| XII. | 1886–1890 | 223 |
| XIII. | 1891–1898 | 252 |
| XIV. | THE BEGINNING OF THE NEW FLEET | 308 |
| XV. | THE VOLUNTEER FLEET | 334 |
| XVI. | THE RUSSIAN DOCKYARDS, ADMINISTRATION | 337 |
| XVII. | THE RUSSIAN DOCKYARDS, DESCRIPTIONS | 340 |
| | 1. New Admiralty . 341 | |
| | 2. Galernii Island . 346 | |
| | 3. The Baltic Works 356 | |
| | 4. Smaller Yards . 365 | |
| | 5. Kronstadt . 366 | |
| | 6. Revel . 389 | |
| | 7. Libau . 390 | |
| | 8. Vladivostok | 394 |
| | 9. Port Arthur. | 399 |
| | 10. Talienwan | 402 |
| | 11. Sevastópol | 403 |
| | 12. Nikolaïf | 409 |
| | 13. Other Naval Ports | 412 |
| XVIII. | NEW PORTS AND SHIP CANALS | 413 |
| XIX. | THE "NEW FLEET" | 417 |
| XX. | EVOLUTION OF TYPE IN RUSSIAN WARSHIPS | 430 |
| XXI. | FINANCE | 435 |
| XXII. | THE SLOWNESS OF RUSSIAN NAVAL CONSTRUCTION | 437 |
| XXIII. | THE RUSSIAN ADMIRALTY | 446 |
| | Naval Intelligence Department | 448 |
| | Personnel Department | 454 |

PAGE

XXIV. ENTRY AND TRAINING OF OFFICERS . . 457
XXV. ENTRY AND TRAINING OF MEN . . . 465
XXVI. PAY . . . . . . . . . 470
XXVII. RETIREMENT, PENSIONS, ETC. . . . 478
XXVIII. WATCHES . . . . . . . . 480
XXIX. RUSSIAN NAVAL FLAGS . . . . . 481
XXX. ORGANISATION . . . . . . . 484
XXXI. DISCIPLINE . . . . . . . . 494
XXXII. DRESS . . . . . . . . . 501
XXXIII. DISTINGUISHING MARKS FOR RANK . . 507
XXXIV. PERSONAL CHARACTERISTICS OF RUSSIAN OFFICERS AND MEN . . . . . 513
XXXV. THE ARMAMENT AND EQUIPMENT OF THE FLEET . . . . . . . 520
XXXVI. THE INFLUENCE OF PETER THE GREAT ON THE RUSSIAN NAVY TO-DAY . . . 545
XXXVII. ANGLO-RUSSIAN RELATIONS . . . 549
XXXVIII. SOME CONCLUSIONS . . . . . . 562
XXXIX. RUSSIA IN THE FAR EAST, 1899 AND 1904 . 578
XL. OUR MISTAKE IN DEALING WITH RUSSIA . 590
XLI. OTHER NAVIES AS SEEN BY THE RUSSIANS . 601
XLII. ANGLO-SAXON *V.* SLAV . . . . . 605

APPENDICES—

HISTORICAL APPENDIX . . . . . 613
CONDENSED BIOGRAPHIES OF SOME DISTINGUISHED RUSSIAN NAVAL OFFICERS . 704
CONDENSED BIOGRAPHIES OF BRITISH AND AMERICAN OFFICERS IN THE RUSSIAN SERVICE . . . . . 714
RELATIONS BETWEEN BRITISH AND RUSSIAN OR OTHER FOREIGN OFFICERS IN THE EIGHTEENTH CENTURY . . . 725
INDEX TO SUBJECT MATTER . . . 731

# LIST OF ILLUSTRATIONS


PAGE

The Battleship Rostistav . . . . *Frontispiece*

Map of Turkey, etc. . . . . . . . . 25

The Russian Fleet before Constantinople, a.d. 86 . . 27

Sectional Plan, Earliest Russian Warship . . . 29

A Ship of the Russian Black Sea Fleet, a.d. 865, and the Tri Svititelia of the Present Day . . . . 30

Destruction of the Russian Fleet by Greek Fire outside Constantinople . . . . . . . . 35

"The Little Father of the Russian Fleet" . . . 42

Map of the Baltic . . . . . . . 56

Warships *tempus* Peter the G eat . . . . 59

The Battle of Gangoot (*map*) . . . . . 63

Facsimile of Autograph Letter Peter the Great's . . 65

Map of the Crimea . . . . . . . 72

Map of Black Sea, Turkey, etc. . . . . . 81

Map of the Baltic . . . . . . . 98

The Battle of Viborg . . . . . . 103

Map of the Baltic . . . . . . . 117

Map of Black Sea, etc. . . . . . . 119

Frigate and Schooner, *circa* 1810 . . . . . 125

Russian Warships, 1830 . . . . . . 131

The Battle of Sinope . . . . . . 137

Map of Turkey and Black Sea . . . . . 143

Cliff at Inkerman . . . . . . . 145

Inkerman Heights . . . . . . . 145

Balaklava Field . . . . . . . 145

Kronstadt in 1854 . . . . . . . 149

*Idem* . . . . . . . . . 149

The Kreml . . . . . . . . 154

The Netron Menia . . . . . . . 155

The Kniz-Pojarsky . . . . . . . 157

The Bronònosetz . . . . . . . 159

The British Penelope . . . . . . 159

PAGE
The Russalka (*photograph*) . . . . . . 161
The Admiral Spiridoff (*photograph*) . . . . 163
The Admiral Greig (*photograph*) . . . . . 165
The Peter Velīky . . . . . . . 169
The General Admiral . . . . . . 171
The Gerzog Edinbourski . . . . . . 173
The Popoff . . . . . . . . 176
The Avni Illah . . . . . . . 182
The Feth-i-Bulend . . . . . . . 182
The Assar-i-Shevket . . . . . . . 182
The Lutfi Djel . . . . . . . 182
Hobart Pasha's Torpedo Pond . . . . . 183
Sketch Map of Crimea and Adjacent Coasts . . . 184
Lieutenant (now Admiral) Makaroff (*photograph*) . . 188
Defeat of a Russian Torpedo Boat Attack in the Danube . 191
The Attack on the Assar-i-Chevket . . . . 193
Sinking of the Sulina . . . . . . 197
Return of Torpedo Boats . . . . . . 201
The Minin . . . . . . . . 205
Plan of Vladimir Monomakh . . . . . 207
The Dmitri Donskoi, 1886 (*old rig*) . . . . . 209
Plan of the Nahimoff . . . . . . 212
The Admiral Nahimoff (*photograph*) . . . . 213
The Pāmiat Merkuria (*photograph*) . . . . 215
The Rasboynik (*photograph*) . . . . . 216
The Rȳnda (*photograph*) . . . . . . 217
The Strelok . . . . . . . . 219
The Bobr . . . . . . . . 220
Russian "Flat-iron" Gunboat . . . . . 220
The Asia . . . . . . . . 220
The Afrika . . . . . . . . 221
The Zabiaka . . . . . . . . 221
The Ekaterina ii. (*photograph*) . . . . . 224
The Tchesma in 1890. . . . . . . 225
Plan of Sinope Class . . . . . . 227
Plan of Alexander ii. . . . . . . 230
Plan of Pāmiat Azova . . . . . . 232
The Pāmiat Azova . . . . . . . 233
The Dvenadsat Apostolov . . . . . . 237
Plan of the Dvenadsat Apostolov . . . . . 238
The Gangoot Sinking. . . . . . . 241
The Groziastchy . . . . . . . 245
The Korniloff . . . . . . . 247

PAGE
THE KOUBANETZ . . . . . . . . 249
THE TCHERNOMORETZ . . . . . . . . 249
THE KOREITZ . . . . . . . . 250
THE MANDJOUR . . . . . . . . 250
THE LIEUTENANT ILYIN . . . . . . . 251
THE NĀVARIN . . . . . . . . 253
PLAN OF THE NĀVARIN . . . . . . . 254
THE RURIK (*photograph*) . . . . . . . 255
PLAN OF THE RURIK . . . . . . . 258
PLAN OF THE ROSSĪA . . . . . . . 259
THE ROSSĪA (*photograph*) . . . . . . . 261
PLAN OF THE GEORGI POBEDONOSETZ . . . . . 266
THE GEORGI POBEDONOSETZ AT SEVASTÔPOL (*photograph*) . . 267
THE OUSHAKOFF IN KRONSTADT DOCKYARD (*photograph*) . . 271
PLAN OF THE APRĀKSIN . . . . . . . 273
ENGINES OF THE OUSHAKOFF (*photograph*) . . . . 275
THE TRI SVITITELIA (*photograph*) . . . . . 280
PLAN OF THE TRI SVITITELIA . . . . . . 281
THE SISSOI VELĪKY . . . . . . . 283
PLAN OF THE SISSOI VELĪKY . . . . . . 285
INTERIOR OF THE SISSOI VELĪKY'S TURRET AFTER THE DISASTER (*photograph*) . . . . . . . . 287
PLAN OF THE KHRABRY . . . . . . . 289
THE DMITRI DONSKOI RECONSTRUCTED (*photograph*) . 291
PLAN OF THE ROSTISLAV . . . . . . . 293
THE SVIETLANA (*photograph*) . . . . . . 295
THE KAZARSKI . . . . . . . . 297
THE SOKOL (*photograph*) . . . . . . . 299
THE RUSSIAN FLEET AT TOULON (*photograph*) . . . 301
L'ENTENTE CORDIALE AT TOULON (*photograph*) . . . 303
THE IMPERIAL YACHT STHANDART (*photograph*) . . . 305
THE PETROPAVLOVSK (*photograph*) . . . . . 309
PLAN OF POLTĀVA, ETC. . . . . . . . 311
END-ON VIEW OF THE SEVASTÔPOL . . . . . 313
THE RETVISAN (*photograph*) . . . . . . 315
PLAN OF THE RETVISAN . . . . . . . 315
THE BÖYARIN (*photograph*) . . . . . . 317
PLAN OF THE BÖYARIN . . . . . . . 317
THE BAYAN (*photograph*) . . . . . . . 319
PLAN OF THE BAYAN . . . . . . . . 319
THE SEVASTÔPOL (*photograph*) . . . . . . 321
PLAN OF THE PERESVET . . . . . . . 321
THE VARIAG (*photograph*) . . . . . . . 322

PAGE
Plan of the Variag . . . . . . . 323
The Pobieda (*photograph*) . . . . . . . 323
The Bogatyr (*photograph*) . . . . . . . 325
Plan of the Bogatyr . . . . . . . 325
The Askold (*photograph*) . . . . . . . 327
Plan of the Askold . . . . . . . 327
The Novik (*photograph*) . . . . . . . 331
The Osliabia. New Admiralty Yard from the River . . 342
Facsimile of Permit Card to view a Russian Dockyard . 344
Galernii Island Dockyard . . . . . . . 347
The Pallada (*photograph*) . . . . . . . 349
Plan of the Pallada. . . . . . . . 349
On Board the Pallada—Building . . . . 352
The French Cruiser Guichen (*photograph*) . . . 354
Russian Dockyardsman . . . . . . . 355
*Idem* . . . . . . . . . 356
Outside the Baltic Works . . . . . . 357
Inside the Baltic Works (*photograph*) . . . . 358
Plans of the Gromoboi . . . . . . . 360
The Gromoboi (*photograph*). . . . . . . 361
The Yenesi (*photograph*) . . . . . . . 362
Putting in the Engines of the Amoor . . . . 365
Kronstadt Dockyard . . . . . . . 371
Approaches to Kronstadt . . . . . . . 376
Engine-Room of the Sevastôpol . . . . . 377
On the Road to the Gunnery School, Kronstadt . . 382
Map of Libau and District . . . . . . 391
Map of Vladivostok . . . . . . . 395
Map of the "Far East" . . . . . . . 400
Panorama of Sevastôpol (*photograph*) . . . . 405
Sevastôpol Dockyard (*photograph*) . . . . . 407
House after the Bombardment (*photograph*) . . . 407
The Dockyard. Another View (*photograph*) . . . 407
The Rostislav (*photograph*) . . . . . . 408
Plan of the K. Potemkin Tavritchesky . . . . 411
The Tsarevitch (*photograph*) . . . . . . 419
Plan of the Tsarevitch . . . . . . . 419
Admiral Nakimoff (reconstructed) . . . . . 425
Plan of the Admiral Nakimoff . . . . . . 425
H.I.H. Grand Duke Alexander Mihailovitch (*photograph*) . 461
Russian Naval Flags . . . . . . . 482
Officer's Overcoat . . . . . . . . 502
A Corporal (*photograph*) . . . . . . . 504

| | PAGE |
|---|---|
| Marching Uniform, Russian Bluejacket (*photograph*) | 506 |
| A Russian Bluejacket (*photograph*) | 506 |
| A Mitchman | 507 |
| Shoulder-Straps and Epaulettes | 509 |
| Distinguishing Marks for Men | 512 |
| Ivan in Repose (*photograph*) | 519 |
| 6-in. Gun Drill on board the Djidjit (*photograph*) | 521 |
| The Belleville Boiler | 534 |
| *Idem* | 535 |
| Naval War Game Pieces made for H.I.H. Grand Duke Alexander (*photograph*) | 573 |
| Map of the Baltic | 621 |
| Plan of Battle of Gogland, July 1788 | 629 |
| Plan of Battle of Öland, July 1789 | 651 |
| Repulse of the Swedish Fleet at Revel, 1790 | 656 |
| Plan of Battle off Revel, 1790 | 663 |
| Plan of the Battle of Viborg, 1790 | 667 |
| Plan of Battle of Svensksund, 1789 | 671 |
| Plan of Battle of Svensksund (Rotgensalm), 1790 | 673 |
| Plan of Petty Fleet Battle | 687 |
| *Idem* | 695 |
| The Late Tsarvitch | 707 |

# THE IMPERIAL RUSSIAN NAVY

## I

## THE GERM OF THE RUSSIAN NAVY

THE Russian Navy, though generally regarded as a comparatively modern institution, founded by Peter the Great, can, as a matter of fact, lay greater claim to antiquity than the British fleet. A century before Alfred built the first English warships, Russians had fought in desperate sea-fights, and a thousand years ago the foremost sailors of the time were Russians. This navy died, it is true,—it met its end in absolute annihilation,—but the nation that owned it did not die; and to-day the root of all the Eastern Question, and hence of the Far Eastern Question too, lies in the enterprise of early Russian warships.

*Antiquity of the Russian Navy.*

*Its importance.*

Into the details of the expedition of Darius against the Scythians, some two thousand odd years ago, it is unnecessary to enter; the Scythians had no sea power, and adopted in the place of it those tactics which Napoleon at a later period was unable to appreciate without practical test. Had the Scythians

*Darius and the Scythians.*

possessed that "Sea Power" of which nowadays we read so much, Darius would never have crossed into Europe. In connection with the frequent question: "What does Russia want with a navy?" this incident has some bearing. The future may yet see Oriental armies seeking to pour into Europe across the Bosphorus and Dardanelles; the thing that has happened more than once in the past may yet come about again in the future. The probabilities of such an event are small enough to-day, and certainly the Russian Black Sea Fleet does not exist because of such a possibility.

On the other hand, the place where Darius made his bridge of boats would be one of the objectives of that fleet, given certain eventualities; and the most cursory glance at a map will show how in the Turco-Russian War of 1877 thousands of lives might have been saved had Russia but possessed a fleet capable of striking at once at the heart of the Turkish Empire.

*Russia and Constantinople.*

We first hear of Russia in connection with the channel dividing Europe from Asia. More than two thousand years have passed since then,—to-day this same channel is supposed to mark the bounds of Russia's southward ambition in Europe, and towards this channel and the city upon it have Russian efforts been directed for a great many of the two thousand years between. Ever since Byzantium was founded, Russians have at intervals made efforts to take it to themselves;—if persistence goes for aught the two-headed eagle should yet again fly where it used to fly

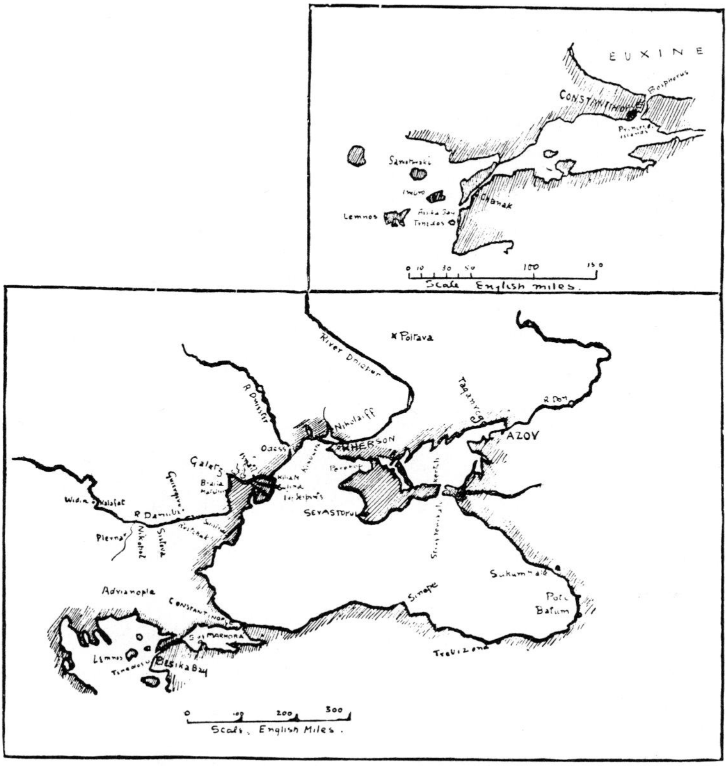


MAP OF TURKEY, THE BLACK SEA, ETC.

before the crescent took its place. Empires have been born and died since then, even the races themselves have changed or died, but always the people inhabiting what is now the Imperial Russian Empire have striven to capture the blue waters of the Bosphorus. It is a thing too little recognised, this hereditary trend of Russia to Constantinople.

In attacks upon the capital of the Eastern Roman Empire we, too, find the earliest mention of Russians on the sea. The Scythians changed into Slavs, the Goths took possession of almost all of what is now European Russia, and founded a sort of empire, which Huns and others a little later overthrew, till in the year 862 Rurik arose, created a central Russian state, and took to himself the title of Grand Duke.

*Rurik.*

Rurik was originally the chief of the Varangians, a Norse tribe, and he appears to have come to the aid of the original Slavs much as Hengist and Horsa came to help the ancient Britons — a fairly close parallel can be drawn; though the Saxon king Edgar is the monarch Rurik would more nearly resemble otherwise.

The Varangians being Scandinavian were originally, of course, a seafaring people, and some faint transmitted original Varangian strain may possibly account for the fact that at the present day moujiks from the interior of Russia can be turned into tolerably capable sailors.

It was not long before the Varangians, working southward, turned their eyes towards Constantinople; their natural instincts led them to naval expeditions both piratical and trading on the shores of the Black

THE RUSSIAN FLEET BEFORE CONSTANTINOPLE, 865 A.D.

*First Russian attack on Constantinople, 865 A.D.*

Sea, and there, naturally enough too, they soon heard of the wealthy city on the Bosphorus. At this period, Cherson (now Sevastôpol) was a Byzantine possession, and with this place the Russians carried on a good deal of legitimate trade. Commercial rivalry, therefore, equally with piratical intent, may have been at the bottom of the first Russian expedition, which in 865 A.D., in the reign of the Greek Emperor Michael III., attacked Constantinople.

*Earliest Russian warships.*

The attacking fleet consisted of 200 small ships—*μονόξυλα* the Greeks called them, which means literally "made of one single piece of wood." They were, however, more than that, the sides being built up with planks above the main boat *b*, *b*, as indicated in the sectional drawing. With all these old-time warships a certain amount of doubt has to be used; but the illustrations convey some idea of their probable form. They were 60 feet long, probably very broad for their length, and the freeboard is always spoken of as 12 feet above the water level. The modern Russians have a penchant for a high freeboard, as the Peresvet and a good many other of their ships attest, but these ancient warships were probably scarcely so high as the old historians make out. On such a scale a ship like the modern Peresvet would have sides nearly 90 feet high! In ancient shipping generally the height

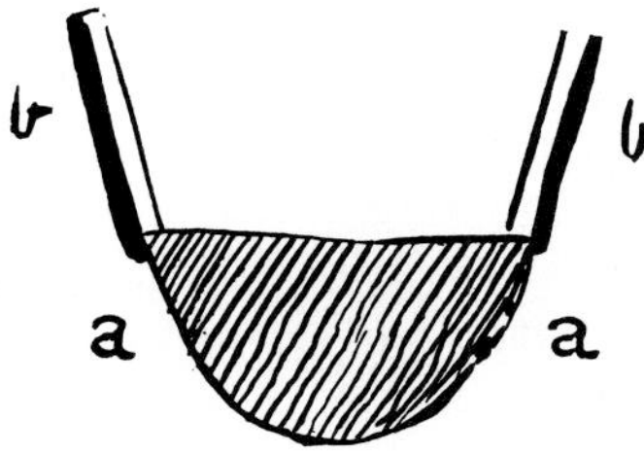

SECTION, EARLY RUSSIAN BATTLESHIP.

of the side took that place in naval ethics now occupied by the "nominal speed." However, for purposes of comparison I have drawn one of these old warships on scale alongside one of the latest completed Black Sea Fleet ironclads, the Tri Svititelia.

Crew.

The crew of these old warships is a doubtful quantity. Twenty is the number stated by Finlay; while Gibbon, with a cautious liberality, says from 40 to 90. Possibly 20 men constituted the normal crew, while 90 could be stowed on board upon special occasions. When we remember that an Athenian trireme of almost the same dimensions as a modern torpedo boat carried 200 men, there is nothing out of the way in these old Russian ships carrying 90. A modern torpedo boat carries less than a score of men; the ironclad Tri Svititelia has a complement of about 580, but machinery now takes the place of the rowers.

Motive power.

It appears that these early Russian ships used sail as a motive power as well as oars, for "by fortune of a favourable wind" they reached and passed the Bosphorus, and anchored at the mouth of the Black

River in the Propontis (Sea of Marmora). Meanwhile the Greek Emperor was away in Asia fighting the Saracens, having left an admiral of the Byzantine fleet to act as governor of the capital. Byzantium was completely surprised by this unexpected attack; and the passing of the Bosphorus by the Russian fleet produced an immediate panic.

After passing the Bosphorus, the Russians under Askold and Dir, princes of Kieff, Rurik's "lieutenants," ravaged the Princes Islands in the Propontis, pillaging the rich monasteries, killing the monks, and laying waste all the country round about Constantinople. Their ferocity and cruelty aggravated the panic in the Byzantine capital; but the Emperor, returning in haste, went out with his fleet, attacked, and utterly destroyed the invaders; the small Russian vessels being helpless against the big Byzantine warships. Nevertheless, so deep a mark had the invasion left, that the Byzantines could at first scarcely credit the news of its destruction, and when finally convinced, at once attributed it to the special interposition of the Virgin.

*Destruction of the Russian fleet.*

In the tenth century the Russians held the highest reputation as sailors. As the Turkish fleet of to-day employs Greeks, so the Byzantine fleet about the year 900 A.D. took to employing Russians. Special and very high rates of pay were offered to them, and history records many specific instances of their employment. Thus in 935 A.D., in the reign of the Emperor Romanus I., we read of Russian ships and 415 men being sent to Italy as part of a Byzantine expedition.

*Russians in demand as sailors.*

In 949, in the reign of Romanus II., six Russian ships participated in an unsuccessful attack on Crete. In 966 again, Nicetas took Russian sailors with him to Sicily.

This recognition of the value of Russian naval auxiliaries did not, however, take place without further experiences on the part of the Byzantines than the abortive expedition of Askold and Dir.

*Second attack on Constantinople, 907 A.D.*

In 907 the Russians made their second attack on Constantinople, being led in person this time by Oleg, regent for the young Igor—son of Rurik. The Russian fleet this time consisted (if the historians are to be believed) of no less than two thousand vessels, which came down the Dnieper with its thirty cataracts.

By means of these cataracts the two thousand ships got somewhat reduced in numbers, but eighty thousand men are spoken of as arriving before Constantinople—"the City of the Cæsars" as the Russians used then to call it.

Outside Constantinople the usual ravaging was carried on, and any prisoners taken were tortured to death in order to keep the invaders amused. Priests in particular were selected as victims, driving nails into their heads in sarcastic emulation of Jael's treatment of Sisera being the favourite method of disposal. Times have changed since then: to-day in Russia, subject of course to the variation consequent upon the lapse of a thousand years, the boot is on the other foot.

Constantinople itself was in no danger of capture, but on the other hand the Russians appear to have had an equal immunity from risk of interference, since the "ravaging" continued without much hindrance for nearly four years; in fine, till in 912, when the Emperor Leo the Philosopher bought their retirement. A commercial dispute appears to have been at the bottom of this war, for at its ending a trade treaty was signed.

To this treaty the Russians adhered until 941, in the reign of Romanus I., when differences arose. This time the Russians are allowed no less than ten thousand ships by some of the historians; others, more modest, credit them with one thousand. The Grand Duke Igor appears to have been in personal command, and, as on the occasion of the two previous attacks, the time appears to have been well chosen, since the greater part of the Byzantine warships were in Italy, and only fifteen vessels at the capital.

*Third attack on Constantinople, 941 A.D.*

In these circumstances the Greek Emperor sent ambassadors to try and buy off the Russians, but all such overtures were rejected; nothing less than Constantinople itself was the prize aimed at this time. In despair the Byzantines, therefore, made ready such ships as they had, fitting them with an extra number of tubes for discharging Greek fire—that awful agent by means of which the fragments of the Roman Empire held out against the barbarian world. Nowadays, when a hundred-pound melenite or lyddite shell is a mere everyday bagatelle in warfare, we are prone to

*Greek fire.*

regard Greek fire as archaic, and in considerable danger of putting it in false perspective; we are unable to realise its potency in those days of unscientific warfare. Yet in comparison with the fighting appliances of those who had to face it, it was in much the same relation as would be the *vril* of Lytton's *Coming Race* pitted against our modern weapons.

On seeing these few ships moving out, Igor, who had heard of Greek fire but apparently had no practical knowledge of its effects, ordered his fleet to charge the Greeks, intent on capturing them at once by boarding,—tactics intelligible enough, and indeed on the face of them reasonable.

*Russian fleet annihilated.*

The Greeks, however, meeting this attack with streams of fire, burnt up the whole attack, and followed up their victory so thoroughly that Igor only escaped with some half-dozen boats. All the rest of his force was annihilated.

*Fourth attack on Constantinople, 1043 A.D.*

After this disaster Constantinople was let alone for a hundred years; then the death of a Russian noble in a street tumult in 1043 was seized on as a *casus belli*. The Emperor Constantine IX. offered compensation, which was refused; subsequently, as the attack drew nearer, he sued for peace. Vladimir, the Russian leader, fixed the price at three pounds weight of gold for each man in his force, and in face of these impossible terms Constantine prepared to resist.

As on the occasion of the previous attacks, very few Byzantine ships were off Constantinople, but these,

DESTRUCTION OF THE RUSSIAN FLEET, 941 A.D.

having loaded up with Greek fire, went out to meet the enemy. An indecisive action was fought; five of the Greek ships, getting cut off from their main body, were captured and destroyed,—an incident which, were reliable data concerning it procurable, would hold a certain amount of almost practical interest even at the present day. For to cut off those ships must have been an operation of something more than difficulty. Guns and torpedoes may miss, but when it is a case of covering the sea with fire the question of accurate aim scarcely enters.

*Indecisive action.*

A second and subsequent action was, however, decisive, and the majority of the Russian ships burnt. The remainder were destroyed in a storm, and practically the whole expedition was annihilated. Thus in slaughter on a scale so complete that to-day we can scarcely picture it, the early Russian striving after Sea Power ended. Those who prophesy that increased means of killing by wholesale will end war may be correct in their surmises, but in the matter of history supporting their theory perhaps the least said the better.

*Total destruction of the Russian fleet.*

This ended the Russian attacks on the decaying Roman Empire, for subsequently a species of alliance grew up; and when at last Constantinople fell before the Turks, Ivan the Great, who had married Sophia Paleologus, took to himself the title of Cæsar (Tsar), and the double-headed eagle of Byzantium that has formed the arms of Russia ever since. For some time the Greek Church had become the religion of Russia; it found its new head city at Moscow, and, as much as the original Constantinople could be transferred, it went to and remained at Moscow till this day. Much of the old Byzantium still lives in the city of the Kremlin.

Nothing of the Greek naval power seems to have gone to Russia owing to the alliance; between the last attack and the fall of Constantinople the struggles of the eleventh to the fifteenth centuries were internal strife, and a battling the Tartar invasion. Till well into the fifteenth century the Tartars more or less overran the country; not till the reign of Ivan III. did Russia emerge as a solid nation. When she did, the Turks were upon Constantinople, and her new birth very nearly coincided with the advent of that nation which has been her hereditary enemy ever since.

*Eleventh to fifteenth centuries.*

In the sixteenth century, however, the Tartars were still too near and great a menace for Russia's reception of the remains of the Eastern Roman Empire to be more than religious and nominal; Moscow itself was burned by the Tartars in 1572; and in 1598, the Roorik dynasty becoming extinct, the whole country was plunged into a civil war, of which the Poles were swift to take advantage, Ladislaus their king being even proclaimed Tsar in Moscow, which he had occupied.

*Minin.*

Then arose Kosma Minin, a butcher of Nijni Novgorod, who started what Sir George Clark has termed the first national movement in Russian history.

Minin was joined by Prince (Kniaz) Pojarski, and between them these two brought about the expulsion of the Poles in 1612. In the following year Mihail Romanoff was elected Tsar of Russia, and founded the present dynasty.

# II

## 1613–1645

THE Russian Navy during all the years of the Tartar invasion was as a fighting force almost non-existent, but the idea that the Russians had no ships at all of any sort is quite incorrect. What they did do, was to remain nautically more or less as they had been in the times of Igor, while England, Sweden, Holland, France, Denmark, Turkey, Venice, Genoa, Spain, and Portugal built seagoing ships and evolved improvements. The huge Russian rivers necessitated craft of elementary kinds for traffic and communication, and there were plenty of rough coasting craft and fishing boats about at Archangel. River boats, too, undoubtedly penetrated at times into the Turkish districts on the Black Sea, and there were some, too, on the Caspian. There is reason to believe that now and again small naval actions—not entirely piratical—took place not only in the Caspian and in the Southern rivers, but also against the Swedes when they were capturing the Neva districts. In 1242 Alexander Nevski won a battle upon the banks of the Neva in which boats participated. Ivan the Terrible (Ivan IV.) made great efforts to promote commerce, and attempted minor naval operations against the Swedes in row-boats upon

Lake Peipus and the rivers round about it. Queen Elizabeth of England sent him a small sailing boat—a present to his navy.

Boris Godunoff, who in 1598 usurped the throne, also had naval designs, and enlisted the services of between two and three thousand foreigners; all drawn from maritime States.

Either in Peter the Great's reign or at some subsequent date, all, or nearly all, records of these events were destroyed. Peter the Great was the founder of Russia's seagoing navy, and people about the Court hastened to abolish anything that might in the slightest degree tend to minimise Peter's claims to be the sole founder. In much such fashion were the records of old Egyptian kings destroyed in the reigns of their descendants. Russian naval operations from the eleventh to the, and of the, seventeenth century were insignificant enough, and probably few, but from historical fragments there is reason to believe that a sort of navy on a par with the English Navy under the Norman kings existed and occasionally acted. In the fights against the Tartars the great Russian waterways must have been used, apart from the evidence of the boat which our Queen Elizabeth sent to Ivan the Terrible. Archangel from the earliest times was a trading port, and Mihail Romanoff engaged English shipwrights there in the period 1620–40; and his successor, Alexei, Peter the Great's father, had an imperial yacht[1] built for him

[1] Charnock.

at the Archangel Dockyard. His son, Fedor, in his brief reign (1678–82), induced one hundred and fifty foreigners, chiefly Scotch and Dutch, to enter his service, chiefly with a view to naval enterprise, both at Archangel, on the shores of Lake Peipus, and at Vorōnege, on the Don. Generally the craft built were flat-bottomed, but there were others built of more shipshape form.

"THE LITTLE FATHER OF THE RUSSIAN FLEET."

The period 1645–89, when Peter and Ivan both nominally occupied the throne, produced internal troubles in which much of this progress went under. But all did not go. Peter at Moscow in 1688 saw Ivan the Terrible's boat, then stowed there, and at once wanted to get afloat in it. An Archangel shipwright (one of Alexei's importations) was sent for, and he repaired and re-rigged the craft, also building a few more.

Queen Elizabeth's boat still exists : Peter christened it "The little father of the Russian fleet," and it is sacredly preserved as the first Russian ship.

It is not the first, and it is not Russian, but English ; none the less it is to this boat that the Russian Navy of to-day owes its origin, and from it the Peresviet, Gromovoi, and Kniaz Potemken Tavritchesky of to-day are directly descended.

# III

# THE BIRTH OF THE RUSSIAN NAVY

## 1645–1725

### Peter the Great

PETER THE GREAT (Peter Veliky) had not been long upon the throne before he realised that if his country was to expand, and grow civilised with that expansion, then the common highway, the sea, must be at his doors. The Baltic was practically a Swedish lake, the Black Sea belonged entirely to the *Russia in 1645.* Turk; Russia was little better than a mass of central territories, bounded on the west and south by more or less hostile nations, on the east by the savage and almost unknown wastes of Asia, while on the north, though she had some coastline, it was only on the inhospitable Arctic seas.

Although Peter was nominally Tsar in 1645, it was *1689.* not till 1689 that he became actual ruler of Russia. His energies were then occupied in the south: a war with Turkey was, as usual, in progress, and Russian efforts were concentrated upon the capture of Azov.

Here failure met them. The Turkish fleet was a

power in those days, and supplies were brought into the town oversea without let or hindrance. Realising the hopelessness of his efforts so long as the seaside of the place was open, Peter made preparations for marine operations. Europe was ransacked for volunteers, naval, artillery, and engineer officers were procured from foreign States, and a flotilla of about two hundred boats and galleys was rapidly constructed with their assistance on the banks of the Don. With these craft Peter secured command of the inland sea, and Azov being closely blockaded, it at length fell in 1696. Fifteen years later the Turks recovered it; and even while Russia possessed it, it was valueless to them so far as larger naval operations were concerned: the Turkish battleships would soon have made short work of Peter's small vessels. Finis, therefore, was written on his operations in this direction; but the very fact of this failure led to Peter's inception of the idea that Russia must become a Naval Power.

*Foreigners employed.*

*Peter's first "fleet."*

*Azov captured.*

Full of this idea, in 1697 he started on his historical tour as Peter Mihailoff, shipbuilder, carpenter, and so on, visiting Dutch and English ports, and learning nautical trades with his own hands. Though his methods were indeed different, yet, broadly speaking, Peter was the Kaiser Wilhelm II. of Russia and of his century: the trades and professions in which he did not seek to shine were few. He was more practical, perhaps, than the Kaiser of the telegrams; still, his greatness ran in the same direction, and our common knowledge of Wilhelm II. to-day will help more than anything else to an

*Peter as a dockyardsman.*

*Peter the Great and the Kaiser Wilhelm II. compared.*

appreciation of the lines upon which Tsar Peter moved.

Peter's travels were not of long duration—a small revolution necessitated his return—but he brought with him a number of British engineers, who proceeded to work upon his first project: the canal between the Volga and the Don.

*Volga and Don canal.*

*Charles XII. of Sweden.*

The following year brought Peter into conflict with the famous Charles the Twelfth of Sweden. Sweden was at that time the principal Baltic Power, and, so far as Russia was concerned, had been frankly recognised as a superior force. Between Swedes and Russians small skirmishes had at different times taken place, but these had nothing of the nature of a regular war in them.

Peter, however, having allied with Denmark, Prussia, Poland, and Saxony, began to attempt active operations against Sweden, which was at first supported by Holland and England. These two Powers, however, were concerned chiefly with Denmark, and withdrew their forces when Sweden made peace with the Danes. Charles having settled matters in the west, then moved eastward, concentrating his force upon the Russians, who under Peter had invaded the Swedish province of Ingria, and were besieging Narva with 67,000 soldiers.

*Russians invade Swedish territory.*

*Battle of Narva.*

On this army Charles suddenly descended with a force of only 8000 men; but such was his genius, and the prestige and impetuosity of the Swedes, that he not only defeated but absolutely scattered and destroyed Peter's host! Peter himself was not present: in his opinion the battle was lost before a shot had been fired, and he acted on the famous maxim that holds out hopes of "another day." His doing so probably spelt Russia's ultimate success against Sweden, for he was the only man in the country possessed of sufficient ability to compete with the Swedish king. With an appreciation of this, characteristic of the great Tsar, Peter left his army to shift for itself, and was busy making preparations for a new campaign even while the smoke was rolling over the field of Narva. It is useless to judge his action in the light of the ethics of personal courage[1]: the result of his flight stands in the Russian Empire of to-day.

Charles, his force now raised to 60,000 men, proceeded southward, invaded Poland, deposed the king, Augustus, and placed Stanislaus Leczmski on the throne. Peter he ignored as a coward who had fled from the battlefield; and though Swedish statesmen and friendly Powers warned him of his error, he marched away from the real menace to his empire, only realising his fatal error when, hemmed in by Peter's forces, his army was crushed and blotted out on the bloody field of Poltāva.

*Poltāva.*

As soon as possible after Narva, Peter resumed his attacks upon the Baltic provinces of Sweden; and while Charles was astonishing Europe, and his Swedish soldiers becoming the wonder of the world, Peter was slowly and surely taking all the country round about where St. Petersburg now stands. Every piece of water that he gained soon saw Russian vessels being built upon its

*Russian ships built in the North.*

[1] See a later chapter on Peter the Great; also the Appendices.

shores, and the Neva, and Lakes Ladoga and Peipus soon had Russian flotillas upon them.

*1702.*

The year 1702 was the real birth-year of the Russian Navy, and is very nearly analogous with the year 998 in English history. In 998 English coasts were almost Danish provinces, and Alfred's new warships first encountered the enemy on his own element about that time. Russia in 1702 was overrun by Swedes, in that year Peter launched two small seagoing warships at Archangel and laid the keel of a 26-gun battleship, while on Lake Peipus a naval engagement resulting in the destruction of a Swedish vessel took place.

*Naval forces on Lake Peipus, 1702.*

Peter's Peipus flotilla consisted of small galleys and *lodkys*. The galleys each mounted four small guns and carried a crew of fifty men ; the *lodkys* were merely four-oared row-boats. Of these there were several hundred : the exact number of the galleys is uncertain, but they were fairly numerous.

The Swedish force was numerically vastly inferior. It consisted of fourteen yachts and sloops, which mounted between them twenty guns and carried about six hundred men. The northern and western portions of the lake were Swedish, but the eastern side was Russian territory. In 1702 the Swedish commodore, Löschern von Herzfeldt, became aware of Peter's intention to try and annihilate the whole Swedish force upon the lake, and in May he went down the lake with four yachts and some sloops, carrying between them sixteen guns and 200 men, on a reconnoitring

*The first naval engagement.*

expedition. In doing so he came suddenly and unexpectedly upon a Russian force of 90 to 100 small craft, carrying about 5000 men, and supported by a shore battery of six guns.

In such contempt did the Swedes hold the Russians in those days, that Löschern unhesitatingly attacked them. They attempted to outflank him, but being received with a heavy and well-directed fire, the flank attack ended in failure. In the middle of it some of the Swedes landed and rushed the battery, while those still afloat, pressing their advantage, inflicted a total defeat upon the Russians, capturing or destroying, besides the battery, nearly half the flotilla, and killing several hundred men.

*Swedish victory.*

After this victory Löschern withdrew to the mouth of the Embach River, in order to refit and to prepare for a larger attack. His preparations being complete about the end of July, he sent the yacht Vivat, Captain Jonas Hökeflycht, four guns, and a complement of fifty men, to discover the whereabouts of the Russians. The wind failing, Hökeflycht ran into a small bay and anchored; and here the Russians getting word of his presence, sent a hundred *lodkys* to cut him out.

*Russian attack upon the yacht Vivat.*

The Vivat opened fire at the longest possible range, with a view to delaying the advance as much as possible, and in the hope of attracting the main Swedish flotilla; but the wind being wanting, Löschern, though he heard the guns, was unable to come to the rescue. Disregarding the Vivat's fire, the Russians came on from all sides, and, after a desperate resistance, captured the yacht's decks. Hökeflycht, desperately wounded, crawled down to the powder magazine and blew up the boat. The Vivat was destroyed, but the action cost the Russians twenty *lodkys*, and over two hundred men killed.

*The Vivat blows up.*

On hearing of these two desperate affairs, Peter withdrew all his remaining forces to the south-eastern shore, where they lay idle under the protection of shore-batteries too strong to be forced. But if the boats were idle their crews were not; and the building of new and larger vessels was at once begun, and pressed forward during the remainder of the summer of 1702 and throughout the following year.

*Russians withdraw.*

*1703.*

On the Neva the Swedes had but two small galleys. These being cut off from retreat, were surprised and taken by the Russian force without much loss on either side. On Lake Ladoga there was no Swedish force; Noteberg was cut off, and surrendered; the Swedes found themselves confronted by a force against which it was hopeless to contend. At the end of 1703 the waters of Neva and Ladoga were practically completely Russian, while Peipus was as completely in the hands of the Swedes.

*Russia gains control of the Neva and Lake Ladoga.*

In 1703 Peter founded the city of St. Petersburg on the banks of the Neva, which at that time was simply a mass of half-submerged mud islets and treacherous swamps.

*Founding of St. Petersburg.*

On Peter's selection of such a dreadful spot to build a city many morals have been drawn: it has been said—and without much exaggeration—that the foundations of St. Petersburg are dead men's bones. But when all is said and done, his choice of locality was extremely limited, and, better than his latter-day critics, he recognised that nothing short of a great city and a capital would consolidate the new seacoast empire that he was building, or attract that trade and merchandise without which the city could not thrive.

*Peter his own architect.*

Like the present Emperor of Germany, Tsar Peter was a man of many parts. He himself plotted-out the new city, himself designed its bridges, its houses, and its palaces: St. Petersburg is essentially a one-man city.

*Difficulties met in building St. Petersburg.*

High tides and inundations swept away his landmarks, quicksands swallowed the foundations of his houses, the unhealthy climate swept off his workmen by the thousand—two hundred thousand men died that St. Petersburg should be an everlasting monument to the persistence of its founder. I write these words on that spot now. All around me the palatial houses, the broad flat roads, the many islands, the great golden dome of St. Isaac's cathedral looming up above the haze, not all smoke as in other cities, but the mist and vapour also from those pestilential marshes underneath the buildings. Intersecting the city are many canals, serving useful purposes as water highways; but in Peter's day the trenches by which he sought to drain the dismal swamps.

*St. Petersburg in 1899.*

And southward, below the wide spans of the bridges, and the lines for the electric trams laid across the frozen river, I see the huge building slips where Peter mapped-out his first dockyard. Alongside its river walls a couple of frozen-in ironclads stand black against the sunset.

Every city was once a desert; but it is only St. Petersburg that vividly recalls the thought to the beholder. And standing looking across it, one has only to think of its name to arouse a longing similar to that experienced by so many travellers on the Nile: to see the past recalled, and to compare it with the very different present.

Peter, when he found the quicksands swallowing his foundations, filled them up with rock, stones, and rubbish till he had created solid ground. When the swift current of the Neva swept away the beginnings of his bridges, he overcame the difficulty of communication by bridges of boats. Every difficulty that met him he combated and conquered, and at last the city rose. Victory could only be accomplished by a total disregard of human life, and probably no one can calculate how many lives it cost—the proverb is true enough, its foundations are dead men's bones.

*Seagoing ships begun.*

At St. Petersburg the building of seagoing warships was at once commenced under Peter's supervision. The designing he seems to have wisely left to his imported naval architects; but he gave all the stimulus he could to the work by sharing any subordinate labour for which his Deptford work had fitted him. The

*Peter's excellent example.*

Tsar himself thus setting the example, his nobles and subjects quickly followed suit, and there was no hampering of the work by officials taking posts for which they were unfitted : labour had its golden age when the Russian fleet was born.

Meanwhile, on Lake Peipus work continued with vigour, and such progress had been made by the early spring of 1704 that preparations were made to assume the offensive against the isolated and unsupported Swedish force then controlling it. Löschern lay in winter quarters at Dorpt, and the Russians evolved the idea of shutting him in there and destroying him.

*Destruction of the Swedish naval force on Lake Peipus, 1704.*

To this end they prepared a big flotilla, erected a strong boom at the narrow part of the river mouth, threw up batteries to protect it, and garrisoned them with 9000 troops. They then brought up their entire force, and waited developments. Löschern, meanwhile, though fully aware that preparations were being made to meet him, made no attempt to frustrate the Russian works. Either he felt that his course was run, or else, bearing in mind his easy victory on a previous occasion,[1] despised his opponents too much to trouble about their movements. In any case, his abilities as a commander were not on a par with his courage. He idled at Dorpt till the 4th of May, then went quietly down the river with his entire flotilla.[2]

The current was strong, and he approached the Russian works at a great rate. They received him with a heavy fire, which he returned as he drifted past, to be brought up helplessly against the boom.

[1] Page 49.

[2] The total crews were 250 soldiers and 350 seamen.

Here all his vessels were crowded together, the Russians firing " into the brown."

The 250 Swedish soldiers leapt ashore, stormed and silenced a battery, then set to work to break up the boom, but the Russians forced them back to their ships. A second attempt was repulsed. The remnant then made a third attack, and, cutting their way through the Russians, escaped to Dorpt.

*Löschern blows up his flagship.*

The sailors of Löschern's force stuck to their ships, fighting like rats in a trap till all their vessels were destroyed and themselves slain. Löschern's yacht, the Carolus, was the last to survive; she was taken by boarding. Löschern, however, managed to reach his magazine, and blew himself up with his conquerors.

*Peter's order about boarding.*

It was a peculiar trait of Peter's to endeavour always to at once adapt his war methods to circumstances. Löschern's action, following quickly upon that of the Vivat's captain, brought about the issue of an imperial order that no Swedish ships were to be boarded till the principal officers had been killed!

*1705.*

*Russian seagoing fleet.*

By the middle of 1705 Peter had got together a seagoing fleet at Kronstadt, consisting of 9 line-of-battle ships, 4 brigs, 5 galiots, 7 large and 8 small galleys, and 12 fire-ships. Forts had been constructed, as well as a boom defence behind which the ships lay.

*The Swedes offer battle.*

In June of this year a Swedish fleet of 7 line-of-battle ships and 5 frigates came off Kronstadt, and offered battle several times. Peter, however, was not to be drawn into losing his new fleet, as assuredly at that early date he would have done had there been a general engagement, despite the difference in numbers. Strict orders were issued that the Swedes were not to be attacked, and eventually they gave up the attempt to provoke an action, and sailed away.

In the meantime, land operations were vigorously pushed, and town after town taken from Sweden on the southern shores of the Baltic. By 1711 all of them, including Riga, had been captured. *1711.*

In the capture of Viborg the new navy participated, the place being taken by Admiral Aprāksin from the sea. The Swedish fleet failed to put in an appearance; the battle of Poltāva the year before had flung Sweden into something very like anarchy. Peter himself was afloat off Viborg, commanding a reserve squadron. *Viborg, 1710.*

Not till his army had been annihilated at Poltāva did Charles XII. realise the fatal error that he had made. Escaping from that bloody field, he spent a couple of years idly careering in the south; then he attempted a counter-irritant, and induced the Turks to fight the Russians. Here the latter met disaster; Peter's army was surrounded, and only saved from annihilation by a peace whereby Azov was restored to Turkey, the Russian Black Sea Fleet destroyed, and a heavy indemnity paid. The peace, however, was fatal to Charles' schemes. *1709. Poltāva.* *1711. Russians hopelessly defeated by the Turks.*

Having disposed of the Turkish War, and captured all the Swedish territory on the southern shores of the Baltic, Peter's genius led him to attack the northern side. In May 1713, therefore, he sent his fleet to sea *1713. Capture of Helsingfors, Abo, etc.*

MAP OF THE BALTIC.

*Note.*—Rogerswick was a small harbour a little west of Revel.

under General Admiral Graf Feodor Matveievitch Aprāksin, the first Russian admiral, to attack the coast of Finland, and himself took the post of second in command, which meant that he did not allow his position as Tsar to affect what he considered his own fighting value.[1] He selected himself as second in command because he considered himself the next best man to Aprāksin—a step characteristic of Peter Veliky, and paralleled by no absolute monarch before or since.

*Aprāksin, first Russian admiral.*

No Swedish ships were encountered, and Abo and a number of smaller places were taken without difficulty: the Swedes, drained by Charles' wild campaigns, could put nothing but raw levies in the field, and Russian soldiers soon overran the southern shores of Finland.

*Abo taken.*

The ships went back to Revel in the course of a month or two; and in July the Swedes, having got their fleet together, sent three ships of 56, 54, and 48 guns respectively, under Commodore Raab, to reconnoitre Revel. On the night of 10th July these ships anchored at Gogland (Högland is the Swedish name), and the next morning, about three o'clock, found the Russian fleet coming under full sail to surprise them. Raab, however, managed to get under weigh and retreat, damaging two of the leading Russians somewhat badly. Scheltinga's flagship, the Viborg, then led the van, supported by Kruyis's ship, the Riga. Both these ships were better sailers than the Swedes,

*Naval engagement off Högland, 1713.*

[1] Peter served always as a *subject*, and was officially known not as Tsar but as Rear-admiral Mihailoff.

and were overhauling them fast when Raab's ship grounded on a bank. She succeeded, however, in sliding over it. The Riga having failed to observe the incident, struck the same bank, and, being of greater draught, stuck fast. The Viborg also struck, but scraped over. The Russians, anxious to save their flagship, stood by to haul her off, and Raab's squadron escaped into Helsingfors.

The state of affairs in Sweden produced by Charles' defeat prevented any large action on the part of Russia's opponents, and not till the following year did the Swedes try to recover the command of the sea.

*Battle of Gangoot, 1714.*

In the spring of 1714 the Swedish Admiral Wattrang put to sea with a fleet of 15 line-of-battle ships, 2 gun sloops or boats, and 2 galleys. Early in May he came off Hangöeud (Gangoot), making for Abo, and here fell in with and captured or sank a number of Russian galleys that were engaged in small isolated operations along the coast. A number of others escaped into the bay formed by the Hangö isthmus, then (the Finnish coast hereabouts rises almost perceptibly yearly) very low and narrow.

In this gulf the Russians were blockaded; but finding themselves shut in, they began to try to move their galleys over the isthmus on rollers. To prevent this, Wattrang despatched Ehrensköld with a 14-gun sloop,[1] six of the captured galleys, and a couple of cutters round the peninsula.

[1] The Elefantin. The galleys carried 8 guns each. The cutters were a species of row-boat.

WARSHIPS *TEMPUS* PETER THE GREAT.

Ehrensköld had gone some twenty-five miles when he sighted 115 Russian ships and galleys, under Peter and Aprāksin, coming up from the southward. He at once retreated into a channel between two islands, and sank one of his cutters astern, so as to protect himself from a double attack.

*Ehrensköld's reply to the request for surrender.*

The Russians, under a flag of truce, demanded his surrender, to which he sent back the historical reply: "My king has not given me ships for the purpose of handing them over to the enemy, least of all to an enemy on whose word none can rely."

Aprāksin sent thirty-five galleys in to attack; but the Swedes, reserving their fire till the galleys were within half-pistol range, easily repulsed them.

*Peter in close action.*

Peter then led the attack himself[1] with the whole galley force, and, after a sanguinary conflict and heavy loss, got his own galley alongside the sloop of Ehrensköld. Defeat being now certain, the Swedish commander made off for the powder magazine; but the Russians, being on the lookout for such a move, shot him, boarded, and took the vessel as well as all her consorts. The Swedes lost 700 men killed or wounded; the remainder of their force, 200 men, were taken prisoners. The loss of the attacking Russians was much more heavy, and has been estimated as high as 3000, while a good half of their galleys were sunk or badly injured. The big ships do not appear to have been engaged on either side.

*Peter and Ehrensköld.*

Ehrensköld, desperately wounded, was brought

[1] He was on board the galley commanded by General Waide.

before the victorious Tsar, who, almost beside himself with delight, ran up to him, wiped the blood from his face, and kissed him. During the time he remained a prisoner, Peter treated the Swedish commander with every mark of esteem, and gave him a gold snuff-box set with brilliants when he liberated him.

*Peter promotes himself.*

On the return of his fleet with the captured vessels, Peter went into the Russian Senate and, describing his victory, announced that he had promoted himself to the rank of vice-admiral.

*1715. England allies with Russia.*

In the following year (1715) England, having some quarrel with Sweden, sent Sir John Norris into the Baltic with 18 ships-of-the-line. The Russians then had thirty 80-gun ships in those waters, and some Danish vessels also joined: the whole fleet, to the number of 80 ships, being under command of the Tsar himself. The Swedes remained shut up in their harbours, and nothing warlike was attempted.[1] Moreover, Peter appears to have had a secret alliance with Charles XII. about this time,[2] and was even suspected of having designs on the capital of his Danish friends. Charles XII. managed to run such blockade as the Danes kept up, and returned to his kingdom, but any naval operations on his side were out of the question. The Anglo-Russian fleet cruised yearly off the Swedish

[1] The Swedish version (Admiral Gyllengranat) says 10 English, 18 Danish, 8 Russian ships-of-the-line *plus* some galleys; and that a descent on the coast of Sweden was meditated but prevented owing to the existence of a Swedish fleet of 14 battleships and 6 frigates.

[2] He had an intense personal admiration for the meteoric King of Sweden.

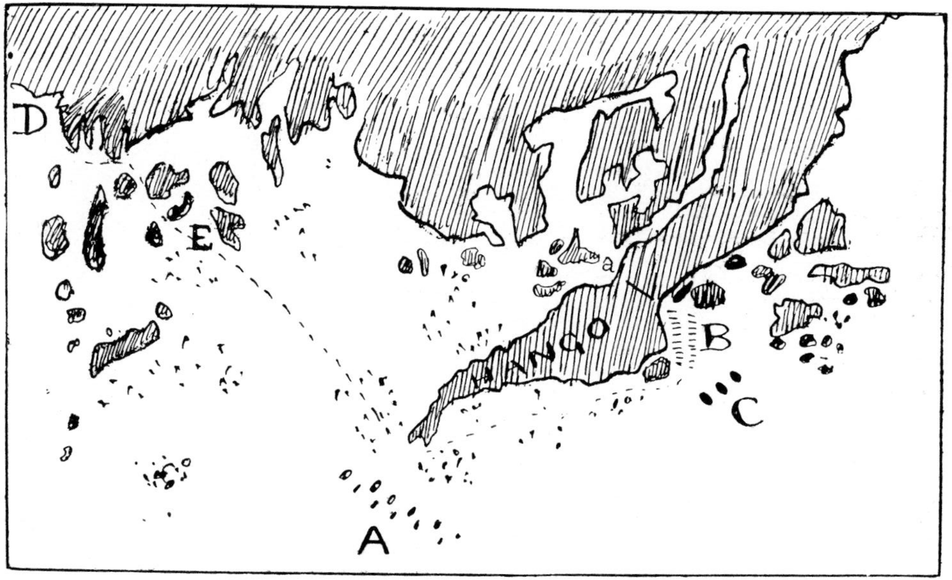


THE BATTLE OF GANGOOT (HANGÖ HEAD).

*A.* Swedish fleet. *C.* Swedes under Lillje.
*B.* Russians. *E.* Ehrenskjöld.
*a.* Point where Russians tried to bring their galleys over the isthmus.

ports till 1718,[1] in which year Charles, who had invaded Norway, was killed by a cannon ball at Frederickshald.

*24th May 1719. Capture of the Wachtmeister and other vessels.*

On the morning of 24th May of 1719 three Russian 50-gun ships cruising off Gotska Sandön (to the N.W. of Gotland) fell in with a reconnoitring force of Swedes — a 2-decker (Wachtmeister, 48 guns), a 24-gun frigate (Rushenfeldt), a 16-gun brig, and a schooner. They immediately gave chase, and being better sailers soon overhauled and captured the three smaller Swedish vessels. The 2-decker, however, kept on, and brought down the foremast of the leading and fastest Russian, steering for Sandhamn. The Wachtmeister seemed likely to show her heels, but about midday two more Russian 50-gun ships appeared between her and the Swedish coast, and brought her to action. The Wachtmeister having lost her foremast, maintopmast, and 110 men *hors de combat* out of a crew of 260, was forced to strike. This was apparently the first sea-fight in which Russian big ships were ever engaged as victors.

*Russian expedition to Sweden, 1719.*

Following upon this action a Russian fleet of 30 battleships and 150 galleys and transports, with 30,000 men under Count Aprāksin and Prince Galatzin, sailed for Sweden, and on the 9th of July appeared off the coast of Upland, to the north of Stockholm. Here they sacked and burned a great many villages, factories, and private residences, after which

[1] In 1717 the British fleet under Byng acted chiefly with the Danes only, and entirely off the south-west coast of Sweden.

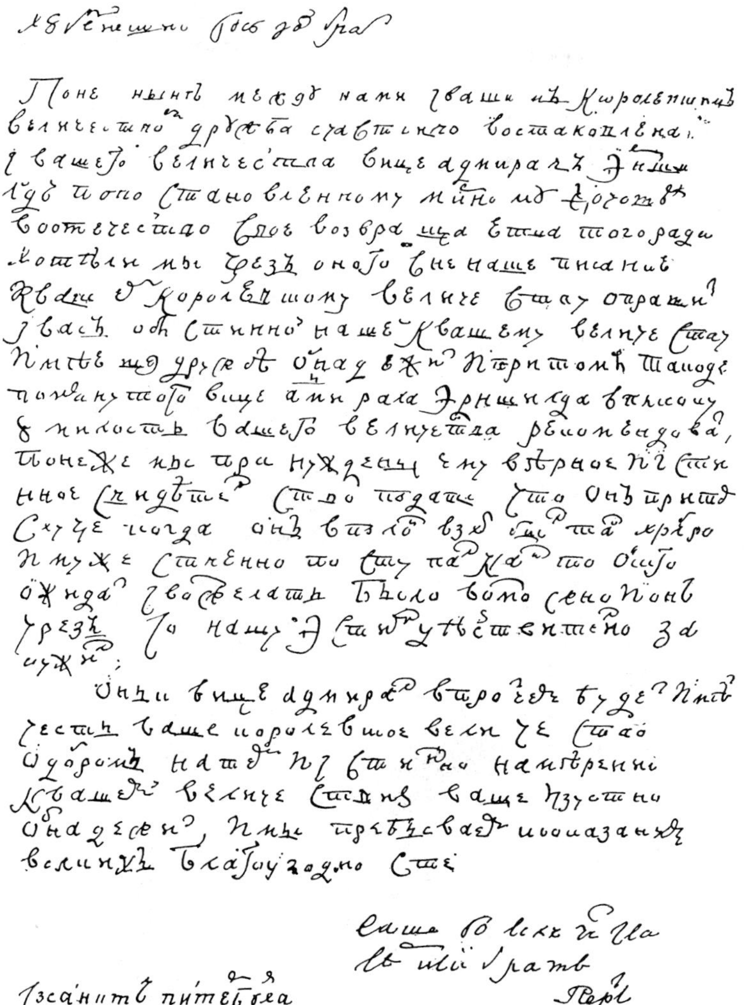

REDUCED FACSIMILE OF PETER THE GREAT'S LETTER TO THE KING OF SWEDEN CONCERNING EHRENSKIÖLD.

(*Only the first line and the signature are in Peter's own hand.—See* Appendix.)

the fleet was split into three squadrons. One squadron remained in the Stockholm Archipelago, the others went, one north, the other south. The northern expedition lasted from July 13th to August 19th, and during its continuance it destroyed the ironworks and sawmills at Harg and Ortaloo, the towns of Östhainmar and Öregund, the factories at Forsmark, Löfsta, Äkerby, Vestland, Harnäs, and Ostanö, then terminated operations with the destruction of Norrtelge on August 19th.

The southern squadron sacked and destroyed between July 14th and August 3rd all the property down the coast as far as the Kalmar Sound, including the towns of Trosa, Nyköping, Södertelge, and Norrkoeping.

On the 13th of August 6000 Russian soldiers landed at Södra Stäket near Stockholm, and began a march upon that city ; but meeting a repulse at the hands of the Södermanland regiment, they retreated to their ships.

On August 20th the Russians collected in the Stockholm Archipelago and returned to Revel.

Considerable interest attaches to these operations, *Comments* in that they form one of several historical instances of the ignoring of the " fleet in being " and several other pretty theories of Sea Power. The Russians, indeed, seem to have got along very well without any knowledge of these theories. The Swedish fleet, unbeaten, existed somewhere, but it made no attempt against them, though (in theory) it should have been capable of doing a good deal. Of course Sweden was almost in a state of anarchy at that time, and any intelligent operations for defence were probably impossible, and the Russians no doubt were fully aware of it. But at the same time they knew perfectly well that England was premeditating coming to Sweden's assistance, and actually had a fleet *en route*. Denmark, too, was nominally about to change sides, now that Charles XII. was dead.

*British fleet arrives.*

In the spring of 1720 the British fleet under Admiral Norris in the Sandwich, 90 guns; consisting of one 90, one 80, seven 70, six 60, and five 50-gun ships, altogether, 20 ships-of-the-line, came with orders to attack the Russians. Forty-nine Swedish ships joined them under Count Sparre. Sparre and Norris spent much of their time in squabbling as to precedence, and though they stayed three weeks off Revel, they did not fight any Russians. The Russian fleet under Apraxine visited the coast of Upper Norrland in May of this year (1720), destroyed the town of Umea and the surrounding villages, without interference from the Anglo-Swedish fleet.

*Second Russian expedition to devastate Swedish coast, 1720.*

*Third Russian expedition to devastate Swedish coast, 1721.*

In the following May the Russians, again directly in face of the powerful Anglo-Swedish "fleet in being," devastated and destroyed the entire coast of Norrland for a month (May 17th–June 17th). Thousands of farms, villages, and private estates were destroyed, including the towns of Söderhamn, Sundsvall, Hernosand, Pite, and Hudiksvall, and a number of important factories.

With this final exhibition of Sea Power of a most unclassical sort the war ended, leaving Russia mistress of the Swedish Baltic provinces and a good deal of the Finnish coast. Sweden, exhausted by twenty-two years of warfare, was prostrate: Russia was the predominant Baltic Power.

*Russian naval demonstration, 1723.*

In July 1723 Peter, being anxious to seat the Duke of Holstein upon the Swedish throne, indulged in a big naval demonstration. Twenty-four ships-of-the-line and 10 frigates, together with a large coast flotilla, sailed about in the Baltic under the general command of Aprāksin, the General Admiral, who personally commanded the central body. An advance guard, with the 60-gun ship Svataya Ekaterina as flagship, was commanded by Vice-admiral Peter Mihailoff (the Tsar himself); the rear-guard was under Vice-admiral Gordon, a Scotchman.

*Death of Peter 1725.*

Two years later Peter the Great died, leaving Russia an important Naval Power. This new navy was brave perhaps, rather than efficient, but under Peter's guidance it had served its purpose and accomplished all that could have been hoped or expected of it. That it did so was due to Peter's grasp of the real meaning of "Sea Power," to his recognition of the fact that his sailors were more or less amateurs, to his evolving tactics suitable for them, and, above all, to his realising that to defeat the enemy or to paralyse him were objectives, while mere "glorious actions" might be valueless.

His order about Swedish officers and their partiality

for powder magazines at the close of an unsuccessful battle, has already been referred to. A second order, one that was to bear queer fruit later,[1] was that no Swedish force was to be attacked unless the Russians had at least a one-third majority over the enemy.

[1] See p. 75.

# IV

## 1725–1762

## EKATERINA I. TO PETER III

PETER THE GREAT was succeeded by his widow the ex-Livonian peasant Ekaterina; and the consequent change in policy produced a naval demonstration in 1726. Twenty English and 12 Danish line-of-battle ships came off Kronstadt when the Russians had only 16 effective ships-of-the-line. The Russians were under Admirals Gordon and Saunders — both of them Scotchmen imported by Peter. Nothing came of the demonstration; nor did a repetition of it in the following year lead to any fighting. In 1727 Ekaterina I. died, and was succeeded by Peter II., who was followed in 1730 by the Empress Anne.

*British and Danish naval demonstration off Kronstadt, 1726.*

Poland was responsible for the next war; and Stanislaus having gone to Dantzig, where an allied army of Russians, Saxons, and Poles besieged him and a French force that had been thrown in to his assistance, the Russian fleet sailed under Gordon to look for the French. No French were forthcoming; but

*Dantzig, 1733.*

"The Putrid Sea" is a local and old name for the Sea of Azov.

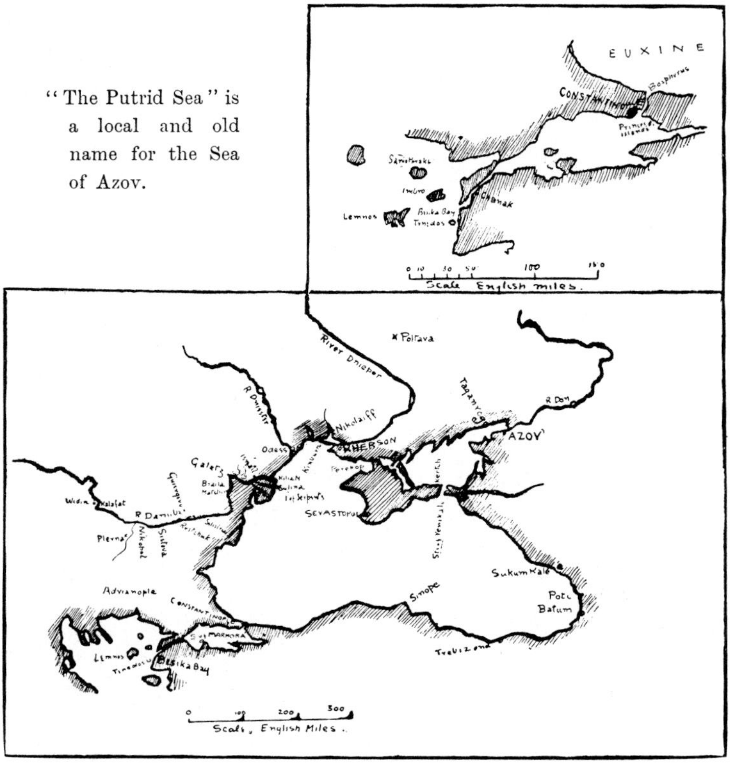


SKETCH MAP OF THE CRIMEA AND ADJACENT COASTS.

*Note.*—It is not clear which part of the Sea of Azov was marched over by the Russians dry shod. Creasy (*History of the Ottoman Turks*) seems to imply that it was the Straits of Yenikalé, that the phenomenon was locally known to occur with certain winds, and that Lascy marched down there to avail himself of the circumstance.

the fleet effectually blockaded Dantzig by sea, and produced its surrender.

In 1736, other relations being peaceful, Russia embarked upon that campaign against Turkey which Peter had had to abandon. Count Münnich in the following year assembled a fleet of flat-bottomed boats to attack the Crimea, and Bredal, a Russian admiral, supported him with a force of gunboats and armed rafts.

*1736. War with Turkey.*

*1737. Invasion of Crimea.*

Lascy now took supreme command, and by a bridge of casks and rafts crossed the Straits of Yenikalé. Azov was captured in June, but no very important operations took place, and in August the Russians left the Crimea by a bridge over "the Putrid Sea."

*Capture of Azov, 1737.*

In the following year these semi-military, semi-naval operations were resumed by Lascy, and a curious incident took place. The waters of "the Putrid Sea" are very shallow, and at times a strong west wind drives back the water, leaving dry land. On 7th July 1738 Lascy marched his army across the sea, which returned just as the last Russian reached the Crimean shore. The parallel to a well-known incident in the Book of Exodus was sufficiently striking to make an immense impression upon the superstitious Russian soldiers, and perhaps it led to Austria's joining the attack on Turkey—a move that cost her dearly.

*1738. A chapter of Exodus in the Putrid Sea.*

Bredal's fleet did not take any great share in the operations. In August 1737, while lying under a battery, it was attacked by a Turkish flotilla, which it

*Operations of the Russian flotilla under Bredal.*

repulsed; but venturing to sea in the following year, it was so damaged in a storm that it was practically useless. Along the Dneister the Russian soldiers won some victories; but, on the whole, the war was very barren of results to either side, save to Russia's ally, Austria, which was heavily defeated in several actions.

*Treaty of Belgrade and the Euxine fleet, 1739.*

In the following year the treaty of Belgrade was signed. By it Russia gained a little territory; but Azov and Taganrog were dismantled, and an agreement entered into that Russia should maintain no ships in the Sea of Azov or in the Black Sea, nor build any vessels on the shores of the Euxine.

In 1740 Anne died, and in that same year the War of the Austrian Succession began to loom. Ivan VI., the new Tsar, started hostilities against Sweden, and gained some land advantage; a revolution then disposed of him, and set Elizabeth, Peter the Great's daughter, on the throne.

*1741.*

Under Elizabeth the Russian arms were more successful, and Lascy brought about the capitulation of an entire Swedish army near Helsingfors.

*Naval operations, 1743.*

In 1743 Lascy got together at Kronstadt a fleet consisting of 17 line-of-battle ships,[1] 5 frigates, and 48 galleys, the command of which fleet was given to Admiral Gollovin.

Off Hango Point (Gangoot) lay a Swedish fleet, numbering 16 ships-of-the-line, 5 frigates, 2 brigs, 2 bomb ketches, and 1 fire-ship.

[1] Some accounts say 15 battleships.

Lascy sent Gollovin to attack this fleet; but when the Swedish admiral, Johan von Utfall, moved out to meet him, Gollovin at once retreated to Revel, and merely a few long-range shots were exchanged. Gollovin excused his inaction by quoting Peter the Great's order that the Swedes were not to be fought unless the Russians were in a big majority.

*Gollovin declines action with the Swedes, May 1743.*

*His reasons.*

Probably Gollovin was right. The Swedes had a heavy naval prestige,—the past gave no hope or record of equal forces of Russian sailors beating Swedes; to attack would have been but to court disaster. By retiring to Revel he occupied the Swedish fleet, and by remaining intact prevented their operating elsewhere.

*Comments.*

In August a peace disadvantageous to Sweden was concluded.

*Peace, 1743.*

In the general fighting which preceded the Treaty of Aix-la-Chapelle in 1748, Russia, though subsidised by England, took no active part, notwithstanding that 37,000 men and 40 galleys were kept in readiness to participate. Lack of transport appears to have been the reason of this inaction, and no attempt of any sort was made to remedy it by utilising the Russian Navy.

*1748.*

The Seven Years' War found Russia in conflict with Prussia, and in 1757 a fleet of 15 Russian battleships bombarded and captured Memel. Thence they blockaded the Prussian coast, till in 1758 the Russian land forces were compelled to withdraw from the scene of several victories owing to shortness of provisions.

*The Seven Years' War, 1757.*

In 1758 the Russian Admiral Mishukoff was joined by 6 Swedish battleships and 2 frigates under Lagerbjclke, and some Danes under Schoutbynacht Fisher, and spent the summer looking for an opposing English fleet, that did not appear.

1760. In 1760 the fleet, now brought up to 27 vessels, under Admiral Mishukoff, attempted but failed to take Colberg in conjunction with a land force. The
1761. next year, increased to 40 ships and having been joined also by Swedish vessels, they tried the same thing, and Colberg was taken on 16th December 1761.

1762. Some three weeks later the Empress Elizabeth died, and was succeeded by Peter III., who at once joined forces with Prussia and became at war with Sweden. Nothing, however, seems to have happened: Peter's energies were principally occupied in trying to rid himself of his wife, Ekaterina, a German princess. Then Ekaterina, having got some regiments of guards to espouse her cause, dethroned Peter, proclaimed herself Tsarina, and Peter, thrown into prison, was strangled by her orders a week after his deposition.

V

## 1762–1796

## THE RUSSIAN NAVY UNDER EKATERINA THE GREAT

EKATERINA II. (the Great) was undoubtedly the most able woman who ever sat on the Russian or, for that matter, any other throne. The means whereby she came to rule were ethically reprehensible enough, and, like every woman who has written her name in the pages of history, her morals were hardly such as meet with favour. But in this respect she was no worse—perhaps even she was better—than her predecessors, Anne and Elizabeth, while she was infinitely more able as a ruler. She introduced many wise reforms into the government, was a great patron of art, literature, and science, and, from the imperial standpoint, raised her country to a pinnacle it had never before occupied. To the Imperial Navy her services were second only to those of Peter the Great: from some points of view they were indeed greater. During her reign appeared the most famous of Russian admirals, Samuel Greig, a Scotchman, who had previously served in the British Navy, and participated in the battle of *Samuel Greig.*

Quiberon in 1759. He joined the Russian Navy in 1762, two years after Ekaterina came to the throne, and soon rose to high rank. Ekaterina also induced a number of other British officers to enter her service, Elphinstone (who entered as a rear-admiral), Dugdale, Mackenzie, and Mitchell being those most celebrated after Greig. Under Peter the Russian Navy had been to some extent a child of the British one, Gordon and Saunders had already been heard of, but under Ekaterina these good offices were increased a hundredfold, and British officers entered her service in scores. At one time more than half the entire list of officers were of Anglo-Saxon and Celtic nationality — Scotchmen, in particular, showed a partiality for the service.

*Other British officers.*

*War with Prussia.*

The first event when Ekaterina assumed the reins of government was a reversal of her husband's policy and a return to that of Elizabeth. No operations of much importance, however, on the part of Russia marked the close of the Seven Years' War; and the small use that the fleet was may have turned Ekaterina's thoughts to the utilisation of British officers. Russian history was full of instances of British fleets entering and operating in the Baltic; the power of the Swedes, though nearly dead in 1762, had been great and decisive upon the sea in earlier years. Contemplation of these facts must have fired Ekaterina's imagination; and she it was who, having reorganised her navy, gave orders for the first attempt of a Russian fleet to operate in foreign waters.

In 1768 war was declared against Turkey; and in

the following year Ekaterina ordered Admiral Count Alexis Orloff to take his fleet from Kronstadt, and operate against Turkey in the Levant. Such an absolutely novel departure made considerable stir in Europe at the time, and the Turks, amongst others, heard of Ekaterina's intentions. They, however, looked upon the projected expedition as so foolhardy and impossible that they made absolutely no preparations to meet it, contenting themselves with the assurance that Orloff would not manage to enter the Mediterranean.

*Russian fleet ordered to the Mediterranean, 1769.*

Count Orloff left Kronstadt with a fleet consisting of 12 ships-of-the-line, 12 frigates, and a number of transports and store-ships. After experiencing some bad weather in the German Ocean, he picked up English pilots and reached Portsmouth in a very bad condition. At Portsmouth the dockyard was put at his disposal; and having refitted, he sailed again, to meet more bad weather in the Bay of Biscay; but eventually he got through the Straits of Gibraltar and anchored at Port Mahon, then occupied by the British. Here again he found himself among friends, his battered ships were put into trim, and his sea-sick and diseased men treated in the hospitals.

*Orloff sails.*

*Reaches Portsmouth.*

*Orloff at Port Mahon.*

The Mediterranean Powers generally regarded the advent of a Russian fleet with extreme dislike: the Venetians, in particular, would have none of it. They issued an order that no Russian ships were to be admitted into the ports, and sent out a fleet with orders to attack Orloff should he try to enter the Adriatic. The Turks, meanwhile, were astounded to

*Views of Mediterranean Powers.*

*Venetian action.*

*Views of the Turks.*

hear of the Russian fleet's arrival; and promptly addressed a complaint to the representatives of Austria because the Venetians "had allowed Orloff to pass the Straits of Gibraltar."

*The Turkish fleet in 1770.*

Mustapha III., the then Sultan of Turkey, had paid great attention to his fleet, and it was in a fairly efficient condition—efficient, at least, for the Turks.

*Hassan of Algiers.*

Its chief admiral was Hassan of Algiers, a man of some fame and mark in his time. Born on the frontiers of Persia, Hassan when a boy was captured and sold as a slave in Algeria. After a time he became a boatman, then a soldier, and later still a pirate, in which capacity he gained so much renown that he became Port Admiral of Algiers. Here he quarrelled with the Dey, and was exiled or escaped to Italy; and his fame having preceded him, he secured a post in the Turkish fleet, and soon became a leading admiral.

*Orloff moves, Feb. 1770.*

Orloff having refitted his ships, left Port Mahon in February 1770, and sailed for the Morea. Here he issued proclamations and produced a revolt, and occupied Navarino, Modon, Patras, and several other ports. His soldiers, however, were too few to help the insurrection to any extent, and the Turkish army coming down in force, he first withdrew to Navarino and then left Greece altogether.

*Orloff's opinion of his fleet.*

He had written to Ekaterina a most trenchant criticism upon his fleet, describing it as nearly useless even against the Turks; but the Tsarina was not to be discouraged. Rear-Admirals Elphinstone and Spiridoff, with Greig, then a commodore, were despatched with

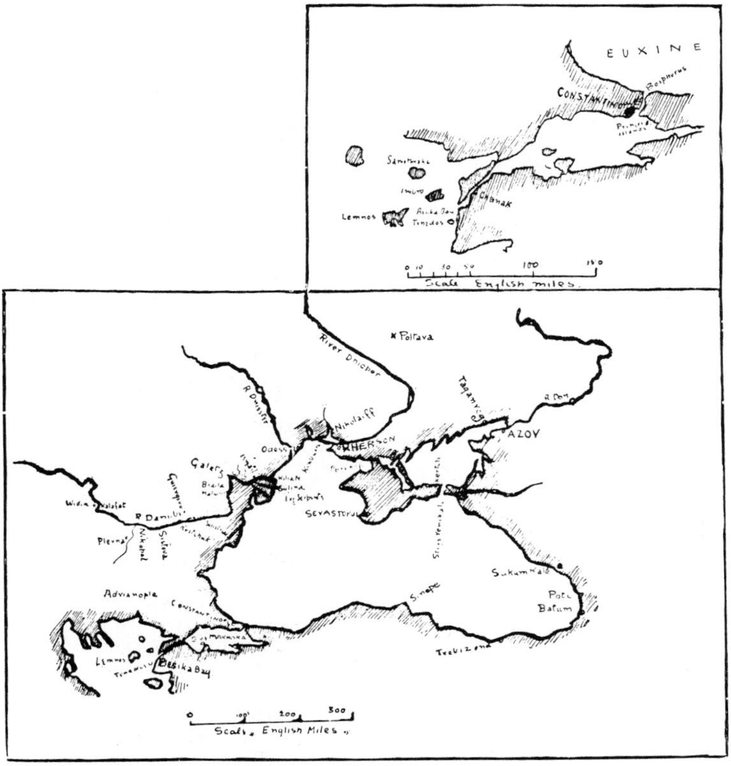


MAP OF BLACK SEA, TURKEY, ETC.

*Ekaterina sends reinforcements.*

reinforcements viâ Portsmouth and Port Mahon, and these reached Orloff early in 1770. In May, Hassan of Algiers came down the Dardenelles with a large fleet, and the rivals tried each other's metal in a number of small long-range engagements that produced little or no loss on either side.

*Small encounters.*

*Battle of Chios and Tchesma, 5-7 July 1770.*

On the 5th of July 1770 Admiral Spiridoff, with ten[1] ships-of-the-line and five frigates, was cruising off Chios, when he encountered Hassan of Algiers. The Turkish fleet consisted of 15 ships-of-the-line (one of 100 guns, one of 96, four 84, one 74, one 70, one 62, and six 60 guns), 8 galliots, 5 xebecques, and 2 corvettes. Hassan ran his ship alongside that of Spiridoff, and both vessels took fire. They continued fighting till they blew up. Nearly the whole of the crews were killed on either side, but in both cases the admirals and principal officers escaped unhurt. The majority of the Turks were at anchor, and so remained during the battle, which led to no very decisive result, though such advantage as there was rested entirely with the Russians. Night fell before the Turks could be destroyed; but the fortunes of the day had gone against them enough to create panic in many of their vessels. Hassan's authority was set aside, and, bent only upon avoiding a repetition of the action on the morrow, the Turks cut their cables and drifted in disorder into the Bay of Tchesma, where they were more or less safe from Russian attack.

[1] Creasy's *History of Turkey* says eight ships-of-the-line and seven frigates. The biggest Russian ship was the Rostislav, 108 guns.

They were not, however, protected against fire-ships (the old-time equivalent to torpedo boats), and Admiral Elphinstone prepared four. None of the Russians knew anything at all about fire-ships, and they evinced no desire to start learning off Tchesma. Consequently the famous battle of Tchesma was practically a British affair with Russian crews, and not invariably even with these, as those in the fire-ships deserted at the critical moment.

*Tchesma a British affair.*

Practically, what Spiridoff did was to very wisely decide not to interfere with an operation concerning which he had neither experience nor knowledge; and when we make allowances for the natural gall that dependence upon foreigners must have produced, Russian behaviour at Tchesma was correct enough. The Russian officers folded their hands, and left the work to those who understood it. History has many instances of our people co-operating with foreigners, the foreigners busy hampering as much as possible. Spiridoff did no hampering, and the command of the entire fleet seems to have been in the hands of Elphinstone that night.[1]

*Spiridoff's wisdom in not interfering.*

The plan of attack was as follows:—

*Plan of attack.*

Elphinstone, with the main body of the fleet, lay outside in case the Turks should attempt a rush.

Commodore Greig, detached with four ships-of-the-line and two frigates, entered the mouth of the bay, and stood by to cover the attack.

*Greig.*

[1] Spiridoff may have been incapacitated from wounds.

The four fire-ships were under Dugdale, with Mackenzie as second in command.

Dugdale.

Three of the fire-ships ran aground and were wasted, as the whole of the Russian bluejackets jumped overboard before the Turks were reached. Dugdale, however, managed to run his vessel alongside a Turk and grapple her. He then fired his ship; the flames spread rapidly amid the crowded shipping, and in five hours only the 62-gun ship and a few small craft remained: the Turkish fleet was annihilated.

In consequence of this action, which ranks as one of the most famous battles in Russian history, Orloff received the surname of Tchesmeski. Naturally the Russians have to some extent concealed their dependence upon their British officers, and the critical have remarked that the names of Elphinstone, Dugdale, and Mackenzie are not to be found alongside that of the Tchesma in the Russian Navy List. Neither, however, is that of Orloff, and Spiridoff's name is perpetuated for other actions than this one.[1] On the whole, we need not grudge the Russians the triumph of their flag at Tchesma: *après tout*, the ships and flag were theirs. Is it not taught in Belgium that Waterloo is a place where in 1815 the Belgians thrashed the French? And at Waterloo the panic-stricken Belgians nearly flung our troops into confusion; while at Tchesma the Russians refused to hamper naval operations that they did not understand, and helped in what was really the most effective way.

[1] "Admiral Greig" is a Russian ship-name.

After Tchesma the whole Levant was at Russia's mercy, and Elphinstone blockaded the Dardenelles. Numerous Turkish merchantmen were captured, and generally the Russians met with success, causing revolts in Egypt, and at one or two places in Greece. Elphinstone wished to force the Dardenelles, but Orloff, who, as before mentioned, had a very low opinion of the value of his fleet, hesitated. The Dardenelles, as it chanced, were at this time practically undefended, there being nothing save a few old tumbledown forts of scarcely any value at all between the Russian fleet and Constantinople.

*Elphinstone proposes to force the Dardenelles.*

While Orloff hesitated, the Turkish ex-Vizier Moldowendji was sending round men with pails of whitewash. Every old fort was carefully whitewashed; and when Orloff came to make a reconnaissance, he found what appeared to be a series of brand-new defences. It is indeed a curious freak of Fate that a few pails of whitewash should have barred Russia in 1770 from the city of her eternal desire!

*How Constantinople was saved from Russia after Tchesma.*

Orloff would doubtless have discovered the deception sooner or later, but his chance was only a transient one. The Turks had then in their service a Frenchman, one De Tott, and under De Tott's supervision real and efficient fortifications were rapidly constructed. Realising at length what was in the wind, Orloff attacked one of these forts, but failing to make any impression on it whatever, he abandoned the Dardenelles and sailed away to attack Lemnos.

At Lemnos he landed all the men at his disposal,

*Russians defeated before Lemnos, 1770.*

and besieged the Castle sixty days. Provisions being exhausted, the garrison had already begun to treat for surrender and sent hostages, when Hassan of Algiers, who had been saved from the holocaust at Tchesma, appeared on the scene. He had got together a number of light vessels, and these he manned with 4000 volunteers, the riff-raff of Constantinople, armed only with pistols and sabres. De Tott, the Frenchman at the Sultan's court, considered the plan ridiculous, but the Grand Vizier approved of it. "If it succeeds," said he, "Lemnos will be saved: if it fails, it will rid Constantinople of 4000 ruffians and rogues."

Hassan landed secretly on the east side of the island of Lemnos, and in the early morning of the 10th of October fell suddenly and unexpectedly upon Orloff's lines. The Russian artillerymen were cut to pieces, their guns captured and turned upon the rest of the besiegers. A great many were killed, and only a percentage managed to reach the ships, which at once sailed away. For this, Hassan of Algiers was made chief admiral of the Turkish Navy.

A little later, Hassan encountered Orloff again in a hard-fought battle at Munderos. Both sides claimed the victory. After the battle Orloff sailed away, first giving up to Hassan the hostages who had been handed over at Lemnos and sent on board his fleet.

After this the Russian Mediterranean fleet did

practically nothing. The ships were in sad need of repairs, battle and sickness had seriously depleted their crews; and for the rest of the war they spent such energies as were left them in attacks upon small towns, in order to get supplies of the necessaries of life.

*Peace of Kainardji, 1784.*

In the Crimea and elsewhere the Russian soldiers had carried all before them; and in 1784, when the Peace of Kainardji was signed, Russia gained Kinburn, Kertch, Yenikalé, and the country between the Bug and Dneiper. She also retained Azov and Taganrog, secured the right to build and maintain a Black Sea fleet, while the Bosphorus and Dardenelles were thrown open to her merchant ships. In securing all these results the Russian Navy may be said to have borne a full if indirect share: Orloff's unexpected attack in the Levant drained and divided the Turkish defence. Directly peace was signed, Orloff, viâ English ports, returned to Kronstadt with his fleet.

*Anglo-Russian war prevented owing to most Russian naval officers being British.*

One curious circumstance remains to be recorded. In 1780 Ekaterina joined the Armed Neutrality—allied with Prussia, Austria, Sweden, and Portugal nominally for the protection of neutral commerce, but practically a pro-French combination. Russia, however, though opposed to Great Britain, found herself unable to act against her for the simple reason that most of her naval officers were British, and her only bases outside her own coasts British harbours!

*New war with Turkey, 1787.*

In 1787 a new war with Turkey broke out. Mindful of the effect that Orloff's fleet had produced, Ekaterina gave orders for Greig—now an admiral — to take eighteen ships-of-the-line, with a number of frigates and store-ships, to the Levant from Kronstadt.

*Greig ordered to the Mediterranean.*

*British and other hostility prevents Greig from sailing.*

The fleet, however, never sailed. On hearing of the projected expedition, every State in the Mediterranean, except Genoa, refused to assist it, or admit it within its ports: the strained relations with Great Britain precluded the hope of friendly offices such as had been accorded to Orloff, and though some British packet lines agreed to provide transport for stores, the British Government forbade such assistance. Finally, through Turkish diplomacy, a rupture occurred between Russia and her old enemy Sweden, which of course necessitated the retention of Greig's ships in the Baltic.

*Rupture with Sweden, 1788.*

*Turco-Russian War.*

The Russian Navy was not, however, altogether idle against Turkey. Hassan of Algiers, now Ghazi and commander-in-chief of the Turkish forces both on land and sea, attacked Kinburn. The afterwards famous Suwarroff marched to its relief, supported by a large fleet of gunboats. The Turkish fleet (galleys and small craft of the gunboat order) was allowed to enter the Liman without resistance, and began to bombard Kinburn, when Suwarroff suddenly attacked the besiegers by land. While the Turkish ships bombarded, they were attacked in the rear by the Russian gunboats, and all, or nearly all, of them, caught between so many fires, were destroyed.

Later, these Russian gunboats operated with Suwarroff on the Danube. Larger ship fighting there was none: so far as big ships were concerned, the Euxine was still a Turkish lake.

*Kapitan Saken's death.*

One naval incident is worthy of record. Captain Saken, of a 15-gun galley, fell in with thirteen small Turkish galleys, that cut him off and surrounded him. Seeing that the day was lost, Saken ordered his men into the boats, but himself remained on board. When four galleys had grappled his ship and were about to board, he blew up his magazine, destroying himself, his vessel, and her four antagonists. A torpedo gunboat commemorates this achievement. Saken was a native of the erstwhile Swedish province of Esthonia.

*The first appearance of "The Russian Menace" in England, 1790.*

In 1790 that hardy annual "The Russian Menace" first made its appearance in England. In that year Pitt asked for an increase of the navy to balance Russian shipbuilding, much as to-day our Governments do every year. Fox, being Pitt's political rival, advocated a Russian alliance. Pitt attempted to end the Turco-Russian war, and Ekaterina declined to listen to his proposals; in consequence of which Pitt, enacting a rôle much akin to that of Beaconsfield ninety years later, nearly brought about an Anglo-Russian war. Popular opinion, however, was not in those days educated up to the good qualities of the Turk, or the necessity of retaining him in Europe, and Pitt obtained little support from even his own party in his anti-Russian crusade. Speaking generally, we entertained in those days much the same kind of "tenderness" of public sentiment for Russia that now, a hundred odd years later, we have for Japan.

The French Revolution put a sudden end to Pitt's views and designs, if he had any, against Russian conquest in the South of Europe. As for Russia, her armies on land pursued a more or less victorious course, but much of her energy was occupied in dealing with Sweden; and in those days, when most nations were liable to change sides a time or two in the course of a general war, Russia's distance from the centre of operations demanded a large amount of circumspection in her movements. If it were not "history," a good deal of what took place in the general wars of the eighteenth century would strongly suggest the Gilbert and Sullivan opera of to-day. Many books have been written on the strategical and political aspects of the Seven Years' War and other conflicts of the eighteenth century, but when one comes to regard them with an open mind, it is difficult to believe that any very serious strategical purposes were ever at work. So long as their armies fought a battle now and again, most of the rulers and their generals seem to have been fairly indifferent as to who they fought, or what was secured or lost by the fighting! The position of the Russian Navy in the foregoing pages has usually been one of strategical inutility, or else of tactical impotence—

*Gilberterian aspect of European politics in the 18th century.*

occasionally of both combined; but in none of the movements of Russia's allies or foes is any much greater purpose to be discerned, unless we look with a very fixed determination to discover one.

*The war with Sweden.*

Mention has already been made of the rupture with Sweden in 1788. When Ekaterina declared war against Gustavus III. of Sweden (then subsidised by Turkey), she had for allies Austria and Denmark. Great Britain, then involved with France, Spain, and Holland, was, as regards Russia, a species of malevolent neutral. She sent no ships to attack Russia, having none to spare, but a number of British naval officers, including the famous Sir Sidney Smith, went to Sweden, and served in the Swedish fleet. Elphinstone resigned his command in the Russian Navy and re-entered the British service,[1] but Greig and most of the others remained in the Russian fleet. England, so far as her naval officers were concerned, was occupying a sea position very nearly analogous to that occupied by the Swiss on shore — nearly every nation had Swiss mercenaries in its armies — most navies carried British or ex-British officers in some of their ships.[2]

*Battle of Högland (Gogland), 17th July 1788*

The first naval battle of the new Russo-Swedish War was that of Högland (Gogland), 17th July 1788, the Swedes having penetrated the Gulf of Finland with a view to attacking St. Péterbōurg.

[1] He served with Byron and Rodney as captain of the Magnificent, 1774-80.

[2] In the Russian Navy there were also many British seamen.

The Russian fleet under Greig was constituted as follows:—

| | | |
|---|---|---|
| 1 ship of | 108 | guns (Rostislav) |
| 8 ships of | 74 | ,, |
| 8 ,, | 66 | ,, |
| 8 frigates | 28–32 | ,, |
| 8 smaller ships, various | | |
| with a total of | 1452 | guns |

The Swedes under their Prince Carl (afterwards king) had a fleet consisting of—

| | | |
|---|---|---|
| 4 ships of | 70 | guns |
| 11 ,, | 60 | ,, |
| 5 big frigates | 40 | ,, |
| 2 frigates | 32 | ,, |
| 4 smaller ships | | |
| with a total of | 1286 | guns |

The Russians had therefore some considerable superiority in number of guns; but so far as number of line-of-battle ships went, their superiority was not very great—17 ships-of-the-line against 15, aided by 5 40-gun frigates capable of "lying in the line," and certainly equal to a couple of third-rate 60-gun ships-of-the-line. Individually, of course, the Russian ships were larger, and history has always shown—except, perhaps, to the perennial contributor of "Pleas for Moderate Dimensions" in Brassey's *Naval Annual*—that, other things being equal, one big ship is always worth two smaller ones.[1]

[1] *Two* brains, that must vary, pitted against one, work the mischief. In naval warfare the individual captain must act largely at times on his own judgment, and "tot homines, tot sententiæ." Had Greig, instead of 17 sail-of-the-line of various sizes, had a dozen, or perhaps even ten, big three-deckers, he would probably have won the battle of Gogland.

The battle began at 3.30 in the afternoon, and was commenced by Admiral Greig, who in the three-decker Rostislav charged right into the Swedish flagship. A seventy-four following, attacked her from the other side. Three Swedish 60-gun ships, the Vasa, Äran, and Fadernistandet, came to the assistance of their prince, and for some while the battle was carried out by these vessels only. The two Russian ships fought desperately, but were eventually forced to retire on their main body, certain ships of which had evinced no great desire to fight. Peter's standing order about the correct proportion of Russians to Swedes was not a dead letter and not forgotten: Greig had broken it by attacking, and Swedish prestige was yet a real thing to the Russians. On the other hand, the Swedes had to combat against the prestige of Greig and his British officers and men, two things that helped to make the action indecisive.

*Greig at Gogland.*

The Swedish Prince Gustav, which failed to change tack, got involved in the Russian line and was captured; but almost at the same moment the Russian seventy-four Vladimir was forced to strike to the Swedes for a precisely similar cause.[1] The rest of the ships did a good deal of firing without doing any great harm on either side save to "sticks"; the greatest loss was in those vessels that had begun the battle. In these it was very heavy. At 10 p.m. the fleets separated, and went back to their harbours. Greig

[1] There was very little wind, and all manœuvres were somewhat disorderly and difficult to carry out effectually.

returned his loss at about 1000 men *hors de combat.*[1] Prince Carl sent in his as 130 killed and 334 wounded —about half the Russian loss. It was in this action that the captain of the Swedish Vasa, Count Balzar Horn, being mortally wounded and having to pass the command to a junior lieutenant, made to that officer the historical and oft-quoted speech: "You shall answer me before the Almighty if you yield!"

The Swedes regarded the battle of Gogland as almost equivalent to a victory, on the score of the front that they showed to a British admiral with a certain number of British officers and seamen under him.[2] Their attack of St. Péterbōurg was, however, frustrated by it.

Details of the fleets engaged[3] at Gogland will be found on the two pages following. The names of British commanding officers in Russian vessels are indicated with asterisks.

[1] He was himself wounded. He reported the Vladimir captured, and a second ship "missing."

[2] There were also a good many picked Danish and Norwegian seamen in the Russian fleet.

[3] A number of additional details, official reports never before published, plans, the correspondence, etc. etc., of this and other battles, will be found in the General Appendix at the end of this book. The whole correspondence and Russian admissions as to the use of inflammable shell at the battle of Gogland will be found in the Appendix.

## RUSSIAN FLEET

### Ships-of-the-line

| *Name.* | *Guns.* | *Commander.* |
|---|---|---|
| Rostislav | 108 | Captain Odenzoff (Admiral Greig *). |
| Mistisloff | 74 | Captain Mautovski. |
| Péter Veliky | 74 | ,, Dennison.* |
| Vladimir | 74 | ,, Berch. |
| St. Helena | 74 | ,, Brayer * (Rear-Admiral Grigorovitch Spiridoff). |
| Retwisan | 74 | Captain Todd * (Rear-Admiral van Oessen). |
| Yaroslav | 74 | Captain Beakes.* |
| Viestnik | 74 | ,, Makaroff (Rear-Admiral Constantinoff). |
| Ivan Bohnslaff | 74 | Captain Narland.* |
| Tchinslav | 66 | ,, Carston.* (?) |
| Rossia | 66 | ,, Trevenna.* |
| Doris | 66 | ,, Kukosoff. |
| Gremiastchy | 65 | ,, Borinoff. |
| Victor | 66 | ,, Obolianoff. |
| Miceslaff | 66 | ,, Borizoff. |
| Vzadnik | 66 | ,, Elphinstone * (not the admiral). |
| Boteslav | 66 | Captain Dennison.* |

### Frigates

| *Name.* | *Guns.* | *Commander.* |
|---|---|---|
| Briantislav | 32 | Captain Seniavin. |
| Priamislav | 32 | ,, Severs * [1] (or Siever). |
| Pozadnik | 36 | ,, Lomen.[1] |
| Sdwan | 32 | ,, Chiroliskoff. |
| Mistisloff | 28 | ,, Stamontoff. |
| Nayezdnik | 28 | ,, (?) |
| Penderaklia | 32 | ,, Lolgnet.[2] |
| Vzadnik | 32 | ,, Liskovski. |

2 bomb ketches, 1 cutter, and 3 transports.

Total broadside, 614 guns. Total guns, 1452.

[1] Uncertain whether Dutch or English.

[2] Said to have been English—name cannot be identified.

## SWEDISH FLEET

| *Name.* | *Guns.* | *Commander.* |
|---|---|---|
| Hedwig Elisabeth Charlotte | 60 | Lieut.-Colonel Modée. |
| Gripen . . . . | 44 | Captain von Hoorn. |
| Ömheten . . . . | 60 | Lieut.-Colonel Kuylenstjerna. |
| Prince Gustav . . . | 68 | Colonel Count Wachtmeister. |
| Rättvisan . . . . | 60 | Lieut.-Colonel Fust. |
| Camilla . . . . | 40 | Captain Dufva. |
| Enigheten . . . | 68 | Lieut.-Colonel Eneskiöld. |
| Froja . . . . | 40 | Major Puke. |
| Dygden . . . . | 60 | Lieut.-Colonel Raab. |
| Vasa . . . . | 60 | ,, Count Horn. |
| Gustaf III. . . . | 68 | Flag-Captain Nordenskjöld (Admiral, Prince Carl—and Count Wrangel). |
| Fäderneslandet . . . | 60 | Lieut.-Colonel Kuylenstjerna. |
| Äran . . . . | 60 | ,, Hysingsköld. |
| Minerva . . . . | 40 | Major Nauckhoff. |
| Försigtigheten . . . | 60 | Lieut.-Colonel Fahlstedt. |
| Thetis . . . . | 40 | Major Wollyn. |
| Prins Carl . . . | 60 | Lieut.-Colonel Psilanderhjelm. |
| Sophia Magdalena . . | 68 | ,, Linderstedt. |
| Prins Fredrik Adolf . . | 60 | ,, Leijonankar. |
| Prins Gustaf Adolf . . | 60 | ,, Christiernin. |
| Yarramas (frigate) . . | 32 | Major Billing. |
| Yarislawitz ( ,, ) . . | 32 | Lieutenant Hokenflykt. |
| Hector ( ,, ) . . | 22 | ,, Kullenberg. |

### Repeaters and Scouts not in the Line

| *Name.* | *Guns.* | *Commander.* |
|---|---|---|
| Sprengtporten . . . | 24 | Lieut.-Colonel Stedingk. |
| Trolle . . . . | 24 | Major Gyllenskold. |
| Patrioten . . . . | 16 | Lieutenant Virgin. |
| Esplendian (yacht) . . | | Ensign Ekholm. |

Total broadside, 568 guns. Total guns, 1286.

Greig, annoyed at his failure to win a victory, hastily refitted his fleet, collected a few reinforcements, then sailed for Sveaborg, whither the Swedes had retired and were still refitting. Here he made a bold attempt to destroy the lot of them, but failed. He managed, however, to capture a line-of-battle ship. He then blockaded;[1] but was taken ill and died; after which his fleet withdrew, losing two frigates.

*Battle of Sveaborg, 1788.*

*Death of Greig.*

In the following year the British, Dutch, and Prussians intervened to the extent of neutralising Denmark, and Gustavus III. made a great and final effort to get together a fleet strong enough to defeat the Russians, of which, now that Greig was dead, he was sanguine.

After Greig's death the command of the Russian fleet passed to the Prince of Nassau-Siegen.[2] He had with him 21 ships-of-the-line and 10 frigates, and with this force met the Swedish Crown Prince Carl, also with 21 ships-of-the-line and 9 frigates. The battle lasted six hours, from 2 to 8 p.m., and was again indecisive. Probably both sides had more ships than they could manage. The

*Battle of Öland, 1789.*

[1] An anecdote of the blockade is as follows. One of Greig's frigates captured a Swedish transport laden with cordage. Greig liberated the crew, a petty officer and seven men, and sent them under a flag of truce to the Mjölö Roads, where Prince Carl was lying. In return Prince Carl sent to Greig a Russian petty officer and seven men from the Vladimir, and also returned the master of a captured Russian merchantman with his wife and three daughters. In a letter of thanks for this courtesy Greig expressed his pleasure, and "regretted that he was unable to exchange presents of the fair sex with the Prince, but he had not had the fortune to make any such prisoners."

[2] Possibly, however, Tchitchagoff was in command at Öland.

MAP OF THE BALTIC.

Swedes, however, never had their full force engaged, as Liljehorn, who commanded their rear-guard, failed to support the main body.[1] He subsequently gave as a reason his opinion that "two-thirds of the Swedish force were quite sufficient to defeat the Russians." His inaction has always remained inexplicable, as he had been noted hitherto for his bravery. He certainly, however, lacked the ability to know what Nelson always knew and acted on: "Numbers only can annihilate," and that mere gallant engagements are useless. In this case the Swedes did not even win, and appear, if anything, to have had rather the worst of an encounter in which decisive victory would have rehabilitated their nation. Indeed, Liljehorn's inaction may be said to have sealed the fate of Sweden: the last chance to break the Russian Naval Power was thrown away. To all intents and purposes this battle was what the Russians claim it—a Russian victory; and after it they felt themselves fully competent to meet the Swedes on equal terms.

*Liljehorn seals the fate of Sweden.*

They retired, however, after this meeting,[2] and Swedish coast-vessels began to penetrate the Gulf of Finland. A coast-flotilla[3] under Ehrenswärd came off Korkiansaari, and was there attacked by a miscel-

[1] The Russians fought a retreating action. The Swedes say that they had several ships disabled in consequence of an epidemic caught from the crew of the captured Vladimir.

[2] The Russian version is that they did not want to fight till reinforcements that were expected arrived. Their plan was to collect a huge force and annihilate the Swedes.

[3] One frigate, 11 coast-frigates, 5 galleys, and 23 small gunboats.

laneous Russian coast-defence force, consisting of 2 frigates, 3 xebecques, 19 galleys, and 37 small gunboats, on the 15th of August. A desultory action ensued for five hours, the Swedes, little hurt, being driven into Rotchensālm (Svenksund) and there blockaded.

*Rotchensālm (or Svenksund), 24th August 1789.*

The Russians now collected a fleet to destroy the entrapped Swedes, and brought up two divisions, one under the Prince of Nassau-Siegen, the other under Admiral Kruse. Altogether they totalled 107 vessels, of which 8 were frigates and 22 galleys—the rest being small gunboats.[1] The action was begun by Kruse, who arrived a little too soon, and sustained a defeat. The Swedes, however, had not come off scathless; and they were also getting short of ammunition when

[1] The coast-flotilla galleys and gunboats of this period were of various types. The principal were:—

| Name of Type. | Dimensions in Feet. | | | Masts. | Oars. | Complement. | Guns. |
|---|---|---|---|---|---|---|---|
| | Long. | Broad. | Draught | | | | |
| Hemmema | 146 | 36 | 10 | 3 | 40 | 250 | 24 36-pounders<br>2 12-pounders |
| Turuma | 126 | 31 | 11 | 3 | 38 | 170 | 24 18-pounders<br>16 3-pounders |
| Udema | 121 | 29 | $8\frac{1}{2}$ | 2 | 36 | ? | 4 12-pounders<br>2 8-pounders (in bow) |
| Poyema | 93 | 27 | $6\frac{1}{4}$ | 2 | 32 | ? | 4 24-pounders (2 in bow, 2 in stern)<br>2 3-pounders |
| Gun sloops | 64 | 17 | 7 | 2 (square sail) | 28 | ? | 1 18-pounder<br>1 12-pounder<br>4 3-pounders |
| Galley | 140 | 21 | 7 | 2 | ? | ? | 2 12-pounders<br>2 6-pounders<br>8 3-pounders |
| Small gunboats | 42 | 10 | $2\frac{1}{2}$ | 0 | 10 | 30 | 1 24-pounder |

the Duke of Nassau-Siegen came up. Ehrenswärd, despite his protests, was ordered by the King of Sweden (Gustavus III.), who had watched the battle from a neighbouring height, to attack the Russians. He did so, and sustained a total defeat, losing his frigate, 3 coast-frigates, 1 galley, and 16 gunboats. 1400 of his men were killed, wounded, or taken prisoners. As a result of this action the Swedes had to withdraw from Finland. The Russian loss was 1 gun sloop; 15 officers and 368 men killed; 38 officers and 589 men wounded.

*1790. Sweden's last effort.*

The following year Sweden made her final effort. The Duke of Sudermania[1] was put in command of the Grand fleet, while the king (Gustavus III.) took command of a large galley fleet, said to have consisted of 19 transports, 27 galleys, and 236 gunboats, mounting altogether nearly 2000 guns.

Operations began by an attack upon the stores at Port Baltic, which were destroyed by Cederstroim with two frigates.

*Sudermania sails.*

On the 30th of April Prince Carl left Carlscrona with a fleet of 52 sail, of which 22 were ships-of-the-line, 12 frigates, and the rest small craft.

*Revel, 14th May 1790. Russians repulse Sudermania.*

On the 14th of May he was off Revel, and attempted to force the harbour and destroy ten Russian ships-of-the-line at anchor there under the batteries. He was driven off, losing one ship-of-the-line captured and one other sunk.[2]

[1] *I.e.* Prince Carl.

[2] This attempt was made in a strong gale. Another account gives

*Gustavus III. forces Fredrikshamn.*

On the same day the King of Sweden forced an entrance into Fredrikshamn harbour, in face of a heavy cannonade from the forts and coast-flotilla, which had a base there. Twenty-nine of these coast-ships were captured or sunk, while the docks and naval stores were destroyed.[1]

Thence the king made course to Viborg, where he landed his troops within easy distance of St. Péterbōurg, and then waited for Sudermania at Bjorno.

*Action off Revel.*

Sudermania, with 21 ships-of-the-line and several frigates, meanwhile met the Kronstadt division of the Russian fleet, 17 ships-of-the-line and 7 frigates, under Kruse on 3rd June. A fierce but indecisive action ensued. Next day fighting went on at intervals, and Kruse was reinforced by Tchitchagoff, with 13 battleships and 11 frigates.[2] Before this combined force Sudermania retreated to Bjorno, and thence to Viborg, where the Russians caught him. Practically the entire naval force of Sweden was here blockaded for a month, at the end of which time their provisions ran short. Outside, the whole available force of the Russian Navy was collected.

the Russian force at 2 ships of 108 guns, 6 of 74 guns, 6 frigates, and some coast-ships. The Swedes lost 51 killed and 81 wounded, besides prisoners.

[1] The Russians lost 1 turuma, 2 gun barges, 22 small and 4 galliots. Only 6 officers and 180 men were made prisoners. The Swedes paid for their victory with 1 gun yawl, 30 wounded and 30 killed.

[2] From Revel.

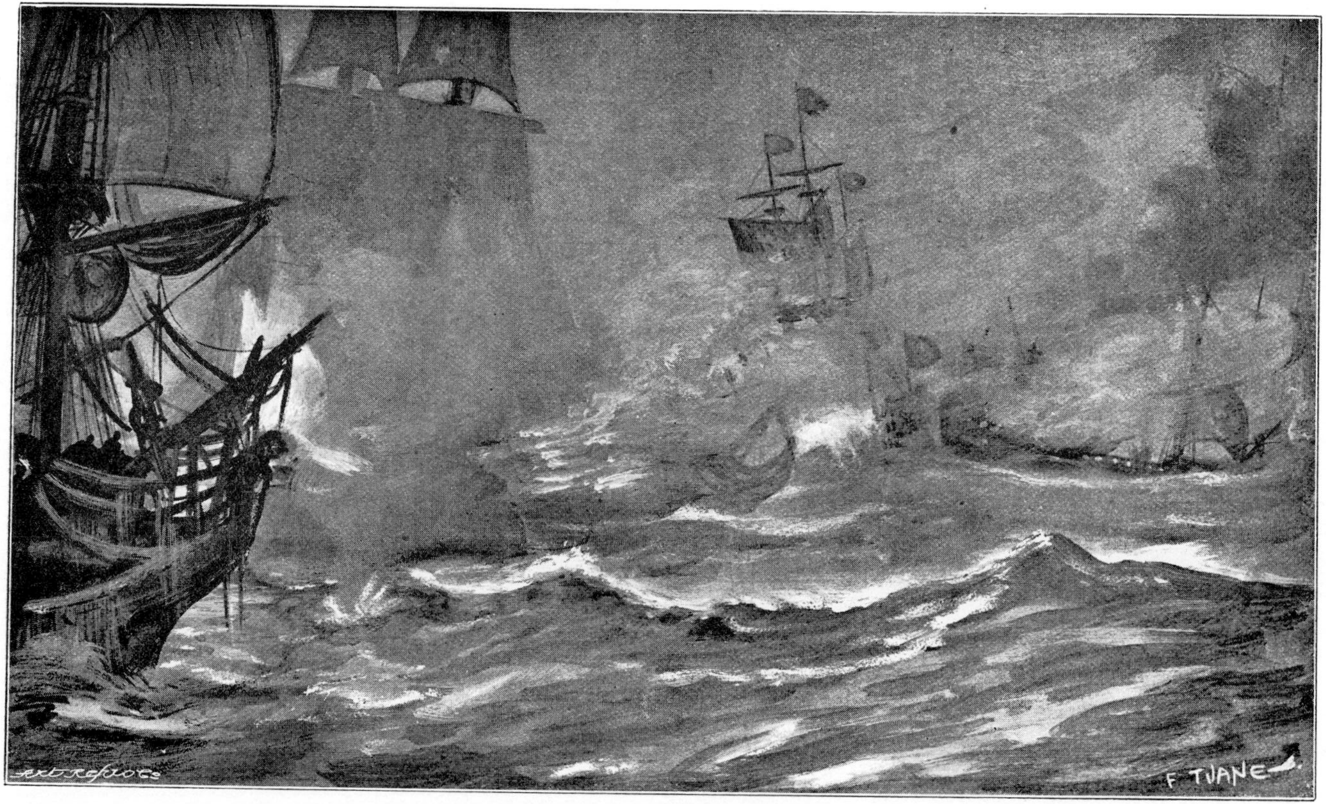


BATTLE OF VIBORG, 1790.

The Swedish force consisted of—

| | | | |
|---|---|---|---|
| 1 | ship of | 74 | guns (Vladimir *ex* Russian). |
| 5 | ships of | 70 | ,, |
| 10 | ,, | 64 | ,, |
| 2 | ,, | 62 | ,, |
| 2 | ,, | 60 | ,, |
| 2 | ,, | 44 | ,, |
| 6 | ,, | 42 | ,, |
| 3 | frigates | 32 | ,, |
| 1 | frigate | 26 | ,, |
| 1 | ,, | 18 | ,, |
| 1 | ,, | 16 | ,, |
| 1 | ,, | 12 | ,, |

In addition, there were a large number of schooners, galleys, gunboats, and transports. A good deal of uncertainty prevails as to what really took place; but the Swedes attempted to break the blockade, and lost of their fleet 7 ships-of-the-line, 3 frigates, 1 schooner, 7 galleys, 4 gun sloops, 4 gun yawls, and 30 transports.

They forced the blockade in the night,[1] launching four fire-ships on Tchitchagoff's fleet. Several vessels had slipped out, when one of the fire-ships broke adrift and, coming on the Swedish rear, set a battleship and frigate on fire. Both these ships blowing up, the remainder were thrown into confusion, colliding and running aground. Those that escaped were hotly pursued by Tchitchagoff, and two ships-of-the-line were captured. The line-of-battle ships were as absolutely put out of it by this battle as were those of

[1] See Appendix for official reports, plans, etc. Swedish accounts say it was in the daytime.

France and Spain at Trafalgar: Viborg, indeed, was the Trafalgar or Ægospotami of the Baltic; and ever since that day Russia has been the principal Baltic Naval Power. Whether she will always remain so—whether she could prove herself so were war to suddenly happen—is a moot point: the German fleet is possibly a full match for such force as Russia maintains in her northern harbours. Sweden, again, is slowly but surely creeping up; and though her battleships are small in size and still insignificant in numbers, their organisation is very complete, and their crews said by the Russians to be exceedingly efficient. Sooner or later Russia and Germany stand to be involved in hostilities, and the scale would be turned by Sweden throwing her forces into either side. That she should do so is not at first sight probable; but the Norwegian question is always liable to produce unexpected developments, which Great Britain—to whom the relations of Sweden and Norway have always been held up as an example of the benefits of Home Rule—little suspects or comprehends. Norway is Sweden's Ireland; and, unlike Ireland, having Home Rule, is able and waiting to seize an opportunity to assert herself.

To return to the battle of Viborg. After Sudermania had got out, the King of Sweden followed with his galley fleet, and reached Rotchensālm (Svenksund) with the loss of thirty ships of his command.

The force left to him still counted 195 vessels mounting 1124 guns, and 14,000 men. Mostly his craft were very small; the largest were merely coast-frigates—of which he had five. He had also a couple of brigs and sixteen galleys.

Against this force the Prince of Nassau-Siegen moved, with a fleet of—

8 frigates.
6 xebecs.
14 galliots.
10 cutters and bomb ketches.
3 floating batteries.
22 galleys.
8 small galleys.
80 gun sloops.

In all 151 vessels, carrying between them 18,500 men and 1412 guns.

Rather rashly the Russians assumed that the Swedes were altogether crushed by the Viborg affair; and so sure were they of victory that a cabin was specially fitted up on board the Prince of Nassau-Siegen's flagship for the accommodation of the King of Sweden when he should surrender, and the 9th of July, Ekaterina's birthday, was fixed as the day of battle as a compliment to the Tsarina. Unfortunately for Russia, the prince was a little too premature; and he seems to have made few if any preparations for finding a vigorous resistance awaiting him.

*Battle at Rotschensälm (Svenksund), 9th and 10th July 1790.*

The battle began at 9.30 on the morning of 9th July, and lasted without intermission till 10 o'clock on the morning of the 10th.

The Russians at first went in without much order or precaution, and being received with a reserved fire, were thrown into tremendous confusion and suffered great loss. For the rest of the fight they made most gallant and vigorous attempts to get in, but each was as gallantly met and repulsed.

Eventually they were forced to retire, half their men (9500) having been killed, wounded, or captured. They also lost a third of their fleet, 52 ships and vessels, namely, 4 frigates, 4 xebecs, 1 coast-frigate, 16 galleys, 6 bomb ketches or cutters, and 21 other vessels.

The Swedes only allowed having suffered the loss of 1 coast-frigate, 3 yawls, and 300 men *hors de combat.*

The Russian estimate fixed their loss considerably higher; and it would appear probable that they must have lost more, if only on account of the close quarters at which the battle was fought. That redoubtable Englishman Sir Sidney Smith was fighting for the Swedes. English, both officers and men, were present in large numbers in *both* fleets:[1] of these, Captain Sir F. Thesiger particularly distinguished himself on the Russian side.

*Battle of "Sissoi Veliky," 27th July 1790.*

*Sweden makes peace, 14th Aug. 1790.*

This repulse of the Russians at Svenksund was, however, too late to save Sweden,—the Swedish force was still blockaded, and Russia had command of the sea with thirty ships-of-the-line, some of which defeated a few Swedes off Gogland on 27th July, the festival-day of the Saint Sissoi Veliky. The battle of Svenksund, however, saved Stockholm for the moment; and peace

[1] Swedes deny the presence of any foreigners in their fleet except Smith, and attribute the legend to the adventures of Mr. Chucks in Marryat's *Peter Simple.*

proposals were made. These Ekaterina accepted, and peace was signed on the 14th of August 1790.

Russia was thus left with a free hand to deal with Sweden's ally, Turkey; and after some land defeats, the Turks were driven to sue for peace; the preliminaries were signed at Galatea in August 1791, and ratified at Jassy on 9th January 1792.

*End of war with Turkey. Peace of Jassy, 9th Jan. 1792.*

Ekaterina now turned her attention to Poland, the partition of which was completed in 1795; and one great source of trouble removed from Europe. By it Russia secured the rest of Courland, and the coastline from long. 23°, lat. 58°, to long. 21° 50′, lat. 56°—from Dome Ness to a few miles north of Memel, the present frontier with Germany.

*Increase of Russian coastline, 1795.*

In this year there was an Anglo-Russian alliance, and the British Admiral Duncan was joined off the Texel by the Russian Admiral Hanickoff, with 12 ships-of-the-line and 6 frigates.

*Anglo-Russian alliance, 1795.*

Russia was then the second Naval Power in the world,—a position to which she had been raised by the genius and foresight of Ekaterina, who died in 1796, and was succeeded by the more or less mad Tsar Paul.

The great Ekaterina's policy did not at once die with her. The British mutiny at the Nore put a temporary end to the fleet combination in 1797; but when the Dutch fleet capitulated in August 1799, the Russian ships Retwisan and Mistisloff, under Mitchell, an English rear-admiral in the Russian service, went into the Texel.

# VI

## 1796–1801

## PAUL

BOTH under Paul, the erratic successor of the great Catherine II., and under Alexander I., the son of Paul, Russia fought on both sides in the general war produced by the French Revolution and Napoleon. Paul, however, was naturally disposed to Napoleon's side, while his successor, Alexander I., though circumstances at one period drove him to become an ally of France, was distinctly anti-Napoleonic in sentiment.

Paul came to the throne in 1796, and almost immediately afterwards the French plan of trade campaign against Great Britain was put into execution. This action on the part of France naturally placed Russia against her, since by the decree of the Directory issued
1798. in January 1798 any neutral vessel found to contain a single British article was to be seized as a prize. Aimed originally at the British, this decree caused most trouble to the neutrals, and four months after it was issued Paul despatched a fleet of twenty-two line-of-battle ships and fifty galleys to protect Russian merchantmen in the Sound. Very shortly afterwards,

Nelson's crushing defeat of the French fleet at the Nile settled the Russian course of action : war was formally conducted against France, and England, Russia, Austria, Turkey, Naples, and Portugal formed a great anti-French alliance.

*Effect of the battle of the Nile.*

Russian armies overran Switzerland, while a combined Russo-Turkish fleet, under Admiral Oushakoff, passed the Dardenelles and captured the Ionian Islands in September. Incidentally, it may be mentioned that the Russian fleet, with that eye to the main chance which her enemies always accuse Russia of possessing to an abnormal degree, troubled very little about its allies, and seemed rather bent on capturing harbours than operating against the French. The letters of Nelson at this period clearly indicate that the great admiral was of opinion that the capture of Malta for themselves was all the Russians in the Mediterranean really aimed at. They had with them eleven ships-of-the-line and a number of frigates and smaller vessels ; but if Malta was their real objective, they did no more than long for it.

*Ancona, 1799.*

In Nelson's eyes Oushakoff was a very inefficient person. Beyond bombarding Ancona in 1799, an operation attended with more damage to himself than to Ancona, he did nothing. Probably some of his inactivity may have been due to his ships being in little better condition than Orloff's had been.

Russian troops, conveyed from the Baltic in British vessels, operated for a short while in Holland ; but very little military advantage was obtained there, and eventually the British stored their Russian allies in the Channel Islands.

In the meantime Suwarroff met defeat in Switzerland, and eight thousand of his men were taken prisoners. Napoleon, with clever forethought, put these troops into new uniforms and sent them back to Russia, a thing that appealed very much to Paul. In addition to that, he was filled with an immense personal admiration for Napoleon on account of his brilliant Italian victories. The little else that was needed, Napoleon managed, and Paul laid an embargo upon all British ships in Russian ports. As a result, there was angry correspondence between London and St. Petersburg, the principal result of which was that negotiations were opened between Russia, Sweden, and Denmark for the "Armed Neutrality," which in one of Captain Marryat's novels is described as "generally meaning a charge of bayonets."

*1800.*

*The case of the Freya, 25th July 1800.*

The gathering trouble was brought to a head by the Danish frigate Freya. She, being out with a convoy, refused to allow the British the "right of search," to which the British replied by coming alongside and forcing her to surrender.

*British method of dealing with the question.*

Lord Whitworth was then sent on an embassy to Copenhagen; and by way of assistance to his arguments, he was accompanied by nine ships-of-the-line, four-bombs, and five frigates, under Admiral Dickson.

*Paul's anger.*

All this Paul took as a personal insult. He got himself created Grand Master of the Knights of St.

John at Malta, which place was then threatened by the British, as the only means of getting possession of the island in face of the British fleet. Oushakoff's fleet being unlikely to effect anything in the Mediterranean, Paul, just at the time when Dickson's squadron reached the Sound, seized all the British merchantmen (about three hundred) then in Russian harbours, and published a declaration that he would keep them till Malta was handed over to him. The British Government making no sign that it intended to acquiesce, and Tsar Paul being further irritated by the fashion in which, disregarding his embargo, some British merchant ships sailed away and escaped, he clinched the matter by ordering all the rest to be burned.

Denmark, Sweden, and Prussia having by now signified to Paul that their sentiments towards the British were at one with his, the Tsar wrote a letter to Napoleon and despatched an ambassador to Paris. At about the same time the island of Malta surrendered to the British.

*British capture Malta.*

On the 16th of December 1800, Russia and Sweden signed the "Armed Neutrality" treaty, and three days later Prussia and Denmark were also signatories.

*Armed Neutrality, 1800.*

Pitt and the British Government were under no delusions as to what was intended. At once an embargo was laid on all Russian, Danish, and Swedish ships (Prussia was excluded), and letters of marque were issued for the capture of any ships belonging to these Baltic Powers. In the meantime British ships were excluded from every port from the North Cape to

*British reply.*

Gibraltar. Exactly four weeks after the signing of the treaty a British fleet, consisting of eighteen line-of-battle ships and thirty-five smaller vessels, sailed for the Baltic.

*Russian fleet in 1801.*

The total Russian fleet at the day was eighty-two ships-of-the-line and forty frigates. Forty-seven of these were in the Baltic or at Archangel, but of that number only fifteen were ready for active service.

The British fleet, with Sir Hyde Parker in command and Nelson under him, were under orders to try diplomacy first—"diplomacy" in this case representing great show of force. Denmark was to be the first point of attack in any case,—an impression was abroad that the Danes, despite the Freya incident, had been acting more or less under compulsion; Denmark, therefore, was to be detached by whichever means might seem best. The instructions proceeded :—that after settling matters at Copenhagen the fleet was to go to Revel, to destroy all Russian ships, forts, and arsenal there, after that to treat Kronstadt in the same way, and generally to cause the Russian flag to disappear from the waters of the Baltic.

At the time these instructions were issued a suspicion began to grow that the Danes would not easily give in. Nelson was in favour of attacking the Russians, and wrote to Sir Hyde Parker for permission to take ten ships-of-the-line, one bomb, or else a couple of fire-ships, to Revel and destroy the Russian fleet with them, leaving the remainder of the British fleet to attend to Copenhagen. By this means the "Armed

Neutrality" would have been smashed at a single blow. However, Sir Hyde Parker was of a different opinion to Nelson, and the famous attack on Copenhagen took place. With Russian naval history this has small concern, save that when Nelson was treating for the armistice he demanded fourteen weeks "in order to allow him time to go and destroy the Russian fleet, and come back again to destroy the Danes if they wanted more." Eventually Denmark was detached. Before much more could be done, news arrived that the mad Tsar Paul had been assassinated, and his successor, Alexander I., had no desire to continue hostilities.

*Nelson goes to Revel.*

Nelson, now in supreme command, was ordered to open negotiations with the new Tsar, to find out what Russia intended doing, and not to fight unless he found the Russians bent on it. He at once made a dash for Revel with eleven ships-of-the-line, a frigate, and two sloops, his intention being to impress upon the Russians that he meant business, and to prevent their Kronstadt fleet joining the ships at Revel. However, he found that, the ice having broken, the Russians were all inside Kronstadt. At Revel, he wrote, he could have destroyed the whole lot of them.

Nelson, indeed, appears to have been exceedingly annoyed at having been compelled to let the Russians slip through his fingers, and the Russian Government seem to have had a fairly clear inkling of his sentiments and a mistrust of his intentions—while his views, freely expressed about their fleet under Oushakoff in the Mediterranean, had been both free and uncomplimentary.

A good deal of correspondence passed between Count Pahlen, the Tsar's secretary, and Nelson, and on the 16th of May the Tsar's astonishment was expressed that such a force as Nelson's should be brought to Russian waters in view of the reputed pacific intentions of the British Government. It looked a good deal like pressure, to an appearance of which the Russians were particularly anxious not to yield. It was further demanded that Nelson's fleet should withdraw.

Nelson's reply was to the effect that it was a mark of friendship, and that his fleet would be of great service in assisting to navigate to England many of the English vessels which had remained all the winter in Russia—a rather neat hint that the principal business in hand had more to do with the merchantmen Paul had seized than with the now purely theoretical and innocuous "Armed Neutrality." Privately he wrote to St. Vincent and said that had any of the Russian fleet been inside Revel, the Tsar would never have made the demand he had.

However, Nelson left the gulf, and the Tsar removed the embargo from British shipping. He also invited Nelson to come and see him, if he would come with a single ship; but acceptance was postponed, and as Nelson soon afterwards left the Baltic, nothing ever came of it.

*Treaty with England.*

On 5th June a treaty was signed between England and Russia, by which Russia secured the right to trade between the ports of a belligerent. A concession so considerable, at a time when the British fleet was clearly in a position to deny it without trouble, indicates that there can have been no particular hostility to Russia on the part of the British Government. Apparently Paul's action was regarded as the freak of

MAP OF THE BALTIC.

a mad ruler. Its ultimate result was advantageous to Russia rather than otherwise. But the whole affair seems to have arisen out of the tailoring enterprise of Napoleon, when he re-clad those 8000 captured Russian soldiers.

# VII

## 1801–1825

## ALEXANDER I

WHEN general war broke out again after the Peace of Amiens, Russia was engaged in completing the subjugation of Georgia, which was annexed in 1801, but gave some trouble for a while afterwards. Not till

*1805.*

the beginning of 1805 did Alexander enter into the alliance with England, Austria, and Sweden against France, though for a twelvemonth before some such act had been foreseen. Nelson's letters on the subject are couched in the usual strain: a hope that he would not have the assistance of a Russian squadron, and a firm conviction that if they joined with the Allies, they would merely use it as an occasion to capture the Ionian Republic and the whole of Turkey. In this he

*Russian fleet in the Levant.*

was incorrect. Russia entered honestly into the war, and her fleet stood to bar the French from going towards Egypt. Subsequently the French fleet met annihilation at Trafalgar,[1] but the battle of Austerlitz upset all the projects of the Allies on land.

[1] There were one or two Russian officers serving in Nelson's fleet at Trafalgar.

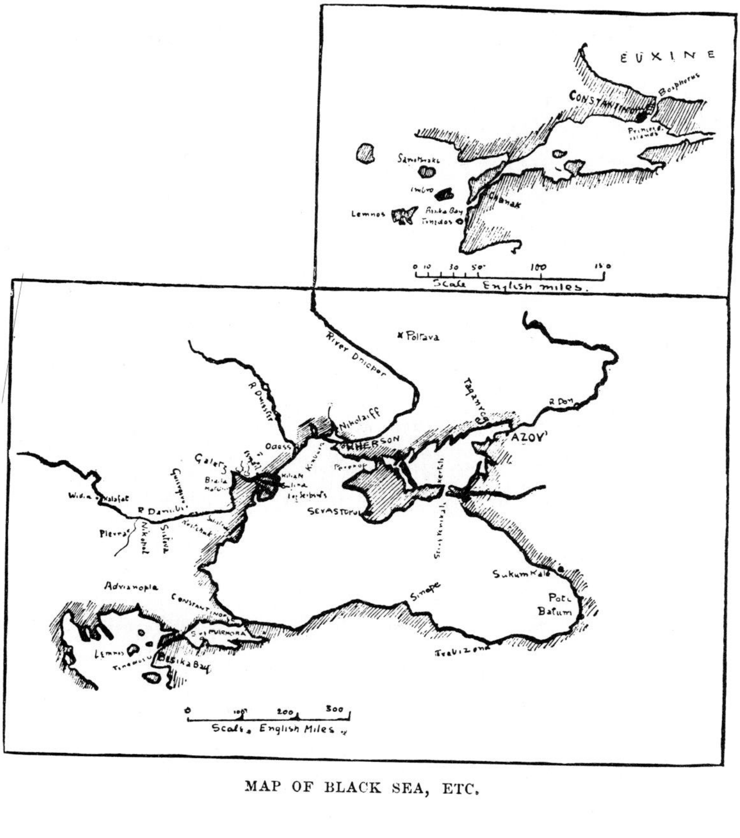


MAP OF BLACK SEA, ETC.

*Austerlitz.*

Owing to Austerlitz an Anglo-Russian expedition to Naples fell through. The Russian troops in this projected expedition were employed in the capture of Cattaro, while the fleet operated without success against Ragusa.

*1806.*

About this time Napoleon was busy over his projected alliance with Turkey and Persia, in order to harry Russia by their means; and in the case of the Turks, getting them to close the Dardenelles and Bosporus to Russian warships.

*1807.*

In February 1807 a British fleet forced the Dardenelles. Senyavin, the Russian admiral, had been ordered to co-operate with four line-of-battle ships, but he failed to arrive in time to do more than meet the British fleet coming back in a very disabled condition. He had with him then eight ships-of-the-line, and was anxious that the Anglo-Russian fleet should again essay the passage of the Dardenelles. England, however, if the first fiasco[1] had not been sufficient, was otherwise engaged in operations in Egypt. Senyavin was left blockading the Dardenelles, which he does not seem to have considered passable by his squadron—at least he made no such attempt. In the Black Sea a second Russian fleet blockaded the Bosporus.

*Operations against Turkey.*

Seeing the English go away, and having had ocular

[1] Although the damage sustained was very small compared with what might have been expected, it was none the less pretty heavy. Further, at Constantinople nothing had been effected, and the ships were in imminent danger of having their retreat cut off by new batteries that the Turks erected. They probably only retired in the nick of time. A second attempt would likely have led to total disaster.

demonstration that they had done them some harm, the Turks got together a big fleet and came down the Dardenelles on the 19th of May. Almost immediately they fell in with Senyavin, but not caring to try conclusions, they made back again. In their haste three ships ran aground and were captured by the pursuing Russians.

*May 1807.*

*Senyavin chases back the Turkish fleet.*

A month later the Turkish fleet came down again, accompanied by transports carrying between four and five thousand men. These—in defiance of all the theories of "Command of the Sea"—they landed at Tenedos. On the same day that the landing took place, Senyavin's squadron met the Turkish fleet off Lemnos and inflicted a severe defeat upon them. One ship was captured in action, five were driven ashore in flight, and the rest dispersed. Four weeks later the troops landed in Tenedos had to surrender to Senyavin.

*Battle of Lemnos, 22nd June 1807.*

If victorious at sea, on land the Russian arms were anything but successful, and Alexander had to sign the Peace of Tilsit, whereby Russia became an ally of France and at war with England, Austria, and Sweden.

*Russia again changes sides.*

This sudden change of policy put Senyavin in rather a tight place. The French fleet was well-nigh non-existent, the British fleet was the commanding unit in the Mediterranean, and his new friends the Turks, who had so recently experienced disaster at his hands, were perhaps hardly to be trusted. He had with him altogether eleven line-of-battle ships and a number of smaller vessels. To stay where he was simply meant destruction by the British fleet, and he formed the project of a rush for the Baltic. He, however, detached Greig,[1] his rear-admiral, to capture the Ionian Isles, allowing him for this service two ships-of-the-line and four frigates. With the rest of his fleet he sailed out of the Mediterranean and reached the Tagus, where a British fleet promptly blockaded him.

Greig's ships were not attacked by the British, and for some time wandered aimlessly in the Levant. In the end they were run to earth and taken possession of by an Austrian fleet, which conducted them to Trieste, where later on Napoleon's soldiers re-captured them.

*August 1808, loss of Senyavin's fleet.*

Senyavin stayed inside the Tagus for some while. Eventually, however, he surrendered his ships to the British, on condition that he and his men should be free to go back to Russia, and that at the end of the war his ships should be returned. These terms were granted without question. A curious feature of the case is that when Senyavin went into the Tagus there was at that time no war between Russia and England, so far as any formal declaration was concerned. Senyavin's evacuation of the Mediterranean and the British blockade of him in the Tagus were merely "precautionary measures." No direct English attack on the Russians was made till some while after the Peace of Tilsit. As a precautionary measure against a renewal of the Armed Neutrality, however, the British seized the entire Danish Navy.

[1] Rear-Admiral Greig was the son of the ex-British officer, Samuel Greig. See pp. 80 *et seq.*

This left the Baltic Powers with somewhat reduced forces; but in May 1808 the Russians had in those waters twenty line-of-battle ships and fourteen frigates, all effective, while Sweden possessed eleven line-of-battle ships and seven frigates, which by dint of military pressure counted upon the Russian side.

A British expedition entered the Baltic in June *1808.* 1808, under Sir James Saumarez, with a view to assisting the Swedes to detach themselves from the Russian alliance; and two months later two British ships-of-the-line reached Oro Sound, where six Swedish battleships were lying. Off this place a Russian fleet of eleven ships-of-the-line under Hamkoff appeared the very next day, and the next day again four more Swedes arrived. The entire Anglo-Swedish fleet, now consisting of twelve battleships and five frigates, then put out to fight the Russians, who made off towards Rogerswick; and one of the two British ships, the Implacable, being swift, succeeded in overhauling and engaging the Russian Svlod. She had, however, to haul off, as the entire Russian fleet turned about to attack.

The Svlod did not long escape, as the Centaur—the other British ship—managed to block her entry into Rogerswick harbour.

*Fight between the Svlod and British Centaur.*

A fierce engagement took place, and, after a gallant resistance in which she lost over three hundred men, the Russian ship, dismasted and disabled, struck. She was burned immediately afterwards.

The rest of the Russian fleet were blockaded in

Rogerswick, and showed no signs of coming out. They erected a boom to keep out fire-ships, and being well protected by the shore-batteries, attacks upon them were futile. After a couple of months the blockading fleets withdrew, and the Russians went back to Kronstadt, where they remained.

*August 1808.*

On neither side were operations conducted with much vigour. The British Government, with their hands full enough elsewhere, had no desire to press matters against the Tsar, whose alliance with Napoleon already showed signs of weakness. Russian troops overran and captured Finland, but the Swedish ships do not seem to have attempted any counter attack as a diversion. Such naval actions as took place were minor operations conducted by flotillas. At Grönvik, Palva, and Äland the Russian coast-flotilla met with some small losses at the hands of the Swedes.

*Capture of Finland, 1809.*

The British line-of-battle ship Implacable, on the night of 7th July, sent seventeen boats to attack eight Russian gunboats, which, with some store-ships, lay at Porcola Point, in the Gulf of Finland. After a sanguinary conflict, seven of the gunboats and twelve store-ships were captured.

*British capture seven Russian gunboats at Porcola, 7th July 1809.*

A fortnight later Sub-lieutenant Korobka, with four gunboats convoying a brig with stores to Rotchensālm, fell in with nineteen English boats.[1] One gunboat managed to show her heels; but with the remaining three Korobka made a most stubborn resistance for

*Aspe, 25th July 1809.*

[1] Mortar-boats, according to Russian accounts, but more probably the ships' boats of the Implacable and Centaur.

FRIGATE AND SCHOONER *CIRCA* 1810.

over two hours, and when finally forced to surrender, all but seven of his men were killed or wounded.

At the very time that these minor operations were in progress, British merchantmen were trading at Russian ports, and the operations of 1810 were purely pacific ones of trade. Russia being nominally at war with England still, and this trade being in any case directly contrary to Napoleon's "Continental system," Franco-Russian relations soon grew very strained. The end was Napoleon's fateful invasion of Russia, and the destruction of the Grand Army, in which the crews of the Russian ships at Kronstadt, being landed, participated.

*1810.*

*Anglo-Russian Alliance.*

Russia and England, from having been in a practical state of peace while nominally at war, were now formally allies once more, and the ships of Senyavin captured in the Tagus were restored.

Beyond some boat affairs in the Danube, no naval operations on the part of Russia marked this new and final phase of the Great War.

Alexander I. died in 1825. During his reign the dimensions of the Empire were considerably increased, and fresh coastline was gained on the shores of the Black Sea.

# VIII

## NAVARINO AND THE CRIMEAN WAR

### 1825–1855

### Nikolai I

ALEXANDER was succeeded by his younger brother Nikolai, an elder brother, the Grand Duke Constantine, having renounced his succession to the throne. For the first few years of his reign Tsar Nikolai was occupied in a Persian war, but the problems produced by the Greek revolt against the Turks naturally engaged Russian attention. In June 1827 Nikolai joined France and England in a league originally started to suppress Greek piracy in the Levant, but which soon became an engine for Greek freedom. A naval demonstration was decided upon, and Rear-admiral Count Heyden, flying his flag in the Azov, 74, and having with him three 74- and three 48-gun frigates, joined an Anglo-French fleet in the Levant. The whole force was under the British Vice-admiral,

Sir Edward Codrington, as senior officer, and was thus made up :—

| | | | |
|---|---|---|---|
| 4 | (Azov, Gangoot, Ezekiel, Alexander I.) | 74-gun ships. | Russian, under Rear-admiral Count Heyden ; flag in Azov, 74. |
| 3 | | 48-gun frigates. | |
| 1 | (Asia) | 80-gun ship. | British, under Vice-admiral Sir E. Codrington ; flag in Asia, 80. |
| 2 | (Genoa and Albion) | 74-gun ships. | |
| 1 | | 50-gun frigate. | |
| 1 | | 48 ,, | |
| 1 | | 42 ,, | |
| 1 | | 28 ,, | |
| 1 | | 18-gun brig. | |
| 3 | | 10-gun brigs. | |
| 3 | (Scipion, Trident, and Breslaw) | 74-gun ships. | French, under Rear-admiral de Rigny ; flag in Sirene. |
| 1 | (Sirene) | 60-gun ship. | |
| 1 | | 44-gun frigate. | |
| 2 | | schooners. | |
| 26 | | | |

In the harbour of Navarino—the ancient Sphakteria, rendered famous many centuries before by that Athenian triumph when Spartans for the first and only time laid down their arms and surrendered—lay practically the entire Turkish and Egyptian fleet, consisting of—

*Turkish fleet.*

3 ships-of-the-line,
1 rasée frigate,
16 frigates,
27 corvettes,
5 fire-ships,
19 brigs,

and a large number of gunboats and transports (about 40 to 50).

*Allied fleets dispositions.*

Into this harbour the Allied fleets sailed, intent upon a "naval demonstration" of the type that recent years have rendered familiar to us. They found the Turks lying in a crescent, and cleared for action, whereupon Codrington anchored his vessels to leeward on the outside of the curve, so that in the event of hostilities none of his ships would be exposed to a concentrated fire. He also sent a message to the Turkish Admiral warning him that any hostile demonstration would be construed as an act of war, and punished by the destruction of the Turkish fleet.

*Navarino, 27th October 1827.*

A little later some English boats taking a message to a Turkish ship were fired on, and a lieutenant and several men killed, and the remainder only returned in safety through the ship to which they belonged firing on the Turks. The Turk replying, a general action ensued, and lasted four hours. The Turkish ships were concentrated on, one after the other, and as they were disabled the Turks set them on fire and abandoned them.

*Turkish ships destroyed.*

About two-thirds of their force—one ship-of-the-line, three 2-decker frigates, nine frigates, twenty-two corvettes, nineteen brigs, one schooner, and five fire-ships were thus burnt, and the remaining vessels severely mauled. Details of the battle vary according to the nation giving the account. The English version is that the Russians took small part in the affair; while Russian history states that Count Heyden's flagship, Azov, herself sank the Turkish flagship, two frigates, and a corvette. The present-day Russian cruiser Pāmiat Azova is so named in remembrance of this action, and her ensign carries the badge of St. George (for valour) in commemoration. French accounts give, of course, yet a third version. So far as can be gathered all the ships-of-the-line took their share,[1] and most were a good deal knocked about—the battle was by no means a "walk over." The English line-of-battle ships were the most damaged, and presumably the most hotly engaged,—all three had to be sent home for repairs, the damage done to them being beyond Malta's resources to put right.

*War with Turkey, 1827-29.*

Almost immediately after Navarino a regular war came about between Russia and Turkey, and Navarino more than anything else contributed to Russian success. Owing to that holocaust Russia had an excess of "Sea Power" which, judiciously utilised, enabled her to take Anapa and Poti, and keep up the communications of those land forces which penetrated as far south as Adrianople, at which place peace was signed in 1829.

*Peace signed at Adrianople, 1829.*

*Pāmiat Merkuria, 4th May 1829.*

Naval operations in this war were useful rather than showy. Kapitan-Lieutenant Kazarski of the brig Mercury, 20 guns, however, earned some laurels in an action the exact facts of which are probably not procurable. The Russian version is that off Constantinople he was attacked by two Turkish ships-of-the-line, one of 110 guns, the other a 74. After a four hours' action, in which the Turks were badly injured, and silenced, Kazarski sailed away! For this affair Kazarski and his officers were promoted, and a pistol added to the arms, because they had

[1] The frigates were less engaged.

RUSSIAN WARSHIPS, 1830.

determined to blow up the Mercury *à la Suède* should she be overcome. Kazarski's name, and also that of his brig, are perpetuated as Russian ship-names to-day.

*Remarks.*

Now, despite the notoriously bad condition of the Turkish Navy at that period, this account is evidently in need of some "editing." It is a moral impossibility that so small a craft as the Mercury could have disabled two ships-of-the-line in four hours, even had they done no shooting; and the most natural assumption is that the Turks were frigates, that have grown to ships-of-the-line since.[1] That Kazarski distinguished himself there is little doubt; the Russians have so rarely perpetuated the names of distinguished naval officers in ships, that the fact of their having done so in this case presupposes a gallant action against heavy odds.

*Treaty of Turkomachai, 1828.*

*Control of the Caspian.*

The war with Persia ended in 1828 with the treaty of Turkomachai. By it territory was gained as far as the Aras (Araxes) River; naval control of the Caspian was also secured.

*Russian fleet in 1836.*

In the thirties the Russian fleet had a fairly high reputation for efficiency. A certain number of definite types were adopted; but being built of fir, the life of the vessels was short—only about eight years, though the Russians tried to keep them going for double or treble that period.

[1] See 1877–78: action between the Vesta and a Turkish ironclad. It closely resembles the Kazarski story, and at the time was proved in some quarters to have been a pure invention.

The types were—

| Name of Type. | Guns. | Length. | Beam. | Depth. | Tonnage. |
|---|---|---|---|---|---|
| | | Feet. | Feet. | Feet. | Tons. |
| Warsaw . . . . | 120 | 206 | 55½ | 22 | 4857 |
| Brave . . . . . | 120 | 201½ | 52⅓ | 21½ | 4184 |
| Imperator Alexander . | 110 | 197 | 53 | 21¼ | 4244 |
| Imperatritza Ekaterina II. | 84 | 191 | 52 | 21 | 3516 |
| Imperatritza Marie . | 84 | 196 | 51 | 20½ | 3575 |
| Ezekiel . . . . | 80 | 176½ | 49 | 19⅓ | 2918 |
| Smolanck . . . . | 74 | 177 | 49 | 20 | 2876 |
| Vienna . . . . | 60 | 171 | 44 | 17½ | 1884 |
| FRIGATES. | | | | | |
| Penelope . . . . | 46 | 152½ | 40 | 16½ | 1452 |
| Marie . . . . | 44 | 160 | 42 | 16½ | 1664 |
| Swift . . . . | 44 | 153½ | 40¼ | 16½ | 1419 |
| BRIGS. | | | | | |
| Favourite . . . . | 20 | 106⅓ | 30 | 11¼ | 488 |
| Merkur . . . . | 20 | 94 | 30½ | 12¼ | 428 |

All ships built for the navy from 1830 till the introduction of steam, and even for some while after that, were copies of one or other of these thirteen types of ships constructed after the year 1800.

*Sevastôpol made into a naval arsenal.*

In 1830 Sevastôpol was made into a fortified naval arsenal, English engineers being employed to design the forts and docks.

*Sea of Aral flotilla, 1847.*

In 1847 a flotilla was first formed on the Sea of Aral.

*Steamers.*

The adoption of steam left the Russians somewhat behind—in 1853 two small steamers of 6 guns were commissioned in the Black Sea. In the Baltic about twenty-three steamers were built or building, but not more than a dozen or so were efficient.

The "paper" force of ships in 1853 was as follows:—

Russian fleet in 1853. Official list.

BALTIC

| | | |
|---|---|---|
| 25 ships-of-the-line | . | (120 and 84 guns). |
| 18 frigates . | . . | (46 and 44 guns). |
| 40 corvettes and smaller craft. | | |
| 20 steam corvettes | . | (paddle) (6 guns). |
| 3 ,, ,, | . . | (screw) (6 guns). |

BLACK SEA

| | | |
|---|---|---|
| 5 ships-of-the-line | . | (120 guns). |
| 13 ,, ,, | . . | (80 guns). |
| 3 ,, ,, | . . | (60 *or* 74 guns). |
| 7 large new-type frigates | | (54 guns) (*razées*). |
| 25 corvettes, brigs, etc.. | | (mounting 170 guns between them). |
| 2 steam corvettes | | (paddle) (6 guns). |

Of the Baltic fleet only 17 ships-of-the-line, 10 frigates, and 10 corvettes were considered effective by the Russians. The Black Sea ships were all nominally effective, but (with about three exceptions) owing to the bad durability of the fir were unseaworthy.

The nominal crews in each fleet were 20,000 officers and sailors, and 10,000 marines and artillery.

Shell guns were adopted into the Russian service about 1852. *Shell guns.*

In 1853 hostilities with Turkey were embarked on. The naval feature of the war was the battle of Sinōp, wherein the best part of the new Turkish Navy that replaced the one destroyed at Navarino was annihilated. It is—or was—usual to speak of this affair in England as "the Massacre of Sinope," but political exigencies are the only grounds of justification; the battle was

*War with Turkey, 1853. Battle of Sinōp, 30th Nov. 1854.*

really a brilliantly conceived and executed surprise. Its absolute decisiveness created a great stir, and this being the first time in which *shell* were used by ships against ships,[1] the fight is enrolled upon the annals of naval history as one of the most important of epochs. Fight, in the sense to which we are accustomed, there was none, the affair was as short as that of Santiago in the Hispano-American War of 1898. There was neither time nor need for tactics: the Turks had no shell, the Russians had. In five minutes the Turkish fleet was on fire, and, with the exception of a solitary steamer that escaped, every single vessel was annihilated. The Turks fought exceedingly well,[2] and in the brief space allowed them managed to kill 34 Russians and wound 230, a not insignificant number in view of the comparative smallness of the forces engaged. The Turkish loss is unknown, but it practically amounted to their entire *personnel*, either killed, wounded, or prisoners.

*Russian losses.*

*Turkish loss.*

The forces engaged were—

RUSSIAN

| | | |
|---|---|---|
| Tri Sviatitelia . . | 120 guns (flag). | Admiral Nahimoff. |
| Rostislav . . . . | 120 ,, | |
| Imperitritza Marie . | 80 ,, | |
| Paris . . . . . | 80 ,, | |
| Tchesme . . . . | 80 ,, | |
| Grand Duke Constantine | 60 ,, | |

TURKISH

| | |
|---|---|
| 7 razée frigates. | 2 steamers. |
| 2 corvettes. | Covered by a small shore-battery. |

[1] The combustible shell used by Greig (see Appendix) were not fired from the ordinary ship's gun.

[2] The Turkish *personnel* had lately been thoroughly reorganised and improved.

BATTLE OF SINOPE.

The Turkish version of the affair, one, too, that was very generally current on the Mediterranean at the time, was that, finding themselves caught and overmatched, the Turks set their ships on fire at once, fighting them till they blew up. There is probably some truth in this version. *Apropos* of this, it may be mentioned that at Santiago in 1898 the Spaniards did something of the same sort.

The lesson of Sinope was variously taken. Some argued that the shell[1] had made naval warfare impossible (a thing, by the way, that is claimed for nearly every new invention nowadays); others attributed the holocaust more to Turkish inefficiency than to Russian ability or the power of the shell. None the less, a marked impetus was given to the old idea of armouring ships; the ironclad was no longer an idle dream, no longer the resurrection of the fad of some long since dead and gone Dutch sailor, but the only answer to the historical cry, "For God's sake keep out the shells!"

France, usually to the front with any new invention, began the construction of ironclad floating batteries; and a little later England followed suit. *Ironclad floating batteries.* From these, as every schoolboy knows, grew the sea-going ironclads, which were shell-proof for many years. Gunnery science, however, evolved a means of penetrating armour, and in this battle with the gun, armour grew thicker and thicker. In this growth its area was naturally diminished, and in the struggle to keep out

[1] See Greig's use of shell in Appendix.

shot, that are at the most merely mildly dangerous, the shell was absolutely forgotten. A small patch of impenetrable armour was the one thing sought after, and such caricatures of the whole theory of armoured ships as our Benbow class, the Italian Lepanto, or the French Magenta, and to some extent all modern ironclads, arose. The man who in an Italian dockyard designed the ironclad cruisers of the Garibaldi and Cristobal Colon types may truly claim to be the only ship-designer able to realise the purpose for which armour was introduced!

*Crimean War begins.*

To resume. The shell at Sinope did not cause the British and French Governments to hesitate one moment in coming to hostilities with Russia in the following year. The causes of the Crimean War can hardly be traced, but one of many was whether the Roman Catholics (France) or the Greek Church (Russia) should be the predominant guardian of the Church of the Holy Sepulchre.[1] A certain amount of "protecting the poor Turk" was thrown in, but England's interests or concern in the matter were absolutely *nil.* We were blessed, or cursed, at that time, however, with that faddist Lord Palmerston, who was full of the idea of bringing about an Anglo-French understanding on the "love your enemies" principle. Nothing deeper seems to have existed. In addition, there was in England at that time a great taste for the penny dreadful literature[2] about Siberia and Russian tyranny,

*Its silly causes.*

[1] Kinglake's *Crimea.*

[2] The Russians have a very similar sort of literature detailing the

and Lord Palmerston was an ardent reader and devout believer in these sensational inventions. Suffering from that particular form of insanity known as "love of freedom,"—which usually works out at nothing more logical than judging unknown things by a man's own experience of something else,[1]—Lord Palmerston was distinctly Anti-Russian in sentiment, without a thought of any reasons of importance or policy. To a great extent the country, carefully prepared, echoed these sentiments. The "massacre of Sinope" was the key and watchword. Consequently strained relations ensued. War might, however, have been averted but for the action of the Peace Society. A self-constituted deputation of these amiable maniacs visited St. Petersburg, and were received by the Tsar Nikolai. They begged him not to make war: and the Tsar, incapable of comprehending that the deputation was unofficial, fell into the error of crediting it with being a direct embassy from the British Government.[2] In consequence, this country was no longer a factor in his mind, British protests were disregarded as intentionally meaningless,

*The Peace Society and Tsar Nikolai.*

horrible tortures inflicted upon the Irish by the English and Scotch. The one series is, of course, about as truthful as the other.

[1] The term insanity is used advisedly. The plea for "Home Rule for India" raised here by politicians who have never seen that country; the description of Jew stockbrokers in the Transvaal as "patriots struggling for freedom"; the hysterical rubbish talked on the eve of the Græco-Turkish War,—can only be explained on such an hypothesis. The primary factor, the absolute ignorance of the agitators concerning the subject they shriek about, is completely ignored.

[2] Kinglake.

and when war was declared no man was probably more puzzled than Tsar Nikolai. To this day the Imperial mind in Russia has never comprehended the situation, a distrust of England is ingrained into every member of the House of Romanoff, and "British deceit" on the eve of the Crimean War is a stumbling-block to any understanding between Russia and England. More: *an expression on the part of our Government of a desire for any understanding is regarded as a danger signal that England meditates a war!*[1] One way and another, those amateur diplomatists, the friends of Peace, have a good deal to answer for.

*Naval history of the Crimean War, 1854-55.*

The naval history of the Crimean War is not lengthy or important. In all cases—in the Baltic, Euxine, White Sea, and Pacific waters, Russian ships wisely kept inside their ports.

*Odessa bombarded, 20th April 1854.*

On the 3rd of January 1854, French and English warships had entered the Black Sea; on the 20th of April Odessa was bombarded by eight frigates.

The fleets then cruised before Sevastôpol, while frigates did some small damage along the Caucasian coast. In September a huge fleet of Turkish and French warships, crowded with troops, crossed the Euxine to descend upon Sevastôpol, protected by a British fleet of ten ships-of-the-line, two 50-gun frigates, and thirteen armed steamers. The Russian fleet then intact at Sevastôpol was nominally superior

[1] This is not a mere opinion of my own; I heard it in Russia many times in circles where the holding of it meant very much indeed.

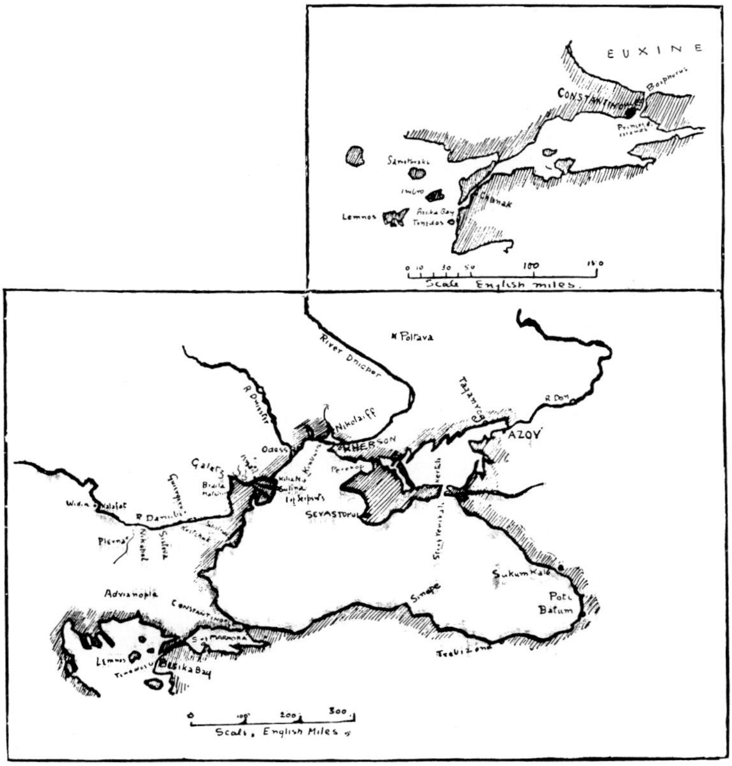


MAP OF TURKEY AND BLACK SEA.

to the British force; the Allies were absolutely, or nearly absolutely, ignorant of its condition or strength; the whole move was in direct defiance to all the principles of "Sea Power," "fleets in being," and the other theories of which we hear so much to-day. It was purely a matter of fortune that Prince Mentschikoff had decided to fight on land only, otherwise the transports must have been more or less annihilated. Korniloff, the Russian Admiral, who had earned promotion over his share in the battle of Sinope, desired to attack, and, indeed, began preparations; but Mentschikoff countermanded. By the Prince's orders the fleet that might have done so much waited idle in harbour till the Alma was lost. Then all, or nearly all, of the Russian ships were sunk to block the harbour mouth, and the crews landed under Korniloff devoted themselves to throwing up fortifications. It was chiefly to the efforts of these sailors (aided, it is true, by the hesitation of the Allies) that Sevastôpol was not taken immediately after the Alma. Mentschikoff had counted upon defeating them on shore, and he had been holding the fleet in hand with the idea that after this expected victory the Russian warships would serve to totally destroy or capture the escaping remnants. Something of Scythian tactics is observable in his plans; but he undoubtedly threw away an almost certain chance for a problematical greater effect; and he cannot be free from suspicion of having been filled with a desire to obtain military glory at the expense of sound strategy. When all

*The Alma, 21st Sept. 1854.*

*Sinking of the Russian fleet.*

*Why the Russian fleet was inactive.*

1. CLIFF AT INKERMANN OVER WHICH THE RUSSIANS MARCHED, REGIMENT AFTER REGIMENT, IN THE FOG.
2. THE HEIGHTS OF INKERMANN.
3. THE FIELD OF BALAKLAVA. THE WINDMILL WAS THE CENTRE OF THE BATTLEFIELD.

[*From Photographs kindly supplied by* MR. C. DE GRAVE SELLS.]

is said and done, however, Russian strategy was "sounder" than that of the Allies. Still, luck was with the latter, and it atoned, as it so often has, for errors that would else have been fatal.

After the immolation of the Russian ships, the war, of course, became purely military. Sevastôpol was invested, and the Allied fleet bombarded its forts without impression, though many of their ships were badly injured. Inkermann and Balaklava were fought, and after nearly a year's siege Sevastôpol was abandoned. In the course of this siege Korniloff was mortally wounded. Subsequently Kinburn was bombarded and captured by the Allied fleet.

*The war in the Baltic, 1854-55.*

A large English fleet, with some French vessels, was sent up the Baltic, but here again the Russian ships ran to cover. Nothing could be done against Kronstadt, and the English Admiral was wise enough to see it. In the following year Sveaborg was bombarded, the town and dockyard being destroyed.

*Bombardment of Sveaborg.*

*Defence at Kronstadt.*

At Kronstadt the Russians were not entirely idle, and a large force of steamers was extemporised with a view to attempting a naval action. It is not clear, however, whether these intended to meet the small craft of the Allies, or to attempt conclusions with their big ships. In any case peace came before any use was made of them.

*War in the White Sea and Pacific.*

Allied ships visited the White Sea and some Siberian harbours, but no naval actions were fought. Petropavlovsk was attacked, and the attack defeated.

When the English came back the next year they found that the Russians had evacuated it.

*Remarks on the war.*

The war, of course, was not one of the first importance. It demonstrated the extreme difficulty of attacking Russia ; any other results secured by it have long since been negatived.

One other thing, however, was indirectly demonstrated by the " Crimean " War, though curiously enough no attention seems ever to have been bestowed upon it in England. This is, that, so far as the British Empire is concerned, Russian expansion of coastline offers the best chances of a successful war against her. For instance, the more Chinese coast that may come under the Russian flag, the greater is the possible area against which England could act. Port Arthurs and Vladivostoks may be impregnable, but posts of this sort cannot be indefinitely multiplied, and the Power holding undisputed command of the sea (as England certainly would in a war with Russia) also has undisputed power to destroy the coast between the fortified spots. In craving for an extended coastline, Russia is merely creating elements of weakness for herself ; no land force, however excellent, can be mobile enough —or anything like mobile enough—to defend a long line of coast. And if the damage sustained is not great, to meet it is exceedingly expensive, and a heavy drain on resources. To believe that Russia's occupation of the Port Arthur peninsula is a menace to England, is to credit her with a stupidity for which there is no warrant.

*Coast extension. Russia's weakness.*

KRONSTADT IN 1854 (NAVAL HARBOUR).

KRONSTADT IN 1854 (MERCANTILE HARBOUR).

[*From Sketches made during the war by* CAPTAIN W. P. BURTON, R.M.A.]

# IX

# THE EARLIER IRONCLADS

## 1855–1877

IN one way and another, as much by "suicide" as by anything else, the Russian Navy had become nearly non-existent when the Crimean War ended. As has already been shown, however, many of the destroyed vessels were well-nigh useless when the Russians scuttled them; the better, and only really efficient ships, were kept out of danger during the war.

Directly the war was over, Russia began to re-organise her navy. Steamers were hastily laid down, old ships overhauled or reconstructed; the *personnel* too came in for the general revision. *Reorganisation.*

In 1859 the Russian fleet (according to their navy lists of that year) consisted of 73 steamers and 85 sailing vessels, besides a number of small gun vessels, chiefly screw steamers. *Condition in 1859.*

Details of the fleet in 1859 are as follows :—

| *Steam.* | | *Sailing.* | |
|---|---|---|---|
| 7 | screw line-of-battle ships. | 12 | battleships. |
| 11 | ,, frigates | 7 | frigates. |
| 12 | ,, corvettes. | 7 | corvettes. |
| 1 | ,, lugger. | 7 | brigs. |
| 41 | various steamers. | 11 | schooners. |
| 1 | tender. | 7 | xebecs. |
| 73 | | 5 | luggers. |
| | | 3 | clippers. |
| | | 4 | yachts. |
| | | 15 | transports. |
| | | 7 | baranes. |
| | | 85 | |

A fair proportion were probably ineffective.

Personnel.

The *personnel* was constituted as follows :—

16 admirals.
30 vice-admirals.
39 rear-admirals.
111 captains, first class.
95 captains, second class (commanders).
257 senior lieutenants.
607 lieutenants.
296 "mitchmen."

Marine artillery, 281 officers. Marines afloat, 131 officers.
*Personnel* of all ranks, about 40,000 sailors and 20,000 marines.

This *personnel*, I gather, is the purely nominal paper force; it is identical with what Russia had before the Crimean War. Probably about half this number of sailors and marines were actually available.

The Navy Staff consisted of—

The General Admiral.
A Deputy.
Master of ordnance of reserve artillery.
Inspector of naval architects.
Chief of Marine Chancery.
2 adjutant-generals.
4 vice-admirals.

To the Ministry of Marine, a president, ten admirals, a vice-admiral, six officer-inspectors, a lieutenant-general at the head of the hydrographic department, a medical director-general, an auditor-general, and ten chief clerks were allotted.

Other departments were the Engineering Department, for the care of naval fortresses; the Marine Training Department, under an admiral as director; the Marine Intendancy, under a lieutenant-general of marines; the Naval Commissariat; also shipbuilding, timber, and Naval Artillery Departments.

The guns then in use were as follows:—

| *Denomination of Gun.* | *Weight of Solid Shot.* |
|---|---|
| 36-pounder | 32 lbs. $7\frac{1}{2}$ oz. |
| 24-pounder | 21 lbs. $10\frac{1}{2}$ oz. |
| 18-pounder | 16 lbs. 3 oz. |
| 12-pounder | 10 lbs. 13 oz. |
| 8-pounder | 7 lbs. 3 oz. |
| 6-pounder | 5 lbs. $6\frac{1}{2}$ oz. |

The 36-pounder was 9 ft. 7 in. long, and weighed just under $3\frac{1}{2}$ tons. The 24-pounder was 9 ft. 4 in. long, and weighed a trifle over 2 tons.

For coast defence a monster gun was in process of adoption. This gun was $16\frac{1}{2}$ ft. long, $11\frac{1}{3}$ ft. in circumference at the base, 7 ft. at the muzzle. The bore was 13 in. diameter, and the length of the bore $13\frac{1}{4}$ ft.

This piece weighed 22 tons, threw a 340-lb. shot, and had a charge of nearly 80 lbs. of powder. There is no record of any attempt to use it on shipboard. The Americans, who then, as now, were prone to be the first to take up and experiment with any new weapon, were at that time engaged with the Niagara and her sisters, carrying 11-in. 135-pounder guns; and the 68-pounder was a recognised piece in all navies except the Russian. Russia for a long time stuck to the 32-pounder as the most easily handled gun.

This affection for a light piece is still to be found in the Russian Navy. As we shall see later, Russia at the present day has adopted the 3-in. quickfirer when other nations use the 4·7-in., and in lieu of the 4·7-in. The 12-in. is the heaviest big gun she has ever gone in for, and a tendency to prefer the 10-in. has been manifest lately,—that being the heaviest piece in the Peresvet class, and in the Rostislav. Russia, in fine, is the only Naval Power that has never been bitten with the craze for monster guns in her ships.

*First ironclad.*

Gradually, however, the 68-pounder found its way on shipboard, and the coming of the ironclad produced other changes in *matériel.* The Russians early took to iron for ship construction, and, following in the wake of their opponents in the Crimean War, decided to have an ironclad navy. In

*Pervenetz.*

England, therefore, they ordered the Pervenetz, launched in 1863. Practically this ship (she still exists) is, and always was, a floating battery. She carried at that time about two dozen 68-pounders, and was a formidable ship, plated all over with $4\frac{1}{2}$ in. iron. The dimensions are :—

| | |
|---|---|
| Displacement . . . . . . . | 3279 tons. |
| Length . . . . . . . . | 220 ft. |
| Beam . . . . . . . . | $52\frac{1}{2}$ ft. |
| Draught . . . . . . . . | *circa* 16 ft. |
| Present armament . . . . . . | Six 8-in.<br>Nine 6-in.<br>Four 9-pounders.<br>Seven small Q.F. |

The engines were made by Messrs. Maudslay, Sons, & Field of Lambeth, London, and were of 1067 horse-power. The trial speed was 9 knots—the ship was never built to be a "flyer." Rectangular box boilers were fitted, and are still in her. She was launched at Blackwall, having been built by the firm of which the present Thames Ironworks Company are the lineal descendants.

It is interesting to note that despite the Crimean War, Russia turned to Great Britain for assistance in reconstructing her navy, just as she had turned in the past.[1]

In the following year (1864) she launched the Kreml at St. Petersburg, and the next year again the Netron Menia (Touch-me-not), sisters to the Pervenetz.

*Kreml and Netron Menia.*

[1] A Scotchman imported about this time to supervise construction, is still at the Baltic Works.

*Sevastôpol and Petropavlovsk.*

In all navies the best of the old wooden line-of-battle ships on the stocks were cut down, and armoured. In this fashion Russia added to her navy the seagoing broadside ships Sevastôpol (1863) and Petropavlovsk (1865).

Details of these are :—

| | |
|---|---|
| Displacement . . . . . | 6210 tons. |
| Length . . . . . . | 295 ft. |
| Beam . . . . . . | 52 ft. |
| Armament . . . . . | Twenty-one 9-ton guns. |
| Armour . . . . . . | $4\frac{1}{2}$ in. iron. |
| Horse-power . . . . . | 2800. |
| Trial speed . . . . . | 11 knots. |

These ships are now broken up.

*Effect of American Civil War.*

The monitor and its deeds in the American Civil War made a great impression upon the Russians. They immediately began to lay down a number of iron

*Monitors.*

monitors, and in the year 1864 most of these were launched, though they were not completed till some years later. Originally each carried a couple of big smooth-bore guns, but these were long ago replaced by 9-in. 15-ton breechloaders, of no great power or strength.[1]

These monitors still figure to some extent in the Russian Navy list, but they have of course no present value, unless it be as tertiary fortifications. Several have been broken up, and the rest

[1] Muzzle energy, 3035; muzzle velocity, 1260; weight of shell, 275 lbs.; length of gun, 13 ft.; nominal muzzle perforation, $10\frac{1}{2}$ in. of iron—inferior to that of a modern 6-in. quickfirer. War game value, D.

THIRD-CLASS BATTLESHIP KNIAZ POJARSKY.

distributed about at minor ports. Their names are as follows:—

Brononosetz, Edinorvg, Koldoune, Latnik, Lava, Ouragan, Peroune, Streletz, Tiphoon, and Vestchoune.

THE BRONONOSETZ.

Displacement from 1400 to 1800 tons. Side armour, five plates, each 1 in. thick; turret armour, eleven such plates. This turret armour is in value equivalent to about 3 in. of modern armour, the series of plates offering very small resistance.

Having taken to the monitor, Russia practically adopted it. Nothing in the nature of a seagoing vessel was attempted for some time, saving only the broadside, iron-hulled ironclad Kniaz Pojarski *Kniaz Pojarski.* launched in 1867 at St. Petersburg. She was inspired by the British Penelope, and is one of the earliest examples of a ship with recessed ports. She is still on the navy list, but is scarcely worth reconstruction, though some tinkering was recently attempted.

Her principal details are :—

| | |
|---|---|
| Displacement . . . . | 5000 tons. |
| Length . . . . . | 272 ft. |
| Beam . . . . . | 49 ft. |
| Draught . . . . . | *circa* 25 ft. |
| Armour . . . . . | $4\frac{1}{2}$ in. on complete belt and over battery. |
| Guns . . . . . | Originally eight 8-in. and two 6-in., but several of these have been removed. |
| Horse-power . . . . | 2835. |
| Trial speed . . . . | 12·5 knots. |
| Sea speed . . . . | 9 knots. |

*English influence.*

At this time England had the semi-seagoing turret-ships Wivern and Scorpion,[1] as well as the seagoing turret-ships Captain and Monarch. Russia, following the English lead, commenced to build a species of Wivern, and also laid down the Minin, a vessel of the Monarch type.

*Smertch.*

Before the Wivern type she had, however, gone in for the double-turreted monitor, and the Smertch of 1460 tons was launched in 1864. She carried the same armament as the Brononosetz type, but only one gun in each turret. These turrets had 6-in. armour in one solid thickness on them.

This ship is now relegated to harbour service, and is practically removed from the list.

*Tcharodeika and Russalka.*

In 1867 the Tcharodeika and Russalka, vessels of about 2000 tons, of the same type as the Smertch, but

[1] Originally U.S. Confederate rams.

RUSSALKA.

ADMIRAL SPIRIDOFF.

ADMIRAL GREIG.

carrying two guns in each turret, were launched. The Tcharodeika still exists for harbour service and coast defence; the Russalka was lost in the Gulf of Finland three or four years since. She put to sea in a gale, and no trace of her has ever been found since.

*Wivern type.*

Four ships of the British Wivern type were launched in 1868—two types, one a copy of the Wivern, the other an adaptation of the old British Prince Albert and Royal Sovereign[1] with several turrets.

Details of these ships are:—

*Spiridoff and Tchitchagoff. Wivern type.*

Admiral Spiridoff and Admiral Tchitchagoff.

| | |
|---|---|
| Displacement | *circa* 3500 tons. |
| Length | 234 ft. |
| Beam | 42½ ft. |
| Draught (*mean*) | 18 ft. |
| Armour (belts and turrets) | 6 in. |
| Armament | Two 11-in. B.L.[2]<br>Six small Q.F. or machine. |

(Two turrets.)

*Greig and Lazareff.*

The Admiral Greig and Admiral Lazareff are of exactly the same dimensions. The only difference is that the belt is thinner (4½ in. only) and that there are three turrets—each with one 11-in. B.L. gun in in it.

*Remarks.*

None of these ships are seaworthy; the Russians, however, consider that they may still possess some

[1] Not, of course, the present Royal Sovereign.

[2] 19 calibres long; muzzle energy, 8000; muzzle velocity, 1496; weight of projectile, 1000 lbs.; date of manufacture, 1867. War game value, C.

coast defence value, and the Lazareff was reboilered last year. The reboilering of the others is either under consideration or in process of being carried out. Eventually it is likely that they will be rearmed with lighter and more powerful pieces — the Lazareff, at least, will probably be so treated.

*Minin.* The Minin was launched in 1869, but the capsizing of the British Captain soon afterwards produced a strong distrust in the Minin, although she was more of the Monarch than the Captain type. Work upon this ship languished, she was never properly completed, and at a later date practically rebuilt. Details of her will therefore be found upon a later page in the proper chronological order of her rebuilding.

The turret-ship being at this time in full favour in the British Navy, and great things expected of the Devastation and Thunderer, the Russians laid down a larger edition of these ships, the Peter Veliky, launched in 1872.

The details of this ship are :—

| | |
|---|---|
| Displacement . . . . . | 9665. |
| Length . . . . . . | 328 ft. |
| Beam . . . . . . | $62\frac{1}{3}$ ft. |
| Draught . . . . . | *circa* 26 ft. |
| Armour . . . . . | Belt, 14–8 in. (iron). |
| | Redoubt, 9 in. ,, |
| | Turrets, 12 in. ,, |
| Guns . . . . . . | Four 12-in.[1] |

[1] 17 calibres long ; weight, 40 tons ; model, 1877 ; muzzle velocity, 1705 ; muzzle energy, 10,000 ft. ; tons weight of projectile, 990 lbs. War game value, C.

PETER VELĪKY, SECOND-CLASS BATTLESHIP.

A proposal to rearm this ship is under consideration, but nothing had been done in January 1899.[1]

Armoured cruiser General Admiral.

With the Peter Veliky the construction of seagoing ironclads stopped for nearly ten years, and armoured cruisers—which Russia may almost claim as her own invention—were commenced. The original idea of an armoured cruiser was a vessel protected at the water line by armour, but otherwise a cruiser pure and simple. The original armoured cruiser was the prototype of the deck-protected cruiser of to-day,[2] and the Russians were the first to devise this kind of ship. In 1873 they launched the General Admiral, a vessel without any protection to her guns, but with what was in those days a fairly efficient protection against being sunk.

Details of the General Admiral are as follows :—

| | |
|---|---|
| Displacement | *circa* 4600. |
| Length | 285 ft. |
| Beam | 48 ft. |
| Draught | *circa* 25 ft. |
| Armour belt | 6-in. belt. |

[1] See description of Kronstadt dockyard, later.

[2] The curved deck inside is merely a substitution for the heavier outside belt.

| | |
|---|---|
| Armament . . . . . . | Six 8-in. B.L.[1]<br>Two 6-in. B.L.<br>Ten machine or small Q.F.<br>Two torpedo tubes above water. |
| Horse-power . . . . . . | 4472. |
| Trial speed . . . . . . | 12 knots. |
| Present sea speed . . . . | *circa* 8 knots.[2] |

The guns are carried in an overhanging battery, on the upper deck. Originally she had but one funnel, but having been recently reboilered, now carries two. A peculiar turtle-back stern is a feature of this ship, which, with her sister the Gerzog Edinburgski (launched 1875), is now relegated to training service.

*Gerzog Edinburgski.*

*The circular ironclads.*

The year in which the General Admiral was launched (1873) saw also the launch of a still more unique Russian warship invention, the circular ironclad Novgorod, of about 2500 tons displacement. She was designed by the late Admiral Popoff, and launched at Nikolaiff on the Black Sea. The idea of this extraordinary craft was in theory most admirable.

*Novgorod.*

The circular turret then claimed to deflect any shot hitting it,—6 in. on a circular turret were held equal to something like 10 or 12 in. of ordinary vertical armour. Popoff's idea was to apply to the hull what other designers had applied to the gun protection.

With this end in view he designed the Novgorod, a circular hull 121 ft. in diameter, and drawing $13\frac{1}{2}$ ft. of water. Two 11-in. guns were mounted in a barbette

[1] War game value, D. [2] May be a little more.

ARMOURED CRUISER GERTSOG EDINBOORSKI.

amidships, and this barbette, as well as the whole side, is covered with armour 9 to 7 in. thick. Engines developing 2000 horse-power moved the vessel at a speed of about 6 knots, and six screws formed the propelling power.

Two years later a larger edition, the Vice-Admiral Popoff, of 3550 tons, was launched. She was of the same draught, but 120 ft. in diameter. The guns (12-in. 40-tonners, similar to those in the Peter Veliky) were mounted on the disappearing system. The sides are 16 in. thick,—the barbette 9 in., and there is a flat 3-in. deck; 3066 horse-power gave a trial speed of 8½ knots. There are four screws. *The Popoff.*

Had these ships been able to make anything like a decent speed, it is by no means impossible that Europe would have imitated, and circular ships might be found in every navy to-day. The low speed, however, at once relegated them to the rank of floating forts, and they remained as unique curios of naval architecture —nothing more. *Remarks.*

Such mobility as they had was soon heavily discounted. On a trial cruise they went up the Dneiper very nicely for some distance, till they turned to retire. Then the current caught them, and they were carried out to sea, whirled helplessly round and round, every soul on board hopelessly incapacitated by vertigo. *Their attempt to cruise.*

The lesson was read. Since then the Popoffkas have abandoned the rôle of the ironclad for that of floating forts, and in the Turco-Russian War that followed soon afterwards, no attempt to use them was made.

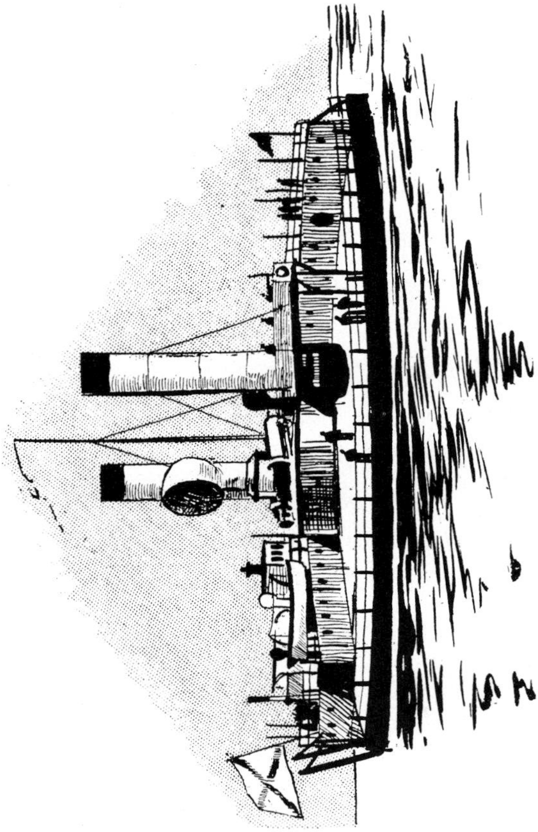

CIRCULAR IRONCLAD VICE-ADMIRAL POPOFF.

During this period, 1855–1877, a number of unarmoured ships were built. Of those which still survive, mention may be made of the "flat-irons" Stichit (1856), Mina (1861), Pistchal and Siekira (for the Caspian Sea) (1866), and Jorsh (1874), — all carrying one big gun.

The unarmoured cruisers Kreysser and Djijdit, 1450 tons, which took some five years to build, were launched at St. Petersburg in 1875 and 1876. They have no fighting value.

Other vessels launched in this period are Abrek [1] 1069 tons, Askold [1] 2229 tons, Bayan [1] 1998 tons, Bombory (Black Sea) 760 tons, Don (Black Sea) 354 tons, Japonec 1472 tons, Jemtchug 1781 tons, Ermak [1] 706 tons, Kasbek (Black Sea) 692 tons, Kelasurz (Black Sea) 307 tons, Morz 456 tons, Narra 379 tons, Pitsunda (Black Sea), 335 tons, Psezuappa (Black Sea) 335 tons, Salgair (Black Sea) 360 tons, Skobeleff (originally some other name) 2397 tons, Sobol 456 tons, Sokol [1] (Black Sea) 1057 tons, Souk-Su (Black Sea) 307 tons, Svetlana [1] 3200 tons, Tunguz 706 tons, and Voyin (Black Sea) 1652 tons.

In 1877 nearly all these were obsolete and of very small fighting value. Some are still on the list, others have been broken up. New vessels have taken the old names in many instances. The ships built in England for the Russian Governments during the period were the transports, etc., Artelstchik 550 tons (Millwall), Sextant and Kompas 251 tons (Blackwall),

[1] All these are now broken up, and new ships bear their names.

Krasnaia Gorka 1166 tons (Blackwall), the yacht Strielna 185 tons (Millwall), the paddlers Erckhik 920 tons (Low Walker, Newcastle), Baku 440 tons (Blackwall), Tchihischlar 177 tons (Low Walker, Newcastle), and the training ship Beresan 3050 tons (Greenock).

About the end of this period the total of warships in the Russian Navy was 223,[1] thus distributed :—

| | |
|---|---|
| Baltic Fleet | 137 |
| Black Sea Fleet | 31 |
| Caspian Flotilla | 19 |
| White Sea | 3 |
| Sea of Aral Flotilla | 6 |
| Siberian Fleet | 27 |
| | 223 |

The *personnel* was—

| | |
|---|---|
| Admirals of all ranks | 95 |
| Other officers of all ranks | 2345 |
| Civil functionaries | 966 |
| Seamen | about 25,000 |
| Cadets, etc. | 169 |

It will be noted that marines no longer figure separately. In the period under review the marines—who were analogous to the military element afloat in the British Navy at the time of the Armada, and in the French Navy during the Great War, rather than to marines as we understand them—the "marines" were absorbed into the navy generally. Longer than any

[1] These figures probably include torpedo boats, a number of which were ordered from Yarrow about 1876; while numerous third-class boats were built or building in Russia. It also includes transports, etc.

other nation, Russia held out against the change whereby the difference between those who *fought* the ships and those who *sailed* them was abolished. To-day there are those who predict some similar fusion[1] between the executive and sailor branch, who do the fighting, and the engineering branch, who to a partial extent represent the old branch who sailed the ship. There is, however, less analogy—the engineers have nothing to do with navigation or steering the ship : their work is limited to attending to the main engines and every other species of machinery on board. Practically, they are the modern equivalent of the rowers in ancient warships, and these, in thoroughly efficient navies like the Athenian, specialised as strictly as the engineering department in the British Navy to-day—more strictly, possibly, as a stoker nowadays receives a certain amount of deck training and drill.

[1] The U.S. Navy has taken steps toward some such fusion.

# X

## THE TURCO-RUSSIAN WAR, 1877–78

Russian fleet.

WHEN the Turco-Russian War of 1877–78 broke out, the only seagoing Russian battleships were the Minin, Kniaz Pojarski, Petropavlovsk, Sevastôpol, Peter Veliki, General Admiral, and Gerzog Edinbourski. Of these the Minin was under reconstruction, some of the others were on distant stations, and the Petropavlovsk was the only one anywhere near the spot. She was a very old ship, of next to no value even in those days, and in the face of the large Turkish fleet remained inactive at Spezia throughout the war,—an operation of circumstances that might be held worse than a defeat both on her own crew and on the Russian sailors generally.

Black Sea Fleet.

In the Black Sea there was nothing; or rather, there was worse than nothing, a number of old tubs of no fighting value whatever. About twenty merchant steamers were purchased and armed, and a number of torpedo boats (launches we should call them nowadays) were sent across country by rail from Pétersbourg, but practically at the outbreak, and in the early stages of the war, Russia was worse off than she would have been without a fleet at all. For the consequent forced inactivity, as in the case of the Petropavlovsk at Spezia, might be assumed to have a fatal effect on the *morale* of the men. Inaction soon neutralises the finest fleet, and its effects are likely enough to spread to the military in a long campaign.

The Turks, on the other hand, had what passed for a very fine fleet in those days—about a dozen[1] sea-going ironclads, and six or seven light draught monitors, up the Danube. As has been before observed,[2] Russia had no "Sea Power," and in this case at least "Sea Power" had a full meaning. With a fleet like she now has in the Black Sea, Russia could have settled the war in a week or two.

*Torpedoes.*

In those days the torpedo was a new weapon, and though possessed by all Powers, was more associated with the name of Russia than any other. These torpedoes the Turks were supposed to be particularly afraid of, and this has been put forward as a reason for their extraordinary inactivity; actually, however, circumstances, lack of ammunition, or defects in machinery, may be considered more probable causes.

*Hobart Pasha.*

The Turkish admiral, Hobart Pasha, was an ex-British officer hardly likely to have been frightened by such an untried weapon as the torpedo then was. The most of his subsequent actions, moreover, point clearly

[1] Specific numbers are dangerous where Turkish ships are concerned—as many as fifteen could be named, but the Turks have a way of doubling their ships by re-naming them. The superiority, however, was so tremendous that two or three, or for that matter half a dozen, ships more or less would have made no difference.

[2] See p. 24.

AVNI ILLAH AND MOYINI ZAFFIR.

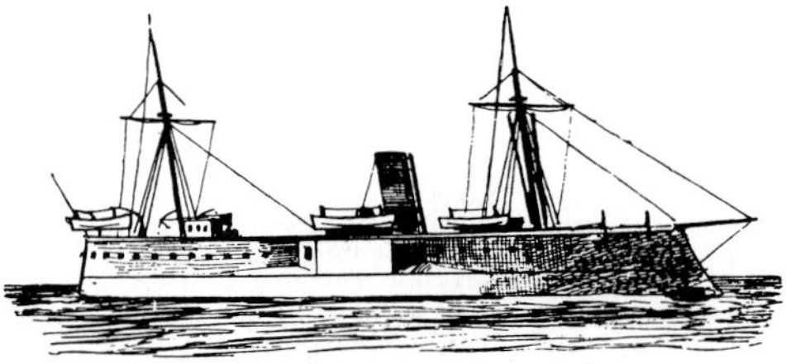

FETH-I-BULEND AND MUKADIM-I-HAIR.

ASSAR-I-SHEFKET AND NEDJIM SHEFKET.

LUTFI DJEL AND HAFIZ RAHAM.

SOME OF THE TURKISH WARSHIPS, 1877.

enough to a considerable study of defence against torpedo attack, and, further, that defence was successful as a passive defence could be.

In this connection it may not be without interest to mention that near the village of Upottery, in

HOBART PASHA'S TORPEDO POND AT THE PRESENT DAY.

Devonshire, is a pond, or rather the remains of one, which rustics have pointed out to me as where the Turkish admiral during a visit to England had played about with torpedoes. This was some two or three years previous to the war, and so far as I could glean from the very non-technical descriptions of the village blacksmith (who as a boy had been employed to fish things out of the water), experiments, which if rough and ready were certainly very catholic, had been carried out. Certain it is that this village blacksmith knew a good deal more about torpedo defence some twelve years ago than the ordinary citizen knows even in these days of Navy Leagues. All of which goes to help prove that Hobart Pasha was not the cipher subsequent historians have made him

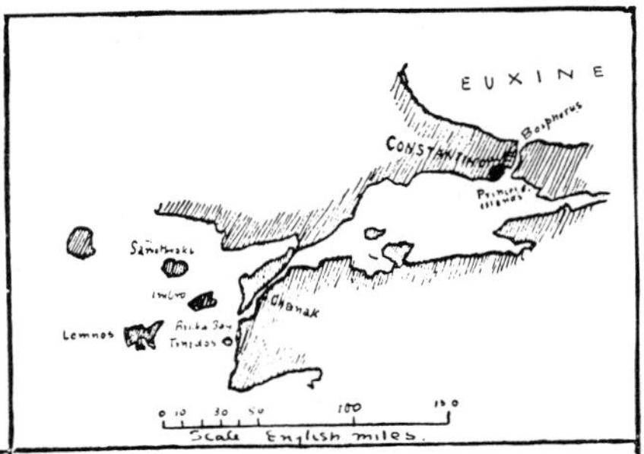


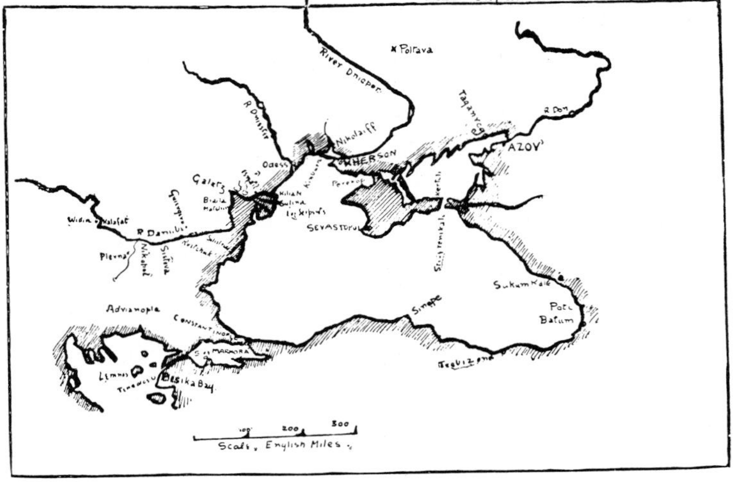


SKETCH MAP OF THE CRIMEA AND ADJACENT COASTS.

out to be; if he was paralysed it was more through the way the Russian conducted operations than from any general inability. What the Turks failed to recognise was that a vigorous offence was the best defence against torpedo attack, and that nothing else could possibly avail. This neither Hobart[1] nor his officers seem to have grasped, while the Russians saw and acted on it.

The first place where the Turkish fleet should have been in evidence was the Danube, but the Russians were swift to concentrate efforts on preventing that. Nor was the river easy for Turkish ironclads to ascend; in the upper reaches things were left to the little monitors already there, lower down Hobart did get a few ships up the river, and the Russians promptly dropped mines around them.

*Sinking of the Lutfi Djel.*

This fixed the Turks, who stayed there exchanging shots with a Russian mortar and small gun battery, a shell from which struck an ironclad, Lutfi Djel, and blew her up. The Russian theory was that a shell had dropped down her funnel; the Turks had some vague tale of an accident in the engine-room. As the Russians gave the Iron Cross to a gunner who was considered to have fired the lucky shot, and none of the Turks immediately concerned ever survived the explosion to give evidence, the balance of such evidence as there is is in favour of the shell.

*Instances of mysterious endings of warships.*

It may be remarked *en passant* that mystery surrounds the fate of almost fifty per cent. of the ships that have been sunk in modern warfare. To take the last decade only, the monitor Javary went down in the Brazilian Civil War in much the same style as the Lutfi Djel—a puff of white smoke, a great cloud

[1] Assuming that a good many Turkish ships were not merely hulks through parts of the engines being missing—a perfectly possible contingency.

of black, then—nothing. In this case a shore-battery was being engaged. How the King Yuen went down at Yalu has never been described, the loss of the famous Chih Yuen has a good deal of uncertainty still about it,[1] while the sinking of the Isla de Cuba and Isla de Luzon at Manila in the Hispano-American war—ships that were subsequently, according to official reports, got up almost undamaged—puzzles one when taken in conjunction with earlier and most detailed accounts of how they were blown to bits.

*The first successful torpedo flotilla attack ever made, 25th May 1877.*

Having disposed of the seagoing turret-ship, the Russians next decided to sink the river monitors Seifé and Feth-ul-Islam and a gunboat, which were attacked by torpedo boats on the night of the 25th of May, about ten days after the destruction of the Lutfi Djel. Four boats, the Tsarvitch, Xenia, Djidjit, and Tsarevna, set out from Braila on an excellent night for such work, very thick weather and heavy rain. The flotilla was under Lieutenant Doubasoff in the Tsarvitch, with Lieutenant Tchestakoff in the Xenia, second in command, abreast of him. Astern came the other two boats under Sub-lieutenants Persin and Bali.

This attack is of special interest, and the order followed has therefore some importance. Doubasoff directed the attack to be made by the Tsarvitch and

[1] A Japanese officer who served in the Takachiho at Yalu told me that they hit this ship *near the funnel* with a 10-in. shell. Previously to that she had been steering very wildly, and apparently was quite out of control, and looked to be foundering. From an officer in the Chinese service, on the other hand, I heard that one of the Chinese ironclads put a big shell into her by mistake.

Xenia, the Djidjit was to support them in case of defeat, the Tsarevna to be in reserve, and act according to circumstances.

The boats were all armed with spar torpedoes, and the greatest speed they could manage (without being so noisy that the enemy's attention would be attracted) was about five knots. *Armament and torpedoes.*

Having got within 150 yards unnoticed, the two attacking boats put on full speed ahead, and were within 70 yards before they were hailed from the monitor. In a modern attack, of course, torpedoes could have been fired long before the boats were seen, the spar torpedoes, however, necessitated close contact.

The alarm given, the Turks trained their big guns at the boats, but owing to miss-fires, or because the interval was too short, nothing happened. The Tsarvitch struck the monitor with her torpedo in the stern. The explosion was very violent, nearly swamping the boat, and the men were ordered to jump overboard, the impression being that she was going down. *The Tsarvitch's attack.*

The monitor does not seem to have been very much injured, since as the boat went astern she fired her turret guns at her, and the crew opened a rifle fire.

The Xenia now steamed at the monitor, and struck her under the turret just as the big guns went off. The explosion hurled a lot of wreckage into the air, some of which fouled the Xenia's screw, and she was only got clear by her crew pushing along the side. All this while rifle fire was being exchanged, but no Russian was hit, and at the most only three Turks. *The Xenia's attack.*

As day broke the Seifé went down, still firing, but only one hit was made, a bullet that struck the stern of the Djidjit and disabled her. No Russians were even wounded, and the loss of life on the Turkish side appears to have been very small: the importance of the affair is not, however, to be gauged by this. The

ADMIRAL MAKAROFF.

object of the expedition was achieved, and it stands in history as the first successful torpedo boat flotilla attack.

It was not the first attempted, as a few days earlier an attack with towing torpedoes had been made at Batûm. The towing torpedo, however, does not lend itself to flotilla attacks like the spar and the

Whitehead, and this particular attack was a dismal failure.

The Grand Duke Constantine was an armed merchant steamer of about 1500 tons, and the command of her was given to Lieutenant (now Admiral) Makaroff. Practically the Grand Duke Constantine was an anticipation of the British Vulcan or French Foudre of the present time, though the boats of 1877 being much smaller than those of to-day, they were carried, to the number of six, on the davits. *Makaroff.*

The very first Russian naval movement in the war was to send Makaroff to Batûm, where some Turkish ironclads lay at anchor behind a partially completed boom. Four boats, Tchesma, Sinôp, Navārin, and Sukhum Kalā, were sent in, but finding a small vessel on guard outside, which opened fire upon them, their efforts were concentrated on her. Nothing came of the torpedo which they tried to tow under this ship, and the attack had to be abandoned as the enemy were on the *qui vive*. *Makaroff at Batûm, 12th May 1877.*

On the 12th of June the Turkish ironclads Idjalalieh, Feth-i-Bulend, Mukadim-i-Hair, and a gun-boat, were lying at Sulina. Hobart had devised a protection for these ships,—a circle of guard-boats, each connected to the next with a rope,—a very sound passive defence, which under certain circumstances would be valuable enough in the present day. *Makaroff at Sulina, 12th June 1877.* *Hobart Pasha's defence scheme.*

Off Sulina arrived Makaroff in the Grand Duke Constantine, with a sister ship, the Vladimir, as consort. Having located the enemy, he dropped his boats, ordered them to attack in two divisions and rejoin the flag at a rendezvous off the coast.

The boats were—

| | | |
|---|---|---|
| 1st division, | Tchesma, | Lieut. Zatzarennyi (in command). |
| | No. 2, | Lieut. Rojdestvenski. |
| | No. 1, | Lieut. Poutschine. |
| 2nd division, | Sinôp. | |
| | Navārin. | |
| | Sukhum Kalā. | |

The Tchesma still had the towing torpedo; the other boats were all armed with spar torpedoes, consequently the former had to act independently.

*Fate of No. 1.*

The first division, thus reduced to two boats, ran at the nearest ironclad, the Idjalalieh, and No. 1 running into the rope between the picket-boats, she was capsized, the torpedo was exploded, and the boat sunk. Six of her crew who escaped were captured by the Turks.

Rojdestvenski's boat managed to jump the boom, but sustained some damage in doing so. Proceeding, she struck her spar against the Idjalalieh's torpedo nets, and in the explosion sustained further damage, which put her out of action. The Turks, who had kept up a heavy fire all along, also did some damage to the boat, though no men were hit. The ironclad steamed forward in pursuit, failing to capture or destroy No. 2, but quite neutralising the remainder of the flotilla. The Tchesma's towing torpedo proved altogether useless, and the whole attack was a complete failure.

*Attack defeated.*

*20th June 1877.*

On 20th June a Turkish monitor off Rustchuk

attacked some Russian boats laying mines in the daytime. One of them attempted to torpedo, but the wire for firing was cut by a bullet and the boats routed.

*23rd June 1877, off Nikopolis.*

Three days later this same monitor was up the Danube at Nikopolis, and the torpedo boats Mina, Sub-lieutenant Arens, and the Toutchka, Sub-lieutenant Niloff, were ordered to attack her. The monitor, however, dropped nets at once, and also rigged out booms with explosives at the end of them. She likewise steamed at the boats, and very nearly caught that of Sub-lieutenant Niloff between her booms and the river bank.

The boats being armoured with boiler plates, the Turkish rifle fire did them little harm; on the other hand, they were absolutely powerless against the monitor, the captain of which, an Englishman or an American, stood on the bridge waving his cap and jeering at his assailants, who were doing what they could with small arms. After a time he disappeared, and the monitor promptly steamed away, the boats retiring also.

*Reported naval action, 23rd July 1877.*

On the 23rd July the Russian armed merchantman Vesta is supposed to have been engaged with the Turkish ironclad Assar-i-Chevket. Considerable uncertainty hangs over this action, and it has been denied *in toto.* In any case, in view of the disparity of the combatants, it cannot have been more than partial, and was probably nothing but a stern chase in which a few long-range rifle-shots were interchanged. The only sure thing in the matter is, that if the action really took place, the Turkish captain ought to have been shot for failing to capture or sink the Vesta.

*Makaroff at Sukhum Kalé, 24th Aug. 1877.*

On the night of 24th August Makaroff came off Sukhum Kalé, which a Turkish squadron had attacked and occupied. He despatched four boats—

| | |
|---|---|
| Tchesma (flag) . . | Lieut. Zatzarennyi. |
| Sinôp . . . . | Lieut. Pifarefsky. |
| Torpedoist . . . | Sub-lieut. Hirst. |
| Navārin . . . | Lieut. Vishnevetski. |

These, armed with the towing torpedoes, after some delay came to the roadstead where two large ships, one of them the Assar-i-Chevket, and a number of feluccas were lying. They found the Turks in full occupation, a huge fire burning on the beach, by the light of which the attack was able to proceed fairly easily.

*Attack on the Assar-i Chevket.*

There was an eclipse of the moon that night, and in the middle of the eclipse the four boats rushed the

THE ATTACK ON THE ASSAR-I-CHEVKET.

Assar-i-Chevket under a heavy fire from the vessels and from a battery on shore.

*The Sinôp's attack.*

Alongside the ironclad a boat was lying, and the Sinôp's torpedo was exploded by hitting this. Drifting closer alongside, the Sinôp got entangled with this boat, and a good deal of hand-to-hand fighting took place, in the course of which Lieutenant Pifarefski was wounded, and very nearly made prisoner. Eventually, however, the Sinôp got free and retired.

*The Navārin's attack.*

The Navārin, attacking at the same time, fouled her torpedo and exploded it, nearly swamping herself thereby.

*The Tchesma's attack.*

The Tchesma fouled the ironclad's accommodation ladder and was so compelled to cut loose her torpedo, which drifted to the beach. A moment later she fouled the accommodation ladder herself, and the ironclad, rolling from the effect of the Sinôp's torpedo, nearly forced her under. As it was she escaped, but badly disabled.

*The Torpedoist.*

The Torpedoist missed the way, and was supposed to have been lost. Zatzarennyi went back under fire to look for her, and eventually picked her up.

*Effect on the ironclad.*

The ironclad was quite uninjured by the torpedo—a slight dent on the armour belt being the sum-total of her injuries. At the time, however, the Russians were under the impression that they had sunk her.

Just as the flotilla reached Makaroff's steamer the Grand Duke Constantine, a large Turkish ironclad was sighted through the morning mists. The Russian expedition was not, however, sighted in return, and it went back to Odessa unmolested.

*Mouth of Danube.*

The next naval operations did not take place till the winter. In November there left Odessa an expedition consisting of—

*Attack on Turkish fleet.*

| | | |
|---|---|---|
| Voron (gunboat) . . . | 3 mortars | 2 small guns |
| Outka (gunboat) . . . | 3 ,, | 2 ,, ,, |
| Lebedi (gunboat) . . . | 3 ,, | 3 ,, ,, |
| Mortar barge . . . . | 2 ,, | 1 ,, ,, |
| Armed tug, No. 1 . . . | 1 ,, | 2 ,, ,, |
| Armed tug, No. 2 . . . | 1 ,, | 2 ,, ,, |

and seven torpedo boats. It carried with it ninety torpedoes, some of them Whiteheads, and mines, and seventy-five high-explosive rockets.[1] Two of the boats were fitted for Whitehead torpedo discharge.

This expedition reached the Danube without molestation, and ascended by the Kilia mouth, where one of the torpedo boats was wrecked.

*Turkish fleet.*

The Turkish fleet consisted of the broadside ironclads Medjenieh, Assar-i-Chevket, Moini Zaffir, and the turret-ship Hafiz-i-ul-Raham (a sister to the lost Lutfi Djel). The Admiral, Mustapha Pasha, flew his flag in the Moini Zaffir. This fleet lay between two breakwaters, across and between which a chain was stretched; strong batteries defended the position to seaward, and up stream another battery had been placed, with the ironclad Mukadim-i-Hair, the gunboat Sulina, and an armed tug to reinforce it. Here also was a chain and a mine field.

*Its defence scheme.*

The Turkish position was practically impregnable to the means at the Russian disposal, nor, owing

[1] Loaded with gun-cotton.

to the marshes, swamps, and quicksands surrounding the place, could any military assistance be obtained. Practically the Russian tactics resolved themselves into an attempt to shut in the Turkish squadron by sowing mines broadcast above and below it.

*The Russian tactics.*

The torpedo boats having gone up the Danube to

Toultcha, now descended toward Sulina, laying mines under fire that did them no harm.

*Sulina blown up.*

The following day a Russian steamer reconnoitred. The Sulina and the tug came out to attack her, but the former getting on to the Russian mines was blown up and sank in shallow water, and the tug busied herself rescuing the survivors of the crew. The

Mukadim-i-Hair now came up, opening fire at long range, but no hits appear to have been made on either side.

*General action.*

The whole Russian flotilla attacked next day, and a sort of naval battle took place at long bowls. The turret-ship Hafiz-i-ul-Raham was hit by a shell somewhere in the machinery[1] and put out of action. The Mukadim-i-Hair continued the fight till all her ammunition was expended, but again without securing any hits. On the other hand, if the Russians hit her they did no harm—she is a ship largely coated with armour, and shell-fire therefore likely to be comparatively innocuous to her.

*Makaroff at Batûm, 21st Dec. 1877.*

After the Sukhum Kalē affair the Russians began to discard the towing torpedo, and the Tchesma and Sinôp were armed with Whitehead tubes. The boats were too small to carry the tubes as tubes are carried nowadays, and that of the Tchesma was lashed under the boat's bottom, the intention being to cut it loose as soon as it had been used.

*Method of carrying the Tchesma's tube.*

*Method of carrying the Sinôp's tube.*

That of the Sinôp was secured to a raft which was lashed alongside the boat. For practical purposes each, therefore, was fitted with a sort of bow tube. These torpedoes had a 60-lb. gun-cotton charge, and besides being smaller, were, of course, far slower and more uncertain than the Whiteheads of to-day.

*Hobart Pasha's precautions.*

Hobart Pasha lay at Batûm with seven vessels, presumably defended in the usual fashion. A very sharp lookout was kept, picket-boats were out, and all lights carefully hidden both on shipboard and on shore.

[1] Said to have been hit in the boilers, but this is doubtful.

As a result of this the Russians had some considerable difficulty in finding the place; it was also a dark, rainy night. At last, however, the masts of ships were made out, and for these, guided also by the sound of the Turks' voices, the Russians steered.

*Difficulty in finding the quarry.*

Without being sighted they crept up, and the Tchesma discharged her torpedo; but it hit nets or some other obstruction and exploded harmlessly. The Sinôp's torpedo missed altogether; and the Turks opening a heavy fire, the attack was over.

In the retreat the Russian boats nearly attacked the Grand Duke Constantine—taking her for a hostile vessel. The Torpedoist and the Navārin had previously sighted Makaroff's vessel, and steamed away from her under the impression that she was an enemy best avoided.

*Batûm, 26th Jan. 1878.*

The last naval action in the war was also off Batûm. On this occasion, Makaroff only sent the Tchesma and Sinôp into the attack. There was a sea on, but the harbour was fetched, fairly visible in the bright moonlight. The two boats both fired simultaneously at the same ship, a large gunboat, which sank at once. The Turks appear to have known nothing about this affair till they found their ship going under, and the Russians retreated after the event without any loss.

*General remarks.*

The results of this guerilla warfare cannot be said to have been particularly conclusive. They produced *negative* rather than positive results. That, in the nature of things, is likely always to be the effect of torpedo warfare. A few ships were sunk; but the destruction of ships is merely an item in naval warfare. "Moral effect" on the Turks seems to have been little, or at anyrate less than might have been expected; the Turk is a case-hardened person, and he seems to have taken the then novel and new-fangled torpedo as being quite as commonplace a Kismet as a shot or a shell. In the absence of full knowledge as to the state of the Turkish fleet it is almost impossible to gauge how much, if at all, that fleet was paralysed by the torpedo boat menace.

On the other hand, the credit due to the Russians is immense. They had no fleet to start with, and they used an almost unknown weapon. We cannot judge Makaroff's exploits by the light of present-day knowledge: he had to *invent* his tactics, and to invent tactics is a very different thing to executing evolutions of the drill-book. Nor, because their loss of life was small and insignificant, can this be held to detract from the individual bravery of the Russian torpedoists; on going into action there were absolutely no reasonable prospects of such an extraordinary survival. Possibly they lost more men than they have admitted to—but that is a side issue. The main fact is, that they accomplished a good deal with the slenderest materials, and if Farragut is worthy of being called the Nelson of ironclads,[1] Makaroff certainly deserves a similar

[1] This comparison is of course made in a purely relative sense. Neither Farragut nor Makaroff occupy a niche anywhere near Nelson, for the simple reason that the operations in which they did so well were purely local ones, having no world-importance like those in which Nelson participated.

status for torpedo work ; the planning of torpedo attacks requires quite as much brain and ability as the same sort of thing with ironclads. In a sense—the torpedo boat being a novel weapon—it requires more.

# XI

## 1878–1885

THE immediate result of the Turco-Russian War was Russia's recognition of the necessity of a Black Sea fleet, and she decided on the construction of vessels which have put Constantinople at her mercy ever since. The decision that a fleet there was necessary did not, however, lead to much at first, since nothing was actually laid down for five years. This, for a variety of reasons, was due chiefly to the British Government. In the first place, the armistice with Turkey was soon followed by the forcing of the Dardenelles by a British squadron, which, with guns loaded and ships cleared for action, steamed up the Dardenelles in a heavy gale and snowstorm. It was anticipated in the English vessels that the Turks would offer opposition; it is almost probable that something of the sort had been decided on; but the move was of the nature of a surprise, and it is not impossible that the Turks knew little about it till it was a *fait accompli*.

*British fleet forces the Dardenelles.*

In any case, the British ironclads had Constantinople at their mercy, and beyond Constantinople and the Bosphorus lay the Russian Black Sea Coast also at the fleet's mercy. A fleet in the Black Sea would control the Danube, and, once a beginning was made, ships capable of operating in the Danube and cutting communications would soon be got up if required. By occupying the Turkish Dardenelles' forts, the Russians would, indeed, have put the British fleet in a tight place, but Austria, hungering for a share of the spoil, had also to be considered. The British game was chiefly one of "bluff" on this particular occasion: however, it was bluff that succeeded in its immediate objects. The precise value of those objects is a debatable point; but that is not our concern here. *Result of the move.* The precise ultimate result was that Russia recognised that the Dardenelles were not necessarily a closed door, and a good deal of energy was for some years expended in strengthening Sevastôpol and Nikolaieff and fortifying other ports. Hence the laying down of Black Sea battleships did not take place till 1883.

The period directly following the war was one of naval stagnation. The Minin's reconstruction was completed, and the Vladimir Monomakh laid down: that, saving the building of a few minor craft, is the naval history of the two or three years following the war.

*Minin.* To the Minin some reference has already been made.[1] The altered Minin was quite a different type of ship: from an English turret-ship type she was converted into a barbette ship of French style—the direct antithesis of what she had been.

The turrets amidships were abolished, and the four heavy guns mounted in sponsons, one on each beam

[1] See p. 168.

and one on each quarter. The low bulwarks amidships were raised and built up to the height of the old flying deck, and all along the old maindeck 6-in. guns were placed. Originally she was to have carried four 11-in. guns in turrets, and four 6-in., two in the forecastle, two in the poop. Full details of the ship—a photograph of which is on the opposite page—are as follows :—

| | |
|---|---|
| Displacement . . . . . . | 6000 tons. |
| Length . . . . . . . | 298½ ft. |
| Beam . . . . . . . | 49¼ ft. |
| Draught (*mean*) . . . . | 25 ft. |
| Armour . . . . . . . | Complete iron belt, 7–4½ in. |
| | Barbettes, 8 in. |
| Armament . . . . . . | Four 8-in. |
| | Twelve 6-in. |
| | Sixteen small Q.F. |
| Horse-power . . . . . . | 6000 |
| Trial speed . . . . . . | 12½ knots. |

At present (1899) the ship is laid up for reconstruction,[1] and some of the guns have been or will be removed. Belleville boilers will also be fitted to her. For a considerable time she was employed on training service.

*Vladimir Monomakh.*

The Vladimir Monomakh, once a very famous ship, is practically a copy of the altered Minin. She was launched in 1881. Her dimensions, etc., are—

| | |
|---|---|
| Displacement . . . . . . | 6000 tons. |
| Length . . . . . . . | 295 ft. |
| Beam . . . . . . . | 52 ft. |
| Draught (*mean*) . . . . | *circa* 24 ft. |

[1] See article on Kronstadt.

THE MININ (MĒĒNIN).

| | |
|---|---|
| Armour *was* . . . . . . | Belt and barbettes, 6 in. |
| | Compound armour. |
| Armament *was* . . . . | Four 8-in. |
| | Twelve 6-in. |
| | Twenty small Q.F. |
| | Three torpedo tubes. |
| Horse-power . . . . . . | 7000. |
| Trial speed (*max.*) . . . . | 15 knots. |
| Sea speed . . . . . . | 13 knots. |

She was then a fully rigged ship, with double topsails, and reckoned one of the finest cruisers afloat.

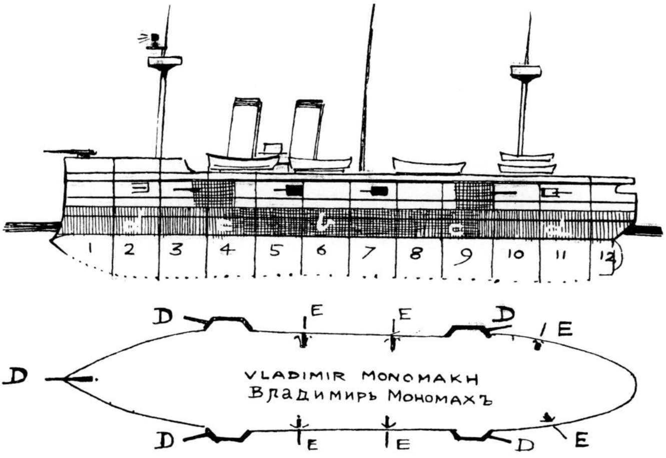


PLAN OF VLADIMIR MONOMAKH WITH PRESENT RIG.

Since then she has been a good deal reconstructed. As soon as possible after completion she was sent out to the Pacific.

In 1883 the Vladimir Monomakh was followed by *Dmitri Donskoi.*
her sister the Dmitri Donskoï, which also has since been reconstructed.[1] She differed in armament and

[1] For details of reconstruction, see a later chapter.

its arrangement, but otherwise was identical with the Vladimir Monomakh. Instead of four 8-in. 9-ton guns, she only carried two of these pieces, and these were in sponsons upon the upper deck, the influence of French type being here visible.[1] In the maindeck battery fourteen 6-in. guns were carried. All these have since been removed. The Dmitri Donskoi was, if possible, more heavily masted than the Vladimir Monomakh; indeed, a tale was current in the Mediterranean, where she presently appeared, that her topsails had never been set for fear she should capsize. She evoked considerable interest, and was in service for some long while.

Both she and the Vladimir Monomakh have steel hulls, and are sheathed and coppered. On trial, the Dmitri Donskoi made 16 knots, and she is to this day rather faster than her sister.

*Admiral Nahimoff.*

The next ship of importance to take the water was the Admiral Nahimoff, launched in 1885. She is in part an evolution of the Dmitri Donskoi, and in part a "reply" to the British Imperieuse and Warspite, which she closely resembles. The influence of French type is again fully manifest.

The following are the details of the Admiral Nahimoff,[2] and for purposes of comparison the details of the British Imperieuse are also given. "War game" notation of the armour and guns is given for the benefit of immediate comparison:—

[1] See Evolution of Type.

[2] She is reconstructing at present (1899).

ARMOURED CRUISER DMITRI DONSKOI—OLD RIG.

| | NAHIMOFF (Russian). | IMPERIEUSE (British). |
|---|---|---|
| Displacement | *circa* 9000. | *circa* 9000.[1] |
| Length | 333 ft. | 315 ft. |
| Beam | 61 ft. | $62\frac{2}{3}$ ft. |
| Draught (*mean*) | 25 *ft.* | $27\frac{1}{3}$ *ft.* |
| Armour belt | *b – c.* | *b.* Bulkheads, *b.* Deck. at ends = *d.* |
| Proportion of belt to length | complete. | about $\frac{1}{2}$ (rather less). |
| Armour barbettes | *c.* | *b.* |
| Shields to big guns | *f.* | *d.* |
| Armament[2] | Eight D (8-in.). Ten D (6-in.). Ten small Q.F. Four torpedo tubes. | Four C (9·2-in.). Six D (6-in.). Eight small Q.F. Six torpedo tubes. |
| Horse-power | 8000 natural. | 8000 natural, 10,000 forced. |
| Trial speed (*max.*) | No reliable data. | |
| Sea speed | Nahimoff was about $\frac{1}{4}$ knot slower than Imperieuse. Both about 15 knots then. | |
| Coal carried | (?) 1200 tons. | 900 tons. |
| Bunker capacity | 1300 tons. | 1130 tons. |
| *Nominal* radius with full coal supply at 10 knots | 8000 miles. | 7000 miles. |

On paper the Nahimoff here looks to have a good deal the best of it, but it is very doubtful whether such a colossal armament could have been properly fought, nor is it certain that her protection is quite so good as is usually supposed. It so chanced that both

[1] The Navy list "nominal" displacement is 8400.

[2] Data of armour-piercing guns—

| *Gun.* | *Muzzle Velocity.* | *Muzzle Energy.* | *Penetration at 1000 Yards.* |
|---|---|---|---|
| 20-ton 9·2-in. (C) | 1780 | 8356 | *c* |
| 9-ton 8-in. (D) | 1794 | 4400 | *d* |

ships went out to the China Station, and becoming "chummy ships" there, the question as to which was the better naturally cropped up for discussion. The palm was eventually given to the British vessel—by her own officers at anyrate. Probably they were right.

Like the Imperieuse, the Nahimoff was originally brig-rigged—the former vessel, however, had a single military mast substituted at an early stage. The

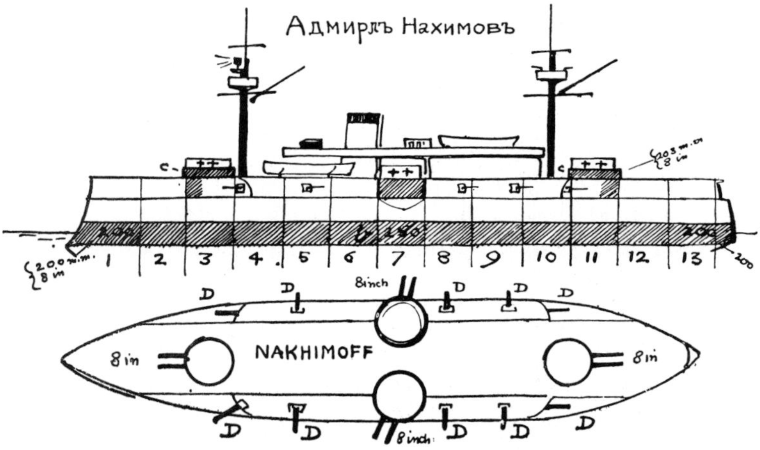


Nahimoff, on the other hand, though her bowsprit was after a time removed, retained her top hamper. The plans and photograph will give a clear idea of her general appearance. The rig in the plan is that which will probably be given to her.

The Nahimoff was not repeated, but followed instead by an enlarged copy of the Dmitri Donskoi, the well-known Pāmiat Azova. She was not launched till 1888, and several battleships took the water before her. Before proceeding to describe her, and the

THE ADMIRAL NAHIMOFF.

battleships which stand as the earliest non-obsolete vessels in the Russian Navy, some attention may be given to the unarmoured ships constructed in this transition period after the war.

The Pāmiat Merkuria, originally called the Yaroslav, a vessel of 3050 tons, launched at Toulon in 1880, was the first effort at creating a modern Black Sea Fleet. She is long since obsolete, and was never of any great *Pāmiat Merkuria, 1880.*

THE PĀMIAT MERKURIA.

account, though her original armament of four 18-ton guns rendered her a formidable opponent on paper fifteen years ago. These guns have since been replaced by 6-in. and 4-in. breechloaders. Further details of her, and of other unimportant vessels, being given in the Appendix, it is unnecessary to delay over her here.

In 1885 the first Russian deck-protected cruiser, the Rȳnda, was launched at Kronstadt. She too has *Rȳnda, 1885.*

rather outlived her sphere of usefulness, though she is a vessel that has been much employed in the last ten years. She is about on a par with the British "C" class cruisers—the Calliope and her sisters.

THE RASBOYNIK.

The details of the Rўnda, and her sister the Vitiaz (subsequently wrecked in the Pacific), are :—

| | |
|---|---|
| Displacement . . . . . . | 3506 tons. |
| Length . . . . . . . | 269 ft. |
| Beam . . . . . . . | 45 ft. |
| Draught (*mean*) . . . . . | $16\frac{1}{6}$ ft. |
| Armament . . . . . . | Ten 6-in. breechloaders. |
| | Ten small Q.F. |
| | Five torpedo tubes. |

RȲNDA.

| | |
|---|---|
| Armour deck[1] . . . . . | $1\frac{1}{2}$-in. curved deck over machinery only. |
| Horse-power (*forced* draught) . . | 3000. |
| Trial speed . . . . . | 15 knots. |

She is a very fine-looking craft, with what the French call "robust" engines.

Other vessels of this period are a number of useless corvettes, many of which, however, are still employed. These are the Oprïtchnik, Plastoune, Naiezdnik, Rasboynik, and Strelok. They are similar to the Djijdit and Kreysser,[2] and carry three old-type 6-in. guns. A photograph of one of these guns on board the Djijdjit will be found further on. The Oprïtchnik is now struck off the list and used as a hulk; some of the others serve as seagoing training-ships. Officially they are known as second-class cruisers. *Corvettes, 1878–80.*

STRELOK

In 1884 the Sivoutch was launched at Stockholm, and in the following year the Bobr at Kretona. These, though out of date now, were in their day rather remarkable vessels, being nothing more nor less than an attempt to create seagoing "flat irons." They displace about 1000 tons and carry a large armament for their size—a heavy 9-in. gun forward, a 6-in. *Bobr and Sivoutch, 1884–85.*

[1] The war game value of this deck would be *f*; it would keep out nothing save the very smallest projectiles.

[2] See p. 177.

gun aft, and half a dozen smaller guns—the old nine-pounders. They have flat bottoms, their horse-power is 1150, which on trial gave 13 knots. At sea they make about 8 knots; and are employed in the Pacific. They are 187 feet long and draw about 9½ feet of water.

*Other "Flat irons," 1879-81.*

The "flat irons" Dodje, Groza, Grad, Snegue, Toutcha, Vikhr, and Bouroun were added to the fleet in this period. They are merely the ordinary flat-bottomed gunboat, carrying a single old-type 11-in. gun fore and aft. Some of them are fitted for spar torpedoes; but their speed being very low indeed, it is difficult to conceive of conditions in which they could effectually use their weapons.

*"War scare cruisers."*

A war scare with England caused the Asia (ex Columbus), Afrika, and Zabiaka to be purchased as commerce destroyers. The first two are of 2500 and 2800 tons, the Zabiaka 1234 tons. They are single-

screw ships, originally American merchantmen, and were not particularly new when purchased. They are of no use except for transport service, and even at the time of their purchase could hardly have done much harm to British commerce had war broken out.

APRICA (RUSSIAN)

Torpedo boats, 1878–85.

The Turco-Russian War gave Russia a trend to torpedo craft. In the period under review about 100 torpedo boats were added to the fleet. These included the Thornycroft boat Sokhum (1883) of 64 tons, the Yarrow-built Batûm, and a number of boats of 30 tons, either built by Shichau or copies of them constructed in Russia. The Yalta, launched during the war, is the more remarkable of these boats, as she was of 160 tons displacement—not far short of the displacement of the earliest destroyers. The Yalta is one of the earliest examples of a seagoing torpedo boat.

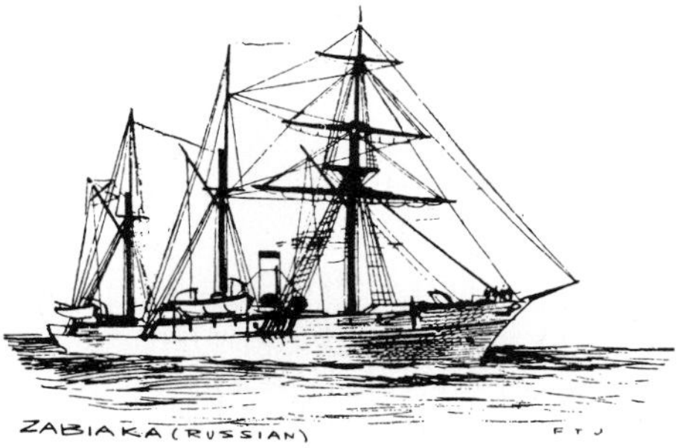

ZABIAKA (RUSSIAN)

F. T. J.

The yachts Marevo (1878), 58 tons, and Lividia

(1880) were added during the period under review. The latter is a curious vessel, and was intended to be an imperial yacht. She was built by John Elder & Co., at Govan, and in some ways is an adaption of the circular ironclad Popoff. She has three funnels abreast, three screws, and four signal masts. The displacement is 4000 tons, the trial speed, with 10,500 horse-power, nearly 16 knots. The dominant idea of the design was to produce an unsinkable vessel—the Nihilists were active in those days,—but she did not fulfil expectations, and so was converted into a transport, and rechristened Opit—the Experiment. She is able to carry 4000 men. Another interesting vessel is the iron storeship Penderaklia, of 1052 tons. She was originally the Turkish transport Mersina, and was captured in the War of 1877. No "history," however, attaches to her capture.

*Penderaklia.*

# XII

## 1886–1890

### Armoured Ships

May of the year 1886 saw the launch of the Ekaterina II. at Nikolaiff, and of the Tchesma at Sevastôpol: in June of the following year the Sinōp took the water at Sevastôpol. The first two ships were on the stocks for nearly three years, the Sinōp was three years and two months.

*Black Sea Fleet, 1886. Ekaterina II., Tchesma, Sinōp.*

These remarkable vessels are practically identical; such differences as exist between them are of a very minor nature. They are distinctly Russian in type; and the only foreign vessels which can be said to appear even remotely connected with their design are the British Téméraire, and our Inflexibles, or the Italian ironclads, from the Duilio to the Lepanto, with their big guns *en échelon* to get a strong end-fire.

At the bombardment of Alexandria, just about the time the Tchesma was being designed, the Téméraire, carrying two guns on the disappearing system, acquitted herself as well, or better, than any ship, and she was in high favour in the British Navy for other reasons. *The* feature of the Téméraire was the mounting of guns on a naval adaptation of the Moncrieff system: possibly the germ of the Russian thought lay here. On the other hand, the Vice-Admiral Papōff, with disappearing guns inside a strong redoubt, was already in existence, and the idea may equally well have come from her.

EKATERINA II.

In any case, the Tchesma and her sisters represented a unique type of a very powerful kind. The details of these ships are as follows :—

| | |
|---|---|
| Displacement | 10,300 tons. |
| Length | 339 ft. |
| Beam | 69 ft. |
| Draught (*extreme*) | 29 ft. |

The ships are built of iron and steel, with powerful rams. The entire water-line is armour-belted, and this belt is of compound armour 16 in. thick, tapering to 10 in. There is also a flat 3-in. protective deck on top of the belt. Amidships, above the armour belt is a

THE TCHESMA IN 1890.

huge triangular redoubt, at the rounded angles of which the big guns are mounted. This redoubt is 14 in. of compound armour at its maximum thickness, but probably thinner in places. In the Ekaterina II. and Tchesma, as will be seen from the photographs, it overhangs the sides somewhat—in the Sinope it is flush. The top of this redoubt is finished off with a glacis, over which the guns fire. Owing to error in design, the Ekaterina's armour has no backing.

The big guns are six in number, 12-in. pieces,[1]

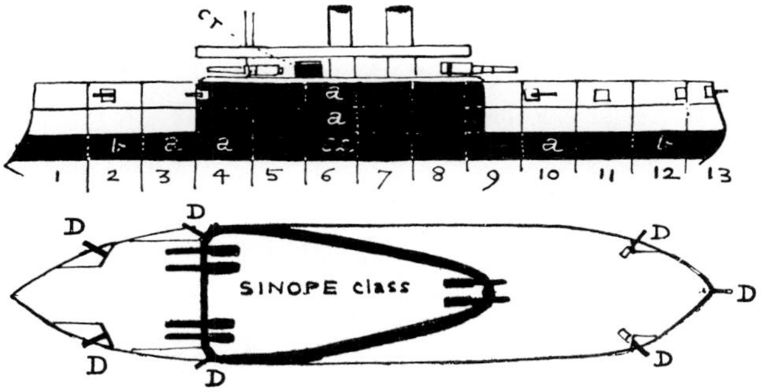


mounted in three pairs. They are short pieces of no very great power, 30 calibres long. Those of the Tchesma are of Krupp's make, and cannot be fired with full charges owing to some defect. The other two ships have Obukoff guns, also of 30 calibres in length. The disappearing mountings of the Tchesma were made at the Motala Iron Works, those of the other two ships at the Obukoff factory. Practically the mounting is identical with that used in the British

[1] Muzzle energy with full charges, *circa* 19,000 ft.-tons ; velocity, 1940 ; weight, 50 tons ; war game value, B.

Téméraire—the recoil causes the gun to duck down when fired, and presses in a hydraulic rammer, by means of which it is elevated again after loading.

The secondary armament of these three ships consists of seven 6-in. breechloaders of 35 calibres long, four of which are in an unprotected battery before the redoubt, the remainder being abaft it, also unprotected. One gun is right aft, and can be trained on either broadside. A reference to the plan will show that these ships can fire four 12-in. and four 6-in. ahead, and six 12-in. and three 6-in. astern. Theoretically, at least, they can—practically, upper works are rather in the way of this stern fire from the big pieces.

*Torpedo tubes.* There are seven torpedo tubes, above water and unarmoured. Four are before the redoubt, two on each broadside; the others are one each side well aft, and one in the stern.

*Machinery.* The engines of the Tchesma and Ekaterina II. were designed to develop 11,000 horse-power, and are of the compound vertical three-cylinder type. Those of the Tchesma were made by the Cockerill Company, Belgium, those of the Ekaterina II. were made at the Baltic Works, St. Petersburg. The Sinōp's engines are of the triple-expansion type, and were made by Napier of Glasgow. With natural draught they develop 10,000 horse-power; and with forced draught, 13,000 horse-power.

*Boilers.* In each ship there are fourteen cylindrical boilers, three furnaces to each boiler. Those of the Ekaterina II. are about to be replaced by Belleville boilers.

The trial results were as follows:— *Trial speeds.*

| | Natural Draught. | | Knots. | Forced Draught. | | Knots. |
|---|---|---|---|---|---|---|
| Tchesma[1] . | 9,058 | = | 13·5 | 11,000 | = | *circa* 16 |
| Ekaterina II. . | — | | — | — | | 16·5 |
| Sinōp . . | 10,000 | = | 15 | 13,000 | = | 17·8 |

The present-day continuous sea speeds are roughly about 13½ knots for the Sinōp, from 12 to 13 for the Tchesma, for the Ekaterina II. considerably less. This last ship is reported to be in a very bad way; but possibly popular report has mixed up the defective boilers with the general condition of the ship.

The building of these vessels was a lengthy affair— *Cost.* though laid down in 1883, they were not fully completed till the latter part of 1889. They cost about £900,000 each.

Shortly after the launch of the Ekaterina II., the Dvenadsat Apostolov (Twelve Apostles) was laid down at Nikolaiff. She was not, however, launched till 1890, and will be described in that year.

On the 26th of July 1887 the Alexander II. was launched at the New Admiralty Yard, St. Petersburg, and in the spring of 1889 her sister-ship the Nikolai I. was launched at Galernii Ostrov (the Franco-Russian Works). The details of these ships are as follows:— *Imperator Alexander II., 1887; and Imperator Nicholai I., 1889.*

| | |
|---|---|
| Displacement . . . . | Alexander II. 9900.<br>Nikolai I. 9700. |
| Material . . . . | Iron and steel, wood-sheathed and coppered. |
| Length . . . . | 326 ft. |
| Beam . . . . | 67 ft. |

[1] The Tchesma's natural-draught trial was with a very dirty bottom.

| | |
|---|---|
| Draught (*extreme*) . . | *circa* 26½ ft. |
| Armament . . . | Two 12-in.[1] forward. |
| | Four 9-in. 19-ton in battery. |
| | Eight 6-in. 4-ton ,, |
| | Eighteen small quickfirers. |
| | Torpedo tubes: one in bow, one in stern, four on broadsides. |

Here similarity ends. Both have complete belts of compound armour, 14 in. thick at its maximum,

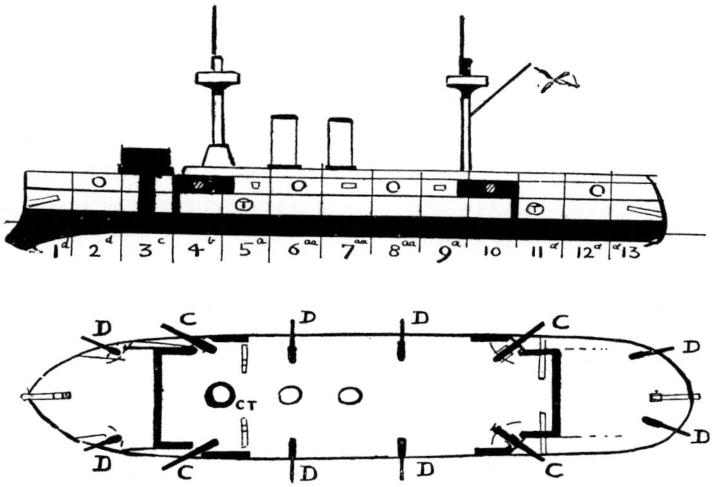


and dwindling to 6 in. at the ends; but that of the Alexander is 9 ft. wide, while that of the Nikolai is only about 8 ft.[2]—a considerable difference where

*Belt.*

armour belts are concerned. The Alexander has 12-in. bulkheads above the belt, protecting the battery and lower deck. At the sides, over the 9-in. gun ports, this is carried to a thickness of 6 in. The Nikolai

[1] It is not certain whether these are the 50-ton 12-in. or the older 40-ton 12-in. See tables in the chapter on Guns.

[2] The Nikolai's belt is from 3 ft. above to 5 ft. below the water-line.

has no such bulkheads, but the 9-in. guns are protected by armour screens 9 in. thick. *Bulkheads.*

The Alexander has a 12-in. barbette, with a thin shield over the breeches of the guns; the Nikolai has a 10-in. thick closed turret revolving in the 12-in. barbette. Both ships have a strong 3-in. protective deck, curving up above the belt. *Big guns.*

In appearance they are much alike: far less clumsy-looking ships than they generally appear in photographs. The Alexander II. has vertical compound three-cylinder engines of 8000 horse-power, which gave a maximum of 16·5 knots on a short trial. The Nikolai has vertical triple-expansion engines, which on trial developed 8000 horse-power, and gave a speed of just under 16 knots (15·94). This, however, was a maximum speed, and she proved the slower vessel of the two. In 1898 she was reboilered with sixteen Bellevilles, and with eleven of these made 14 knots. Her present continuous sea speed may therefore be put at that. *Machinery.* *Nikolai reboilered, 1898.*

On the 1st of June 1888 the Pāmiat Azova was launched at St. Petersburg in the presence of the Tsar and Tsarina. She had been two years and three months on the stocks. As previously observed, she is an enlarged edition of the Dmitri Donskoi, and closely follows that vessel in all her main features. *Pāmiat Azova, 1888.*

The details of this ship are as follows:—

| | |
|---|---|
| Displacement . . . . . . . | 6700. |
| Length . . . . . . . . | 377 ft. |
| Beam . . . . . . . . | 50 ft. |
| Draught (*mean*) . . . . . . | 23 ft. |

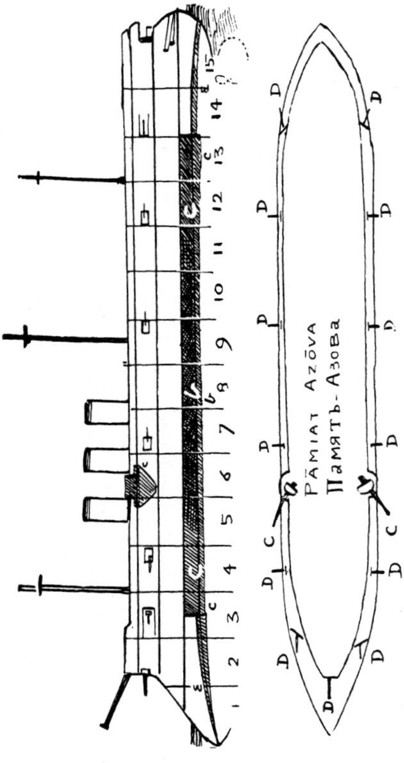


PLAN OF THE PĀMIAT AZOVA.

ARMOURED CRUISER PĀMIAT AZOVA.

| | |
|---|---|
| Armament . . . . . | Two 8-in.<br>Thirteen 6-in.<br>Fifteen small Q.F.<br>One torpedo tube on the stern, and one on each broadside. |

There is a belt of compound armour 259 ft. long by $8\frac{1}{6}$ ft. wide, 10 (*b*) to 8 (*c*) in. thick. 8-in. (*c*) bulkheads terminate this belt. Beyond them is a curved steel deck, $2\frac{3}{4}$ in. thick (*e*) on the slopes. There is a strip of 8-in. armour upon each barbette, but the shields are merely thin bullet-proof ones. The 6-in. guns have no protection. There is no armoured conning tower. *Armour.*

The machinery consists of two sets of triple-expansion engines: cylinders, 41, 60, and 90 in. in diameter; stroke, $3\frac{1}{4}$ ft. *Machinery.*

There are two screws, $16\frac{1}{2}$ ft. in diameter, 19 ft. pitch. *Screws.*

There are six double-ended boilers, with corrugated flues. These boilers are $15\frac{1}{4}$ ft. in diameter and $16\frac{1}{4}$ ft. long. There are thirty-six furnaces. The total heating surface is 19,946 square ft.; working pressure in boilers, 130 lbs. The total weight of machinery with full boilers is 1150 tons. On trial, this ship made 17 knots with 8500 horse-power, and 18·8 knots with 11,000 horse-power, forced draught. Her present continuous sea speed is about $14\frac{1}{2}$ knots. *Boilers.*

The ship is barque-rigged, with a sail surface of 16,000 square ft. The three funnels and curious ram make the ship more or less unique in appearance—that is to say, there is no other ship that could be mistaken for her. *Sail surface.*

*The Tsarvitch's tour in the Pāmiat Azova.*

Soon after her completion the Pāmiat Azova went on a tour with the Tsarvitch, the late Grand Duke George, on board. In the course of this tour the first sod of the Trans-Siberian railway was cut at Vladivostok by His Imperial Highness. The Pāmiat Azova was accompanied by the cruiser Korniloff;[1] and at the end of the tour all the officers of the squadron were decorated with the special Tsarvitch medal, a small lifebuoy, in commemoration of the cruise.

The Pāmiat Azova is named after the Azov, Russian flagship at the battle of Navarino,[2] 27th October 1827, and on account of this carries the badge of St. George on her ensign.

*1889.*

In 1889 the battleship Navārin was laid down at St. Petersburg, and the Georgei Pobiedonosets at Sevastôpol.

*Dvenadsat Apostolov, 1890.*

In the Black Sea the Dvenadsat Apostolov was launched at Nikolaiff on the 11th October 1890.

Her dimensions, etc., are as follows :—

| | |
|---|---|
| Displacement . . . . | 8500 tons. |
| Length . . . . . | 330 ft. |
| Beam . . . . . . | 60 ft. |
| Draught (*mean*) . . . | 25½ ft. |
| Armament . . . . | Four 12-in. 35 calibres.<br>Four 6-in. Q.F. 35 calibres (converted guns).<br>Twenty-five small Q.F.<br>Six torpedo tubes: one of them in the bow, one in the stern, the other four amidships behind thick armour. |

[1] See p. 247. [2] See p. 128.

SECOND-CLASS BATTLESHIP DVENADSAT APOSTOLOV.

*Armour.*

Like the other ships in the Black Sea Fleet, she is of original design, and there is a tremendous piling-on of defence to the 6-in. guns, which are the best protected 6-in. guns in the world. This is done at the expense of the belt and barbettes.

*Belt.*

The belt is 212 ft. long, and has a width of only $5\frac{1}{2}$ ft., and all, or nearly all, of it is under water. The bulkheads at the ends of this belt are 12 in. thick, compound armour, furnished from Creusot. The belt

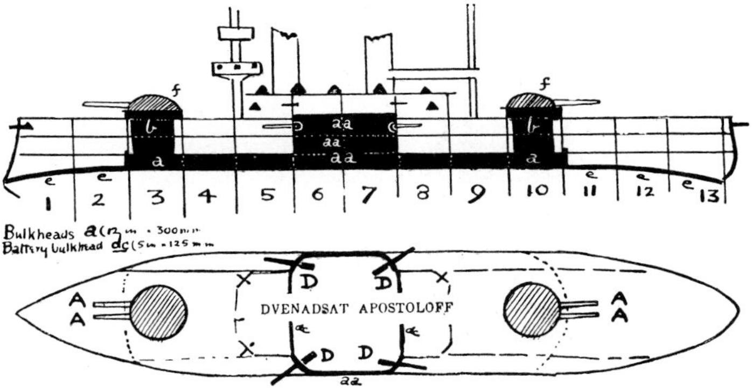


itself varies from 16 to 12 in., most of it being only 12 in. The protective deck is $2\frac{1}{2}$ in. on the slopes, and 2 in. on the flat on top of the belt. At each extremity of the belt rise circular armoured towers, about 9 to 10 in. thick—protecting the gun-hoists, etc. The gun shields are about 3 in. thick, hardened steel. Amidships, the belt is carried up in the old fashion, central box battery, and is 12 to 16 in. thick.

*Machinery.*

The propelling machinery consists of two sets of vertical triple-expansion engines, made at the Baltic

Works. There are four double-ended boilers and four single-ended ones. The indicated horse-power is 8500, natural draught; forced draught is put at 11,500. On trial, 1892, she steamed 16·6 knots with 8000 horse-power; the coal used was bad. Forced draught was not tried. This ship was completed for sea in the early part of 1893. As originally built, she had two very short funnels; a year or two ago these were considerably heightened, and a great change effected in her appearance.

*Boilers.*

*1892.*

*Funnels.*

Regarded as a ship, the Dvenadsat Apostoloff is a very good second-class battleship; as a tactical unit of the Black Sea Fleet, chiefly composed of Sinôps, she is somewhat of a mistake, or else they are. In action, one type must hamper the other.

The year that saw the Dvenadsat Apostoloff launched on the Euxine, saw the small battleship Gangoot launched at St. Petersburg. Her details are :—

*Gangoot, 1890.*

| | |
|---|---|
| Displacement . . . . . . | 6600 tons. |
| Length . . . . . . | 278 ft. |
| Beam . . . . . . | 62 ft. |
| Draught . . . . . . | 21 ft. |
| Armament . . . . . | One 12-in. 35 calibres. |
| | Four 9-in. 19-ton. |
| | Four 6-in. 35 calibres. |
| | Twelve small Q.F. |

This ship has been described as a small Alexander II., but perhaps a diminutive of the Dvenadsat Apostolov would describe her better. The thickness of the armour belt (compound) was 16 in. at the

*Armour.*

maximum, thinning at the ends; and this belt was a very partial one. A $2\frac{1}{2}$-in. protective deck was fore and aft of the belt. The turret was 8 in. thick. The 9-in. gun battery appears to have had a little armour on it, but not much.

*Machinery.*

The machinery was of 8300 horse-power, and gave 14·7 knots on trial. The Gangoot was finished in 1893. In 1897 she had been out for target practice, when she suddenly began to sink. Much mystery surrounds her loss, and surmises as to the reason have run the gamut from a Nihilist outrage to faulty construction. Either is possible. The more generally accepted tale is that she was badly put together, and that the strain of firing opened her seams. The official version was that she struck a rock. This version is quite discredited outside of Russia, but it is at least as probable as either of the others.

*Loss of the Gangoot, 1897.*

The only details that I have so far been able to procure of the occurrence are that the ship was leaking for some hours before she went down, that the water gradually gained, and she had to be abandoned. This was accomplished without loss of life or undue haste; and one of the officers took a snap-shot photo of her as she made the last plunge. She listed slightly to starboard, with her bow depressed, and went down slowly and gently in that position.

From time to time since, hopes of raising the vessel have been entertained; and at the moment of writing, a Swedish firm have a contract to attempt it. The ship must, however, be pretty soaked by now; and

THE GANGOOT SINKING.

[*Drawn from a snap-shot Photo taken as she made her final plunge.*]

judging by the British experience in raising the Sultan, the operation will not be worth the cost. The Sultan, it may be remembered, had to be almost rebuilt—a work of some years and very great expense—on account of the insanitary conditions produced by the stagnant water and slime that had soaked into everything, and was only got rid of with the greatest difficulty. And the Gangoot, at the best of times, was a very inferior fighting unit.

To return to the year 1890. In this year there was considerable naval activity. The celebrated Rurik was laid down at the Baltic Works on 31st May 1890. The ironclad gunboats Gremiatschy and Otvajny, sisters to the Groziatschy, were also laid down. A battleship that had been commenced at a private yard at Nikolaiff was, however, abandoned after about 36 tons of steel had been put together for her. *1890.*

The Groziatschy, which was launched in 1890, and her sisters Gremiatschy and Otvajny, launched in 1892, are a type of ship whose principal use would seem to be to swell paper lists of ironclads: it is not easy to conceive of circumstances in which they would be of use as tactical units of a fleet. For coast defence, however, they might be of some service, though the smallest guns could quickly put them out of action. *Groziatschy, 1890. Gremiatschy and Otvajny, 1892.*

Their details are:—

| | |
|---|---|
| Displacement | 1500 tons. |
| Material of hull | Steel. |
| Length | 223 ft. |
| Beam | $41\frac{2}{3}$ ft. |

| | |
|---|---|
| Draught . . . . . | $13\frac{1}{3}$ ft. |
| Armament . . . . . | One 9-in. forward. |
| | One 6-in. aft. |
| | Ten to sixteen small Q.F. |
| | Two torpedo tubes. |

*Armour.* The armour consists of a narrow belt from the stern to within 40 ft. of the bow, where it ends in a bulkhead $3\frac{1}{2}$ in. thick. This belt has a maximum thickness of 5 in., and dwindles to $3\frac{1}{2}$ in. The protective deck is 1 in. thick on top of the belt; forward it is curved, and $1\frac{1}{2}$ in. thick on the slopes. There is a cellular backing behind the belt.

*Machinery.* The machinery consists of two sets of vertical triple-expansion engines. Those of the Gremiatschy were made by Maudslay, Sons, & Field of London; the others were constructed at the Baltic Works. On trial, the Gremiatschy made a mean of 13·6 knots with 2034 indicated horse-power, forced draught. The others did about 13 knots. All are able to make 12 knots continuously at sea. All three have Belleville boilers.

## Unarmoured Ships, 1886–90

*The Admiral Korniloff, 1887.* The only important unarmoured ship launched in this period was the deck-protected Admiral Korniloff. She was a vessel of which great things were expected. A special interest further attaches to her in that, just after she was laid down, a Russian officer wrote a book entitled *The Russia's Hope*, which glorified the Korniloff much as the Chilian Arturo Prat type is glorified in Mr. Laird Clowes' *Captain of the Mary*

*The* **Russia's Hope.**

GROZIASTCHY.

*Rose.* The "agile cruiser," in more ways perhaps than one the invention of Lord Armstrong, was very much to the fore in the eighties, and there was a tendency to altogether forget its limitations. Not that the Russia's Hope performed ridiculous feats, any more than did the Mary Rose: her operations were matter of fact and possible enough. True, they were aided by seventeen similar vessels that have not yet been built

ADMIRAL KORNILOFF.

—but that is a detail. This interesting story of the Russia's Hope—interesting because, being written by a Russian naval officer, it gave an insight into the Russian Navy and its aims and theories such as has never been given before or since—was translated into English some twelve years ago, but did not, I fancy, have the vogue that it might have had and deserved. The Russia's Hope was more or less of a "commerce destroyer."

The British ships she met, she either ran from or else was easily able to destroy, owing to her superior armament. Generally they were the "old tubs" that we kept on foreign stations in those days. By the device of sending in an oil ship and flooding the harbour with oil, which they set light to, the whole of the British shipping in Bombay harbour was burnt. The Russia's Hope was given luck; still, in view of the sort of craft we then had on the East Indian and adjacent stations, there was very little straining of the probabilities. Certainly our failure to send out anything to hunt down the Russia's Hope, and the deserted island base, are against the tale; still it stands on its merits, apart from these things. It will be a long day before Russian warships are able to treat our ships in such fashion now; a longer day, perhaps, before they will attempt it.

To return to the Korniloff. Her principal details are:—

| | |
|---|---|
| Displacement . . . | *circa* 5000 tons. |
| Length . . . . . | 350 ft. |
| Beam . . . . . | $48\frac{1}{2}$ ft. |
| Draught . . . . | $23\frac{1}{2}$ ft. |
| Armament as designed . . | Two 8-in. |
| | Fourteen 6-in. |
| | Six small Q.F. |
| Armament, present day . . | Fourteen 6-in. Q.F. 40 calibres. |
| | Sixteen small Q.F. |
| Torpedo tubes (above water) . | Six. |
| Horse-power (*forced*) . . | 9000. |
| Machinery . . . . | Horizontal triple-expansion, which can be disconnected to work as compound. |

| | |
|---|---|
| Boilers . . . . | (new in 1895) Eight cylindrical. |
| Armour . . . . | Deck, 2½ in. on the slopes. |

About 1000 tons of coal are carried. On trial she made 17½ knots with natural, and 18½ knots with forced draught. The present-day sea speed is said to be 17 knots; but this is perhaps a rather favourable estimate. The ship was built in France, at St. Nazaire. She is built of steel, and wood-sheathed for service in the Pacific, to which fleet she belongs.

KOUBANETS (RUSSIAN)

In 1886–87 eight vessels of the gunboat order were launched. The Donetz, Tchernomoretz, and Zaporetz, at Nikolaiff; the Uraletz, Teretz, and Kubanetz, at Sevastôpol; the Koreetz, at Stockholm; and the Mandjur, at Copenhagen. Practically they are all identical, though there are minor differences in tonnage, rig, and form of bow. The details are:— *Gunboats.*

TCHERNOMORETZ (RUSSIAN)

| | |
|---|---|
| Displacement . . . . | 1500[1]–1300 tons. |
| Length . . . . . | *circa* 210 ft. |
| Beam . . . . . | 35 ft. |
| Draught (*mean*) . . . | *circa* 11 ft. |
| Armament . . . . | Two 8-in. (old type). |
| | One 6-in. (old type). |
| | Four 4-in. (old type).[1] |
| | Six small Q.F. |

[1] Koreetz and Mandjur only.

KOREIETZ (RUSSIAN)

MANDJOUR (RUSSIAN)

There is a very thin (half-inch) steel deck over the machinery, and thin shields to the guns. The horse-power is about 1500, which on trials gave about 13 knots, and some of them can make 11 knots to-day. The first six belong to the Black Sea Fleet,[1] where they might be of some use; but, speaking generally, they have no fighting value. The Koreetz and Mandjur belong to the Siberian Fleet in the Pacific. The Koubanetz, Teretz, and Uraletz are to be reboilered with Belleville boilers.

*Reboilered.*

*Lieut. Ilyne, 1886.*

Two other vessels remain to be mentioned—torpedo cruisers. The Lieut. Ilyin is of 714 tons displacement, 230 feet long, and armed with seventeen small Q.F. (three-pounders, one-pounders, etc.). She has seven torpedo tubes. Her sea speed is, or was, about 17 knots; on trial she made 20 knots.

*Kapitan Sāken, 1889.*

The Kapitan Sāken, of the same type, belongs to the Black Sea Fleet. She is somewhat larger—750 tons—but carries only ten Q.F. guns. She has six

[1] The Nikolaiff ships were engined by Napier of Glasgow, the Sevastôpol ones by the Motala Company, Sweden. This firm also engined the other two.

torpedo tubes. In 1897 she was given water-tube boilers, and is probably good for 18 knots.

In the period 1886–90 the special service paddle-wheel steamer Krasnovodski, of 147 tons, was set afloat in the Caspian, as were also the stern-wheelers Tsar and Tsarina. *Caspian flotilla.*

Twenty-seven first and second class torpedo boats were added to the fleet in this period, as well as a number of third-class ones. *Torpedo boats.*

# XIII

## 1891–1898

1891. THE principal vessel launched in 1891 was the turret-ship Navārin, which took the water at St. Petersburg on the 20th of October.

Her details, etc., are :—

| | |
|---|---|
| Displacement . . . | 10,000 tons. |
| Material of hull . . | Steel. |
| Length . . . . | 338 ft. |
| Beam . . . . | 67 ft. |
| Draught. . . . | 29 ft. |
| Armament . . . | Four 12-in. 40 calibres. |
| | Eight 6-in. 35 calibres. |
| | Thirty small Q.F. |
| | Six torpedo tubes: four broadside behind thick armour; the others, one in bow and one in stern. |

Armour. The armouring is very complete, and practically identical with that of the British Trafalgar—the Navārin being like her—a low freeboard ship. There is a partial belt of compound armour, 16 to 14 in. thick, about 212 ft. long, finished off with 12-in. bulkheads. The curved protective deck before and abaft this belt is 3 in. thick on the slopes. On top of the belt it is flat, 2½ in. thick.

SECOND-CLASS BATTLESHIP NAVĀRIN.

Above the belt is an octagonal armoured redoubt about 200 ft. long, 12 in. thick, enclosing the turret bases. The turrets at either extremity are also 12 in. thick.

Between the turrets is a rectangular battery about $4\frac{1}{2}$ in. thick. The conning tower is 16 in. There are four funnels in pairs abreast, with a very heavy single military mast abaft them.

*Machinery.* The machinery consists of two sets of vertical

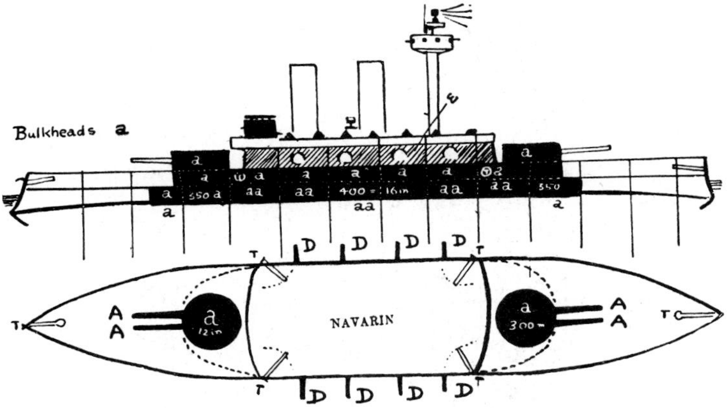


triple-expansion engines, which on trial made 9000 horse-power and 16 knots on the measured mile. The sea speed is about 14 knots. The ship is supposed to carry about 1000 tons of coal.

*1892.* In November 1892 the Rurik, laid down in May 1890, was launched at the Baltic Works. Her launch made a considerable stir, and led to the laying down of the Powerful and Terrible in this country as a "reply."

ARMOURED CRUISER RURIK.

Data of the ship are as follows :—

| | |
|---|---|
| Material of hull . . | Steel. |
| Displacement . . . | 10,950. |
| Length . . . . | 426 ft. |
| Beam . . . . | 67 ft. |
| Draught (*maximum*) . | 30 ft. |
| Armament . . . | Four 8-in. in sponsons behind shields. |
| | Sixteen 6-in. Q.F. on main deck. |
| | Six 4·7-in. Q.F. on upper deck. |
| | Twenty-two small Q.F. (3- and 1-pounders). |
| | Six torpedo tubes. |
| Horse-power . . . | 13,250. |
| Speed . . . . | 18 knots (on a 6 hours' trial). |
| Machinery . . . | Four sets triple-expansion engines, made at the Baltic Works; 48 furnaces; 2 screws. |
| Continuous sea speed . | 17·5 knots. |
| Complement . . . | 768. |
| Coal capacity (*maximum*) | 2000 tons. |
| Nominal radius . . | 19,000 miles at 10 knots. |
| Actual radius at *full speed* | *circa* 2300 miles. |

The Rurik carries a belt of Creusot steel, 341 ft. *Armour.* long, amidships. This belt is 6½ ft. deep, and is terminated at the ends by armoured bulkheads, the forward one being 12 in., the after about 10 in. The belt varies from 10 to 8 in. in thickness. The ship is an enlarged Pāmiat Azova, and, like her, has armoured protection to the sponsons, but of no great thickness. The big 6-in. battery is entirely unarmoured, save for thin screens here and there. The protective deck is 2¾ in. thick on the slopes, and about 2 in. on the flat on top of the belt.

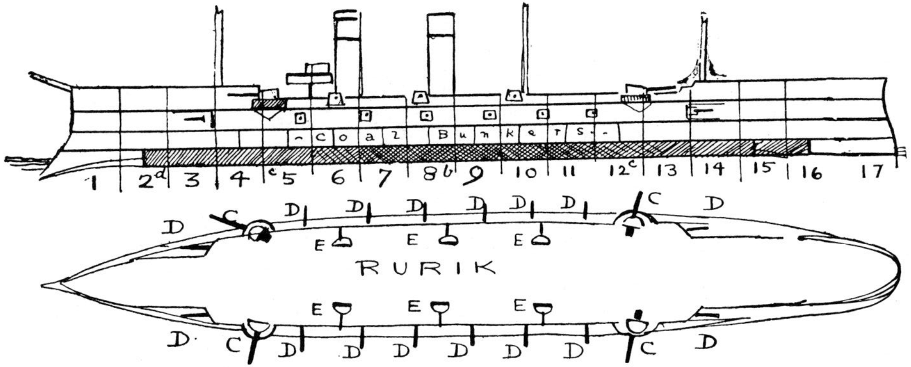


RURIK.

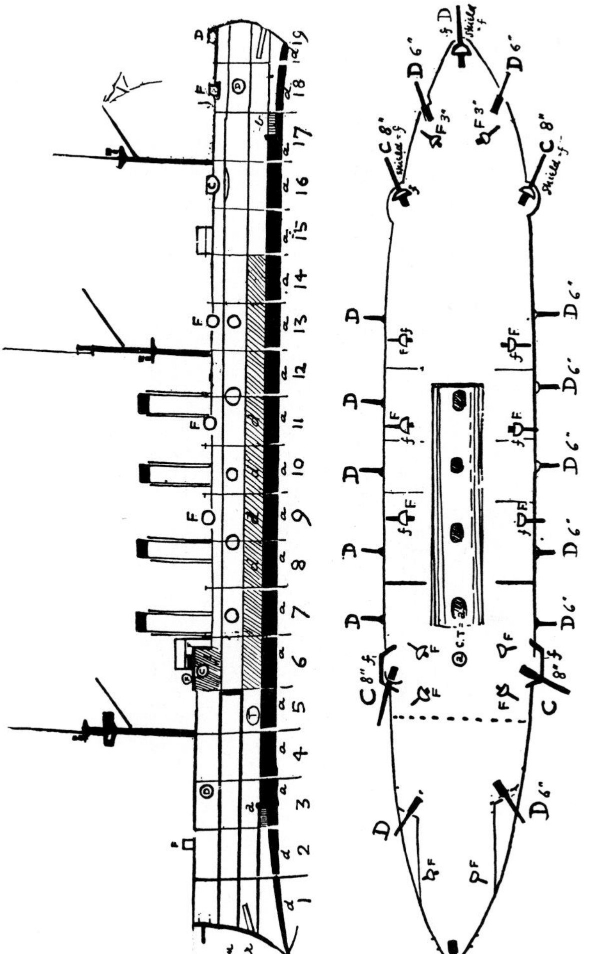


ROSSIA.

The ship represents the maximum of offence with the minimum of defence. So slight, indeed, is this last, that in the ship laid down immediately afterwards, the Rossia, some very distinct changes were introduced.

*Rossia, 1896*

The Rossia, launched from the same slip as the Rurik in May 1896, is not the next ship in chronological order, but is more conveniently described here in juxtaposition with her prototype.

Details of the Rossia are :—

| | |
|---|---|
| Material of hull . . | Steel. Sheathed and coppered. |
| Displacement . . . | 12,100 tons. |
| Length . . . . | 480 ft. |
| Beam . . . . | 68 ft. |
| Draught (*mean*) . . | 26 ft. |
| ,, (*maximum*) . | Probably same as Rurik. |
| Armament . . . | Four 8-in.<br>Sixteen 6-in. Q.F.<br>Twelve 3-in. Q.F.<br>Thirty-six small Q.F. |
| Machinery . . . | Three sets vertical triple-expansion engines, made at the Baltic Works. |
| Screws . . . . | Three. |
| Horse-power . . . | 18,446. *Trial maximum* gave a mean of 19·74 knots in ten runs. |
| Boilers . . . . | 32 Belleville. |
| Coal supply (*maximum*) . | 2500 tons, and petroleum. |
| Sea speed . . . | *circa* 19 knots. |
| Speed with central screw only . . . . | 9 knots. |
| Radius (*nominal*) . . | 19,000 miles. |
| Radius at *full speed* . | 3000 miles, nearly. |
| Protection . . . | Belt, 359½ ft. long by 6 ft. wide 9¾ in. Harvey steel. |

| | |
|---|---|
| Protection (*contd.*) . . | Bulkheads to belt, 9 in. forward, 8 in. aft. |
| | Armour deck, 2·7 in. on slopes. |
| | Bulkhead to battery fore and aft, 6-in. Harvey. Screens and shields to battery guns. Casemates for forward 8-in. guns, 2 in. |
| | Patch of armour amidships on lower deck, 4 in. Coal behind this and in water-line. |
| Complement . . . | 735. |

A comparison of the plans and these details will bring out the quite vital differences that exist between these two ships, often erroneously spoken of as sisters. The Rossia is as far in advance of the Rurik as that vessel is of the Pāmiat Azova—indeed, is perhaps more in advance.

The chief essential differences are :—

*a.* Much wider distribution of the armament.

*b.* The bulkheads to the maindeck battery entirely proof against the 6-in. gun.

*c.* Abolition of 4·7-in., and substitution of a large number of 3-in. 12-pounders,—an important point in a ship like the Rossia, one of whose main defences is the frightful power of her armament.

*d.* Armour on the lower deck amidships.

*e.* Shields to all guns (this may or may not be advantageous).

The Rossia is not a perfect ship, but she is a great deal better ship than is usually supposed. She was heavily discounted at one time owing to the false impression concerning her protection: the existence of the 6-in. bulkhead to the battery, which makes all the difference, was unknown. An action between the Powerful and Rossia would not be won by virtue of material on either side: the human element only would be the dominant factor. Like the Italian Lepanto, the Rossia is designed to rush in and destroy her antagonist with her overwhelming fire; unlike the Lepanto, she is protected in a fashion to enable her to do it. She can choose her range to that extent, and there is no doubt that did she get her guns on the target, neither the Powerful nor any other cruiser would be any better than a wreck inside a few minutes. On the other hand, as Russian officers have admitted, her own life in battle must be short. "She can fight five minutes, at the end of that time will have won, or"—

All Russians, however, do not hold this view. One of their most favourite war-game duels is an action between the Rossia and the Powerful, and I have seen a good many of these played with every method to secure realism that an utter disregard of time or trouble could suggest. The absolute maximum of realism was secured by rules that few others would care to labour at. I do not remember a single decisive action in these duels, or a single one that was short. The actions lasted for periods representing anything from twenty minutes to two hours, and always ended with the two ships, much disabled, sheering off from each other. The way in which the Powerful was fought indicated that *her* good points were fully known, while the Rossia was generally fought by some officers who had served in her. Each side knew what would serve the other best, and tactics were governed by preventing its consummation. Hence the battles were at ranges usually beyond 3000 yards, at which hits are necessarily few. And there is every reason to suppose that a duel between the real Rossia and Powerful would have a like result.

It was originally intended to fit full rig to the Rossia, like the Rurik; but finally the idea was abandoned.

The Georgi Pobedonosetz was launched at Sevastôpol on the 9th of March 1892, having been building since July 1889. *1892.*

Her details are as follows:—

| | |
|---|---|
| Displacement . . . | 10,280 tons. |
| Material of hull . . | Steel. |
| Length . . . . | 339 ft. |
| Beam . . . . | 69 ft. |
| Draught . . . . | 27½ ft. |
| Armament . . . | Six 12-in. of 40 calibres, Obuchoff. |
| | Seven 6-in. Q.F. of 45 calibres, Canet. |
| | Eight 3-in. Q.F., Barinofsky. |
| | Eighteen small Q.F. |
| Submerged torpedo tubes | One in bow, four in broadside. |
| Above-water tubes . . | One in stern, two forward. |

In general type this ship follows the Sinōp and Tchesma class, the six big guns being carried in the same unique fashion—in pairs in a triangular redoubt. With this, however, resemblance ceases. *Armour.*

The weak point of the Sinōp class was the totally unarmoured secondary battery. To resolve these ships into some other equivalent, they practically followed the style of ships like the British Alexandra, Téméraire, Superb, and so on,—a complete belt, and amidships a redoubt. In the broadside ironclads this redoubt is pierced with gun ports; in the Sinōp the guns are inside, and fire over the top. The triangular form of

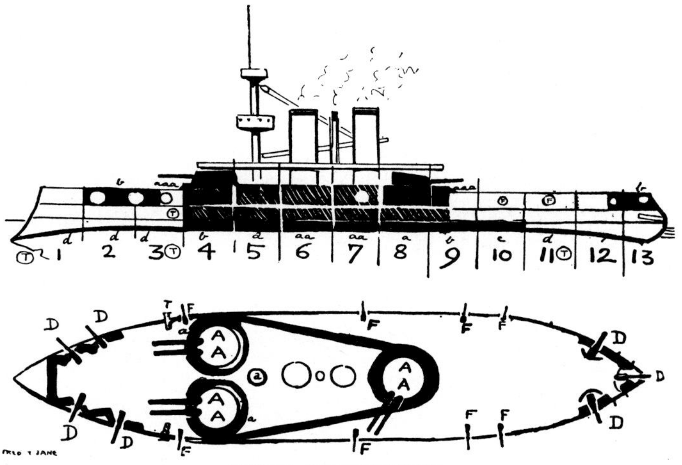

GEORGI POBEDONOSETZ.

redoubt saves weight by doing away with the need of an after bulkhead. There being nowhere inside to carry the secondary armament, they had to be placed before and abaft the big guns,—a reversion of the usual process; and there being no weight to spare, they were entirely unarmoured. In the Georgi Pobedonosetz the 6-in. guns have been protected at the expense of the water-line.

The water-line amidships is protected by a belt about 175 ft. long, with bulkheads at the ends. The

THE FIRST-CLASS BATTLESHIP GEORGI POBEDONOSETZ AT SEVASTÔPOL.

[*This Photograph was taken before the big guns were put on board.*]

greatest thickness of this belt is 16-in. Creusot steel, equal in resisting value to the later forms of compound armour. This belt at the ends diminishes to 8 in. thick. The bulkheads are 12 in.

Fore and aft of this belt runs a curved armoured deck 2½ in. thick on the slopes. On top of the belt this deck is flat.

About 130 ft. of the side above this is plated with 6-in. armour. Above again is the triangular redoubt, 12 in. thick under the big guns, but diminishing to about 6 in. in the middle portion. Forward and aft along this maindeck are large casemates about 9½ in. thick. In the forward one are four 6-in. guns; in the after one, three 6-in. guns, the aftermost firing astern or on either quarter. Between these casemates the 3-in. quickfirers, unprotected, are carried.

Unlike the Tchesma class, the Georgi Pobedonosetz does not carry her big guns on disappearing mountings; they are too long to admit of it. They have simply the ordinary barbette mounting, firing over a glacis. There are shields to these guns of hardened steel 6 to 8 in. thick in front, and about 4 in. thick at the sides. A 12-in. conning-tower is abaft the bow guns. The propelling machinery of the Georgi Pobedonosetz *Machinery.* consists of two sets of vertical triple-expansion engines, *Engines.* made by Messrs. Maudslay, Sons, & Field of Lambeth, London. On a twelve hours' trial these worked up to *Trial.* a mean indicated horse-power of 13,468, and a mean speed of 16·5 knots. The estimated horse-power was *Horse-power.* 10,600 with natural draught, and 16,000 with forced draught. At this the speed was to have been 16·5 knots, so that the contract speed was reached with considerably less than the maximum horse-power. No full power trial appears to have been made.

*Coast defence ironclads, 1893.*

In June 1892 the Admiral Oushakoff—"coast defence battleship"—was laid down at St. Petersburg, and launched in September 1893. In August of the following year a sister-ship, the Admiral Seniavin, was launched, and in May '96 a third, the General Admiral Graf Aprāksin, was launched at the New Admiralty. A fourth, the Admiral Bubakoff, is supposed to be building, but I saw no signs of her anywhere, and doubt if she is more than a projected ship that will never be built. All these ships belong to the Baltic Fleet.

*1894.*

*Difference between Aprāksin and the others.*

Save in the matter of heavy guns they all resemble each other—the Aprāksin has three 10-in., the others four 9-in. The Aprāksin being the latest, is the best to select for description, and my acquaintance with her is greater than with the others. She is, moreover, the entirely Russian one of the three.

The displacement of this class is about 4200 tons. The dimensions are: Length, 277 ft. 5 in.; beam, 52 ft.; extreme draught, 17 ft. 6 in. They are low freeboard vessels, and more fitted for work in the Baltic than for wider cruising. There have been rumours that the Aprāksin will be attached to the Siberian Fleet, but there do not appear to be any valid grounds for this report. It seems more probable that she will be utilised for home service.

THE "COAST DEFENCE BATTLESHIP" ADMIRAL OUSHAKOFF IN KRONSTADT DOCKYARD.

The armour of the ship is arranged in the following fashion :—A protective deck of Harvey steel 3 in. thick upon the slopes, about 2 in. on the flat. Forward and aft this deck is curved, amidships it comes flat on top of the belt. The belt is a rather narrow strip amidships, rising to no great height above the water-line. It is about 175 ft. long, and has a maximum thickness of 10 in. Harvey steel, diminishing at the ends to 8 in.

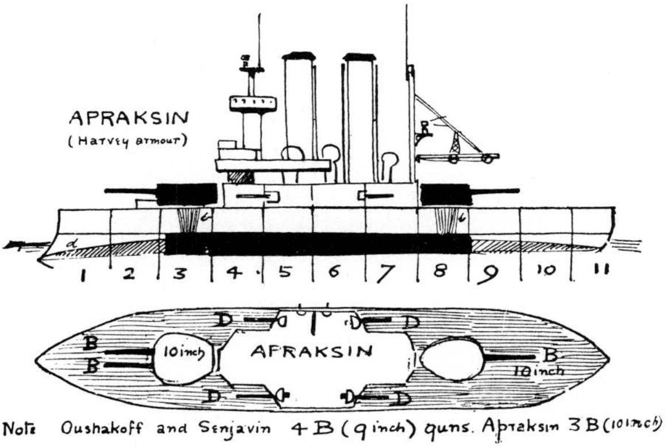


GENERAL ADMIRAL GRAF APRĀKSIN.

The ends are joined by 8 in. bulkheads, slightly curved.

On the lower deck the ship carries four torpedo tubes—one in the bow, one in the stern, and two training tubes amidships, situated a little abaft the foremast. These two tubes, like those which Elswick fitted to the Japanese Takasago, can be unshipped in order to increase the accommodation for the crew. Unlike the Takasago's tubes, which are hinged, those of the Aprāksin unscrew at the muzzle end of the tube, and are then stowed, much as the maindeck guns are stowed in British casemated battleships and cruisers. In such a small vessel this is a decided boon.

On the maindeck all the guns are carried : three 10-in., four 6-in. 45 calibres quickfirers, and some 6-pounders. The 10-in. guns, which are the new 45 calibre Oboukhoff pattern, are carried in the usual Russian turrets, the prototype of the "gun-houses" now fitted to most cruisers. The forward turret, which carries a pair of guns, is oval in form, with a central loading position between the guns. The guns revolve upon the armoured hoist, 6 in. to 8 in thick; the turret is practically a big shield revolving with the guns. It works on circular rails laid on the deck. The thickness of this turret varies from 8 in. to 4 in. It is very lofty, and the guns are mounted high up in it, the muzzles being a good 6 ft. above the deck, perhaps more.

The after-turret is circular, and contains only one gun, otherwise it corresponds to the fore-turret.

The turrets of the Oushakoff and Seniavin are both oval, and carry a pair of guns each.

The main engines of the Admiral Oushakoff were designed and constructed by Messrs. Maudslay, are of 5000 I.H.P., and consist of two sets of triple-expansion engines having cylinders 31 in. diameter H.P., 46 in. diameter I.P., and 68 in. diameter L.P., with a stroke of 33 in.

The crank-bearing frames are of cast iron, and the cylinders are supported by four cast-iron standards, with guides bolted to their faces. The piston-rods, connecting-rods, and shafts are all of forged steel, the

ENGINES OF THE ADMIRAL OUSHAKOFF.

[*From a Photo kindly supplied by* MESSRS. MAUDSLAY, SONS, & FIELD.]

journals in crank and shaft being well provided with large bearing surfaces. The condenser, constructed of gun-metal and fitted with ¾-in. tubes, having 7500 square feet of cooling surface, is placed athwartships, the shafting being carried underneath.

A single acting air-pump is driven off the L.P. engine crosshead, conveniently placed for repairing or overhaul.

The feed-pumping engines are of the duplex type, and these, with circulating pumps, fan engines, and all other auxiliaries, are supplied by Messrs. Maudslay.

Steam is supplied by four double-ended boilers, constructed at the contractors' East Greenwich Boiler Works, each boiler being 18 ft. long by 13 ft. in diameter, and working at 160 lbs. steam pressure.

The engines of the Aprāksin are almost identical, but were made at the Baltic Works, St. Petersburg. Those of the Seniavin were built by Messrs. Humphrys & Tennant.

The trial results, natural draught, were as follows :—

*Trials.*

| | | | | | |
|---|---|---|---|---|---|
| 1895. Oushakoff, | 12 hours, | 5769 mean | I.H.P.= | speed | 16·1 kts. |
| 1896. Seniavin, | 12 ,, | ? ,, | ,, | *circa* | 16 kts. |
| 1898. Aprāksin, | 7 ,, | 5757 ,, | ,, | [1] | ? |

The contract power was 5259 I.H.P. and 16-knot speed.

*Sea speed.* At sea, these ships can do 14 knots steadily, unless there is a sea on, when of course their low freeboard soon reduces their speed.

[1] Variously reported at from 17 to 15 knots.

| | Russian. | | German. | | Swedish. | |
|---|---|---|---|---|---|---|
| | Apräksin. | Oushakoff and Seniavin. | Hildebrand. | Ægir. | Thor. | Dristigheten. |
| Displacement | 4126 | 4126 | 3496 | 3600 | 3400 | 3500 |
| Armament, heavy | 3 B. (10 in.) | 4 B. (9 in.) | 3 B. (9 in.) | 3 B. (9 in.) | 2 B. (10 in.) | 2 (C. 8 in.) |
| ,, Q. F. | 4 D. (6 in.) | 4 D. (6 in.) | 8 F. (3·4 in.) | 10 F. (3·4 in.) | 6 E. (4·7 in.) | 6 D. (6 in.) |
| ,, light | 22 | 22 | 6 | 8 | 16 | 16 |
| Submerged tubes | *nil* | *nil* | *nil* | two | one in bow | two |
| Belt | *a* | *a–b* | *b–d* | *a–b* | *aa–a* | *aa–a* |
| Ratio of belt to length | 55 % | 55 % | 100 % | 55 % | 55 % | 55 % |
| Deck | =*d* | =*d* | =*e* | =*d* | =*d* | =*d* |
| Protection to vitals | =*a* | =*a* | =*b* | =*a* | =*aa* | =*aa* |
| Lower deck | *nil* | *nil* | *nil* | *nil* | *nil* | *nil* |
| Bases of big guns | *nil* | *nil* | *nil* | *nil* } | *b* [1] | *b* |
| Hoists | *c* | *b* | *f* | *f* } | | |
| On big guns | *b* | *a* | hoods *e*<br>barbette *b* | hoods *c*<br>barbette *b* | *b* | *b* |
| On secondary armament | *nil* | *nil* | *nil* | *nil* | *dc* | *c* |
| Speed (sea) | 14 | 14 | 13·5 | 14 | 14·5–15 | 15 |
| Coal supply {normal capacity | 260 | 260 } | 225 | 270 | 300 | 300 tons |
| Coal supply {maximum ,, | 400 | 400 } | | | | |
| Date of launch | 1893 | 1896 | 1892 | 1895 | 1898 | building |

[1] In the Oden, which has but four 4·7-in. guns, the bases are *a*.

A comparison of these ships with Swedish and German vessels, which they may be more or less designed with a view to meeting, may be of interest. War game notation of guns and armour is followed—the Aprāksin's armour, it will be noted, is better than that of the others (being Harveyised), though it has the same thickness.

The Oushakoff may be called, and presumably is, an "answer" to the Hildebrand and some earlier sister; the Aprāksin to the Ægir; while the Thor was probably built with an eye to both.

The Tri Svititelia, laid down in 1891, was launched at Nikolaiff on the 12th of November 1893, but has only quite recently (1899) been completed for sea. She did not cruise in 1898. She is the heaviest iron-clad in the Russian Navy, and the most strongly protected ship in the world, offering, as an inspection of the plan will indicate, exceedingly few points for attack. *Tri Svititelia, 1893.*

In general type she is an improved Navārin,—a British Trafalgar with best hardened steel armour instead of compound. Her principal details are:—

| | |
|---|---|
| Displacement . . . | 12,500 tons. |
| Material of hull . . | Steel. |
| Length all over . . | $377\frac{3}{4}$ ft. |
| Length between p.p. . . | 371 ft. |
| Beam . . . . | $72\frac{1}{3}$ ft. |
| Draught (*mean*) . . | 27 ft. |
| Armament . . . | Four 12-in. 40 calibres, Obukoff. |
| | Eight 6-in. Q.F. 45 calibres, Obukoff. |

BATTLESHIP TRI SVITITELIA.

[Photo by favour of H.I.H. Grand Duke Alexander.

Four 4·7-in. Q.F. of 45 calibres, Obukoff.

Fifty small Q.F. (3- and 1-pounders).

Six above water torpedo tubes.

The armour consists of a belt 250 ft. long by 7 ft. 10 in. high, Creusot nickel steel 16 in. in thick- *Armour.*

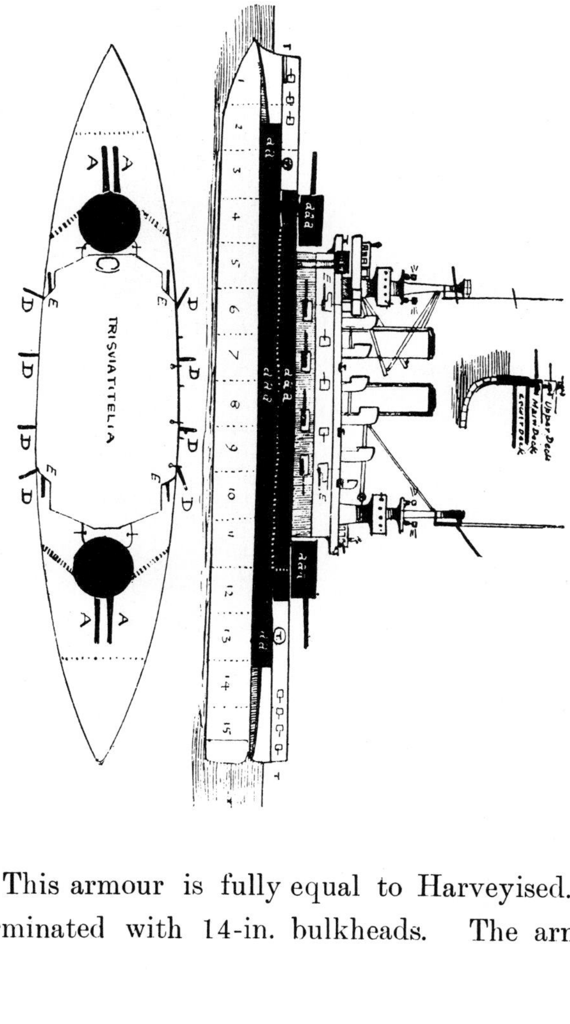

ness. This armour is fully equal to Harveyised. This is terminated with 14-in. bulkheads. The armoured deck, inclined fore and aft, is 3 in. thick, and is flat upon top of the belt. Above the belt is a redoubt about 225 ft. in length, with rounded ends enclosing the turret bases. This redoubt is 16 in. thick. The turrets are the same thickness. Between the turrets is the battery with continuous 5-in. armour and screens, 2 in. between the guns. Above this battery again is an upper-deck battery, unprotected, with a 4·7-in. Q.F. at each angle, and small Q.F. along the side. Above, again, on the boat deck, the remainder of the 3-pounders are carried. The foremost and aftermost 6-in. guns have end-on fire. It is worthy of note that the torpedo tubes are all placed outside the redoubt, not behind armour.

The engines were built by Messrs. Humphrys & Tennant, of Deptford, London, and in a 12 hours' trial, natural draught, developed a mean of 11,400 I.H.P. and an average speed of 17¾ knots.

She has a bunker capacity of 1000 tons, and can also carry liquid fuel, which is abundant and easily procurable in the Euxine.

The Tri Svititelia is, it will be noted, a low freeboard ship, and is in consequence not a homogeneous unit of the Black Sea Fleet. In the Euxine, however, this low freeboard is a matter of less consequence than it might be elsewhere.

*1894.* In June 1894 the Sissoi Veliky was launched at St. Petersburg, and got ready for sea with unprecedented despatch. She is a second-class battleship of consider-

SECOND-CLASS BATTLESHIP SISSOI VELIKY.

able power, and, for her size, exceedingly well protected. Her details are :—

| | |
|---|---|
| Displacement . . . . | 8880 tons. |
| Material . . . . | Steel. |
| Length . . . . | 345 ft. |
| Beam . . . . | 69 ft. |
| Draught (aft) . . . | 24 ft. |
| Armament . . . | Four 12-in. Obukoff, 40 cals.<br>Six 6-in. Q.F., Canet, 45 cals.<br>38 small Q.F.<br>Six torpedo tubes above water. |

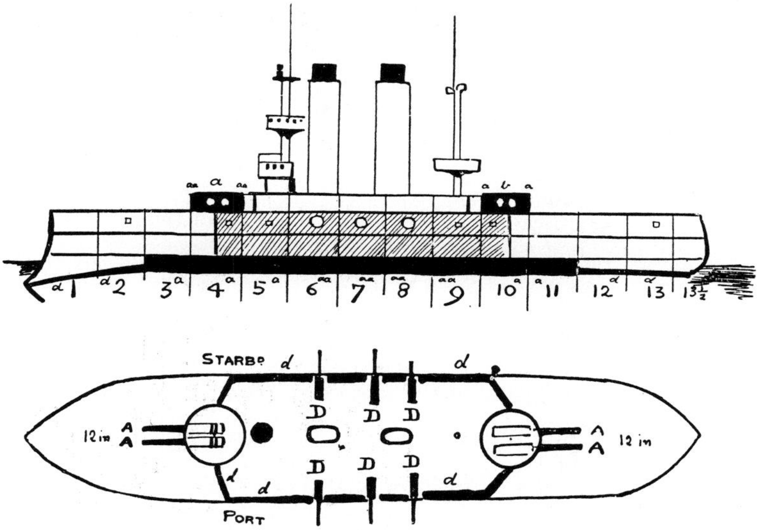


SISSOI VELIKY.

| | |
|---|---|
| Horse-power . . . | 8500. |
| Speed (continuous) . . | 15 knots. |
| Screws . . . . | Two. |
| Complement . . . | 600. |
| Armour . . . . | Belt, 247 ft. long by 7 ft. wide, $15\frac{3}{4}$ to $11\frac{1}{2}$ in., terminated by 5-in. bulkheads. |

Above this is her especial feature, a redoubt 5 in. thick, which covers all the lower and main decks for a space of 195 ft. amidships. This redoubt is of Creusot steel, and protects the turret bases. The fore-turret is 12 in. thick, the after one 10 in. The funnels are very high,—the casing stopping short some way below the tops gives them a peculiar appearance. The mainmast is used as a huge ventilator.

*Turrets.*

*Funnels.*

The normal supply of coal is 500 tons; the capacity is 800 tons. The engines are two sets vertical triple-expansion, and made 16 knots on trial. The boilers are Belleville, there being twelve of these in three groups of four each. So soon as she was completed, the Sissoi Veliky was sent to the Mediterranean, where, off Crete, she became notorious for a terrible gun explosion while at target practice. The cause of this disaster is that she had been rather hastily supplied with her big guns, and in the after-turret two with different breechpieces were mounted. The starboard one of these, an experimental gun, when unlocked, looked like the other locked. This gun was fired unlocked by mistake, and the breechpiece blown off. The explosion killed or wounded everybody in the turret, and some men on the upper deck, upon which the top of the turret was bodily flung.

*Coal.*

*Engines.*

*Disaster on board the Sissoi Veliky.*

*Cause.*

In 1895 the Rostislav, a sister to the Sissoi Veliky, was laid down at Nikolaiff, and the ironclad gunboat Khrabry launched at St. Petersburg.

*1895. Rostislav. Khrabry.*

It will be observed that the Khrabry bears little or no

PHOTOGRAPH OF THE INTERIOR OF THE SISSOI VELIKY'S TURRET AFTER THE DISASTER.

resemblance to her reputed sisters — the Groziatschy class. Indeed, her only real connection with these vessels is that, like them, she is officially designated an armoured gunboat.

Her details are :—

| | |
|---|---|
| Displacement . . . | *circa* 1500 tons. |
| Length . . . . | 230 ft. |
| Beam . . . . | 43 ft. |
| Draught (*max.*) . . | 13 ft. |
| Armament . . . | Two 8-in. forward, one 6-in. 45 calibre Q.F. aft. |

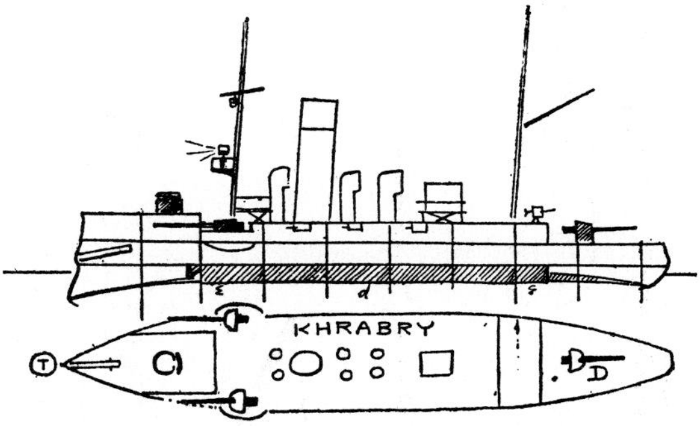


KHRABRY.

| | |
|---|---|
| Torpedo tubes . . . | One fixed in bow. |
| Armour . . . . | Belt amidships of Harvey steel, *circa* 5 to 3 in.; protective deck, $1\frac{1}{2}$ in. on slopes; bulkheads, 5 in. |
| Horse-power . . . | 2642. |
| Speed . . . . | 14·5 knots. |
| Boilers . . . . | Eight Niclausse. |
| Engines . . . . | Vertical triple-expansion. |
| Screws . . . . | Two. |

The freeboard forward is a deck higher than that

of the Groziatschy class. The 8-in. gun sponsons have apparently no armour of any sort.

*Reconstruction. Korniloff.*

In this year the Admiral Korniloff[1] was reboilered and rearmed, fourteen 6-in. 45 calibres Obukoff Q.F. being substituted for her old armament of two 8-in. and fourteen 6-in. breechloaders. She is now the most powerfully armed second-class cruiser in the world, and thanks to her new boilers is able to make a very good speed, 17 knots being her official continuous sea speed.

*Dmitri Donskoi.*

The Dmitri Donskoi[2] was also taken in hand. Her heavy rig was removed and fighting tops substituted. *New armament.* She was reboilered, and a new armament of six 6-in. Q.F. 45 calibres Obukoff, and ten 4·7-in. Q.F. ditto, substituted for her old pieces.

*1896.*

In September 1896 the Rostislav was launched at Nikolaiff. Originally intended to be a replica of the Sissoi Veliky,[3] some important modifications have been since introduced, and her eight 6-in. Q.F., instead of being in battery, are carried in turrets in pairs. The plan indicates the alterations in disposition of armour. *Armour.* This armour also is Harvey, of greater resisting power than the Sissoi's. It is also about three-quarters of an inch thicker; saving in weight having been effected over the big guns, which are 10-in. instead of 12-in.

The Rostislav did her trials in November 1898, using liquid fuel, and made the unexpectedly high speed

[1] P. 244. [2] P. 207. [3] P. 282.

THE DMITRI DONSKOI—PRESENT RIG.

of 18 knots. Like the Sissoi Veliky, she has Belleville boilers.

In December of this year the Svietlana was launched at Havre. *1896. Svietlana.*

She is practically a third-class cruiser, though her dimensions might warrant her being rated in the second class. She is, however, primarily a yacht, the guns and

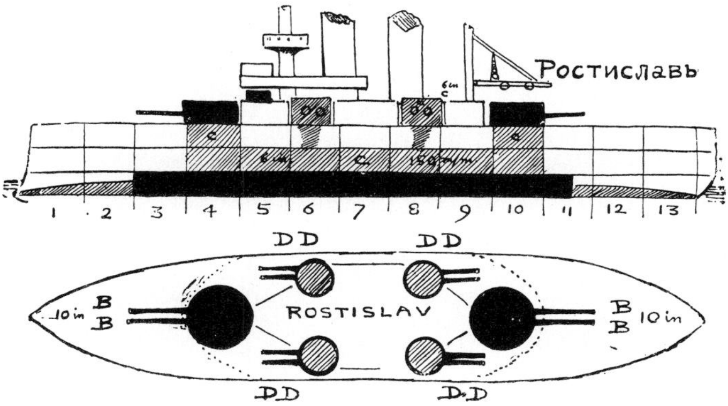


ROSTISLAV.

other warlike things being more or less after-thoughts, as it were, to enable her to be used for war purposes if necessary. The following are the principal data concerning her :—

| | |
|---|---|
| Displacement . . . . | 3900 tons. |
| Length . . . . . | 331 ft. |
| Beam . . . . . | 42 ft. |
| Draught (*maximum*) . . | 19 ft. |
| Armament . . . . | Six 15-cm. (6-in.) 45 cal. Q.F., Canet ; twelve small Q.F. ; four torpedo tubes. |
| Armour . . . . . | Creusot steel deck, $1\frac{3}{4}$ in. on the slopes. |
| I.H.P. (natural draught) . | 8500. |

| | |
|---|---|
| Trial speed (average) . . | 20·25 knots. |
| „ (maximum) . | 21·6 knots. |
| Engines . . . . . | Vertical 4-cylinder triple-expansion; two screws. |
| Boilers . . . . . | 18 Belleville. |

Laid down at Havre 1895, launched 1896.

She serves as the yacht of the Grand Duke Alexis, Commander-in-chief of the Russian Navy, and is permanently fitted for that purpose. The Grand Duke's state-rooms are fairly large, and are wainscoted with yellow pine. A good deal of interior space is taken up by a very broad and shallow mahogany staircase leading to the Grand Duke's smoking-room on the quarter-deck. This staircase is very fine and massive, but it takes up so much space that the smoking-room itself is considerably curtailed.

THE SVĚTLANA.

TORPEDO CRAFT

The Kapitan - Lieutenant Kazarski, launched at Elbing in 1890, was followed by the Posadnik and

Voivoda in 1892. In 1893 the Gaidamak and Vsadnik were launched at Abo, and the Griden at Nikolaiff.

Their details are :—

| | |
|---|---|
| Displacement . . . | 400 tons. |
| Length . . . . | 190 ft. |
| Beam . . . . | $24\frac{1}{4}$ ft. |
| Draught (*aft*) . . . | 11 ft. |
| Armament . . . | Six 3-pounders, three 1-pounders; two torpedo tubes. |
| Horse-power . . . | Natural draught, 1270; forced, 3500. |
| Speed . . . . | *circa* 25 knots on trial. |

They are practically elementary destroyers, but much too broad to give satisfaction,—they look very "tubby" in appearance.

An improved vessel of the same type, the Abrek, *Abrek.* was launched at Abo in 1896, and completed for sea at the New Admiralty Works, St. Petersburg. She is of 534 tons, 212 ft. long, 25 ft. beam, and $8\frac{1}{2}$ ft. mean draught. She did exceedingly well on trials, and left for the Pacific in the autumn of 1898.

In 1895 Messrs. Yarrow of Poplar launched the *Sokol.*

destroyer Sokol, which made a great sensation owing to her remarkable speed. She is constructed of nickel steel, and was the first destroyer to be built of that material. Her details are :—

| | |
|---|---|
| Displacement | 240 tons. |
| Material | Nickel steel. |
| Length | 190 ft. |
| Beam | 18½ ft. |
| Draught | 7 ft. |
| Horse-power | 4400. |
| Boilers | Eight Yarrow. |
| Screws | Two. |
| Speed trial | 29·7 (three hours' mean). |
| Coal | 60 tons. |
| Armament | One 12-pounder, three 6-pounders; two torpedo tubes. |

The excellent photograph of this little vessel was taken just as she was leaving for Russia. The guns, etc., are of course not on board; these were not fitted until she reached Russia.[1]

*Torpedo boats.*

In the period 1891–99 the following torpedo boats have been added to the Russian Navy :—

| | | | | | | | | |
|---|---|---|---|---|---|---|---|---|
| 23 | of | 118 | tons, | 130 | ft. long, | 25 | knots | trial speed. |
| 4 | ,, | 100 | ,, | 152 | ,, | 19 | ,, | ,, |
| 1 | ,, | 130 | ,, | 152 | ,, | 27·4 | ,, | ,, |
| 4 | ,, | 99 | ,, | 127 | ,, | 21 | ,, | ,, |
| 2 | ,, | 95 | ,, | 152 | ,, | 19·7 | ,, | ,, |
| 5 | ,, | 85 | ,, | 128 | ,, | 22 | ,, | ,, |

[1] Photographs of the Sokol are procurable in England, showing her with the guns on board, the officers in British uniform, and the funnels like those of the British Hornet! I heard in Russia that this very mysterious photograph is preserved in the confidential photograph-book at our Intelligence Department; but perhaps that is to be taken with a grain of salt. The boat, of course, is not the Sokol at all.

THE DESTROYER SOKOL.

THE RUSSIAN FLEET AT TOULON.

L'ENTENTE CORDIALE AT TOULON.

IMPERIAL YACHT STHANDART.

## Historical Data

The visit of the French fleet to Kronstadt in 1892, and the return visit of the Russian fleet to Toulon in 1893, are events too well known to need more than a passing reference. By means of the fleets an alliance was cemented through which Russia obtained a good deal of advantage in money, while the French Government presumably acquired the kudos that it desired.

## Imperial Yachts

1890. The imperial yacht Polarnaia Sviezda (Pole Star) was launched at St. Petersburg in May 1890. She is of 3640 tons displacement, cruiser built. She carries six small guns (Baranovski 12-pounders), and with 5602 I.H.P. natural draught made 8·8 knots. She could be of some use as a cruiser for scouting, but has no direct fighting value.

1895. The other imperial yacht Sthandart, launched at Copenhagen in 1895, is much larger—5557 tons; with 10,600 I.H.P. she made 21·18 knots. She has 24 Belleville boilers, and carries eight 3-pounders Q.F. She is not intended for any warlike uses.

BOURIA & YERSCH (RUSSIAN)

# XIV

## THE BEGINNING OF THE NEW FLEET

AS the previous pages have shown, Russian warships are not produced in batches, like British ones are: one ship, or at most two, are all that have generally been produced of a type. The new era quite alters this: of the Poltāva class, the first of which was laid down early in 1892, three vessels have been constructed. Of the Peresviet type, three were built. Then came the Borodinos in a batch of six, and subsequent programmes indicate that like all other nations Russia has taken to the building of squadrons instead of isolated ships, thus following the system long ago initiated by the British Navy.

*Poltāva. Petropavlovsk. Sevastôpol.*

The Poltāva was launched on the 6th of November 1894 at St. Petersburg, the Petropavlovsk followed three days later, the Sevastôpol took the water on the 1st of June in the following year. The greater part of the five years odd intervening was spent in completing them. None of them were in a condition to be commissioned in 1898. The Poltāva was almost completed in January 1899, the Sevastôpol completing.

"Improved Indianas" is what the Russians call these ships, which are best described as a blend of the Indiana and the French Brennus.

*Indiana. Brennus.*

The Indiana is now quite out of date, both by reason of her low freeboard and the crowding of her guns without efficient protection. The Brennus, on the other hand, in type closely resembles the Suffren, a quite modern ship, and even the République class do not differ from her very essentially so far as general design is concerned. Both, with their secondary turrets, are lineal descendants of the Brennus.

In fighting speed the Indiana is probably a knot behind the others. The Brennus only has a curved deck to reinforce the belt. She is a little faster than the Poltāva, and alone of the three has water-tube boilers. Of these she carries thirty-two Belleville. Of the three she is probably the best ship, when considered from every point of view. If she had had a less abnormal thickness of water-line protection,—the equivalent of 30 in. of iron would probably have sufficed,—and the balance had been expended in better protection to the quickfiring guns, and four 12-in. instead of three 13½-in., her superiority would perhaps have been greater still.

*Points of the Brennus.*

The following are the full details of the Poltāva class:—Displacement, about 11,000 tons;[1] dimensions, 367 ft. long by 69 ft. beam; draught, 27 ft.—

[1] 10,960 is the designed displacement as announced when the ships were commenced.

FIRST-CLASS BATTLESHIP PETROPAVLOVSK.

this was the maximum draught on trials, the actual draught is probably rather more.

*Armour.*

In the arrangement of armour they resemble the Iowa or Indiana more nearly than any other vessels; but the freeboard is, of course, higher than in the Indiana class, and the protection better than in the Iowa.

*Belt.*

The armour belt, of Harveyised steel, extends for about three-fourths of the water-line amidships, and has a maximum thickness of 16 in. At the ends are bulkheads 9 in. thick. The deck, which is flat on top of the belt, is about 2½ in. thick; fore and aft of the belt it is 3½ in. on the slopes. The Poltāva was laid down in 1892, and consequently has the water-line protection of an Indiana or a Royal Sovereign, and not the belt reinforced by a curved deck behind it, common to all designs of the present time. In England this reinforced belt first appeared in the Majestic, previously to which it had been confined to the French Navy. Behind the immensely thick belts of all French ironclads, from the Magenta onwards, is a curved protective deck, rising from the lower edge of the armour.

*Lower deck*

Above the thick belt of the Poltāva is a thinner belt protecting the lower deck—a feature she has in common with the Indiana, Iowa, and Royal Sovereign. It is about 5 in. thick. On the main deck are four casemates, armoured with 5 in. of Harvey, built out upon a sort of recess, the nature of which is best understood from an inspection of the illus-

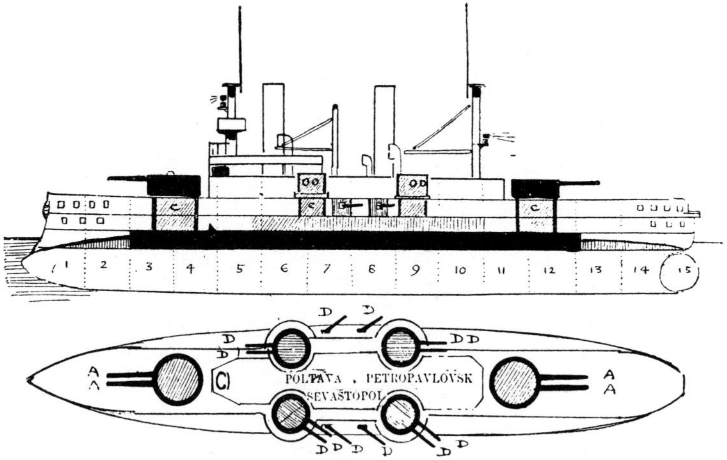


POLTAVA.

trations. On the upper deck are four turrets, originally designed to carry a pair of 8-in. guns each, but 6-in. quickfirers have been substituted. These turrets are very high, and have a very fine arc of fire. They do not resemble those of the Indiana in any way, unless they are regarded as an enormous heightening of that vessel's secondary turrets. These Poltāva turrets are 5 in. thick, and revolve inside large armoured bases going down through the main deck. Not only, therefore, have they a very fine command, but they are not liable to be put out of action by a shell underneath, like the Iowa's are: it being improbable that any shell—except, possibly, a big armour-piercing—will get through a curved 5-in. Harvey plate.

*6-in. turrets.*

*Big gun turrets.*

The big gun turrets, which appear to be 12 in. thick at least, though 10 in. is their reputed size, have the same protection as the 6-in. turrets, a 5-in. armoured base. They differ, however, in one item: the bases of the secondary turrets rise a trifle above the upper deck level, while those of the big turrets do not. The big turrets are "gun-houses," similar to those of the Aprāksin, already described in an earlier article. There is not, therefore, much resemblance to the "barbette turret" of the Majestic, Canopus, etc.

In the Sevastôpol I noticed, on the main deck, doors leading into these armoured bases. Those who have tried to get into the turrets of one of the Majestic class in a hurry will possibly consider this an advantage outweighing any consequent structural weakness.

SEVASTÔPOL—AN END-ON VIEW.

*(Before being sent to the Far East this ship had her funnels heightened.)*

*Armament.* Vessels of the Poltāva class were designed to carry the armament still attributed to them in many statistical tables, namely, four 12-in., eight 8-in., and twenty-five small pieces. The actual armament is as follows for the Poltāva and Petropavlovsk :—

(*a*) Four 12-in. 40 calibres, Oboukhoff.

(*b*) Twelve 6-in. 45 calibres, Oboukhoff quickfirers, carried eight in pairs in turrets, and four on the main deck in casemates. Six guns can fire directly ahead or astern.

(*c*) Thirty-six quickfirers—12-pounder, 3-pounders, and 1-pounders.

When I visited the Sevastôpol no guns were yet on board, nor were the maindeck casemates in position.

There are four above-water torpedo tubes behind 5-in. armour.

Flush with the tops of the secondary turrets, which nest into it, is a spar deck running on top of the superstructure that extends from the foremast to the after-*Superstructure* most mast. There is no wood in this superstructure. The conning-tower stands on this deck just before the foremast. Above the spar deck is a very large wood-decked flying bridge, from which a most excellent all-round view of the whole ship is obtainable. All the guns can be watched from this bridge, and I cannot recall any other warship with so good a "fighting position." It is exposed, of course,—very exposed, for that matter,—but everything that is going on can be seen at a glance from it.

[*Photo, copyright* 1902, *by W. H. Rau.*

FIRST-CLASS BATTLESHIP RETVIZAN.

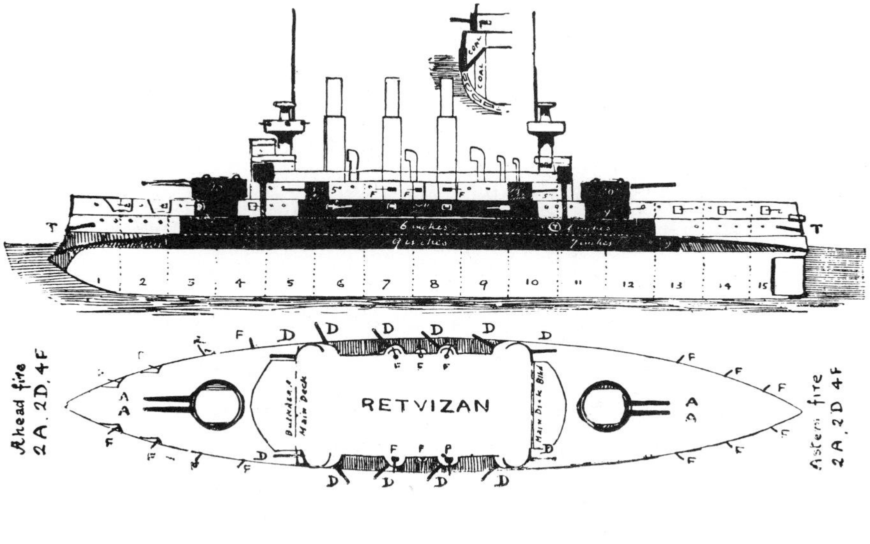

The foremast, which is of French shape adapted to Russian needs, carries a not very obtrusive fighting top very low down, and a platform with two search-lights higher up. Two search-lights are also carried on the main, and two others on the ventilator shaft between the funnels. The other masts are hollow, and used as immense ventilating shafts, — a piece of utilitarianism first adopted in the Sissoi Veliky, where the mainmast is a ventilating shaft. There are also ten good-sized cowls in the Poltāva class. The engines of the Poltāva were supplied by Messrs. Humphrys & Tennant; those of the Petropavlovsk were made by Messrs. Hawthorn, Leslie, & Co.; those of the Sevastôpol are of Russian manufacture.

A good many reports have from time to time been set afloat to the effect that these ships cannot make their speeds, and never have. As a matter of fact, however, on their trials both the Poltāva and Petropavlovsk exceeded the contract forced-draught

*Speeds.*

speed with open stokeholds, an average of about 16½ knots being maintained for twelve hours. This was taken as "good enough," and the forced draught remains what is in the British Navy list called "not yet tried"—the fans are run merely to assist ventilation. The story of the failures on trial came, I believe, originally from Germany, and, if investigated enough, a desire to supply machinery to Russian warships might be found near the bottom of it. It was copied into English newspapers by some who

BÖYARIN. [Photo, Geiser.

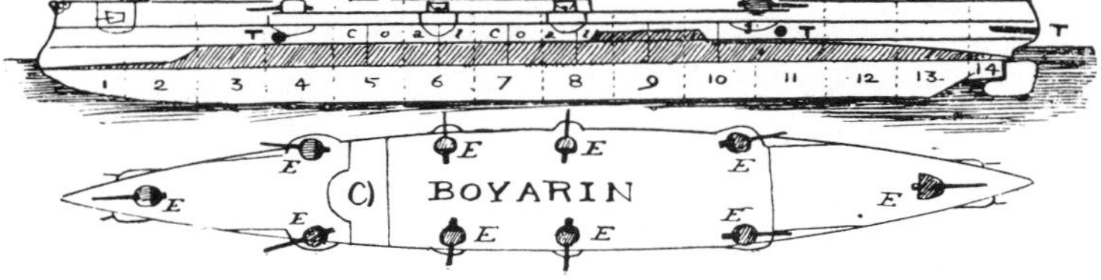

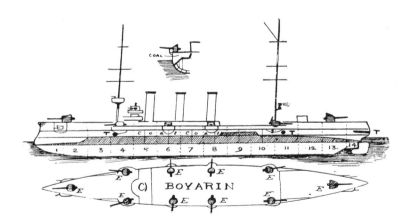

were in all likelihood blissfully ignorant of the fact that in their haste to decry Russian ships they were simply blindly throwing stones at English manufactures!

*Peresvet.*

The following are the principal particulars of the Peresvet, Osliabia, and Pobieda:—

| | |
|---|---|
| Displacement (nominal) | 12,674 tons. |
| Length | 36 ft. |
| Beam | $71\frac{1}{2}$ ft. |
| Draft (*aft*) | $27\frac{1}{4}$ ft. |
| Guns— | |
| In turrets | Four 10-in. 45 cals. |
| In casemates | Ten 6-in. Q.F. 45 cals. |
| In bow battery | One 6-in. Q.F. 45 cals. |
| In battery amidships | Twenty 3-in. |
| Small Q.F.'s | Twenty-six. |

Four torpedo tubes above water in bow, broadside, and stern, and two submerged.

Boilers, 30 Belleville generators with economisers in six groups.

Engines, three sets vertical triple expansion.

| | |
|---|---|
| Screws | Three. |
| Coal supply (normal) | 1063 tons. |
| Bunker capacity, also liquid fuel | 2058 tons. |
| Continuous sea speed | 16 knots (estimate). |
| Maximum speed | 19 knots (estimate). |
| Horse-power, natural | 14,500. |

Armour—Harveyised steel. Krupp steel in the Pobieda.

*Water-line.*

The water-line is protected for nearly all its length by a belt 9 in. thick amidships, tapering to 6 in. at the ends, where, 30 ft. from the bow and stern respectively, are 9-in. bulkheads. A curved deck $4\frac{1}{2}$ in. thick on the slopes runs the entire length of the vessel. In the Pobieda the belt is complete.

BAYAN

BAYAN.

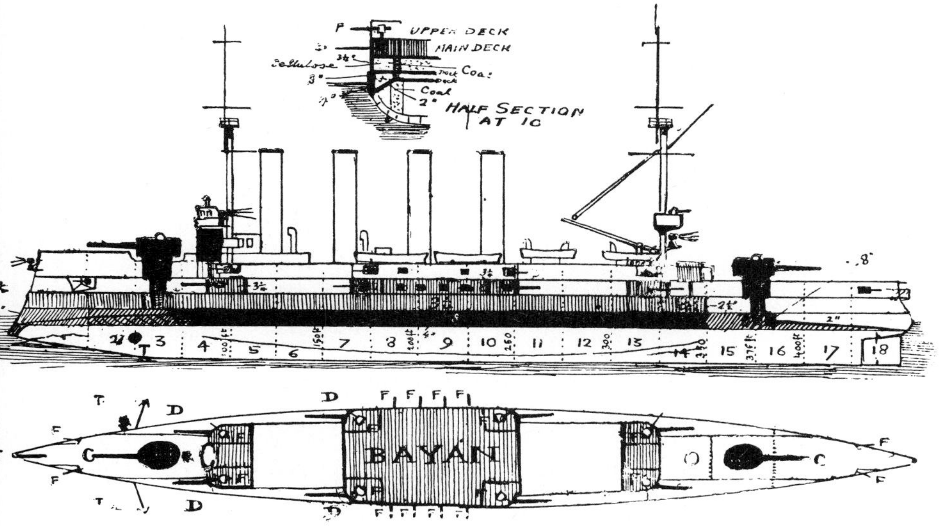
UPPER DECK
MAIN DECK
Cellulose
Coal
Coal
HALF SECTION AT 10
BAYAN

*Lower deck.*

The lower deck amidships is protected by 5-in. Harvey, as are also the ten casemates. The bow 6-in. gun has no armour to it; its arc of fire is also limited—that is to say, it can only train before the beam, and not even be used upon the broadside.

*Turret bases.*

The armouring of the turrets is peculiar. They are 10-in. gun houses with bases 8 in. thick. The peculiarity lies in the fashion in which these bases contract as they descend, and in them much of the Peresvet's novelty consists. For the 12-pounder 3-in. guns stout shields are provided, and great care is taken to mount these free of all obstructions likely to burst shell.

*Armour.*

Relatively to the earlier Poltāva class, it will be seen that the Peresvet presents a larger target, is less heavily armed, and perhaps rather less well protected on the whole. Of course there is a *quid pro quo* somewhere, and in this case it lies in speed. The Poltāva is a battleship pure and simple; the Peresvet is one of those hybrid craft that the French call "intermediates." It is worthy of note, in passing, that the French have built no such ships themselves: their battleships, however open to criticism they may be, have been designed as battleships, and the French in the past have usually proved fairly sound in their ideas as to the best form of fighting ship.

The Peresvet is really an armoured cruiser masquerading as a battleship. She might be called an improved anticipation of the Cressy class. She is slower; on the other hand, she is more powerfully

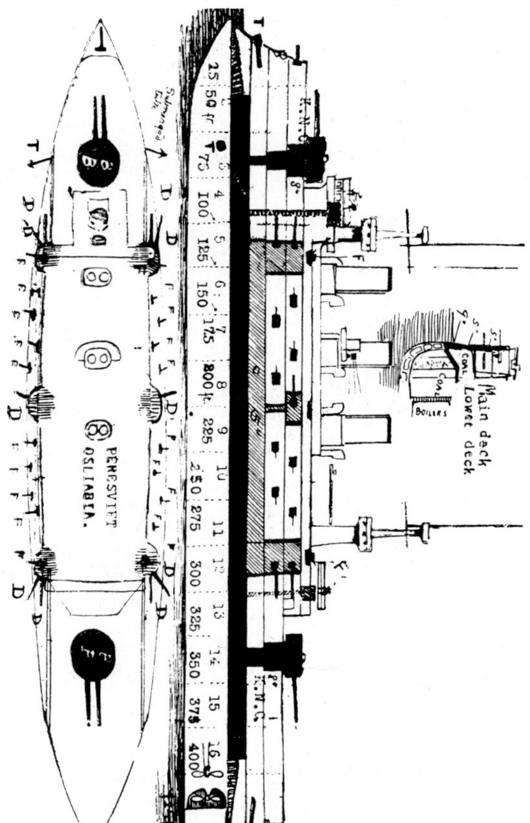
PERESVIET
OSLIABIA.
Main deck
Lower deck
BOILERS
COAL
K.M.G.

armed and better protected. Consequently, if any armoured cruiser, with its extra speed, caught her, the catching (assuming equal gunnery and equal *personnel*) would not be altogether advantageous.

*Asama.*

With some such idea at the back of his head the Peresvet's designer must have gone to work; possibly, as the ship was designed for the Far East, he might be thought to have had the Asama at the back of his head also, only the Asama was not then heard about, I fancy, for all that her launch slightly preceded the

VARIAG.

Peresvet's. There is no ship in either the British or Japanese Navy to which the Peresvet can be called an exact reply, and to call her an anticipatory reply of any seems scarcely correct.

*Kaiser Friedrich III. and Bismarck.*

The Peresvet was laid down in November 1895, the Osliabia being commenced on the same day. The only possible "rival" ships that she could be a "reply" to would be German—either the Kaiser Friedrich der Dritte or, less probably, the Fürst Bismarck, both of which were laid down before the Peresvet.

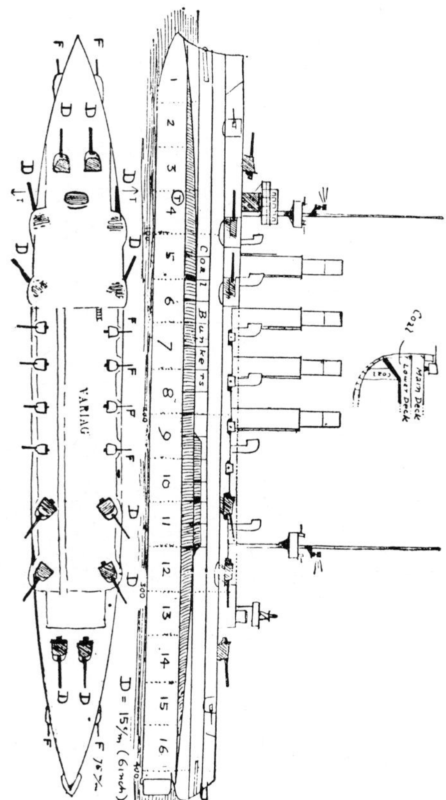
VARIAG
Coal Bunkers
Main Deck
Lower Deck
Coal
D = 15c/m (6inch)

From the purely sailor point of view, the Peresvet class are really splendid ships. The lofty foke's'le, broad clear decks, and fine lines are all things to appeal to the seaman. Then, too, the coal supply is better than that of the British Majestic class—a point of great importance to Russia in the event of war in the Far East.

*Coal.*

*Giliak.*

The river gunboat Giliak was launched in 1897. She is of 1200 tons, $206\frac{1}{2}$ feet long, $36\frac{1}{2}$ feet beam, and 10 feet maximum draught. Armament: one 4·7 Q.F., five 12-pounders, four 3-pounders, and two $2\frac{1}{2}$-pounders Baronovsky. There is a one-inch inclined deck over the vitals amidships. Designed I.H.P. 1000 = 12 knots. Six Belleville boilers. 170 tons of coal carried.

She was sunk by the Chinese when they opened fire on the Allied fleet at Taku, but subsequently raised.

### FOREIGN BUILT SHIPS

Soon after the Peresviets were well in hand the Russians embarked upon a foreign construction programme, orders being given out for the battleships Retvizan (Cramps, Philadelphia, U.S.A.), Tsarevitch (La Seyne), and the cruisers Bayan (La Seyne), Variag or Waryag (Cramps), Bogatyr (Vulcan Co.), Askold (Krupp), and the small cruisers Novik and Boyarin (at Schichan's and Copenhagen respectively). Commenced in 1898 this programme was completed in 1903, and practically completed a year before that.

BOGATYR.

[*Photo, by favour of H.I.H. Grand Duke Alexander of Russia.*

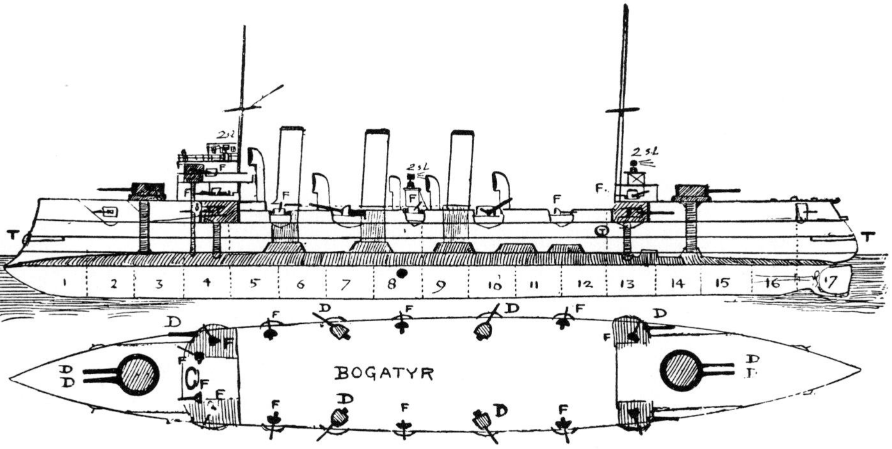

A description of the Tsarevitch is reserved for a later page, because she has become the standard type for Russian battleships. I propose here to deal only with the isolated ships which, having filled gaps, were not perpetuated as types. The Tsarevitch marks the final abandonment of Anglo-American design for French design.

*Retvizan.* The Retvizan is, with a few minor alterations, a replica of the U.S.S. Maine. Particulars of her are :—

| | |
|---|---|
| Displacement . . . | 12,700 tons. |
| Dimensions . . . | 376 ft. long, 72 ft. beam, 26 ft. mean draft. |
| Armament . . . | Four 12-in. 40 cals.<br>Twelve 6-in. 45 cals. Q.F.<br>Twenty 12-pdrs. Q.F. and 26 lesser Q.F.<br>Two submerged torpedo tubes (at 20°).<br>Four above water (two about to be removed). |
| Machinery, etc. | Designed H.P. 16,000 = 18 kts. Niclausse boilers; coal normal 1000 tons, bunker capacity 2000 tons. |

The armour (Krupp) consists of a 9-7-in. belt about 250 feet long, with a 2-in. extension to the bow. It is reinforced by a 3-in. armour deck. Along the lower deck is a 6-in. redoubt, from which rises the armed ships battery 5 inches thick, containing eight 6-in. guns sponsoned out in a recess with 110° arcs of fire. The other 6-in. guns are in case-

ASKOLD. [*Photo, Herr Krupp (builder).*

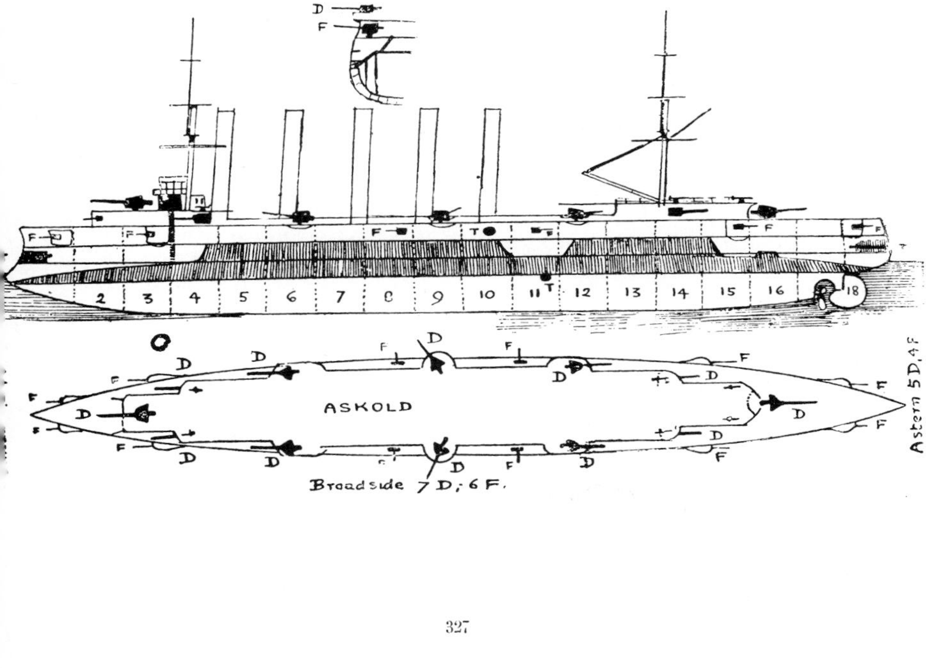

mates on the upper deck with axial fire. There are 10-in. turrets of Russian pattern, with 9-in. bases and bulkheads.

On her first trial she made only 17·75 knots; but after docking and overhaul succeeded in reaching 18·8 knots maximum, and in performing the 12 hours contract of an average 18 knots.

On her way to Russia a boiler tube burst, killing several men, and, in consequence of this and unfavourable reports generally, the Niclausse boiler was condemned in Russia just about the time that it was adopted for trial in the British Navy. It seemed to be doing well enough when I visited the Retvizan, but the prejudice against it was very strong on board on account of this unfortunate explosion. In the British Navy, on the other hand, no water-tube boiler, except the Belleville, is, perhaps, more favourably regarded at the present moment.

As a fighting unit, the Retvizan is, perhaps, about on a par with the British Canopus class. The total weight of armour is about 3900 tons.

*Bayan.*

The armoured cruiser Bayan is, for her size, one of the best designed warships afloat. Particulars are:—

| | |
|---|---|
| Displacement . . . | 7800 tons. |
| Dimensions . . . | 443 × 55¾ × 22 ft. |
| Armament . . . | Two 8-in. Q.F. |
| | Eight 6-in. Q.F. 45 cals. |
| | Twenty 12-pdr. Q.F. and seven 3-pdr. |

| | |
|---|---|
| Armament . . . | Two submerged torpedo tubes (at an angle of 20°). |
| Machinery, etc. . . | Two sets 4 cylinder triple expansion; designed I.H.P. 17,000 = 21 kts.; 26 Belleville boilers. |

The protection consists of a belt 375 feet long extending from the bow. Here it is 4 inches thick: amidship it increases to 8 inches, and is terminated by a bulkhead aft of that thickness. Aft of this is a turtle deck 2 inches thick. The protective deck behind the belt is of this thickness, flat on the main belt. A 2-in deck also rises from the bottom of the belt to meet this. Very stout solid bulkheads, without doors, also run across the ship at intervals rising to the main deck.

The lower deck side is protected for 350 feet from the bow by a $2\frac{1}{2}$ to $3\frac{1}{4}$-in. belt, on which stand three redoubts $3\frac{1}{4}$ inch thick. The forward and after ones contain a couple of 6-in. guns each, the central one four 6-in. at its angles and eight 12-pounders in between. These 6-in. are built into box casemates with 2-in. screens, and all the 6-in. gun shields, instead of being semicircular, are completely circular. The 8-in. guns are in roomy 7-in. turrets with 5-in. bases. Each turret is fitted as a conning tower.

The remaining 12-pounders are disposed, two at each extremity and eight on top of the 6-in. gun positions.

Altogether this ship is in many ways unique. So

far as she resembles any other vessel she is an armoured edition of the French D'Entrecasteaux. In both there is a similar disposition of artillery, in both the secondary guns are protected by armour that is only proof against small pieces, but so arranged that should a 6-in. shell penetrate its effect will be tremendously localised. Here the resemblance ends. The Bayan has at the water-line the protection of a battleship. Most armoured cruisers sacrifice armament and water-line protection to speed : the Bayan sacrifices armament and gun protection to a slight extent only. A 6-in. shell hitting a battleship's casemates would probably disable it by blast and the flying of rivets. Hitting near a secondary gun of the Bayan it would do the same damage on a major scale, but nothing more.

It should further be noted that this remarkable vessel, owing to her solid bulkheads, is not likely to suffer any more from water-line hits and torpedoes than a battleship of twice her tonnage.

It remains to add that, on the defect side, the ship is not a good sea boat, as she rolls a good deal, and its extremely lively. None the less, she probably is the best ship of her size in the world. After a careful inspection of her, I would rate her fittings as modern in every way.

On her trials the Bayan made about 22 knots quite easily and greatly exceeded the designed horse power. So well did she do that, although no fresh orders have gone to the French yard that produced her, the Belle-

NOVIK. [*Photo by favour of Herr Schichau.*

ville boilers which contributed to this result were adopted wholesale for new Russian ships, and six old vessels were ordered to be reboilered with this type. Such a triumph for French industry evoked considerable comment; but it cannot be denied that in the Bayan France exemplified that her old fame for design and speed is still with her. The no less remarkable success of the Tsarevitch, particulars of which will be found in a later chapter, emphasised the same thing, so that Russia's adhesion to French type is no matter of surprise.

When protected cruisers were ordered in 1897–98 a species of competition between two German firms and an American one was instituted. Particulars of the three types are:—

| | Bogatyr. | Variag. | Askold. |
|---|---|---|---|
| Displacement . (tons) | 6500 | 6500 | 6500 |
| Length . . (feet) | 423 | 416 | 426½ |
| Beam . . . (feet) | 52¼ | 52 | 49 |
| Draught (*mean*) . (feet) | 21¾ | 20 | 20¾ |
| Guns . . . . | 12 6-in.<br>12 12-pdrs.<br>8 3-pdrs.<br>2 1-pdrs. | 12 6-in.<br>12 12-pdrs.<br>6 3-pdrs.<br>... | 12 6-in.<br>12 12-pdrs.<br>8 3-pdrs.<br>2 1-pdrs. |
| Torpedo tubes (submerged) . . . | 2 | 2 | 2 |
| Torpedo tubes (above water) . . . | 4 | 2 | 4 |
| Armour deck . . | 3 in. | 3 in. | 3 in. |
| Armoured gun positions | 4 in. | none | none |
| Number of guns protected | 8 | none | none |
| Designed H.P. . . | 19,500 | 20,000 | 19,500 |
| Designed speed . (kts.) | 23 | 23 | 23 |
| Boilers. . . . | Normand | ... | Thornycroft |
| Trial speed (*maximum*) . (kts.) | 23·45 (12 hrs.) | 24·6 (8 hrs.) | 24·5 (12 hrs.) |
| I.H.P. developed . . | 20,000 | 20,000 | 23,600 |
| Coal (*normal*) . . | 900 | 770 | 600 |
| Coal (*maximum*) . . | 1000 | 1300 | 1100 |
| Built at . . . | Stettin | Cramp's | Krupp |

The famous Novik belongs to the same era. Particulars are :—

| | |
|---|---|
| Displacement . . . | 3000 tons. |
| Dimensions . . . | 347 × 39⅓ × 19 ft. |
| Armament . . . | Six 4·7-in., one 12-pdr., eight 3-pdrs., two 1-pdrs., five torpedo tubes. |
| Protection . . . | 2-in. deck, 3-in. engine hatches. |
| Machinery, etc. . . | Triple screw ; designed I.H.P. 18,000 = 25 knots ; twelve Thornycroft boilers ; coal capacity 500 tons (maximum). |

On trial she reached 26 knots, but soon began to fall off, as these small ships invariably do from the effect of vibration. She was built by Schichau. A somewhat similar vessel, the Boyarin, was entrusted to a Danish firm. In her only 11,500 H.P. was provided, and the speed demanded was 22·5 knots. She has only two screws, and was given Belleville instead of Thornycroft boilers. Except for the addition of a poop, and a different rig, she resembled the Novik. It is stated that in service she has proved quite as fast as this vessel, and the better boat of the two despite her lesser nominal speed.

# XV

## THE VOLUNTEER FLEET

THERE is no Russian "bogey" that is quite so really harmless as the Volunteer Fleet.

All these vessels have been built in England, and continue to be so, which possibly may account for many of the stories concerning them, there being no doubt but that the Volunteer Fleet is regarded in England as a serious war factor.

The Volunteer Fleet is primarily no more a war force than, say, the Cunard Line or the P. and O., and it is infinitely less capable of being utilised for war purposes, because, between Odessa and Vladivostok, Russia has no basis at which they could fit out. Under the most favourable conditions a merchant vessel makes but a sorry warship: in no case can she suddenly jump from one to the other.

Altogether there are twenty-five of these ships, of which ten belong to the Black Sea Navigation Company and fifteen to the Volunteer Fleet Association. None of the Black Sea Steam Navigation Company's steamers have the speed to make them of any use, and only four are less than fifteen years old.

The Volunteer ships are better, but not so very much. They date from the Orel, in 1888, to the Moskva and Poltāva of 1898, but only six of them have made 19 knots, or anything like it, on trial; the rest are 13 knotters nominally. Actually all are less. Russian mercantile engineers are not good, and it is exceedingly doubtful whether they could get more than 16 knots out of such a splendid vessel as the Kherson.

For all these ships 8-in. and 6-in. guns are stored at Vladivostok or in the Black Sea. A war would probably be over, however, ere they got them on board, while if we were the other party to the struggle the ships would be caught and captured without any trouble.

The whole "menace" of this fleet has arisen from its name. Its actual object was the exceedingly natural, obvious, and useful one of taking stores to Vladivostok, bringing back tea,—though with the progress of the Trans-Siberian railway more of this comes yearly overland. Gradually the ships will become more and more transports, which the Black Sea steamers always have been. The whole of them are under the Admiralty, just as our Indian troopships used to be, and it is to those old troopships that they are most analogous.

It, of course, suits Russia to allow them to appear likely to be a useful war force, just as it suits the anti-Russian party in this country, but, so far as most of them are concerned, we might just as well speculate on the war qualifications of our cross-Channel steamers. In the event of war they could only operate from Vladivostok and Port Arthur, and would very quickly be captured if they did so, while all *en route* would be laid up for want of coal. This is where Russia's desire for a coaling station in the Persian Gulf comes in; but even did she secure one, our position at Singapore would still control the situation,—apart from all other reasons, geography puts the Volunteer Fleet out of court.

In the event of war with Japan or Germany the vessels might be of some service, but the Japanese fleet has now such a numerical superiority that it is exceedingly doubtful whether the Volunteer ships could trouble her. Against Germany they would serve well to carry troops to occupy those isolated outposts with which Germany is trying to star the Far East.

# XVI

## THE RUSSIAN DOCKYARDS

### I. Administration

THERE is no hard-and-fast rule of administration for Russian dockyards, nearly every group having its own variations. There are, however, certain general regulations common to all.

All ports are divided into two classes :—

*1st Class.* St. Petersburg Yards.
Kronstadt.
Nikolaiff.
Libau.

*2nd Class.* Revel.
Sveaborg.
Sevastôpol.
Baku.
Batûm.
Astrabad.
Vladivostok.
Port Arthur.
Talienwan.

The St. Petersburg yards are under direct supervision of the chief Navy Staff. The other first-class ports have vice-admirals as Commanders-in-chief.

The Navy Staff of first-class ports is thus constituted:

Navy Staff office.
Dockyard Staff under a rear-admiral.
Building and workshops under a chief constructor.
Engineering department under the chief engineer.
Magazine and stores under the chief storekeeper.
Ordnance under the chief gunnery officer.
Torpedoes under the senior torpedo officer.
Medical and Sanitary under the senior doctor.
Dockyard Police.
Workmen.

Each department is responsible through the Navy Staff office to the Commander-in-chief of the port, who again is responsible to the General-Admiral.[1]

Second-class ports vary in their staff according to the requirements and capabilities of the port or dockyard, but they all have the Medical, Construction, Police, and Engineering branches. The chief of the Navy Staff for second-class ports is a rear-, instead of a vice-admiral.

Sevastôpol, Baku, Batûm, and Astrabad are, however, all grouped under separate rear-admirals, each responsible to the vice-admiral at Nikolaiff instead of to the General-Admiral[1] direct; the Commander-in-chief in the Euxine is, in fine, a species of under general-admiral.

[1] See "Personnel," later.

The following sections describe the Russian dockyards, the principal of which, through the kindness of H.I.H. Grand Duke Alexander, I was permitted to inspect as freely as I could any of our own, with which, by the way, they compare infinitely more favourably than in England we are prone to fancy.

# XVII

## THE RUSSIAN DOCKYARDS

### II. Descriptions

THIS section is devoted mainly to a description of the various yards and their resources, supplemented by full particulars of such vessels as were actually under construction in the early part of the year I went (1899). In order to avoid wearisome repetition where the ship dealt with as under construction is merely a replica of some vessel already completed, the prototype vessel is mentioned and a reference made to her in a footnote. The different yards are described in a sort of geographical sequence, and not arranged in order of importance: each Russian dockyard being a complement to some other establishment, to adopt any other arrangement would produce considerable difficulty. Roughly speaking, the whole group of the St. Petersburg dockyards and Kronstadt may be regarded as a complete unit, those of the Black Sea as another unit, while Vladivostok and Port Arthur go to make up a third. The *équipage* system of *personnel* is, in fine, carried out into the dockyard administration.

## ST. PETERSBURG YARDS

### 1. The "New Admiralty"

The depth of winter is not at first sight the best time to view a dockyard situated within fairly easy reach of the Arctic Circle. From the mere sightseer's point of view, however, the winter visit has something to recommend it, and even apart from this, the science of fighting the cold has reached the state of being a "fine art" in Russia to the extent of enabling dockyard work to be carried on without any very great inconvenience from the frost.

The New Admiralty Yard at St. Petersburg is situated well in the centre of the city, being on the banks of the Neva, just below the English Quay, the farthest up the river of the three yards. As regards size, it is, in comparison with Portsmouth or Chatham, a very small place ; in dimensions it approaches most nearly to the dockyard at Sheerness. The buildings, however, are on a considerably larger scale, the shops being very large and the two slips somewhere about the dimensions of cathedrals. A slip in Russia is a much more important thing than in England ; it is not possible there to construct a battleship in the open air, as is often done in England. Hence, not only are the slips enclosed by solidly built stone walls, and covered by roofs, but both ends are solidly built in also. When the ship is ready for launching, the river end is pulled down, to be rebuilt immediately afterwards.

The interior of a slip is very large, and that from which the Osliabia was launched at the New Admiralty has the constructor's office as a sort of cloister to it. It is reached by ascending the permanent ladders that go up inside the slip house.

THE NEW ADMIRALTY YARD FROM THE RIVER.

Work at the New Admiralty was not by any means vigorous at the time of my visit; such as there was

was chiefly concentrated on the Osliabia and General Admiral Graf Aprāksin, which two ships lay alongside the jetty, frozen in.

The Osliabia was the first ship I visited. She was not very advanced, neither funnels nor masts being in place, nor, of course, any guns on board. As she is a replica of the more advanced Peresvet,[1] it is unnecessary to give a detailed description here, and it will suffice to mention that the designed displacement is 12,674 tons, and the dimensions 436 ft. length, by 71½ ft. beam, with a draught aft of 27 ft. 3 in. The Osliabia class are ironclad-cruisers rather than ironclads, and may be best described as mixtures of the Canopus and Diadem. *Osliabia.*

Work upon the Osliabia was chiefly between decks when I boarded her; a none too easy task, as the gangway approximated very nearly to a toboggan slide. Everything on deck was in the grip of the frost, and great icicles hung over the sides. Beyond was the frozen river with its roads across the ice, and the long streams of sledges carting away the snow.

The General Admiral Graf Aprāksin has already been fully described.[2] The remainder of the ships at the New Admiralty were merely small craft—yachts, river gunboats, and sloops; none of any interest. *Aprāksin.*

There are no dry docks in this yard, which is a building, not a repairing one, though minor repairs can be undertaken. There is a very large pond under

[1] For details of the Peresvet see p. 326.

[2] See p. 270.

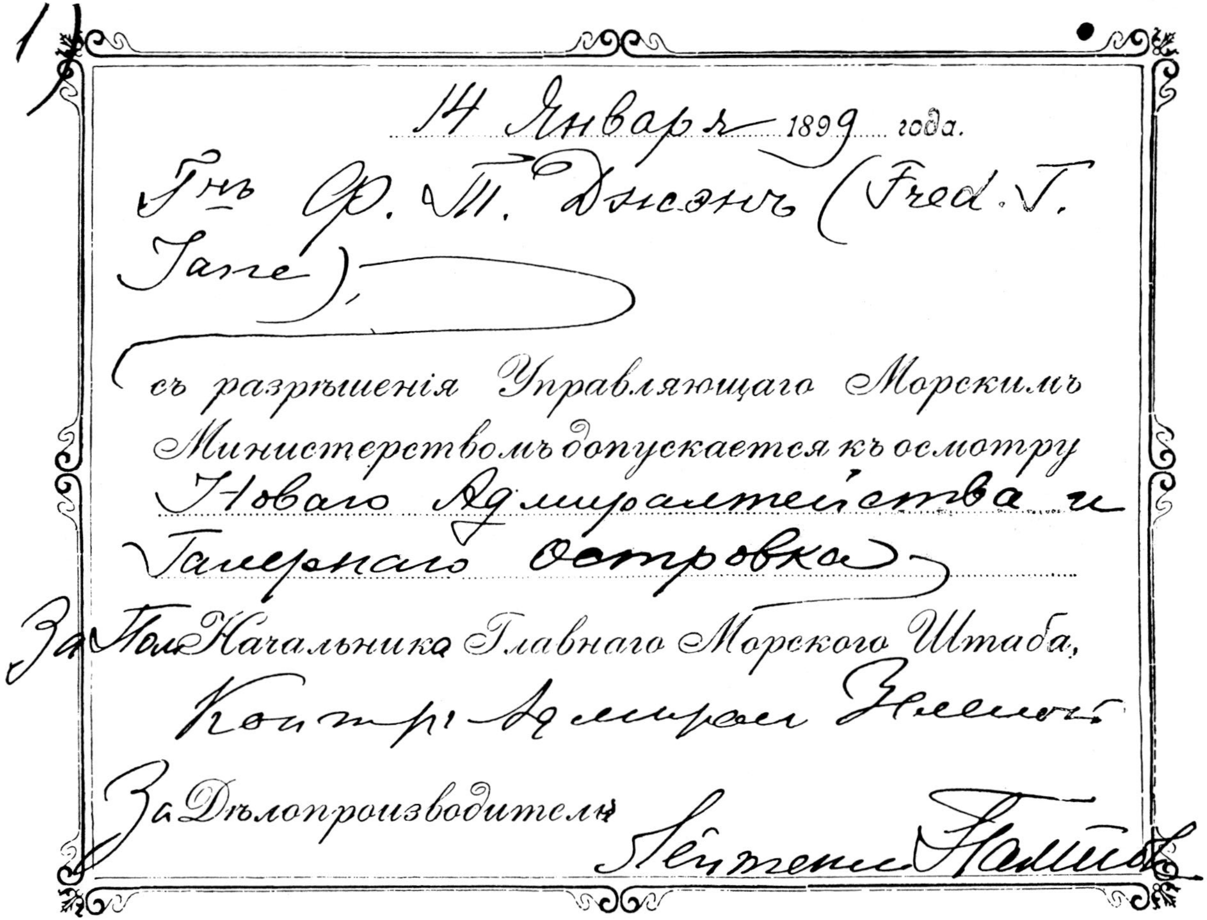
14 Января 1899 года.

Г-нъ Ф. Т. Джэнъ (Fred. T. Jane)

съ разрѣшенія Управляющаго Морскимъ Министерствомъ допускается къ осмотру Новаго Адмиралтейства и Галернаго островка

За Нач. Начальника Главнаго Морского Штаба,

Контръ-Адмиралъ [illegible]

За Дѣлопроизводителя

Лейтенантъ [illegible]

FACSIMILE OF PERMIT TO VIEW THE NEW ADMIRALTY AND GALERNII ISLAND DOCKYARDS.

cover, in which experiments with models are made, similar to those carried out in England at Haslar. A number of submerged tube experiments have recently been tried here, but generally speaking the basin is for experiments in connection with the under-water forms of hulls.

About 2,000,000 roubles have been spent in improving this dockyard during the last few years; the slips and several of the buildings are new erections.

Before concluding this brief sketch of the New Admiralty, reference may be made to one or two items of personal rather than technical interest. In the first place, every building shed in the Russian dockyards, and for that matter every shop also, has standing on the wall in one corner the *ikon* or sacred picture, before which candles are always burning, and on passing which one should uncover. A second item of interest is a barrel of snow usually to be found standing somewhere inside each slip—it probably serves as a rough-and-ready temperature gauge. A third is my permit card to view the New Admiralty Yard, a reproduction of which in facsimile is on the opposite page.

## 2. Galernii Island

From the New Admiralty Dockyard I went on to Galernii Island, which is situated down the Neva, below the New Admiralty and exactly opposite the Baltic Works. The yard occupies a fair amount of space, and gives the impression of being larger than the New Admiralty, though the portion actually occupied by slips and shops is, I believe, of less area.

Exactly to whom Galernii Island belongs I am in some doubt. It is generally spoken of as being a purely Government yard, but I derived an impression from those who showed me over that it was a private Franco-Russian Company, subsidised and under Government control. Possibly the private firm part of the business extends only to the workshops.

That one should visit and minutely inspect a dockyard without discovering whether it is a Government institution or belongs to a private firm, may strike the average reader as arguing considerable lack of something or other, but in self-defence I must point out that the difference in language always creates a difficulty in explanations; and further, that my cicerone here, as in all other cases,—save at the Baltic Works,—was an executive officer, to whom the matter as to who controlled the works would be of no particular

GALERNII ISLAND.

interest. They gave me a set of rivets of various sizes as a souvenir, and these were ticketed "A souvenir of the Franco-Russian Works," but it is just possible that I misunderstood.

At Galernii[1] Island work is entirely devoted to construction. The ships building on its slips in January 1899 were the cruisers Pallada, Diana, and Aurora, of which the first was by far the most advanced.

Diana class.

These three ships, which are sisters, are of 6630 tons displacement, 406 ft. long by 55 ft. broad, and 21 ft. mean draught. The armament consists of eight 45-calibre 6-in. quickfirers, twenty-two 12-pounders, and eight smaller guns.

These guns are grouped fore and aft, the amidships part of the vessel being devoted to the huge 12-pounder battery. This simplifies ammunition supply, which in these ships is as excellent as in the Rossia type it is the reverse. This is a point of very great importance, though it shows little on paper. The Palladas, though 1000 tons heavier, are about on a par with the British Eclipse class. About 350 tons of this is taken up by coal—900 tons against 550 normal, most of the rest of the excess goes to a perfected ammunition supply. It will be noted that there are three funnels close together, instead of wide apart, as in the Svetlana, on which these ships are supposed to be mainly modelled. Actually they represent an entirely novel

Armament.

[1] Since these papers were first written Galernii Yard has been burned. It was, however, soon repaired, and in 1903 in full swing again.

PALLADA.

*[Photo by favour of H.I.H. Grand Duke Alexander of Russia.*

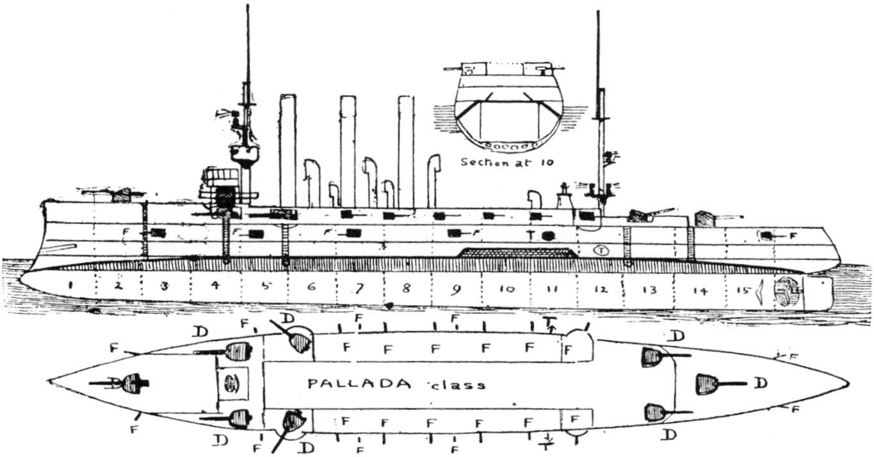

type, being, as they are, examples of the deliberate adoption of the 3-in. 12-pounder quickfirer in preference to the usual cruiser gun, the 4·7-in. 40-pounder.

Whether Russians are right or wrong in this very radical step is a difficult thing to give an opinion on. If worked out on the favourite "energy of fire" system, the Russian cruisers are rather behindhand, but then the question arises whether energy of fire has much to do with cruisers. Energy, the Russians would argue, implies penetration, which has little to do with cruiser fighting. The *shell*, not the shot, is the cruiser's projectile.

*The 3-in. quickfirer.*

In their view the 3-in. is the most accurate weapon and if its shells are small, size is made up for in numbers. Further, there is nothing like the small shell to find the joints in the enemy's armour; in other words, no porthole in a casemate is so small but that 12-pounder shells can enter, and are likely to, if only enough of them are fired.

It is a question that only war can decide. The Diana class, if armed on Elswick lines, would carry, let us say, nearly twenty 4·7-in. instead of twenty 3-in. —that is near the Takasago proportions. And in no paper way of looking at it can the 4·7-in. seem inferior to the 3-in. Actually, much depends on the ammunition supply: on a given displacement a great many more rounds can be carried for the 3-in. pieces. A point to be borne in mind also is that in Russia the naval officer has considerably more voice in the construction of warships than in any other country:

elsewhere the ship designer has it mostly his own way. The ship designer proceeds upon certain theories and upon certain lines of evolution; while the naval officer works from a different standpoint, and tactical questions and needs are the things he thinks of first. Probably, therefore, the Russians have what they consider best for the tactics they intend to adopt in action; and it is exceedingly doubtful whether paper comparisons of the energies of fire in the Diana and in foreign vessels of the same tonnage have any value. If the 12-pounders hit and the 40-pounders miss, then the little guns will have the best of the argument; if the larger pieces are equally accurate, then the smaller guns will be out of court. But this very obvious conclusion does not really help towards a solution of the *pros* and *cons*.

I went over the Pallada from upper deck to double bottom as she lay on the slip at Galernii Island. The electric light was installed everywhere, and a good many men were at work inside her. Considerable care was needed in moving about—the Russian workman has an undesirable fondness for leaving trap-doors open; so the whole ship was a series of pitfalls. But I believe accidents are rare.

The ship was in a very advanced state below, and generally had reached or passed the launching stage; the ice, however, rendered launching impossible till the spring. Many of the cabins were nearly complete

ON BOARD THE PALLADA—BUILDING.

in the matter of fittings, all these being of steel—steel bunks were being put up in some. The quarter-deck consists of metal plates, and it is doubtful whether there will be such a thing as wood anywhere in the ship—the Russians are determined to avoid any bother with fire in action.

It is not quite evident whether the casemates of the Pallada class will be armoured or not—whether, in fine, the ships will be big Eclipses or small Diadems. They have no belts, and the protective deck is not very thick—2½-in. Harvey on the slopes. Coal bunkers are situated immediately above and below the slopes of the protective deck for the greater part of its length. The usual tables describe them as unarmoured; but where Russian ships are concerned the usual tables do not go for much.

The French cruiser Guichen is probably the prototype of the Diana class—a type of swift cruiser carrying but few guns for her size, relying more on her "heels" than on her artillery, and chiefly intended for semi-piratical use in war.

"Commerce destroyers" is perhaps the most correct designation of these craft. They are intended to be of 16,000 horse-power. The estimated continuous sea speed is 19 knots; they will thus be as swift as anything of their type afloat. The Russians are growing very indifferent to measured mile trial speeds nowadays, all their efforts being concentrated upon securing a speed that can be maintained at sea. One step—an important one in this direction—is the new system of officering ships, particularly with the engineers. The captain, commander, gunnery lieutenant, and most of the engineer officers are already appointed to these new ships. They are daily with them as they grow, and will continue with them. The engineers, indeed, will be so far as possible kept to the ships always as though they were regiments. As a body, the Russian

THE FRENCH CRUISER GUICHEN.

*Russian engineer officers.*

naval engineers are not the most efficient in the world; the origin of the new system is a desire to improve their efficiency. It will certainly improve their opportunities—hitherto they have been shifted about from ship to ship a great deal.

The Pallada class have three screws — the Diana was having her sternpost bored when I visited her. The screws are three-bladed, and not particularly large. Steam is to be supplied by Belleville boilers; in the

Pallada these were being put in place. The Aurora was yet in an elementary stage. The Pallada is the prototype vessel, and the completion of the others will stand by till she has done her trials.

*Shops.*

From the ships I made a lengthy tour of the shops, but a detailed description of these is beyond my powers. It will be of interest, perhaps, however, if I mention that a good half of the machinery bore the names of English manufacturers. Leeds appeared to be the usual birthplace. Near each machine stood a duplicate of Russian manufacture, but none of these last were working.

*Russian dockyardsmen.*

Roughly comparing these shops with those in English dockyards, I derived an impression that they were rather more roomy and lofty than ours. Everybody about the place was Russian. So far as I could judge, the men knew their work thoroughly: everything was going on in a very orderly and matter-of-fact fashion in each of the shops. I mention this because there is, I believe, an impression that the reverse obtains.

RUSSIAN DOCKYARDSMAN.

*Wages.*

Wages of skilled mechanics in these shops are very high, as the demand for skilled workmen considerably exceeds the supply. I was given to understand that, taking into account the difference in cost of living and so on, these workmen earn nearly double what English workmen at the same trade earn. But then the Russian workman is a person of less extravagant tastes than his English "opposite number," and the Imperial Russian Government see that he is not loaded with trades-union sentiments. In the course of a year he probably puts in at least half as much work again as an English mechanic,—possibly twice as much. Those in our Royal dockyards certainly give the impression of having to work less hard than the Russian men.

RUSSIAN DOCKYARDSMAN.

There is a particularly fine drawing loft at Galernii Island; its dimensions I should roughly estimate at 500 ft. to 600 ft. long by nearly 90 ft. broad. It is about 25 ft. high inside.

### 3. The Baltic Works

The Baltic Works, exactly opposite Galernii Island, lie in rather an out-of-the-way part of St. Petersburg. As regards accessibility, they bear about the same relation to St. Petersburg as the Thames Ironworks do to London; and the district in which they are situated is also not so very unlike. They have been described as

OUTSIDE THE BALTIC WORKS.

the Elswick of Russia, but such a comparison is purely relative; of course, Russia has no Elswick. However, these works are the only ones in Russia that will bear comparison with big British private firms. Laird Brothers, of Birkenhead, is the British firm that they most nearly resemble in scope.

The Baltic Works have a strong appearance of being a private yard; there is an absence of the usual policeman's guard-house at the entrance. It is hardly a private firm in the matter of being run by private capital; it is heavily subsidised, I believe, and the Admiralty stands for the bulk of the shareholders.

Still, its work is not entirely confined to warship building. Steamers for mercantile purposes are constructed; and when warships are built or refitted, the work is a matter of contract.

The works are divided into two parts, the shipbuilding yard near the river, and the boiler and engine

INSIDE THE BALTIC WORKS.

factories across the road. Russia's adoption of the Belleville boilers is very evident at the Baltic Works; these boilers are stacked all over the place in the shipbuilding yards.

This yard contains the finest slip in Russia. It is 520 ft. long, housed in with the usual cathedral-like structure, the height and span of which in this case are not so very far behind St. Pancras Station in London.

It is an exceedingly fine building of red brick and ironwork; 700,000 roubles were spent on this. On this slip the Rurik was built. Her sister, the Rossia, followed. The Gromoboi, an improved Rossia, was under construction at the time of my visit, and in a very advanced state; but for the frozen river she might have been launched at Christmas, 1898.

Particulars of the Gromoboi[1] are :—

| | |
|---|---|
| Displacement . . . | 12,367 tons. |
| Length . . . . | 472½ ft. |
| Beam . . . . | 69 ft. |
| Draught (maximum) . | 29¾ ft. |
| Armament . . . | Four 8-in. Q.F. 45 cal. |
| | Sixteen 6-in. Q.F. 45 cal. |
| | Twenty 12-pdr. Q.F. |
| | Sixteen 3-pdr. Q.F. and eight 1 pdr. |
| | Two submerged tubes. |

As indicated by the plan, two of the 8-in. and twelve of the 6-in. are in casemates. The heavier guns are on the upper deck.

The belt is 6-ins. Harvey Nickel, over about two-thirds of the length amidships, reinforced by a 2-in. deck inclined to the lower armour shelf. A 4-in. belt protects the lower deck for some hundred feet amidships. There are 6-in. bulkheads fore and aft: the casemates are 5 (or possibly 6) inches. Conning tower 10 inches. The machinery consists of three sets

[1] There are two Russian words Gromovoi (Thunderer) and Gromoboi (a name). The ship is called after the latter.

of triple expansion made at the Baltic works. The boilers are thirty Belleville—the first, I was given to understand, constructed in Russia instead of imported.[1] The designed H.P. of 18,000 was intended to give 20 knots. The chief engineer who took me over her was anxiously awaiting the trials; there were wide differences of opinion as to whether home made Bellevilles would equal the imported article.[2] The

YENESI.

coal carried is 800 tons, with provision for 2500 tons, and liquid fuel also.

The Gromoboi is an unhandy ship, her tactical diameter being quite a thousand yards. She is not thought much of in the Russian Navy, on the grounds that her design was rather obsolete at the time of her completion.

On a slip adjacent to the Gromoboi, a battleship of the Peresvet[3] type, the Pobieda, was under construction. She was, however, barely commenced,

[1] There are now four factories in Russia constructing Belleville boilers (1904).

[2] I have since been informed that no trouble was experienced (1904).

[3] For particulars of this type see p. 324.

and was well under 1000 tons when I saw her. On a third slip a combined "catcher" and mining launch was being built. A sister to this vessel, the Amoor, lay frozen in at the jetty; she was launched in the autumn of 1898. She is not a vessel of any particular fighting value; her claim to interest lies only in the stern. Here, in a tremendous overhang, large ports have been devised, through which the mines will be dropped. The ship is about 200 ft. long.

In a large basin one of the imperial yachts lay dismantled for a refit. In a second basin, or series of basins, were a number of small craft—merchant steamers and such-like. Owing to the snow, it was difficult to make out much of these, or to tell where the basin began or ended. It was possibly a canal.

I did not notice any dry docks, and believe there are none in the St. Petersburg dockyards. Russian ships are launched in such an advanced state, that docking during subsequent construction is not so essentially necessary as in British Royal yards, and when docking is needed, the ships go to the Russian Portsmouth, Kronstadt.

At the Baltic Works all the engines for Russian warships, or nearly all, other than those contracted for by English firms, are made. All the engines of future ships, save for such vessels as may be built by contract abroad, will probably be made here in the future; for reasons that will be entered into later, the construction of engines by British firms for the Russian Government is all too probably a thing of the past. The balance of the machinery is made at the Ijora Works, but attention here is being bestowed chiefly upon the manufacture of armour plates and torpedo fittings. A few years ago Russia imported most of her armour, chiefly from Creusot, the balance from Carnegie in America; nowadays the greater part is made at home.

In closing this sketch of the Baltic Works — a sketch that would have been less "impressionistic" but for the particular severity of the weather on the day I went there—it may not be without interest to mention that the manager, or one of the managers, of these works is a Scotchman. I was given to understand, however, that he had been in Russia something like fifty years. Unfortunately I did not come across him, or learn his name. The fact is by way of being in support of the proverb about the ubiquity of Scotchmen; it has also some further interest in that several of the early founders of the Russian Navy were Scotchmen. Probably this particular Scotchman will be the last of the "connection" established some hundred odd years ago, by the famous Admiral Greig, or before that, again, by Saunders and Gordon.

PUTTING IN THE ENGINES OF THE AMOOR
AT THE BALTIC WORKS.

### 4. Smaller Yards

This concludes the list of yards in St. Petersburg itself, other than a small establishment up the river of no particular interest, where a few torpedo boats are built. This is a semi-private firm, and has a sort of "corresponding connection" with the celebrated British torpedo-boat firm of Yarrow at Poplar.

### 5. Kronstadt

Kronstadt was founded in the days of Peter the Great, and some of his buildings are still to be found there alongside modern shops. A few years since many of them were in a more or less tumbledown condition, but that is mostly all changed now—the hands of the repairer have been busy.

Kronstadt Dockyard is a fitting and repairing one. No ships are built here; the place is essentially a naval station. The Russian system is to decentralise—to specialise, as it were, with different yards; there is, for example, no equivalent to Portsmouth or Toulon to be found in Russia. The system has its weak points; it has, however, its strong points also, in the resulting simplicity.

*Area of yard.* The entire area of the dockyard is about one million square yards, but the whole of this space is not full. In the arctic conditions prevailing at the time of my visit it was not very easy to tell what was land and what was sea; the ubiquitous snowdrifts covered everything, and perhaps made the place look larger than it really is.

*Docks.* There are at Kronstadt four large dry docks—the Alexander, 584 ft. by 85 ft. by 29½ ft.; the Constantine, 490 ft. by 73 ft. by 29 ft.; the Nikolai and the Peter, somewhat smaller, but big enough to take most ships. The Alexander is a very capacious dock indeed, and at the time of my visit it contained the new battleship

Sevastôpol, the destroyer Sokol, and a torpedo gunboat of the Posadnik type. The Sokol, a Yarrow destroyer, *Sokol.* has already been described and illustrated. It suffices here, therefore, to mention that she is a 240-ton boat, and on trial with 4490 horse-power made 30·28 knots. She is 190 ft. long by 18½ ft. beam, carries 60 tons of coal, and is fitted, of course, with Yarrow boilers—eight of these. Those who saw this celebrated little ship in England would find difficulty in recognising her at Kronstadt, wooden sheds on her deck, icicles and snow-drifts over all; but, of course, this was only the winter coat. I noticed that she was painted a peculiar dirty brown-grey colour, a little lighter than that which the British Navy adopted for the earliest destroyers.

The Posadnik was "made in Germany," being an *Posadnik.* Elbing craft, launched in 1892. She is of 400 tons, the same length as the Sokol, but over 24 ft. beam. Her draught is 11 ft. The finer lines of the destroyer alongside made her look a rather clumsy craft. The Posadnik's armament is six 3-pounders, three 1-pounders, one torpedo tube in the bow, and one training tube abaft the funnel. There are two masts. The horse-power with forced draught is about 3500, and the trial speed about 22 knots. She has a couple of locomotive boilers, and carries 90 tons of coal.

I was told that on trial last summer the Russians got 30 knots out of the Sokol,[1] and they seemed exceedingly pleased with her altogether. Copies of the Sokol are being built; altogether twenty-eight are

[1] Sokol, p. 298.

either building or projected. As to the number in hand there is considerable doubt. Two were launched at St. Petersburg, at a torpedo yard up the Neva, last year, and two others were set afloat by a private firm at Abo. Of the remaining twenty-four, perhaps a dozen are at present in hand.[1] Messrs. Laird of Birkenhead have a destroyer in hand of the 30-knot type — the Som. Some of the twenty - four will probably be copies of this craft.

*Destroyers.*

*Russian submarine boats.*

There is some indecision in Russia at the present moment as to whether it is better to have destroyers or submarine boats. The Russians have a special type of submarine boat—semi-submarine would be a better word, as the boat is only intended to sink at the moment of attack. Fifty of these are projected, but nothing is likely to be done till the result of the Tsar's Rescript is ascertained.[2] So far as I could make out, this type of boat is a submarine ram as much as, or more than, a torpedo boat. It is larger than the French craft. However, since it is as yet unbuilt and untried, it is too early to discuss its *pros* and *cons*, and I am, perhaps, exceeding my limits by saying much about it. I may, however, mention that the Russians believe very much in underwater craft, and do not regard the submarine battleship as an idle dream.

To leave the battleship *in nubibus* for the battleship *de facto*. Kronstadt contained specimens of the latest. At the time of my visit the Peresvet, Sevastôpol, Poltāva, and Seniavin were all in dock or

[1] See a later section. [2] Written before the Hague Conference ended.

basin. The Peter Veliky, Nikolai I., Khrabri, Minin, Svietlana, Edinbouriski, Rȳnda, and a number of monitors and old craft were also about.

Dismantled Nahimoff.

After inspecting the Sevastôpol[1] I had a look at the Admiral Nahimoff in the next dry dock close by. This ship, an armoured cruiser of about 8500 tons, formerly carried eight 8-in. and ten 6-in. guns,—a truly mighty armament.[2] All these guns are gone now; and at the time of my visit she was stripped bare, even the gun-houses in which the barbette guns used to be carried being removed. She is to be rearmed, re-boilered, and generally modernised, and will probably not be about for some time to come—not for a year at least, possibly longer. The new armament will probably consist entirely of 6-in. quickfirers. The weak point of this ship is her feeble protection, identical in arrangement with that of the French Magenta type. There is an all-round compound belt, 10 in. thick at its maximum, but it is a very small strip. The barbettes, again, are merely strips.

Intelligence about Russian ships in English newspapers.

*Apropos* of this ship, a few days after seeing her in this dismantled condition I read in one of our principal evening newspapers, which has something of a reputation for its naval intelligence, that: "We learn from an unimpeachable source that . . . the Admiral Nachimoff, now in the Mediterranean, will shortly go to Russia to refit, and thence to the Far East."

[1] For a detailed description of this class see p. 315.

[2] For a detailed description see p. 208.

It is an interesting instance of how loosely statements as to the Russian Navy are made.

Beyond the two dry docks mentioned above is a very large basin of irregular shape. Its exact form I could not make out, the snowdrifts blotted out all configuration. In the same way it was not possible to tell how much of what looked like a long, rather narrow basin was basin, and how much "stream" with a jetty projecting into it—absolutely nothing, save a few elevated narrow pathways, and a glimpse of wall here and there, told what was "water" and what was land. In

*Basins.*

these basins lay the [1] Peter Veliky, Minine, Nikolai, Rȳnda, a number of old turret-ships, and the modern ironclads Peresvēet, Seniavin, and Poltāva.

*Reconstructed Peter Veliky.*

The Peter Veliky is destined to be reconstructed, Harvey or Krupp process turrets replacing the present one, and modern 10-in. guns in place of the old 12-in.

*Nikolai I.*

The Nikolai I. is perhaps the best-known ship in the Russian Navy. The only thing that particularly struck me about her was, how very unlike she is to most of the photographs of her that one encounters; the masts looked much loftier than photographs render them, and the ship altogether less clumsy.

The old Minine is, and has for a long time been, under reconstruction, but progress on her was at a standstill. She will eventually be brought forward as a seagoing training-ship; at present she is merely a

[1] For detailed descriptions see Peter Veliky, p. 168; Minine, p. 204; Nikolai, p. 230; Rȳnda, p. 216; Seniavin, p. 270; Peresvēet, p. 324; Poltāva, p. 315.

KRONSTADT DOCKYARD—SHIPS WINTERING IN THE BASIN.

hulk, with only the fore and main lower masts standing, the mizzen being altogether removed.

The Rȳnda is an old vessel of very small fighting value. She was nearly as much dismantled as the Minine.

*The Svietlana in the ice.*

The Svietlana next claimed attention. She was lying well out in a large basin, but boards were laid to her over the snow that covered the frozen water, so that with a little cautiousness she was easy enough to get at. Some care was indeed needed, as the snow was pretty deep, and the boards, of course, slippery.

Alongside the ship a large square hole was cut in the ice. From this hole water for washing purposes was drawn. So far as the ship being ice-bound was concerned, this hole had no significance; the pressure of the ice has apparently no inconvenient effect upon the hulls. I did not anywhere notice any of those elaborate precautions which being frozen in is popularly supposed to necessitate. The hole in the ice had one other use—the Russian sailors used it for bathing! The Russian bluejacket is a hardy fellow, and a few degrees of frost add zest to his ablutions. He does not, perhaps, wash very often,—"He ain't clean enough for it to be nice to get alongside and chum with him," is the British bluejacket's reason for the absence of that *entente cordiale* between Jack and Ivan that exists between his officers and Russian officers,—but when Ivan does wash, twenty or thirty degrees of frost will not stop his enjoying a swim. When they make a hole in the Neva, and bless the water in front of the

*Ablutions of Russian sailors.*

Tsar and the Court in the New Year festivities at St. Petersburg, plenty of moujiks jump in and seek salvation and cleanliness in the sacred waters. A Japanese naval officer once gave me his first impression of Russian sailors as he had seen them in some northern Japanese harbour, and the thing that most impressed him was Russian sailors bathing in an ice-covered sea.

*Winter quarters.*

As a rule, Russian ships are almost, if not quite, deserted for the winter, but the Svietlana[1] was hibernating with most of her officers and men on board. To the smart cruiser that was to be seen at Havre some while ago she bore very little resemblance. The whole of the deck amidships was roofed in with wood, much as the decks of our hulks used as depôts are roofed in. Little wooden sheds were built over the fore and aft guns, around the chart-house, and over the search-lights on the masts. But for her three funnels and enormous ram she would have stood very well for a frozen-in whaler as we see them in picture-books.

The Seniavin[2] was built-in in much the same fashion. She and the Poltāva[3] have been already so fully described that nothing remains to be said about them here. The Peresvet,[4] too, admits of little but a passing reference. Men were at work on board her, and save for her masts (a couple of temporary poles) she looked fairly complete. She was being pushed forward to

[1] For a detailed description of this vessel see p. 294.

[2] Fully described on p. 270. [3] See p. 315. [4] See p. 324.

relieve some vessel upon the Pacific station—the Rurik probably.

*The Peresvet all made in Russia.*

In the description of the Peresvet some reference should have been made to her construction. The Russians are exceedingly proud of the fact that "everything, down to the smallest rivet, was made in Russia." Whether or no *matériel* has suffered for the benefit of patriotism time alone can show; since the loss of the Gangut an impression has been abroad that home-made construction in Russia is necessarily very bad. The Gangut,[1] it may be remembered, was lost in 1897, and her loss, rightly or wrongly, was attributed to bad construction. Officially, I believe, she was said to have struck a rock in a part of sea where no rocks exist—so at least the story goes. Bad Russian ship construction is no new thing. A hundred years ago Orloff's fleet, going to the Mediterranean, had to put in at Portsmouth for repairs, some of the vessels only keeping together by cables. The cause then was that the ships were built of fir, sometimes green,—a material very cheap in Russia, and very badly suited for ship construction. Some of this reputation has stuck to the Russians ever since.

*Alleged faulty construction of Russian ships.*

On the whole, facts—so far as I can judge—do not seem to point to any general bad construction of hulls in the Russian fleet, the Peter Veliky, which had to undergo something very like a reconstruction at Glasgow, and the Rossia, which split her decks up

[1] See p. 240.

from the strain of firing her enormous armament, being the only two specific instances that can be cited. Stories were afloat once about the Nahimoff, but it subsequently turned out that the origin of these tales lay in the ship having gone on trials before her forecastle was built in. The Ekaterina II.,[1] in the Black Sea Fleet, was muddled over to a certain extent, as her armour has no backing, but that was due to a clerical error. Every navy has a few black-sheep ships; even our own is not exempt. The Penelope, Rupert, Neptune, Ajax, and, to some extent, Nile and Trafalgar, are ships which for one cause and another — "tinkering" sometimes — may be said to have a black mark against them. The Texas in the United States Navy, the Brennus and Magenta in the French, the Oldenburg in the German, the K. E. Stephanie in the Austro-Hungarian Fleet, are merely a few of the better-known instances of ships that have not fulfilled expectations. At the worst the Russian Navy does no more than come near the top of the list; at the best it is not at the bottom. But here one trenches on the unwritten and secret history of modern warships. Even in batches of new ships there is, for one reason or another, usually a "bad egg," and to conceal the fact is naturally a thing to which energies are directed. Even in England there are instances in which this is successfully done. We may take it as a sure thing that it is done to as great—probably much greater—an extent in foreign navies.

*Defective ships common to all navies.*

[1] See p. 224.

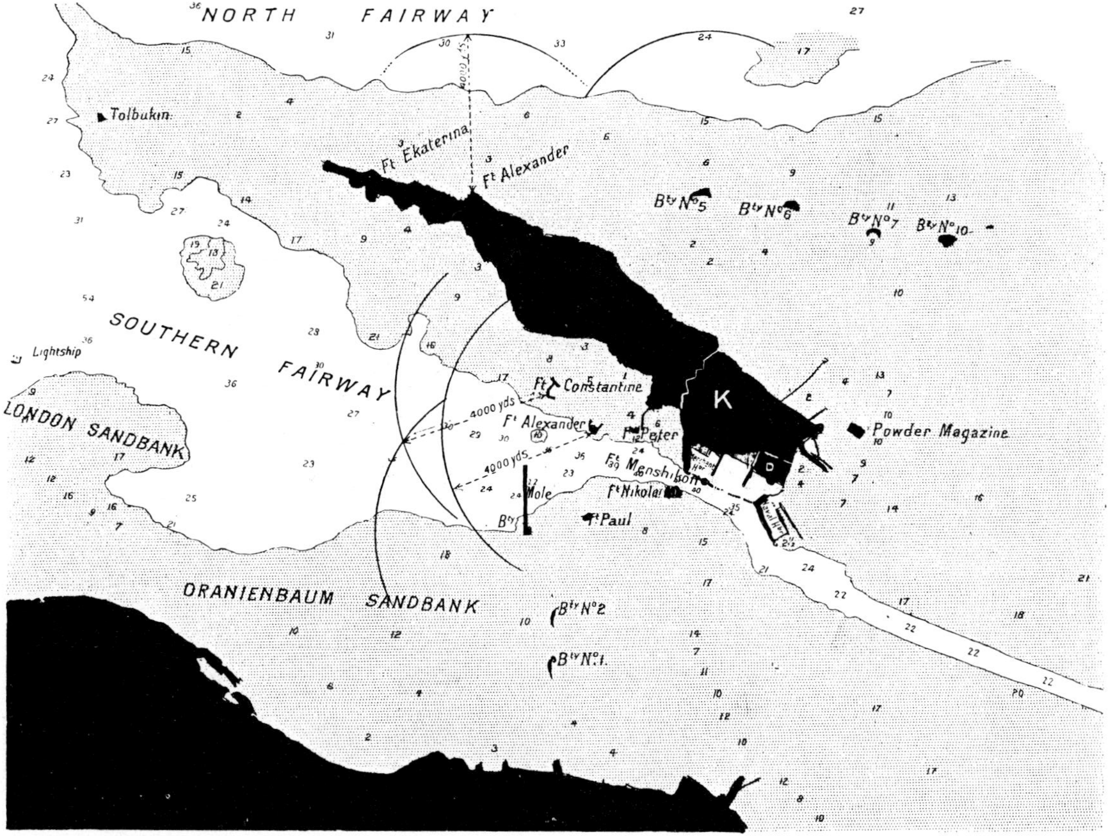


APPROACHES TO KRONSTADT.

To resume the description of Kronstadt. The next ship I directed attention to was the Khrabry, but since she was cut off by snowdrifts, and also housed in with wood, I failed to derive any very clear impression of her details, beyond discerning that she bore a very small relation to the usual description of her. *Khrabry.*

IN THE ENGINE-ROOM OF THE SEVASTÔPOL.

This concluded my tour of Kronstadt Dockyard, so far as ships were concerned. Such of the workshops as I saw were of enormous size, particularly that in which all the hammocks, etc., for the fleet are made. These are—so I gathered—entirely, or almost entirely, made by hand labour. For this several hundred women and girls are employed, and there were two tremendous long rows of them sitting opposite each *Workshops.*

other on forms, laughing and chattering as they worked.

Another item I noticed in the lower part of this building was a row of bow scroll-works for men-of-war. Some of these belong to old vessels now broken up, and hang there waiting for new ships of the same name to bear them. There may be more in this than a mere sentimental idea; at least, if the idea of teaching crews the history of a ship's name has any value, this treating the figurehead or its modern equivalent in the light of a regimental colour should be distinctly useful. In the British Navy we have had for some years a custom of painting up in a battleship the names of actions in which earlier vessels bearing that name have taken part; the idea of preserving and passing on the figurehead is distinctly a Russian novelty. We could hardly copy it, as not only are our new vessels devoid of figureheads, but they are disappearing from the older ships. The Rodney once had a real figurehead, but it is now gone, and when the Royal Sovereign—one of the last ships to have a bow scroll—got her gilt scroll-work knocked off, it was not replaced. The figurehead has never—*pace* the stories, yarns, and anecdotes written in the period when figureheads had a reign—been much of a British institution. Fashion brought it in now and again in the old days, but it was several times ordered to be discontinued.

*Figureheads.*

A feature of nearly all the buildings in Kronstadt Dockyard is the stone spiral staircase—architecturally

*Relics of Peter the Great.*

known as a newel — by which the upper stories are reached. These staircases are relics of Peter the Great's first buildings.

*Accessibility of Kronstadt.*

Kronstadt Dockyard is popularly supposed to be about as accessible to the world at large as Thibet. I doubt whether it is really so strictly preserved as that. True, it is not open to the ordinary casual tourist, but then Kronstadt is not a place that the tourist would seek. It is situated on an island well out in the gulf, to be reached only by steamer in the summer, in the winter by a four or five mile sledge-drive over the frozen sea from Oranienbaum. "Diligences" also labour over this ice road, but there are a variety of reasons for preferring an open sledge.

The thermometer in the winter may stand anywhere between freezing-point and thirty degrees of frost — degrees Centigrade, I believe; and there is always a wind over the gulf which creates a blizzard with the dust of frozen snow. None the less, there is a good deal of traffic to the place every morning, and the people, only a fraction of whom are naval or military, come into and go from the town as easily as even they might come or go into Portsmouth or Devonport.

*Outside the dockyard.*

The yard is enclosed by a low wall—in places a mere palisade—in which are frequent doors guarded by police, who apparently have orders to detach a man to follow whoever enters. My cicerone here as elsewhere was a naval lieutenant, but when we went into the yard a policeman plodded silently along in the snow behind us. All this serves to give the place an air of mystery, but I still think it is much of it more apparent than real. None the less, I must confess, —such are the ideas of Russia that we imbibe almost with our mother's milk and cultivate afterwards with courses of sensational literature,—I must confess that I could not view that plodding policeman with equanimity. The most ridiculous tales of unfortunate Englishmen suddenly seized and transported to quicksilver mines in Siberia suddenly came into my head, and assumed a most painful realism and probability, especially when I was led into an absolutely empty and deserted corner of the dockyard between some snowdrifts.

*Adventure with a policeman in Kronstadt Dockyard.*

I learnt in due course that we had gone into this *cul-de-sac* because from thence a view of the Sevastôpol and Poltāva more or less in line with each other could be seen; while the stolid stare and twitching hand of the policeman, I gleaned, meant nothing worse than that a rouble for his trouble would be cheerfully accepted and expended in liquid good wishes to the Ingliski. Verily our Russian literature has a good deal to answer for!

However, this sort of thing is neither history nor a description of Kronstadt Dockyard.

The dockyard, as already stated, lies very low, and a fair amount of it can be seen from the roads and streets outside, or, at anyrate, could be seen pretty well with a glass. Possibly, seeing that to use a camera or sketch in the streets of even St. Petersburg without permission renders a man liable to be "run in," to attempt to view Kronstadt from the outside might lead to unpleasant enough consequences ; still, some sort of viewing could be done.

The Elswick ice-breaker Ermak will make a vast difference to Kronstadt in future winters, as she will keep the channel and fairway open all the year round. At the time of my visit she had not arrived, but she was almost daily expected, and the interest aroused was very keen indeed—her importance was beyond that of a first-class battleship. *The Ermak.*

From the dockyard I went across to the gunnery school, a species of "Whale Island" standing behind the dockyard. The way to it lies alongside an enormous excavation, empty then, into which all the water in the docks and basins can be turned. It is possibly connected with some system of drainage for the low-lying and marshy land upon which the dockyard is built. Its dimensions I could not very well gauge, as from the pathway the bottom was not properly visible. One side was a perpendicular wall, that looked about 100 feet deep ; the side opposite to that upon which I stood rose in a series of steps, as though excavations would be continued in the summer. My first impression of this sort of embryo replica of a Martian canal was that it was a sandpit or quarry of some kind, but this I heard was incorrect. I gathered that it is regarded as somewhat of an engineering feat, and that its making demanded the overcoming of a good many initial difficulties.

*Description of Kronstadt gunnery school.*

The gunnery school dates more or less from Peter the Great's day. In architecture it is rather after the style of an old cathedral cloister; and the modern guns peeping between the ancient arches in a kind of crypt, the glass doors and pitch-pine partitions under a vaulted stone roof, give a most incongruous and quaint *tout ensemble.*

*Museum.*

The class-rooms and artillery museum are upstairs, reached by the usual old-time spiral steps. The museum is very complete; it contains every type of small quickfirer, the breech-pieces and mechanism of a variety of Canet and Krupp 6-in. guns, revolvers and rifles from the earliest times, chronologically arranged. One case contains rifle bullets, and includes the celebrated Dum-Dum. All the well-known bullets for various rifles are here, as well as a number of others placed by themselves, which I could not name. Some of these were of eccentric shape, probably experimental and theoretically-invented bullets. This museum contains a specimen of the earliest explosive bullet, invented back in the days of smooth-bore muzzle-loaders. Russia bought up the secret of this bullet, and then put it in a museum, making no use of it, except possibly towards the close of the Crimean War.

Round about this room shell are standing, from 12-in. downwards. Mostly these were common shell of the usual pattern, with flat noses for the fuse to be screwed in. There were a few armour-piercing shot,—now abolished in the Russian service,—or they may have been A.P. shell with base fuses. I did not have shown me any of the famous "magnetic" shell or the capped projectile, but these are now served out for all big guns, and have the same penetration as A.P. shot. As noted above, the A.P. shot is abolished. The H.E. shell is not yet in the Russian service.

*The "magnetic" shell.*

The "magnetic" shell,[1] so far as I can gather, was there, and is apparently a short conical shell with another cone fitting on top of it. At least, I saw projectiles which, so far as my limited knowledge of gunnery would carry me, looked to be designed for some such use. In whatever form employed, the shell has no particular advantage over the solid shot, as the shot against thick armour will do all the damage needful in such places, and there is always the risk of the shell breaking up, no matter what its head. In theory,

[1] So called because the Russians set afloat some tale about the cap being fitted to the shell by magnetic attraction.

perhaps, the "magnetic" shell is intended to penetrate armour partially only, and then to shatter by bursting, but that sort of thing is apt to remain theory.

*Class-rooms.* The class-rooms consist of gunnery lecture-rooms, in one of which officers, and in another men, were attending lectures; two rooms for electrical plant and instructions, a large and well-fitted laboratory, a room apparently devoted to hydraulic gear, a room with miscellaneous fittings, and a sort of large central hall. This hall, which looked as architecturally interesting as the Tower of London, has its deep recesses filled with photographs and other details of various Russian battleships. At one end there is a large working turret, armour and all. In place of the guns, however, a couple of tube cannon are fitted, and on the turret roof a Barr and Stroud range-finder.

At the other end of the hall is a very large painted background of sea and sky, with some movable dummy ships. In this arrangement there is, of course, nothing novel so far as the target is concerned. Where the novelty comes in, is in the carefully-painted target producing as nearly as possible the actual sea colours,—a by no means unimportant thing when we remember that the usual Morris tube target is black against white or *vice versâ*,—and the elaborate revolving turret by means of which the guns have to be re-laid each time, more or less as they would have to be re-laid in actual practice.

*Naval war game.* There is also a war game room, but as Kriegspiel belongs rather to strategy and tactics, its chief home is at the Naval Academy at St. Petersburg, or else at the Xenia Palace on the Möika Canal. A subsequent section deals with Naval War Games as played in the Russian Navy. At Kronstadt it is not a compulsory subject.

From the gunnery school, I went on to the drill hall, some account of which, in view of the fact that Russian sailors have—to use an Irishism—to put in more than half their sea-time ashore, may not be out of place.

The hall is a very large tunnel-shaped building, *Drill Hall.* from 80 to 100 ft. wide, and quite 600 ft. long. Possibly the length is greater than that. At either end, this tunnel is continued beyond partitions—a chapel at one end; at the other, behind a theatre stage, a species of gymnasium. The hall is normally some 60 ft. high, but at the gymnasium end the height is considerably increased, and the mainmast of a large ship set up in it. Nets are plentifully spread around, and on this mast the Russian sailor makes his first acquaintance with his profession. Tumbles are frequent, but the nets usually prevent any serious accident. We have this sort of thing of course at Greenwich, and afloat in all our training-ships; but in Russia, owing to climatic conditions, the early mast drills have to be done under cover for a good deal of the year.

After watching the drill for a while, I was taken on to the Kronstadt Naval Club—a place hardly *Naval Club.* sufficiently explained by its name. Like everything of the nature of a public building in Russia, it is architecturally very fine. It is fitted with a theatre, museum, drawing-rooms, a large dining-hall, billiard, and the usual other sorts of rooms one finds in a club; practically it is the "officers' quarters," and nearly all unmarried officers stationed at Kronstadt live here. It is, so far as ornaments are concerned, almost entirely furnished with gifts from the French nation on the occasion of the Toulon affair, when the Franco-Russian alliance was cemented. One way and another these gifts to the Russian Navy from different French towns must be worth over half a million pounds; there are numbers of huge solid silver figures of exquisite workmanship, a few of solid gold, while silk flags, jewelled ornaments, and valuable china-ware are too numerous to be reckoned. There are rooms and rooms of them.

*French gifts.*

The museum is small, and of no special interest. What there is of it is chiefly geological, the balance mostly stuffed birds. There is, however, an interesting collection of harpooning instruments, chronologically arranged; and there are a few models of ships of very early type. This place, however, is in no way on a par with the museum of our United Service Institution, which the Navy Club resembles much more than it does an ordinary club.

*Historical naval pictures.*

A word might be said of the pictures. There is no gallery, but the walls generally are hung with large paintings that form a very complete history of the Russian Navy from the time of Peter the Great onward;

and a high level of technical accuracy being maintained, these are useful as well as ornamental. The finest of these is one of the French fleet at Kronstadt—a masterpiece of bold artistic treatment. Another favourite wall-ornament is weapons. These, lethal and firearms, are arranged chronologically in devices on the walls of the vestibule and staircase.

Did space permit, one could spin out a good deal about the Naval Club at Kronstadt; but perhaps enough has been said.

With regard to the town itself, the streets are extremely wide, but most of the buildings are of wood. A few buildings, like the Navy Staff, are of stone. At the Navy Staff, the hall is hung with half-sectional models of all early Russian ships, but there being nothing of much later date than the Peter Veliky one's interest in these was naturally curtailed.

*The town.*

*Navy Staff.*

Of the famous Kronstadt forts I saw nothing at all; no signs of them were visible anywhere,—probably the snow concealed them; the appended sketch map indicates their positions, and shows pretty clearly that the place is as impregnable as can well be; while the outlying Fort Constantine practically precludes anything in the way of a long-range bombardment. No great study of this map is required to show why Admiral Napier did not attack the place in the Crimean War; nothing save specially constructed monitors would have a chance against it.

*Forts.*

Kronstadt being a commercial port as well as a naval arsenal, there is an English colony there, and this, combined with the floating population of the merchant ships, leads to an English chaplain being permanently stationed at the place. In connection with the English in Russia, it may be of some interest to mention that at Kronstadt I found two Russian officers with English wives, a third whose mother was an Englishwoman, while a daughter of the Admiral commanding is married to a British naval officer; but there no longer remain any English serving as officers in the Russian Navy as in the old days. Half the Russian officers connected with the early days of Kronstadt were, of course, Englishmen; and the Russians do not forget what nation it was that taught them to be sailors. There is at present, as I have already observed, a great craze for everything about Russian ships to be made in Russia; but, as we know, a good many Russian vessels are just now being built or ordered in France, Germany, and the United States. Yet it is only owing to the recent engineering strike that most of these ships are not building in England. Whether owing to this country's help in the early days when the Russian Navy was growing, or whether as the result of experience, Russians have a heavy preference for English over other foreign ship material. Their description of the British workman, however, is "A person who always refuses to work when his employer has undertaken to deliver a job in a certain time!"

*English folk at Kronstadt.*

*A Russian definition of the British workman.*

A bit sweeping and severe, maybe, yet perhaps not altogether without some grains of truth. There is not the slightest shadow of doubt but that the British mechanic has only himself to thank in that he is not working on the Tsarvitch, Bayan, Waryag, Retvisan, and the rest; the Russian officials would sooner far have had these ships built in England than at La Seyne and Cramp's. No question of cost entered: the Russian has not yet learnt to appreciate the cheap and nasty; indeed, so particular are the Russians in the contract specifications, that it is the invariable rule everywhere to charge them more than any other nation.

*Why none of the new Russian battle-ships and cruisers were ordered in England.*

The theory that an anti-British feeling had anything to do with next to no work being sent to British firms is absolutely without foundation. This is not a mere expression of opinion on my part, but a statement resting on the first authority.

## 6. Revel

Revel is an old naval base of no present importance beyond the fact that it is a torpedo boat station, and that there is a dock building there for these craft.

A couple of docks to take large warships are projected, but these are not likely to be in existence for some time to come.

There is no dockyard here for the construction of warships.

## 7. Libau (Port Alexander III.)

Libau has the particular recommendation that it is ice free, or at anyrate that ships do not get frozen in there as at Kronstadt. As yet it is in an incomplete stage, though sufficiently advanced to admit of the Petropavlovsk and Admiral Oushakoff having spent the winter 1898–99 in its basins. These two were perhaps the only modern battleships of the Baltic Fleet in a condition to commission that winter; though the Poltāva and Seniavin could have been added at fairly short notice.

*Reasons for founding Libau.*

The idea of Libau was to have a port from which ships could be sent at any time to the Pacific or Mediterranean. Now that, thanks to the Ermak, Kronstadt is no longer to be considered an ice-bound port, the wisdom of founding Port Alexander III., as Libau naval arsenal is named, is at least open to question.

Before entering into this question, however, some short description of the place is called for. To begin with, it is situated about 450 miles by sea from Kronstadt, over 300 from Revel; but only 50 odd miles from the German town of Memel, where a naval base is projected. Dantzig, the nearest German naval arsenal, is about 100 miles distant from Memel. About half-way between Memel and Dantzig lies the strong German military base of Konigsberg. The

*Its strategical weakness.*

appended sketch map of the coast and railways indicates the strategical weakness of Libau—it is very nearly an isolated outpost. In the event of war, there is little doubt but that the Germans would operate against it; and in the event of a winter war before the days of ice-breakers, they stood to blockade it without risk of interruption from the sea. Speaking generally, the Russian system of defence was always to leave a vast expanse of wilderness between her borders and

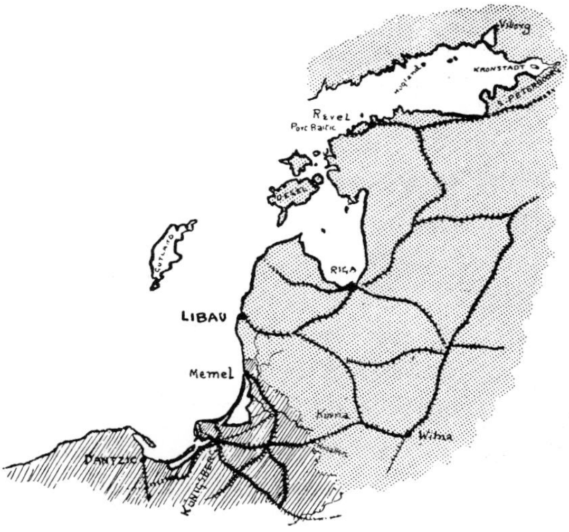


her principal points; in making an arsenal at Libau she has given hostage to fortune to that extent, and the advanced base of Port Alexander III. may yet become another Sevastôpol, the defence of which—successful or unsuccessful—must entail a heavy drain on resources. Port Alexander III. is, or rather will be, a second Biserta. Like the famous French Mediterranean base, it is practically an inland naval arsenal connected with the sea by a canal. Inside a place of this sort ships have practically absolute immunity from capture or damage; but, on the other hand, a vigorous enemy is almost certain to find means to block the canal, in which case for all the good they are the ships might as well have been sunk. The Russians, however, pin great faith on "hiding-places," and a sort of Libau is projected in the Black Sea. Such places may be useful, but their utility is passive, and command of the sea will never be gained by aid of them.

The port is divided into three divisions: (1) the outer harbour, a protected anchorage; (2) a commercial port; (3) the naval port, nearly a mile and a half (about 2200 yds.) inland.

*Description of Libau.*

The outer harbour is now in an advanced state; the commercial harbour has not yet reached any great importance, and is unlikely to vie with Riga for some time to come. Jetties and breakwaters have been constructed to protect the roadstead, and make a harbour of one and a half square miles.

*Naval harbour.*

From the harbour runs a canal about eleven cables (2200 yds.) in length. At the inner head of this is a large basin 800 yds. long by about 240 yds. wide —just beyond and inshore of the town. All round this, storehouses, workshops, and naval barracks are built or building. Into this basin another nearly as large opens. This is the repairing basin, and two dry docks about 600 ft. long open into it. One of these docks is complete, the other is as yet in a rather elementary stage.

All this work on docks and buildings was begun in 1895, and then expected to be completed in 1900; but everything is not likely to be finished much before 1905. In January this year about one and a quarter million pounds had been spent upon Libau—equal, say, to an expenditure of two millions or more in this country. *Cost of Libau.*

## ASIATIC DOCKYARDS

### 8. Vladivostok

The importance of Vladivostok is chiefly of a political nature; as a dockyard or arsenal it is purely a second-class place,[1] on a par more or less with the British station at Jamaica. Much is written about the strength of its fortifications, and a great importance given to it accordingly; but this is usually either for political purposes or else by people who have an idea that the more guns the greater the importance of a station. Actually, of course, there is hardly a naval station in the world that could be reduced by a fleet:[2] consequently to pile on fortifications is mostly a waste of energy. On the other hand, almost any port can be blocked by a determined foe,[3] and a thousand forts will not prevent the eventual capture of a place if the enemy can invest it by land and sea, and prevent supplies and succour reaching it. The defence and attack of naval bases is, in fine, a military rather than a naval question.

From the military standpoint Vladivostok is very nearly impregnable, so far as any foe likely to attack it is concerned. Japan is the only nation in a position

[1] Second-class fortress is its official designation.

[2] The impotence of the American squadron off an exceedingly weakly fortified place like Santiago, is a case in point. It would seem that almost anything in the way of forts, combined with a mine-field, will protect a harbour completely

[3] See Libau, p. 390.

to seriously menace it, and it is unlikely that in the event of war she would attempt it. Vladivostok has so large a garrison, that to duly invest it would need at least 150,000 men.

Much has been said about the Trans-Siberian railway and Vladivostok, but the value of this will scarcely be so great as is made out. It will save Russia having to keep so large a force in the district

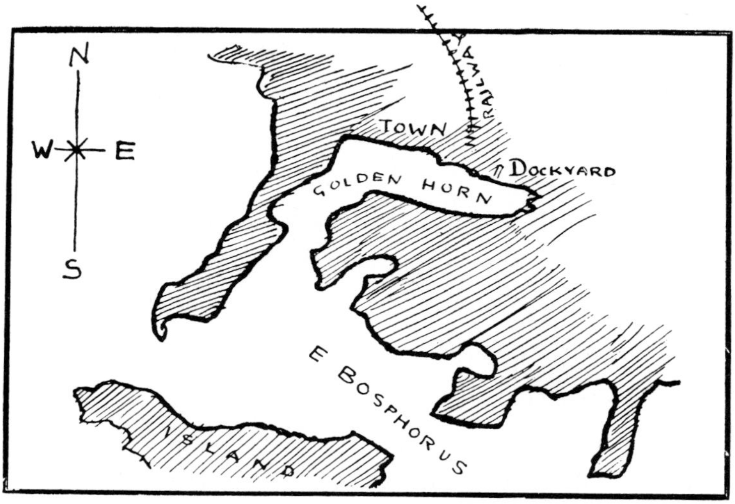


MAP OF VLADIVOSTOK.

(70,000) as she does; but the theory that offence will be much helped is questionable. Russian strategy is not to be in a hurry. In any war upon that coast she is absolutely in a position to take her time; hence the value of ability to move men thither more quickly is heavily discounted. On the other hand, the railway will be of inestimable service in bringing up naval stores and torpedo boats. These last are likely to be needed at Vladivostok in case of war, because, like

Wei-hai-wei, the place is very open to a long-range bombardment. At night, ships (unless kept off by a strong torpedo boat menace) could without much risk steam in and pitch shells over the hills, which would be bound eventually to destroy the dockyard. England or Japan (both stronger than Russia at sea) would undoubtedly do this in case of war,[1] unless the torpedo force were strong enough to make the attempt too absolutely risky. And torpedo boats have very little lasting power; they are bound to be gradually destroyed.

Vladivostok Dockyard is situated at the extreme end of the Golden Horn. It does not contain any slips, and is practically in scope a small Kronstadt, or rather will be.

*Docks.*

There is one dry dock, 550 ft. long, 90 ft. wide, and 30 ft. deep. This dock will take any vessel in the Russian Navy. There is also a small floating dock about 300 ft. long, able at a pinch to take ships like the Vladimir Monomakh, but used chiefly for the armoured gunboats.

*Basins.*

There are two basins of no very great size, and a few repairing shops. The Russian

[1] At Wei-hai-wei the Japanese did the same thing to the Chinese fleet. The damage done to the ships by this wild firing over Leu-kun-tau was infinitesimal; but it absolutely broke the Chinese defence. Its moral effect was enormous. It was this that paved the way for the torpedo attack, and it did as much as the torpedo in the way of effect upon Chinese nerves. Anticipation of these shells destroyed all rest, and when the surrender took place the Chinese had had no sleep worth mentioning for four days. The officer who brought the letter of surrender fell asleep in the wardroom of the Japanese flagship the instant he sat down to await entering the admiral's presence; and the officers of the fleet stated that he attributed all the worst miseries to these aimless shells.

ideal is to make the Yard entirely self-supporting, but so far it is only able to undertake minor repairs. The water alongside the jetties is not very deep,[1] and a good deal of dredging will yet be required before the Yard can be considered of great value. Now that Port Arthur is Russian, Vladivostok is more or less doomed; at Port Arthur none of this depth-of-water difficulty exists. *Jetties.*

However, the fact of the Russians having openly stated that Vladivostok was an unsatisfactory place is always accepted by us as evidence to the contrary, so it is useless to say much about the matter.

An impression prevails that Vladivostok is frozen up the greater part of the year. This is quite inaccurate; small and by no means powerful ice-breakers keep a channel fully open all the year round, and, in addition, it is rare for the entire anchorage to be long frozen thickly. The depth of water—not its tendency to freeze—was the aquatic objection to Vladivostok. *Not ice-bound.*

The anchorage is extremely good in the Eastern Bosphorus, being very well protected, fairly deep, and practically untroubled by tide[2] or current.

Vladivostok is a commercial as well as a naval port, but its commerce is not very great;[3] the Russians have done little as yet towards developing the trade of the district. Stories about the choking of trade and excessively stringent regulations are chiefly moon-

[1] Only about 4 fathoms (24 ft.).

[2] The rise and fall is usually little more than a foot.

[3] About 400 vessels used the port in 1898.

shine: the regulations are identical with those in any other Russian harbour. The idea seems to have been promulgated chiefly through some innocent writers discovering that only two foreign warships are allowed to enter it at one time. Similar regulations exist for nearly every naval arsenal in the world.[1] The curious thing is, that fifteen years ago the Russians had no such regulation at all at Vladivostok, and in 1886 Admiral Sir Richard Vesey Hamilton, being off the place with the British China Station fleet, took it into his head to pay a call. There was a thick sea fog on at the time, and the first the Russians knew about it was the British fleet saluting inside their harbour. They were considerably impressed by the incident,[2] as they would never have credited the possibility of such a thing without ocular demonstration, and they did not altogether like it. When at some later date they framed regulations about the entry of the harbour by foreign warships, Admiral Hamilton was popularly supposed to be the "first cause"; but there is an absence of any very direct evidence to prove this.

The town of Vladivostok is a fine one, with a population of about 30,000 in the town itself. The railway, the first sod of which was cut by the late Tsarvitch, runs nearly 500 miles northward to Khabarovka on the Amoor River; but the new line is destined to run east. It is not likely to be in

[1] Three is the limit in all Italian naval harbours.

[2] See "Our Mistake in dealing with Russia."

complete working order for some years to come, though excursions were advertised to run a couple of thousand miles on it this summer (1899). It is said that owing to bad foundations much of the line will have to be re-laid.

About £150,000 is to be spent on improving the forts at Vladivostok, or in dredging the harbour.

## 9. Port Arthur

Port Arthur[1] is perhaps the most easily defended harbour in the Far East, although the Japanese with a big military force took it without much loss in the late war. The cliffs protect it from a long-range bombardment, while their altitude is such that a strong plunging fire is easily obtained from them. No hostile fleet would be likely to venture within range of its forts, save under exceptional circumstances, such as in the Chino-Japanese War.

Against the place there is to be said that it is not capable of very much expansion; while, standing as it does at the extreme end of a narrow peninsula, it is easily cut off (as it was in the Chino-Japanese War), unless held or covered by a very strong land force; and finally, being round the corner of Korea[2] nearly 1500 miles from Vladivostok, junctions in war-time between squadrons at the two ports would be exceedingly difficult. In the case of hostilities with Japan,

[1] For some political details, see later.

[2] A map will be found on p. 400.

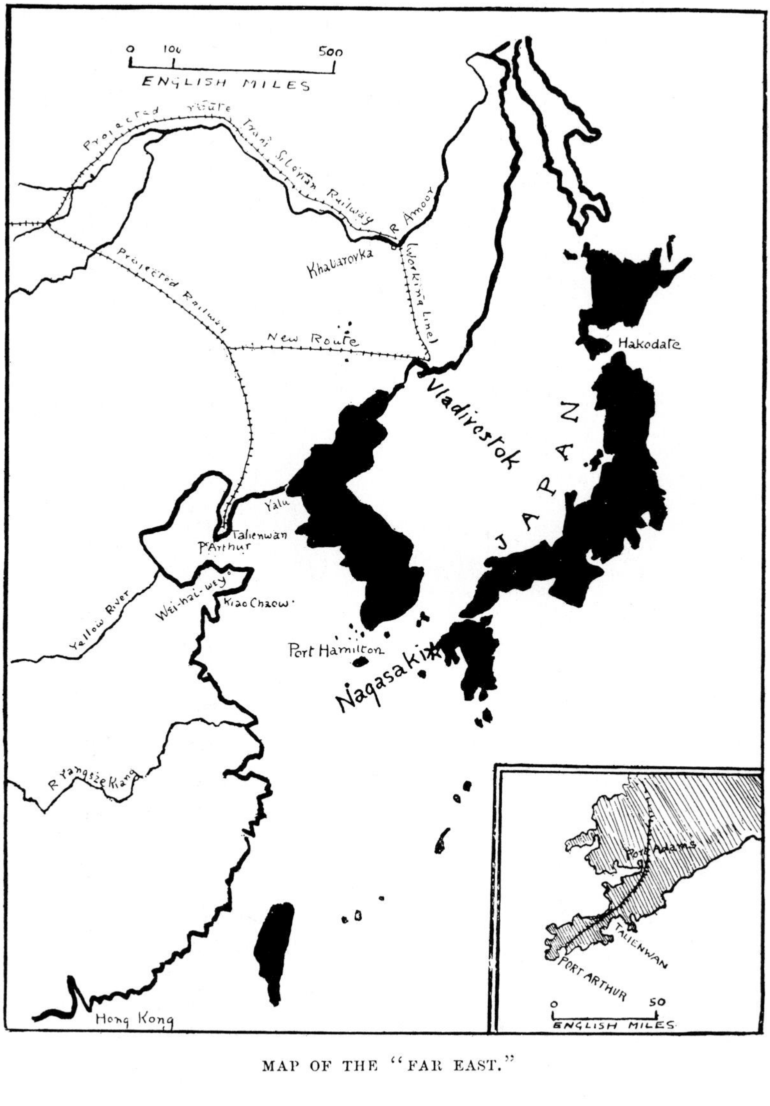


MAP OF THE "FAR EAST."

which has its Nagasaki base dominating the channel, such a junction would be almost absolutely impossible; and in a war with the British the base at Wei-hai-wei (if it could be held) would make the attempt almost equally dangerous. Unless, therefore, she means to virtually abandon Vladivostok as a war base for her squadrons, Russia would look to have very much given hostages to fortune by taking Port Arthur. The two places are bound to be a source of weakness rather than strength; while if Talienwan is added, the weakness will be increased. Certainly, if one studies the map of the district with an open mind, there seems a good deal of truth in the Russian story that they only took Port Arthur to keep Germany out of it. They may be working for a hundred or a hundred and fifty years hence, but it is hard to see any nearer objective. From whatever point of view we regard it, Russia's position at Port Arthur is isolated; nor is it improved by the fact that the steaming radius of several of her ships on the station is good for little more than the 1500 miles between there and Vladivostok. A dry dock capable of taking medium sized warships used to exist at Port Arthur, but it was like most Chinese things—in bad condition. It was freely used, however, during the war. When the Japanese took the place they appear to have destroyed this dock, along with a good many other things. It was about 400 ft. long, 70 ft. wide, and 26¼ ft. deep. It is now being repaired or converted into a new and larger dock.

Port Arthur will be a terminus of the Trans-Siberian railway. It is a purely naval harbour, closed to all merchantmen ; and the only lambs allowed to lie down with the lion there, are Chinese warships. There is an impression that China will not store her new ships there more than she can help, unless, of course, the Russians succeed in doing what the Japanese have already tried to do,—officer the Chinese Navy. Chinese bluejackets are probably among the best in the world, given efficient officers, being intelligent, obedient, and quite indifferent to life. Such, at least, is the opinion of Japanese who have studied and fought them.

### 10. Talienwan

Talienwan is to be turned into a double harbour : one military, one commercial ; but nothing of much importance has yet been done.

## BLACK SEA DOCKYARDS

### 11. Sevastôpol

Sevastôpol is notable chiefly for the part it played in the war which England, France, Sardinia, and Turkey waged against Russia in 1854–55. As a naval port it belongs to the second class, and comes in the same category as Revel and Vladivostok. The dockyard, however, is more important than those of the above-mentioned places, since there are a couple of building slips as well as docks. Except that it builds battle-ships, it is very much on a par with the English dock-yard of Sheerness.

The panoramic view of Sevastôpol on page 405 gives some indication of the extent of the yard. *Dockyard.* In the centre of the illustration the Georgi Pobiedonosetz can be detected on the stocks, and it will be noticed that there is no roofed-in slip as in the northern establishments. Inland, and this side of the slip, shears mark the position of the basin, which has slips the *Slip.* seaward side of it. Inland again are two docks: No. 1, *Docks.* about 400 ft. long by 27 deep; and the Alexandrovski, which was enlarged in 1898 in order to take the Tri Svititelia if necessary. A careful inspection of the photograph will reveal the mast and funnels of the Sinope in this dock.

This photograph was taken in the autumn of 1891. The Georgi Pobiedonosetz[1] was launched in March of

[1] See p. 265.

the year following. Since then no warships have been laid down at Sevastôpol; and though great improvements have been recently made in the fortification, with a view to protecting what exists, it is unlikely that much will be done to improve a dockyard so easily destroyed by long-range bombardment.

*Weakness of Sevastôpol.*

The second page of illustrations is of more recent date (1894 or '95): the first and third are photographs of the dockyard from across the small inner harbour; the second is a Russian monument of the Crimean War—a house (the entire inhabitants of which were killed) left just as it was after the bombardment.

*Captured British guns.*

There are other mementoes preserved at Sevastôpol—the cemetery contains a number of captured British guns, about which our histories are silent. These guns are ranged in rows like the Russian guns that are such familiar objects in most public places in the United Kingdom. It is the reverse side of the medal. The re-captured "Balaklava Charge of the Six Hundred" guns are also in this cemetery.

The warships that have been built at Sevastôpol are the gunboats Teretz, Kubanetz, and Ouraletz, launched in 1887; the second-class battleships Tchesma (1886) and Sinope (1887); and the first-class battleship Georgi Pobiedonosetz, launched in 1892. The gunboats were built on small slips intended for the construction of merchant vessels.

*Fort Constantine.* *North Fort.*

*Inner Harbour.* *Dockyard (with the Georgi Pobiedonositz on the stocks).*

PANORAMIC PHOTOGRAPH OF SEVASTÔPOL FROM THE MALAKOFF REDOUBT.

[*Kindly supplied by* MR. C. DE GRAVE SELLS.]

SEVASTÔPOL.

1. The Dockyard from across the inner harbour.
2. House left just as it was after the Anglo-French bombardment.
3. Dockyard and Coalsheds, with the circular ironclad Popoff at anchor. (The rise in the distance above the Popoff is the Malakoff Redoubt.)

THE ROSTISLAV.

[*Photo. by favour of H.I.H. Grand Duke Alexander of Russia.*

(The Grand Duke Alexander is at present Captain of this ship.)

## 12. Nikolaiff

Nikolaiff, situated on the Boug a little above Kherson, is a strongly protected, comparatively modern place, and one of more importance than Sevastôpol, it being classed as a first-class naval port like Kronstadt or St. Petersburg. Like the St. Petersburg yards, it is purely a building establishment—Pembroke is the British Royal dockyard it most nearly resembles. There is also a private yard belonging to the Russo-Belgian Black Sea Company.

*Ships that have been built at Nikolaiff.*

The ships that have been built at Nikolaiff are the gunboats Donetz, Tchernomoretz, and Zapororosetz, launched in 1887; the torpedo cruiser Kapitan Sacken (1889); the circular ironclads Novgorod and Popoff ('73 and '75); the battleships Ekaterina II. (1883), Dvenadsat Apostolov (1890), Tri Svititelia (1893); and Rostislav, launched in 1896.

*Kniaz Potemkin Tavritchesky.*

At the time of my visit (1899) the first-class battleship Kniaz Potemkin Tavritchesky was building at Nikolaiff.

Particulars of her are :—

| | |
|---|---|
| Displacement . . . | 12,500 tons. |
| Length . . . . | 371 ft. |
| Beam . . . . | $72\frac{1}{3}$ ft. |
| Draught (mean) . . | 27 ft. |
| Armament . . . | Four 12-in. |
| | Sixteen 6-in. Q.F. |
| | Fourteen 3-in. Q.F. |
| | Fourteen smaller Q.F. |
| | Three submerged tubes. |
| | Two above-water tubes. |

The designed H.P. is 10,600 = 18 knots, and this was realised easily on trial.

The coal carried is 670 tons, and 200 extra tons can be shipped. Normally the ship burns oil, and carries 600 tons for this purpose. She can, however, change to coal in about an hour. The oil is carried fore and aft, the 670 tons of coal as extra protection amidships, the 200 tons surcharge in the double bottom —a rather foolish place to stow it in.

The belt is 250 ft. long, 9 in. amidships to 7 in. at the ends, reducing to 5 in. at its lower edge. 9-in. bulkheads enclosed, and an inclined 4-in. deck reinforces it. There is a 6-in. redoubt on the lower deck, with a 5-in. box battery surmounting it. This battery contains twelve 6-in. guns in sponsons, standing on a recess much as on the Ritvizan—of which ship and the Tri Svititelia, the Potemkin, is a mixture. The turrets are 12 in. of the usual Russian type, with reducing 10-in. bases. A noteworthy peculiarity is that the bases, 5 in. thick, are carried below the protective deck.

The ship has two sets of vertical triple expansion engines, steam being supplied by the usual Belleville boilers. Both machinery and boilers were built by the Russo-Belgian Company at Nikolaieff.

*A Russian contract-built ship.*

Some years ago an attempt was made to build an ironclad in a private yard at Nikolaiff, but after a few tons had been built into her the contract was cancelled and the attempt abandoned.

The Imperial Dockyard at Nikolaiff contains a slip dock of 1500 tons, 250 ft. in length over all.

The water at Nikolaiff is too shallow to allow of ships being completed for sea there.

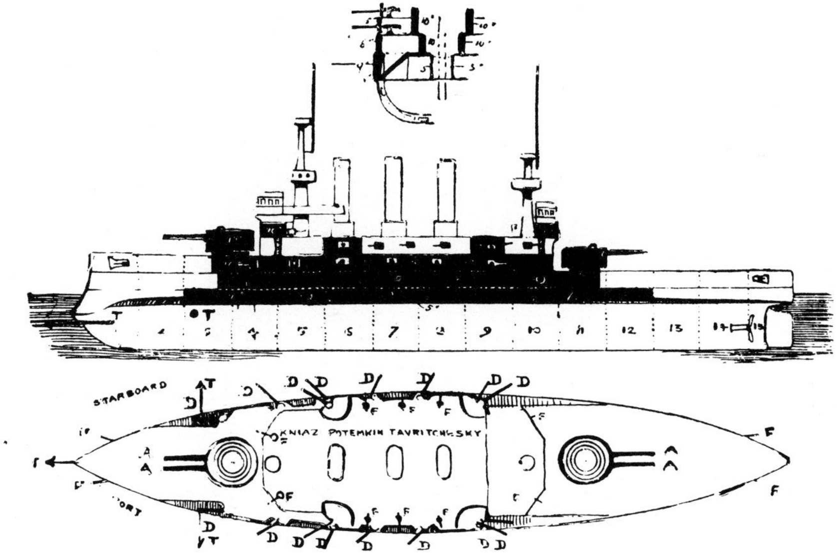


A = 12 in.
D = 6 in.
F = 3 in.

## 13. Other Naval Ports

Other ports and dockyards, calling for no special description, are :—

Abo. Creyton Works; private yard at which destroyers are built.

Ijoro. Private yard. This firm is supposed to be in connection with Yarrow of Poplar.

Sveaborg. Second-class naval port. There are fairly strong fortifications here; and at Helsingfors there is a dry dock, the Oskar Elkund—314 ft. long, 56 ft. wide, and 18½ ft. deep.

Batûm. Naval port, second class. No docks.

Baku (Caspian). Naval port, second class. No docks.

Astrabad (Caspian). Second-class naval port. Base of the Caspian flotilla; and in possession of a small dockyard.

# XVIII

## NEW PORTS AND SHIP CANALS

THE possibility of a British fleet (supported perhaps by allies with military power) forcing the Dardenelles, or being allowed to pass them, is said to have shaken Russian faith in Sevastôpol and Nikolaiff as "safeties." At anyrate, a scheme is in progress for making Kertch in the Sea of Azov into an impregnable first-class naval base. The Straits of Yenikalé should be absolutely impassable to a hostile fleet. *Kertch.*

Kertch, however, is not the only projected base, since this year (1899) a beginning has been made at a new naval harbour in Ekaterina Gulf in the White Sea. It will be connected by rail with St. Petersburg, and visions of a ship canal between the Neva and White Sea are entertained. Without this, of course, the harbour would be of little use; with it the advantages would be theoretically enormous. This new harbour only freezes in the severest winters, owing to the Gulf Stream being close to it, so that by means of it ships could get round the Norwegian coast; and so be free from that easiest *White Sea Harbour.*

of all blockades, a blockade of the narrow seas round Denmark.

Many years must pass before such a prospect can be realised, still it must be regarded as a possibility of the future. A similar project—a ship canal from the Baltic to the Black Sea, is a nearer probability, and likely to be a *fait accompli* ere many years have passed. Russia will then be in a position to concentrate her navy in the Euxine or in the Baltic, as circumstances may require.

*Canals.*

The preliminary steps for this gigantic operation have been undertaken, and the scheme being under the wing of the Grand Duke Alexander Mihailovitch, is fairly certain of ultimate fruition.

*Grand Duke Alexander and Waterways.*

## The Ultima Thule of Russian Ship Canals

There is already a canal for small vessels, and torpedo boats could if necessary go by water from the Baltic to the Euxine. The projected canal will take the largest ships. The proposed route is from Libau to Riga, thence along the Duna River, the Beresina, and Dneiper, with an opening at Nikolaiff. The Sea of Azov would probably be connected also. The length would be nearly 1000 miles. The main difficulties exist in the Dneiper, where 200 miles up there still remain nine cataracts, and a fall of 107 feet in 40 miles. The upper reaches of the

*Baltic-Euxine Canal.*

*Its course.*

*Difficulties.*

Dneiper, too, are very marshy, and engineering difficulties here would be colossal.

When made and all, the canal would be primarily commercial rather than military. Given it, the Dardenelles and the mouth of the Baltic are still as ever at the mercy of a stronger blockading fleet, and the visionary canal to the White Sea would lead to a place too far away from any centre of operations to be of service. For the steaming radius of ships is very small, and only a few British ironclads are able to operate more than a thousand miles from their base. Indeed, 500 miles is more of a limit. So far as England is concerned, the canal would make no very great difference, except in the event of that combination which Russians dream of—Russia, France, and Germany. But a fleet of destroyers at Dover and another at Gibraltar would put France out of touch with Russia and Germany, and the day is far distant when the fleets of these other two Powers would be able to act effectively in concert. In any case, too, we could blockade Wilhelmshaven and the mouth of the Baltic without difficulty. It is the old proverb, Man proposes, God disposes; and geography is greater than canals.

*Its uses.*

Against Germany, on the other hand, Russia would find the Baltic-Euxine Canal of inestimable value. Russian ships would certainly try conclusions with German ones in case of hostilities, and a reinforcement

*Use of the Canal against Germany.*

such as the Black Sea Fleet would mean a tremendous advantage.

So far as England is concerned, for reasons specifically stated in a later chapter, Russia unaided does not dream of a "future on the sea"[1]—yet awhile, at anyrate.

[1] See "Our Mistake in dealing with Russia."

# XIX

## THE NEW FLEET

### Battleships

THE most interesting and powerful vessel completed by the end of 1903 is the Tsarevitch, which, on account of a similarity of armament, was, till she was launched, supposed to be a sister to the Retvizan.

Actually she is the first of a batch of new ships, once destined to be Peresviets, once again to follow the American Maine, finally boldly to carry out French genius as exemplified by M. Lagane of the La Seyne works.

M. Lagane is known as the designer of the French Jauréguiberry, but since that ship was built his great rival, the equally famous M. Bertin, has designed French warships, and the Lagane type was therefore in abeyance, two ships only being afloat—the Chilian Arturo Prat and the French Jauréguiberry—that were characteristic of him till Russia ordered the Tsarevitch.

Her principal details are :—

| | |
|---|---|
| Displacement . . . . | 13,000 tons. |
| Dimensions . . . . | 387 ft. long. |
| | 75½ ft. beam. |
| | Mean draught 26 ft. |

| | |
|---|---|
| Armament . . . | Four 12-in. 40 cals.<br>Twelve 6-in. Q.F. 45 cals.<br>Twenty 12-pdrs.<br>Twenty 3-pdrs., eight 1 pdrs. |
| Torpedo tubes . . | Two submerged at an angle of 25°, two above-water fixed bow and stern. |
| Protection . . . | Krupp cemented belt, 10 ins. amidships, thinning to 4 ins. at the ends, surmounted by a lower deck side belt 6–2½ ins. |

This is reinforced as follows. On top of the upper belt is a flat 2-in. deck as in British ships. Level with the top of the lower belt is a second protection deck 2 inches on the flat, its outer edges depressed to meet the bottom of the belt, and increased to 4 inches in thickness. From the bends of this deck down to the double bottom for the whole length of the ship's side amidships extend two lateral 1⅓-in. bulkheads. These it is hoped will afford protection against torpedoes—the idea being that they are sufficiently strong to resist the weight of water that a torpedo will admit to the wings.

The armour on the big guns is 11 inches, reduced to 10 inches on the bases which grow smaller as they descend, on the now general French and Russian system. She is a great saving of weight over the heavier castle fitted to British ships, and there is no reason to suppose that it is much weaker.

The 6-in. guns are carried in pairs in six turrets 7 inches thick with 5-in. bases to them. In the British Navy the double turret for 6-in. guns has been found anything but a brilliant success ; but its general adoption

TSAREVITCH. [*Photo, Barr.*

A = 12 in.
D = 6 in.
F = 12 pdrs.

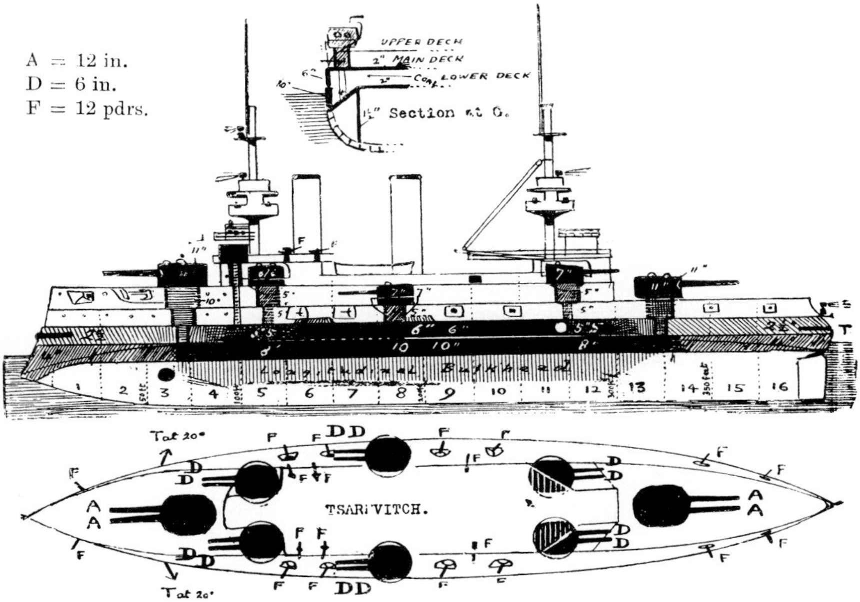

in the French and Russian Navies would seem to indicate that the difficulties we have found have been surmounted.

The Tsarevitch is fitted with twenty Belleville boilers with economisers, designed to give 16,300 H.P. and 18 knots. On trial, however, she enormously exceeded this power and obtained a mean speed of well over 19 knots for twelve hours. The normal coal capacity is about 800 tons, the maximum 1250 tons.

Although of slightly increased displacement, the Borodino class are to all intents and purposes sisters of the Tsarevitch. They are named Borodino, Orel, Imperator Alexander III., Slava, and Kniaz Suvaroff. Save for the last two, which took the water in 1903, these ships and the Tsarevitch were all launched in 1901.

The extra displacement of 566 tons is said to be taken up by increasing the lateral under water bulkheads to 4 inches, but there is some doubt on this point. The maximum coal capacity is increased to 1500 tons.

The peculiarity of the class apart from the bulkheads, lies in the distribution of the 6-in. guns, which, as regards arc of fire, is the best in existence. As will be noted in the illustrations, the amidships secondary turrets are placed on the main deck, while the fore and aft ones are on the upper deck above. By means of this unique arrangement there is no "interference" from blast should the amidships guns be trained ahead. As a result no less than eight 6-in. can be brought to fire directly ahead or astern, so that, so far as secondary guns are concerned, the ship has its best fire axially.

The Tsarevitch at the end of 1903 reached Port Arthur, having made the trip at 10-knot speed. She ran a trial on arriving, and made her trial speed with an economical consumption.

## Newer Ships

At the close of 1903 a new series of ships were ordered and some laid down at the Baltic yards. Two have been named, Imperator Paul I. and Andrei Pervosvanni. The displacement is about 16,500 tons. In general features they are enlarged Borodinos, the points of difference being that 8-in. guns are substituted for the 6-in. of the smaller class. The normal coal capacity is nearly doubled, being 1500 tons, and the maximum capacity is raised to no less than 3000—the highest yet given to any warship. The class will number about five or six ships. Four were believed to be in hand at the end of 1903. The speed for all will be about 18 knots, and Belleville boilers have been appropriated for all the class.

## Cruisers

The species of competition about protected cruisers has already been alluded to. The various points of the Bogatyr, Askold, and Variag were summed up, and eventually the palm was given to the Bogatyr, designed and built by the Vulkan Co. of Stettin, Germany.

Consequently four others of her type were ordered: Oleg, Vitiaz (at Galernii Ostrov) and Kagul and Otchakoff at Nikolaieff and Sevastôpol. Except the Vitiaz all were launched in 1902–03. The Vitiaz[1] was burned when Galernii was destroyed by fire in 1902. Four similar ships have been ordered and laid down in 1903.

All these cruisers are of 6800 tons instead of 6500, but the H.P. remains at 19,500, and 23 knots is still the nominal speed. As they are heavier they should be somewhat slower than the Bogatyr. The coal supply will be 700 tons normal and 1000 maximum. The boilers will be Belleville in all of them, in order to conform with the new Russian scheme of having one type of boiler only.[2] These new cruisers will not have any above-water training tubes.

Two others are projected (1903–04).

## Armoured Cruisers

At the time of writing (January, 1904), a project to reproduce the Bayan type of cruiser is afoot, but nothing appears to have been finally settled.

Two battleships, Efstafi and John Zlatoust, are in hand for the Black Sea Fleet. Both are reported sisters to the Kniaz Potemkin Tavritchesky, but the latter is quite as possibly a Borodino.

[1] This is the second Vitiaz that Russia has lost.

[2] See chapter on Engineering.

### Reconstruction

The Admiral Nakhimoff was in 1899–1900 given a complete overhaul, being entirely re-armed while her worn-out old boilers were replaced by Belleviles. The present armament is believed to be eight 6-in. in twin turrets and ten 4·7's on the broadside, but some of these may be 6-in.

On trial after reconstruction she made the unexpected speed of 19 knots, and kept it up for some hours.

Her rig was substantially reduced.

In 1901–04 the Ekaterina II. and Tchesma came up for overhaul, but little has been done to them beyond the exchanging of their old boilers for Bellevilles.

The Pamiat Azova has been given fourteen 6-in. of 45 calibres and Belleville boilers.

The Alexander II. and Nikolai I. have had their military tops lowered. Only the latter has been reboilered as yet. Neither ship is now regarded as possessing any fighting value.

The Rurik has had most of her yards removed, and the Korniloff has been similarly treated.

The whole of the Teretz type of gunboats have been reboilered with Bellevilles, or are about to be so treated.

### Little Cruisers

One "Novik," the Almaz, was built in Russia and hurried out to the Far East at the crisis in 1904. Two

ADMIRAL NAKHIMOFF (RECONSTRUCTED) [*Photo, copyright, Steinitz.*

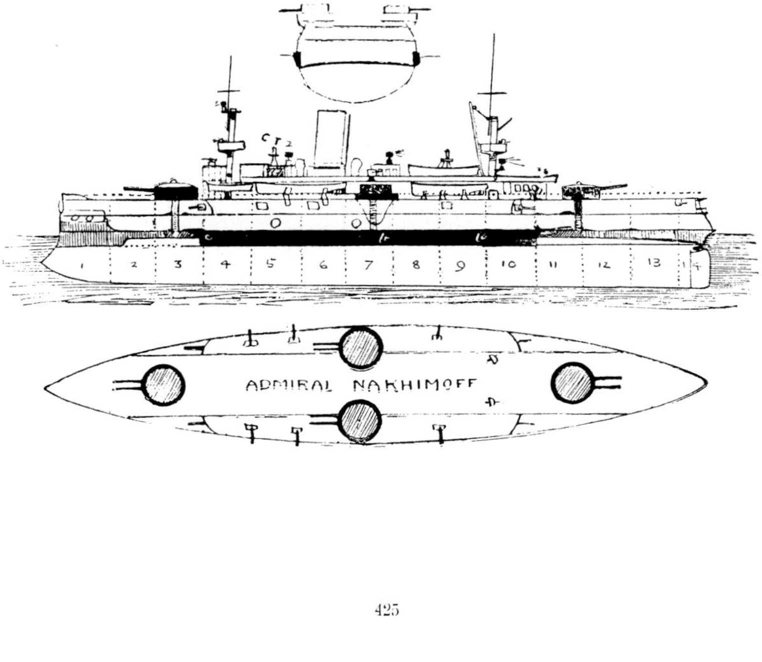

Boyarins are completing—the Jemtchug and Izumrud in 1904 in the Baltic, and two unnamed in the Black Sea. Others projected.

### Mosquito Squadrons

Below is given a statement of the torpedo craft built and building:—

#### DESTROYERS

| | | Tons. | I.H.P. | Kts. | Coal. | Tubes. | Date. |
|---|---|---|---|---|---|---|---|
| | | | | | Tons. | | |
| 17 | Laird type (Som) . . | 350 | 6000 | 27 | 80 | 2 | 1900 |
| 4 | Schichau type (Delphin). | 350 | 6000 | 27 | 80 | 2 | 1899 |
| 16 new | Yarrow ,, (Baklan) . | 350 | 5500 | 26 | 80 | 3 | 1901–1903 |
| 5 | Normand ,, (Forel) . | 312 | 4750 | 26 | 80 | 2 | 1899 |
| 1 | Schichau ,, (Bourakoff) | 250 | 6500 | 32 | 67 | 2 | 1898 |
| 3 | Yarrow ,, (Berkout). | 240 | 3800 | 27 | 60 | 2 | 1898 |
| 8 | Yarrow ,, (Sokol) . | 220 | 3800 | 27 | — | 2 | 1895–1900 |

(Ten of these belong to the Black Sea fleet.)

Fifty-four all told, but the whole of them are not likely to be in service before 1906.

The Yarrow and Laird types have four funnels and one mast, the Schichau and Normand types two funnels and two masts. Except one Laird (the Som) and one Yarrow (the Sokol) all the English types are Russian built. Mostly they were constructed at Ijora, which is practically a branch of Messrs. Yarrow's British establishment. Others were built, or are building, at Abo.

## TORPEDO BOATS

1st Class.

| | Tons. | I.H.P. | Kts. | Coal. | Tubes. | Date. | Type. |
|---|---|---|---|---|---|---|---|
| | | | | Tons. | | | |
| 24 of . . | 120 | 2000 | 24 | 30 | 3 | 1894–1902 | Normand |
| 11 of . . | 130 | 2400 | 27·5 | 40 | 3 | 1893–1902 | Schichau |
| 12 of . . | 120 | 2000 | 21 | 60 | 2 | 1897 | Schichau |
| 12 of . . | 100 | 1250 | 21 | — | 3 | 1893–1895 | (?) |
| (Eight of these not completed in January, 1904. | | | | | | | |
| 2nd Class. | | | | | | | |
| 12 of . . | 85 | 1200 | 21 | 16 | 3 | 1894–1897 | Normand |

Also, about 100 to 125 old boats of various sizes, which have no fighting value. [Of the above—4 of the 130 ton, 5 of the 120 ton, 24 kts., and 1 of the 100 ton, and 3 of 85 ton—total, 13 boats—belong to the Black Sea.]

### Submarines

Russia has aspired to more than she has achieved as yet in submarines. Considerable mystery surrounds her progress in these craft, but all newspaper reports of "considerable successes" should be taken with caution.

There would appear to be one large petrol boat (Holland type), an electric (Kuteinikoff type), and a smaller electric type, something on Goubet lines known as the Poukaloff type.

A British design is also reported as under experiment. This has screws both ends.

The petrol boat is believed to be successful.

The Kuteinikoff boat is unlike the usual submarine, as she has a very flat top. She has been named Peter Kochka. She is a copy of a small 20 ton experimental Peter Kochka I.

The features of the design are that the boat is transportable in sections. She carries two tubes intended to train. From all I can glean she is a complete failure, chiefly on account of some "safety devices" fitted to her and her unwieldy torpedo tubes.

Probably Russia may at the moment (1904) be put down as possessing four more or less "effective" submarines, and four more under construction; but it is possible that she is a little ahead of this. There is little, if any, reason to think that she is as yet at all on a par with France, the United States, or ourselves in the matter of submarines.

The story that Russia's delay in replying to Japan in the 1903–04 negotiations was a desire to delay matters till submarines were got out to the Far East in sections by rail was probably a pure surmise.

# XX

## EVOLUTION OF TYPE IN RUSSIAN WARSHIPS

THE evolution of warship types is a question that scarcely, perhaps, obtains all the attention that it deserves. Nations copy so much from one another, or improve upon each other's improvements to such a degree, that to work out any type without having to drag in so much of this "inter-marriage" that main points are obscured, is not always easy. The persistence of a particular type is, however, fairly noticeable in the armoured cruisers, a species of genealogical table of which is appended. An inspection of the plans of these ships, which are more or less in chronological order, will show that the dominant idea from the Minin, as altered in 1878, to the Rossīa, completed in 1898, is essentially the same. In all cases the water-line has been protected before the guns; these have simply had given to them what weight has been left over from the belt—generally a very slight amount of armour. Offence, not defence, is the main idea from the Vladimir Monomakh onwards, though this first-named ship is now almost a specimen of defence at the expense of offence;

a recent reconstruction and not the original design is the cause of that. In the Gromovoi, indeed, the latest of the type Rurik, protection, as has been shown, is given to the guns nominally at the expense of the belt, but modern improvements in armour have a lot to do with it also; the resisting power of armour has more than doubled in twenty years.

*Armoured cruisers.*

EVOLUTION OF ARMOURED CRUISERS

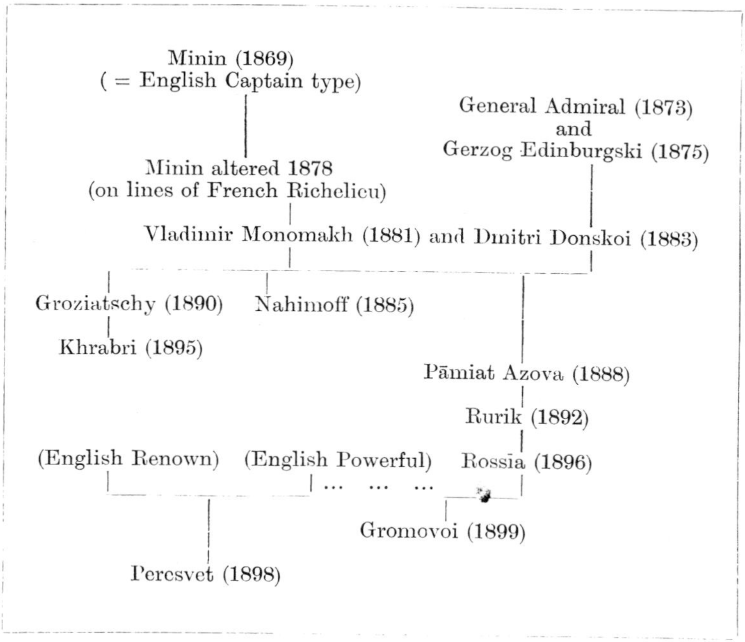


The Peresvet, of course, has no connection with the rest, but as she is an evolution of the British Renown with a little of the Powerful thrown in, and the influence of these types is visible in the Gromovoi, she is included above.

In battleships it is not so easy to trace any evolution, and in the development of the broadside vessels a big gap is felt.

EVOLUTION OF BROADSIDE IRONCLADS

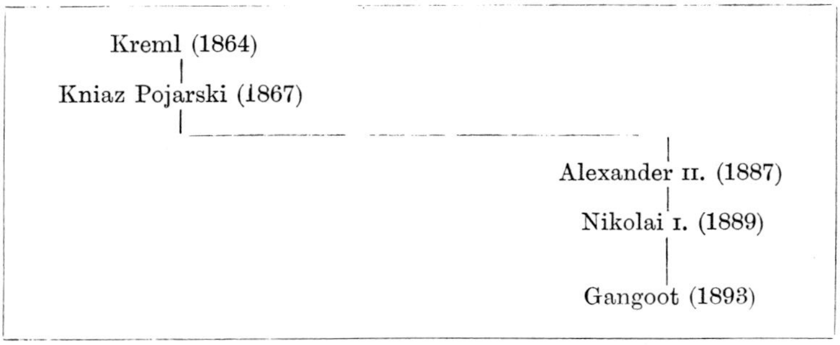


EVOLUTION OF TURRET-SHIPS

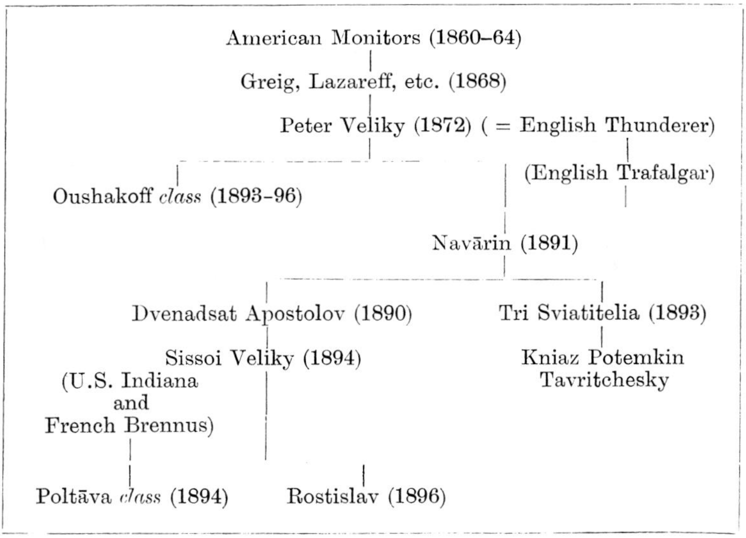


*Turret-ships.* In turret ships, the Peter Veliky idea died with that ship, not to be revived till nearly twenty years later in the Navārin. That ship, however, is practically a Russian version of the English Trafalgar. Unlike the English, whose only advance upon the Trafalgars was the solitary Hood, the Russians have held to this naval man's ideal ship, the Kniaz Potemkin Tavritchesky now building being simply a normal evolution of the Trafalgar type. The United States Kearsarge is the only other modern edition of a Trafalgar. The Dvenadsat Apostoloff is an out-growth of the Trafalgars much as the English Royal Sovereigns are. The same operating cause is at work, the recognition of the tremendous advantages conferred by high freeboard. The Sissoi Veliky is a frantic effort to combine high freeboard with low freeboard advantages; the Rostislav is the same type heavily affected by the Poltāvas. These ships — the Poltāvas — are out-crops of the United States Indiana and Iowa, *plus* the freeboard of the Sissoi Veliky.

*Trafalgar type.*

*Desire for high freeboard.*

The Retwisan does not belong to this lot at all; she is an American new Maine, an evolution of the English Majestic.

The Ekaterina II. class, and the sequel to them, the Georgi Pobiedonosetz, do not appear to be evolved from anything[1] save the inner consciousnesses of Russian designers. There may be, and judging by the non-persistance of the type probably are, practical objections to these vessels, but theoretically they embody a

*Ekaterina II. type unique.*

[1] Unless indeed, as before noted, they can be called developments of the Popoffkas. But these curious craft were still more essentially unique.

splendid idea, and command a good deal of naval admiration. It is, to say the least of it, curious that no other Power[1] has attempted any copy of development of this type. It is not difficult to conceive of a 15,000 ton Georgi Pobiedonosetz which would be in no way inferior to the latest developments of the Majestic class. Probably an undue holding to the theory that a single projectile could "do up" the four forward guns may have had something to do with this. A very moderate screen would, however, prevent anything of that sort, added to which the two pairs would hardly be likely to be often in a direct line. What missed one might very well, of course, hit the other hard by; but in any case, till that happened there would be four big guns instead of two bearing right ahead, while astern perhaps six could bear. Run-away tactics are the best for these ships—so that one or two of them only in a fleet would be a nuisance. But in a squadron of them one can see points, and it is difficult to see the wisdom of the Russian abandonment of them in the Black Sea Fleet, unless there is some practical disadvantage which could only be learnt by long experience of the type. But if that be so, why was the Georgi Pobiedonosetz built?

[1] The Greek Spetsai class and the Austrian Rudolph to some extent embody the Ekaterina II. idea; but, being smaller ships, are necessarily rather "throw backs" than developments.

# XXI

## FINANCE

IN view of the varying price and requirements of naval construction, the £ s. d. of naval estimates do not necessarily prove very much. Still the steady increase of Russian naval expenditure is worthy of note. It is as follows :—

| | | |
|---|---|---|
| 1892–3 | . . . . . | £4,900,000 |
| 1893–4 | . . . . . | £5,100,000 |
| 1894–5 | . . . . . | £5,600,000 |
| 1895–6 | . . . . . | £6,000,000 |
| 1896–7 | . . . . . | £6,440,000 |
| 1897–8 | . . . . . | £6,239,809 |
| 1898–9 | . . . . . | £7,089,106 |
| (Also a special grant of £9,000,000, to be spread over a period of seven years.[1]) | | |
| 1899–1900 | . . . . | £7,089,000 |
| 1900–01 | . . . . | £9,121,321 |
| 1901–02 | . . . . | £10,114,348 |
| 1902–03 | . . . . | £10,500,000 |
| 1903–04 | . (approximately) | £11,000,000 |

These figures, however, cannot be regarded as exact —the purchasing power of the rouble varies very greatly from year to year, and further there is always a varying amount of peculation going on—the figures of which are naturally not obtainable. It should be

[1] Out of this the Tsarevitch, Retvizan, Bayan, Variag, Bogatyr, Askold, Novik, Boyarin and several destroyers were built. Libau, Vladivostok, Port Arthur, and Dalny (Talienwan) consumed the balance.

remembered, however, that broadly speaking peculation is on the decline. The Grand Duke Alexander is at the head of a growing and powerful party which is absolutely opposed to any form of peculation whatever. There is a well known story of the old days when a captain called and ordered a thousand tons of coal. By the time he, the commander, the first lieutenant and the chief engineer had made their pickings, four hundred tons only were delivered.

Those days are gone. A ship now gets all the coal she needs, and also gets it good. However, the peculation phase is dealt with further on. To return to naval expenditure, Russia always has in view a possible naval alliance between herself, Germany, and France.

"We are all building more ships. England can't always go on building. Probably you and I shall not live to see it, but a day must come some time when, to equal the three, England will have to have two hundred battleships and eight hundred cruisers! Your naval superiority cannot last for ever." So said to me the man who, more perhaps than anyone else, may be taken to represent future naval aspirations of Russia, and who is doing all in his power to make the Russian fleet a factor of the future.

Russia never reaches the navy. Foreign residents in Russia are full of stories of money thus intercepted and misappropriated.[1] It is not necessary here to go into the reasons and causes of this state of affairs,—the fact still remains that it exists, and everyone in Russia, or who knows Russia, is more or less cognisant of the why and wherefore. In time it will be stopped: an attempt to stop it explains some of the present naval activity in Russia.

Hence any ship laid down or building in Russia is to be regarded with suspicion, unless very clear evidence of her existence is to be procured: till she is launched no Russian ship should be taken to exist without reserve.

A ship usually used to be completed several months, perhaps a year, sooner in England than in France; in Russia the time distance between these ships and British ones was (with a few notable exceptions like the Rossia) two, or three, or even four years. Russian ships were in consequence to that extent always behind the times, the three Poltāvas, not in service till 1899, are in date and methods of construction equivalent to the British Royal Sovereign class, which were doing duty afloat in 1894.

The instructiveness of all this can best be gauged by tables of the British and Russian first and second

[1] Too much should not be made of peculations, because at one of the finest periods of British naval history peculations was rampant. It should not, therefore, be taken to mean inefficiency. What it does mean is a relative loss of power to the energies expended. This, though serious, is not quite the same thing as inefficiency.

class battleships in 1894 and at the present time. The 1894 table is taken from Brassey for that year, but all ships then incompleted have been put in italics :—

First-Class Battleships in 1894

| England. Launched. | Name. | Russia. Launched. | Name. |
|---|---|---|---|
| 1886. | Anson. | 1886. | Ekatherina. |
| 1893. | *Barfleur.* | 1892. | *Geo. Pobiedonosetz.* |
| 1885. | Benbow. | 1891. | Navārin. |
| 1885. | Camperdown. | Bldg. | *Paris.* |
| 1892. | *Centurion.* | Bldg. | *Petropavlovsk.* |
| 1882. | Collingwood. | Bldg. | *Sevastôpol.* |
| 1891. | Empress of India. | 1887. | Sinôp. |
| 1891. | Hood. | 1886. | Tchesma. |
| 1885. | Howe. | 1893. | *Tri Sviatitelia.* |
| Bldg. | *Magnificent.* | | |
| Bldg. | *Majestic.* | | |
| 1888. | Nile. | | |
| 1892. | Ramillies. | | |
| 1892. | Resolution. | | |
| Bldg. | *Renown.* | | |
| 1892. | Revenge. | | |
| 1884. | Rodney. | | |
| 1892. | Royal Oak. | | |
| 1891. | Royal Sovereign. | | |
| 1887. | Sans Pareil. | | |
| 1887. | Trafalgar. | | |
| Total, 22 ships ; 16 effective. | | Total, 9 ships ; 4 effective. | |

Second-Class Battleships in 1894

| Launched. | Name. | Launched. | Name. |
|---|---|---|---|
| 1879. | Agamemnon. | 1887. | Alexander II. |
| 1880. | Ajax. | 1890. | *Dvenadsat Apostoloff.* |
| 1875. | Alexandra. | 1890. | *Gangoot.* |
| 1882. | Colossus. | 1889. | Nikolai I. |
| 1871. | Devastation. | 1872. | Peter Veliky. |

SECOND-CLASS BATTLESHIPS IN 1894 (*continued*)

| England. Launched. | Name. | Russia. Launched. | Name. |
|---|---|---|---|
| 1875. | Dreadnought. | Bldg. | *Sissoi Veliky I.* |
| 1882. | Edinburgh. | Bldg. | *Sissoi Veliky II.* |
| 1868. | Hercules. | Pro. | *Sissoi Veliky III.* |
| 1876. | Inflexible. | | |
| 1874. | Neptune. | | |
| 1870. | Sultan. | | |
| 1875. | Superb. | | |
| 1876. | Téméraire. | | |
| 1872. | Thunderer. | | |
| Total, 14 ships ; 14 effective. | | Total, 8 ships ; 3 effective. | |

Now of these, the "Paris"—now the Kniaz Potemkin Tavritchesky—reached fruition at the end of 1903! The Tri Sviatitelia was not really complete much before 1901. The Sissoi Veliky, on the other hand, was built and in commission well inside four years. It should be noted that the "Paris" was commenced at a private yard, this order was countermanded and a long spell of idleness followed, before some fragments of her were collected to make the present Kniaz Potemkin Tavritchesky.

Let us now turn to the present year (1904). Russia is turning out ships much more rapidly, but still not quite so rapidly as she would have it appear. The Pobieda is a case in point. In January, 1899, I walked over her keel plate at the Baltic works. In June, 1902, she was at Spithead for the abortive Coronation Review. This was a fine record for swift completion, but,—she was not complete. Not a single casemate was in position. The ship returned to Russia and was a good three months in hand for completion before they began to prepare her for commission. The Osliabia, when I visited her in January, 1899, was (had she been a British ship) in the state of "about one year from completion." She was not completed, however, till 1903, though launched just about the time that the Pobieda was laid down. The Peresviet was completed in 1900. Now she and the Osliabia were both laid down on the same day—November 21st, 1891.

A comparison is interesting :—

| | Laid down. | Completed. | Took to build. |
|---|---|---|---|
| | | | years. |
| Peresviet . . | November, 1895 | June, 1900 | $4\frac{1}{2}$ |
| Osliabia . . | November, 1895 | August, 1903 | $7\frac{3}{4}$ |
| Pobieda . . | October, 1898 | October, 1902 | 4 |

Can we take a mean from this. Hardly perhaps ; for the Osliabia was clearly what is known as a stand-by ship.

The Borodino was laid down in the early weeks of 1900 or thereabouts. She was launched in 1901, and immense efforts made to complete her by the end of 1903. She was not so completed, nor is she likely to be till the middle of the year of writing (1904). This gives us a three and a half years of making—a very good record, and on the whole we may take it that Russia can turn out a battleship in three and a half years if necessary. We can do it in less time than that, but not so very much less. The normal Russian time for the future I should incline to put at four years. For political purposes there is a tendency to put the time at seven years, or three, according to what it may be desired to "prove." Truth, as usual, lies in a mean.

Russian and British and Japanese battleship programmes may be compared as follows :—

| Ready in | Russian. | British. | Japanese. |
|---|---|---|---|
| 1904 | Borodino<br>Alexander III. | Queen<br>Prince of Wales<br>Triumph<br>Swiftsure | |
| 1905 | Orel<br>Slava<br>Suvaroff<br>Efstafi | King Edward<br>Dominion<br>Commonwealth | |
| 1906 | J. Zlatoust | Hindustan<br>New Zealand | |
| 1907 | Imp. Paul<br>A. Pervoswanni | Africa<br>Britannia<br>Hibernia | 2 of 16,400 ton |
| 1908 | 4 new (*pro.*) | 3 new (*pro.*) | 2 or 3 new (*pro.*) |

Completed modern battleships of importance are as follows :—

1*st Rate.*

| Russian. | British. | Japanese. |
|---|---|---|
| K. P. Tavritchesky. | Duncan. | Mikasa. |
| Tsarevitch. | Cornwallis. | Shikishima. |
| Retvizan. | Exmouth. | Asahi. |
| | Montagu. | Hatsuse. |
| | Albemarle. | |
| | Russell. | |
| | London. | |
| | Bulwark. | |

*1st Rate (continued).*

| British. |
|---|
| Venerable. |
| Formidable. |
| Irresistible. |
| Implacable. |
| Canopus. |
| Glory. |
| Ocean. |
| Vengeance. |
| Albion. |
| Goliath. |
| Majestic. |
| Mars. |
| Magnificent. |
| Hannibal. |
| Cæsar. |
| Illustrious. |
| Prince George. |
| Victorious. |
| Jupiter. |

*2nd Rate.*

| Russian. | British. |
|---|---|
| Poltava. | Royal Sovereign. |
| Petropavlovsk. | Hood. |
| Sevastopol. | Empress of India. |
| Trisvititelia. | Repulse. |
| Peresviet. | Resolution. |
| Pobieda. | Ramillies. |
| Osliabia. | Revenge. |
| Rostislav. | Renown. |
| Sissoi Veliky. | Barfleur. |
| Dvenadsat Apostoloff. | Centurion. |

A few older ships are omitted—our Trafalgar and Admiral class balance the Geo. Pobiedonosetz type, and the Navarin.

So far as *matériel* goes the ships in the different rates may be regarded as on a par. There is no question but that at present the British fleet is in no danger from the Russian by itself. Danger lies rather in its combination with others, and the fact that practically all the Russian fleet (other than Black Sea vessels) is concentrated in the Far East. As regards combinations Germany could aid at present by five first and five second-rate ships; France by one first, ten second, and one ship on a par with the Rostislav in fighting value. Germany has five more first rates coming on between now and 1908, France six in about the same period.

# XXIII

## THE RUSSIAN ADMIRALTY

*Russia's advantage.*

RUSSIA has one great advantage over us, in that her Admiralty cannot be changed subject to "the will of the people." True, we are safer now than we have been in the past, and a change of party in power need entail little save a change of figure-head in the person of the First Lord of the Admiralty; and the First Lord, whatever nonsense political exigencies may compel him to talk out of office, when he sits at Whitehall generally adheres carefully to "the custom of the service" and fixed schemes of construction. Should a General Election turn upon whether we do or do not need Protection or Retaliation, or on the evergreen subject of Education, it no longer follows that our entire shipbuilding programme may stand to be upset thereby. But this semi-permanence of the Admiralty is a comparatively modern innovation; nor is it necessarily one that will endure, even though we shall probably always escape carrying the matter so far as our friends the French.

*Weak point in British Admiralty.*

When all is said and done, however, our Admiralty is very much at the mercy of the Treasury; and for party needs, money that should have been voted for the navy may go instead to adorn some parish pump.

There is none of this nonsense in Russia; the money is voted for the navy by a stable institution and dispensed by another stable institution. A good deal too much of the money does not get dispensed much farther than certain pockets for which it was not intended; but that is a personal question rather than one of the system. The superiority of a definite over an indefinite system remains. The collapse of the Athenian, Carthaginian, Venetian, and nearly all other sea empires, from the interference of political or popular meddlers, forms a very unpleasant object-lesson.

*Peculation in Russia.*

*Dangers of democratic interference.*

The Russian Admiralty consists of—

*Admiralty.*

1. The President, who is the General-Admiral—at present a member of the Imperial family; but his having been a naval officer, not Imperial relationship, is the *sine quâ non.*
2. The Minister of Marine, Vice-President.
3. Ten Admirals.

The General-Admiral is the Commander-in-chief of the Navy, responsible to no one save the Emperor. The present holder of the rank is H.I.H. Grand Duke Alexei, the third son of the late Emperor Alexander II., and uncle of the present Tsar.

*General-Admiral.*

The Minister of Marine is a naval officer. His principal duties (apart from those on the Board) are chiefly financial; all save the most important financial questions being settled in his department. The

*Minister of Marine.*

present holder of the office (1899) is Vice-Admiral Tyrtoff.

*Duties.* The special duties of this Board are attending to the Naval Regulations, the more important financial questions, and the inspection of ships, ports, and dockyards. To this Board the various branches of the Admiralty are subordinate.

These branches are :—

1. Chief Navy Staff (Headquarters).
2. Supreme Naval Court.
3. Chief Law Department.
4. Hydrographer's Department.
5. Construction and Supply Department.
6. Technical Committees.
7. Admiralty Department.
8. Medical Department.
9. Record Office,

and a few minor departments.

## 1. Chief Navy Staff

The Navy Staff, with the Chief of the staff at its head, is divided into two departments—(*a*) the Naval Intelligence Department; (*b*) the Personnel Department.

### (*a*) naval intelligence department

The Russian Naval Intelligence Department is said to be, and probably is, the best in the world, though the Japanese "N.I.D." may run it rather close. Of the Russian one it is said over there that they know as much or more about our navy than the First Lord of the Admiralty, and that they consider our Intelligence Department an "interesting institution." They certainly know far more about our confidential instructions than most of our officers are allowed to know. Of course this sort of thing is less essential to the British Navy than to any other, and a blessed thing for us that it is so. Our own Intelligence Department is not much to blame, because it is not allowed enough money to do anything to justify its name. It is a well-known British Navy yarn, that if an officer sends valuable information to the "N.I.D." it sends him stamps to defray his postage,—but no one has yet earned those stamps! On the other hand, he is pretty certain to have been snubbed.

*British N.I.D.*

The Russians work things differently, and the amount of money expended upon Secret Service must be something enormous. Naturally one cannot learn exactly how this money is expended, but in one way and another certain facts leak out. The Russians are justly proud of the efficiency of this department, and it is, of course, rather to their interest than otherwise that the acumen of it should be respected outside Russia. Certain it is that it is no secret in the country that the confidential books issued to the officers in our own and any other important navy, are usually issued to Russian officers before being issued to those for whose sole consumption they were intended!

*Other nations' confidential books used by Russia.*

Again, the Russians possess all the drawings of our submerged torpedo tubes, but, like the French (who also

*Secret of British submerged tubes.*

possess them), these designs are of no use to them, as the man who sold them did not know the prime secret of the weapon. Very few, indeed, do.

*The men who supply information to Russia.*

It is a popular notion in this country that our dockyards and the Admiralty offices at Whitehall contain numbers of Russian spies who collect and sell information. A little of this no doubt is done, but generally speaking this is not the method. Valuable secrets are hardly to be found that way, and information goes to Russia from much higher quarters than humble employés will ever occupy. It does not go directly; it is even possible that those who supply do not know where it goes—they do not officially know, at anyrate.

To be as explicit as one can be over a matter of this sort, certain people own (or feel that they own) the perquisite of selling information to an intermediate quarter, whence it is re-sold to Russia. Nobody concerned asks questions of course. This can hardly be altogether a secret to our administration; indeed, a desire to defeat it may be at the bottom of the niggardliness with which information is dealt out to our "salt horse" officers. Things the secret of which is confined to the Vernon or Whale Island remain secrets; when they are issued as "confidential" to all officers, other people besides naval officers can lay claims to possess them. There are one or two things kept absolutely secret.

*Secrets.*

*Russian Naval Attachés.*

In the usual way, it is the Naval Attachés who are expected to and who do collect information; and if those of Russia collect more than those of other

Governments, it is only because they are more carefully selected.

*Our system.*

In this country of course it is, generally speaking, to our interest to let foreigners see as much as possible of our dockyards, and so on. Nothing could well be sillier than the outcry now and again raised against foreigners being shown over our dockyards. Prepared as we are, it is well to let them know it. Secrecy and stringent regulations nearly always mean defects and lack of preparation; it is the weak points, not the strong ones, that nations chiefly desire to hide. Brand-new inventions are of course exceptions, but these are rare and isolated.

*How Naval Attachés work.*

Naval Attachés, Russian or any other, going round the dockyards of our own or any other navy, are shown, of course, merely what is considered advisable to show them. Of what they see they make notes—the progress of repairs or construction; ability of the workmen; methods adopted for this or that little thing; and so on. All of which they send to their Governments. In addition, they have standing orders with marine photographers for any new photographs of warships to be sent them. They further study all important newspapers bearing on naval matters, extract the wheat from the chaff as much as they can, and send it over to their Intelligence Department.

*Russian "spies."*

The mass of Russian information (other than that referred to specifically above) is obtained in this fashion; the spy people, such as there are, have nothing to do with the attachés. So many absurd stories are and have been written about Russian spies, that most people believe everything or nothing concerning them. The truth lies in a mean, and rather a small mean. The mass of the Russian "spies" in this country belong rather to the police than to the Intelligence Department. At the same time, the work of these agents is not altogether puny; for one thing, Russia always knows when English spies or agents have found out anything about her worth knowing. On the other hand, some of these agents are not chary of inventing information when it cannot be found otherwise. The *actual*, as opposed to the nominal, speeds of our best warships is one subject in which Russia is deeply interested, and one over which she is most liable to be fooled. For instance, the Russians possess the information that our Majestic cannot steam continuously at a greater rate than fourteen knots (13·9 is, if I recollect aright, their exact figure). Now it is perfectly true that the highest *station-keeping* speed of the Majestics is 14 knots; but any of them can steam independently at over 15 knots[1] for days—so long as her coal lasts, in fine. The two speeds have been mixed—an important error.

Still the fact remains that here a piece of valuable enough information had been obtained—one procurable from certain publicly published sources it is true, but not known to the mass of people in this country, interested in the navy though they may be.

Now we possess absolutely no similar data as to

[1] The Hannibal, May 1899, did 16½ knots continuously.

Russian ships, at least none with any official seal of authenticity on them. Yet they could be procured fairly easily if necessary ; we lack the same capacity for taking trouble,[1] and content ourselves with characterising the Russians as "underhand," and the rest of it.

*Other duties, Russian N.I.D.*

Another duty of the Russian N.I.D. is to collect details of coast defences, forts, mines, torpedo stations, and so forth, of any Power with which they are likely to be engaged in hostilities. Knowledge as to how many guns and of what calibre, and how much garrison and ammunition we have in the Isle of Wight, or the exact position of the mine-fields at Spithead, may not seem primarily of much use, still eventualities that might make it so are possible. The sex of which Delilah was so useful an ornament plays its share in things of this sort. In whatever way these things are done the principle is always the same,—the collection of innumerable minor facts [2] of little importance in themselves, which the headquarters Intelligence Department collect and arrange.

*Spies of the fair sex.*

What by common consent is called the "spy business" is, however, merely a small fraction of the work done by the Naval Intelligence Department. All the cruising programmes, stations of ships,

[1] It is, of course, "not worth our while" to anything like the same degree. And there are always a certain number of Members of Parliament prone to consider that all details of expenditure on Secret Service should be publicly announced.

[2] As an instance, I may mention that when I went to the Russian N.I.D. in connection with my tour of the dockyards, I found that they had a photograph of myself there, by means of which I was at once recognised.

positions for coast defence, training and mobilisation, are worked out at the N.I.D., which is a very large building.

*An interesting map.*

The most interesting thing that I saw there—though it has absolutely nothing novel about it—was a huge map of the world, with the positions of every single vessel in the Russian Navy, down to torpedo boats, indicated upon it ; also the positions of foreign vessels in certain quarters. The special interest lay in the fact that this map had been in use some little while, and in the pin-holes upon it one could trace the course of that famous move when the Sissoi Veliky and Navārin were suddenly sent from the Mediterranean to the China station, and the British Victorious sent after them was stranded off the Suez Canal. That "war scare" of the early days of 1898 is almost forgotten now, but this map with the courses of the Sissoi and Navārin, and every possible enemy near their paths, recalled it all very vividly indeed. The pin-holes made it fairly apparent for *whose* benefit the two ironclads were sent out. The Power in question was not England.

### (*b*) PERSONNEL DEPARTMENT

The Personnel Department is under a rear-admiral, assistant-chief of the Navy Staff, and its duties cover recruiting, appointment, promotion, pay, and retirement of officers and men. The Chief of the Navy Staff is head of both these branches, under the Minister of Marine. With the aid of the heads of these two branches, his duties are to draw up all movements of peace and dispositions for war.

### 2. Supreme Naval Court

The Supreme Naval Court is a court of appeal in connection with the local naval courts. Its president is an admiral, and there are five other members of less rank.

### 3. Supreme Law Department

The Law Department is merely a legal branch of the Supreme Naval Court. It attends also to every kind of legal matter connected with the naval service.

### 4. Hydrographer's Department

The Hydrographer's Department supervises and orders all surveying and exploration works, gets out and supplies charts and all nautical instruments; ships' libraries and kindred matters are also under its wing.

### 5. Construction and Supply

The Construction Branch attends to shipbuilding at home and abroad; the Supply Branch has two departments: the first devoted to the supply of stores, the second for all the financial part of supply to the branch generally.

### 6. The Technical Committee

This Committee has for members the directors and assistant-directors of gunnery, torpedo, engineering, construction, and naval works. Every technical matter connected with the navy, including new inventions, goes through their hands; and they are responsible for seeing that the work of the Construction Department is carried out.

### 7. Admiralty Department

This is a literary branch, and attends to the General-Admiral's correspondence, and puts into form all reports received or issued by all the other departments.

### 8. The Medical Department

This attends to all sanitary matters connected with the fleet,--supervises hospitals, sick-lists, reports on officers and men incapacitated by wounds or disease, and everything else within the province of its name.

### 9. The Record Office

This deals with Naval Records Past and Present,—the care of ships' logs, preserves correspondence, reports, and recommendations.

# XXIV

## ENTRY AND TRAINING OF OFFICERS

### 1. Executives

OFFICERS for the Russian Navy are obtained in two ways—(1) by an orthodox system not very different to our Britannia system; (2) by a species of "supplementary list."

The former, who compose the bulk of the executives, are entered by competitive examination. There is no system of nomination as for the Britannia in the British Navy, but what has been called the "close corporation" is secured by a regulation which lays down that only the sons of nobles[1] or officers may compete. The age of entry is very low—twelve to fourteen years,—a very wise provision; naval officers cannot be entered too young.

*Entry of regular executives.*

*Regulations as to social status.*

*Age of entry.*

Those who pass the examination are admitted to the corps of Naval Cadets, in which they serve four years as cadets and two as midshipmen (*guarde-marine*).

*Naval cadets.*

*Midshipmen.*

[1] Gentry is the nearest equivalent English term; so long as the candidate is a man of good family it is not essential that he shall have a handle to his name.

These cadets and midshipmen are divided into six companies, each year's entry forming a company. Each company averages 80 strong, but owing to an increase the two junior companies are stronger, that of 1898 numbering over 100, consequent upon the whole corps having been brought up to 600, its standard number for the future. Previously it was about 500 all told.

For the first three years the cadets receive an ordinary academy training—twenty-eight hours a week;[1] the professional education begins with the fourth year, and is prefaced by an examination. This professional education includes theory, etc., on shore during the winter; during the summer they are sent afloat in masted ships. In the course of these three years they put in three courses, mostly afloat, dealing with the general practical work of their profession. A fourth course afloat is devoted to navigation (the special navigators' branch having, like the special corps of gunnery, been abolished in 1885).

Finally, there is a four months' cruise, usually to the West Indies, after which they have to undergo a final examination for mitchman (*i.e.* sub-lieutenant). About 10 per cent. may fail to pass this; they are then put back for extra training, or discarded altogether, according to circumstances. Seniority as mitchmen is decided by how the *guardes-marine* do in this examination.

The ranks of mitchmen are also filled from outside.

[1] No work is done on Wednesdays or Sundays—both religious days.

Young men of sufficient education are allowed to serve in the fleet, if they have interest enough to obtain permission from the authorities as "volunteers." They are allowed to go in for the mitchman's examination, and if successful, enrolled as officers. They are usually sent to the Siberian or Caspian Fleet—service in the Siberian Fleet proper being anything but popular with the regular officers. *Supplementaries.*

Thereafter mitchmen and officers senior do courses at the Naval Academy. Here they learn strategy, tactics, gunnery, torpedo, war game, etc. etc. There are two year courses, also shorter ones of seven months, and also general ones for the winter months, attended by all officers, from admirals downward. Two days a week are devoted to Naval War Game, details of which will be found in a later section. *Naval Academy.*

There is no exact age for promotion of mitchmen to lieutenants, but if they have gone for ten years without promotion they are placed on the retired list. Promotion to lieutenant necessitates forty months' sea service, and is by seniority. In training-ships, three days' sea service count as four days served.

Lieutenants receive special courses if they specialise in anything — gunnery, torpedo, navigation, etc. Gunnery and torpedo schools are at Kronstadt, musketry at Oranienbaum on the mainland hard by. Lieutenants for navigating duties who do well in their examinations have some special privileges in the matter of promotion—a plan introduced to popularise *Lieutenants.*

this branch when the staff-commanders were abolished.

*Retiring age.*

Unpromoted lieutenants are not retired till they reach the age of forty-seven. Senior lieutenants used to be called kapitan-lieutenant, but that rank is now abolished.

*Kapitans I. and II.*

The next step after lieutenant is kapitan II. rang (commander), the age limit of which is fifty-one years. The majority of commanders that I have come across are, however, much younger men, the average age being thirty to thirty-five years. Unless an officer has a great deal of interest and high social position he does not become a commander, save under exceptional circumstances. Something of the same sort, of course, obtains in the British and most other navies in peace time; promotion must necessarily be by selection if admirals are to be kept young. To become a kapitan, a lieutenant must have done fifty-eight months' sea time as lieutenant, and this may be put at ten to fourteen years' service in home waters, while if he goes to the Mediterranean or Pacific three years will qualify him to be a commander. Kapitans II. rang unpromoted are retired at the age of fifty-one.

*Kapitan I. Rang.*

To become a kapitan I. rang, a commander must have served at least one year as commander of a sea-going ship, and put in other service in addition. The earliest age at which this rank can be reached is about thirty to thirty-two, H.I.H. Grand Duke Alexander, at present a kapitan I. rang, being thirty-three years of age (1899). An unpromoted kapitan I. rang is retired at fifty-five.

H.I.H. GRAND DUKE ALEXANDER MIHAILOVITCH OF RUSSIA
KAPITAN I. RANG.

To become a rear-admiral a kapitan I. rang must have done four years in command of a first-class ship (if in home waters), and spent eight months of that time afloat.[1] If, however, he goes on foreign service, a year's duty qualifies him to be a rear-admiral. Promotion to rear-admiral is entirely by selection. Retiring age, sixty years. The average age of rear-admirals is younger than this by ten to fifteen years. *Rear-admiral.*

Promotion to vice-admiral is as a rule entirely by seniority. The conditions are three years at home on duty with a fleet (twelve months' sea service), or on foreign stations, two years' service. The retiring age is sixty-five. *Vice-admiral.*

Vice-admirals become admiral by will of the Emperor only. There are no conditions to be fulfilled, nor is there a retiring age. *Admirals.*

The highest rank of all, the solitary one of general-admiral, is the next and last step above admiral. The selection is made by the Emperor. The first holder of this rank was Graf (Count) Aprāksin in the time of Peter the Great; the present holder is H.I.H. Grand Duke Alexis, who is fifty years old, and he has occupied his present position some considerable while. *General-admiral.*

It will be noted that foreign service is the only way by which rapid promotion can be obtained. The reason is that the average Russian naval officer hates foreign service, and only those who have no interest

[1] For nearly two-thirds of the year Russian ships in the Baltic are laid up owing to the ice. They are actually frozen in for about five months. In the Black Sea the waters are rather more open.

or else very ambitious officers take it. The Mediterranean may be some exception, and so, too, would be crack ships like the Rossia in the Far East. But there is an utter absence of that contempt for an officer in a "snug shore-going billet" which obtains in the British Navy.

*Inactive List.*

The retiring ages do not at once free officers from liability to serve. When they reach the age limit of their rank they are placed in an intermediate category, in which they form a species of reserve.

*Reserve List.*

In addition, a reserve is created by allowing any officer who has served two years in the active list to enter the reserve till such time as he reaches the age limit. He is only liable for active service in case of war or great necessity.

*Retired List.*

No officer is allowed to "resign" unless he is physically incapacitated from service; and must remain liable till he reaches the age limit of his rank, unless a medical board or court-martial has dispensed with his services.

*Promotion on retirement.*

On leaving the "inactive" list an officer of good character and service is usually promoted as with us, and draws the pay and pension of his retired rank. A second privilege (no mean one in Russia, where officers are never in mufti, and the civilian is looked upon as an inferior sort of person altogether) is the right to go on wearing uniform after being retired.

# XXV

## ENTRY AND TRAINING OF MEN

MEN for the Russian Navy are raised by conscription. Originally this naval conscription was only made in the maritime provinces — Finland, Courland, etc., and the shores of the Euxine, but lately, in part from political reasons, in part because there is a paucity of supply in the original sources, men from the interior have been made into sailors, and these seem to do fairly well.[1] *Conscription.*

Liability to serve does not come till a man is twenty-one years of age, and here is one weak point of the Russian Navy in comparison with ours. In the British Navy the sailor is taken much younger, and trained to *think* as a sailor as well as to do the duties of one. The numbers of men levied in recent years for the Russian Navy have been, roughly— *Age of entry.*

| | | Levied. | Total of all ranks. |
|---|---|---|---|
| 1890 | about | 6,000 | — |
| 1891 | ,, | 6,000 | — |
| 1892 | ,, | 7,000 | — |
| 1893 | ,, | 7,000 | — |
| 1894 | ,, | 8,000 | about 35,000 |

[1] In the British Navy a very large number of sailors are Londoners.

| | Levied. | Total of all ranks. |
|---|---|---|
| 1895 | about 8,000 | — |
| 1896 | „ 9,500 | — |
| 1897 | „ 11,000 | about 40,500 |
| 1898 | „ 12,000 | „ 42,000 |
| 1899 | „ 14,000 | „ 44,000 |

The increase is to some extent more apparent than real, because the population of Russia increases at an abnormal rate. Whereas in 1859 it was 74,000,000, in 1897 it was 129,000,000. A larger increase of officers and men may be expected for 1900–2, when the new ships will be in commission, though a gradual increase to meet this is being made. The Russian Navy has never contained enough men to man all its ships.

*Number of men on foreign service.*

The number maintained on foreign stations is, roughly, a quarter of the entire force.

*Conscripts.*

To resume. In the maritime provinces men only draw the lot once; if they do not draw for active service they are put in the naval militia, and remain more or less "paper" sailors. Exemptions are numerous; numbers of men are physically unfit in Finland, and great pains are taken where possible to avoid drawing men upon whom families depend for support, and so on. If such are taken the probability is that their time of service is shortened or they are not sent abroad. The difficulty of getting enough men under these conditions has led to the recruiting of sailors in the interior of Russia.

*Length of service.*

Every sailor serves normally for seven years on the active list and three additional years on the reserve.

He is not allowed to marry while on the active list.

Sailors are, broadly, divided into two branches—(1) military, (2) civil. *Branches.*

## 1. Military Branch

Bluejackets are drafted to Kronstadt or Sevastôpol, and thence, after a course of instruction ashore, to the training-ships, which are always fully masted. Some of these vessels chiefly carry cadets, others chiefly men. The length of their sea time that they spend at sea depends partly upon the captains of the ships; some do as much time in harbour as they can, others keep the men at sea every moment that they can manage.

From the training-ships men are drafted to the Practice Squadrons and to gunnery and torpedo training-ships, thence to foreign service, which they do not love. When a Russian man-of-war gets home again after foreign service, the men sacrifice their hats in their glee and excitement: every sailor throws his hat overboard in commemoration of his safe return. This is as orthodox a custom as "crossing the line" was in the old days, or as the tremendously long paying-off pennant which British ships indulge in when they come home.

Seamen are divided into two ratings—first and second; the former having better pay. They have no promotion, unless at an early stage they show aptitude and a desire to specialise.

*Corporals.*

In such case they go to a special school at Kronstadt to train for corporal (petty-officer), when they do a seven months' course in shore-going drill and elementary sea duties. After that they go to sea for a year in special training-ships, spending forty weeks afloat in foreign waters.

*Conductors.*

There are no warrant officers in the Russian Navy equivalent to those in the British service; but after a couple of years' service and passing the necessary examinations in technical subjects, corporals can become "conductors" for boatswains, gunnery, or torpedo duties. But "conductors" are never watch-keepers under any circumstances, nor do they undertake any duties higher than those of chief petty officer in the British Navy—the nearest equivalent rank to theirs—and they are practically merely chief corporals. Except in case of war, promotion to the quarter-deck is impossible in the Russian service. In war-time, however, should a man particularly and specially distinguish himself, he would be eligible to rise to any rank that his merits would take him to. In the army such promotions have been known, and I believe I am correct in stating that the great General Suwaroff himself rose from the ranks.

*No warrant officers.*

*Promotion of rankers.*

There are a number of small ranks which corporals fill—gunnery, torpedo, submarine mining, quarter-masters, signalmen, divers, riflemen, etc. For nearly all these there are special schools and classes at Kronstadt, Sevastôpol, or Nikolaiff. Riflemen and gymnastic corporals go to Oranienbaum, where there is a musketry school.

## 2. Civil Branches

These include stokers, engine-room artificers, engine-room corporals in the engine-room; sick-bay men, and writers. All these enter the service for their rank, and have no further promotion. They go to special schools at Kronstadt and Nikolaiff, and are thence passed into service. Their term of service is the same as that of bluejackets.

# XXVI

## PAY

PAY in the Russian Navy is a rather bewildering matter. It may best be described as a pittance eked out with extras that may or may not make it fairly good.

The majority of Russian naval officers have private means; but whether they have or have not it is said to be their characteristic to "chuck about the roubles" periodically when they have them, and then live very quietly in the interim. There is a good deal of the Bohemian about them as a rule—being a "jolly good fellow" is an ideal with most Russians. The same may be said in a way of the men: when they have money they spend it freely, when they have not they lie low. Hence it comes about that pay in the Russian service is variously reputed to be "very good" and "wretchedly bad." As a matter of fact it is neither the one nor the other very much.

*Cost of living in Russia.*

It always varies considerably according to the station,—an exceedingly good arrangement. Living in Russia, it must be remembered, is a great deal cheaper—for Russians—than is living in England, where again it is less than in America. The Russian extra pay for foreign service is partly with a view to popularising it, partly to help cover the increased cost of necessaries,—a piece of consideration practically unknown in the British Navy. In our service, beyond that service on the West Coast of Africa, in ships commissioned for trials (if not in harbour), and torpedo boat duty, brings a little additional money, service on one station is much the same as on another. So, too, the commanding officers and one or two other seniors in the British Navy may draw a little extra; but there is nothing equivalent to the "all along the line" system of the Russian Navy.

The following are the three principal sources of pay in the Russian service, and the rates depending on different stations. The rouble is calculated as roughly worth about 2s. 2d. Its actual value apparently varies daily, and, so far as the traveller is concerned, depends upon whether he wishes to buy or sell it. If one buys, a rouble is worth about half a crown; if one sells, it only fetches about two shillings. I mention this not for the sake of the "wheeze," but to account for a certain appearance of looseness in my Finance. The addition of a nought will bring these figures within about 5 per cent. of the amount in roubles. To obtain the equivalent purchasing power in England, and allow for our more liberal notions as to what constitute the "necessaries" of life, from 50

## RATE OF PAY PER ANNUM OF RUSSIAN NAVAL OFFICERS

| Rank. | Baltic and Black Sea. | | | | Caspian. | | | | Mediterranean or Siberian. | | | | Remarks. |
|---|---|---|---|---|---|---|---|---|---|---|---|---|---|
| | Ordinary Pay. | Mess Allowance. | Extra Sea Pay. | Total. | Ordinary Pay. | Mess Allowance. | Extra Sea Pay. | Total. | Ordinary Pay. | Mess Allowance. | Extra Sea Pay. | Total. | |
| | £ | £ | £ | £ | £ | £ | £ | £ | £ | £ | £ | £ | |
| Mitchman (Sub.-lieut.) | 51 | ... | 40 | ... | 65 | ... | 40 | ... | 84 | ... | 40 | ... | |
| Lieutenant | 58 | 19 | 60 | 137 | 76 | 19 | 60 | 155 | 91 | 19 | 90 | 200 | Specialists get double ordinary pay. |
| Senior Lieutenant (after 5 years) | 78 | 20 | 106 | 204 | 98 | 20 | 106 | 126 | 127 | 20 | 130 | 277 | Mess allowance may rise to £40. |
| Kapitan II. Rang (Commander) | 91 | 37 | 180 | 308 | 112 | 37 | 180 | 329 | 145 | 37 | 250 | 432 | Mess allowance may rise to £80. |
| Kapitan I. Rang (Captain or Commodore) | 110 | 55 | 250 | 415 | 145 | 55 | 250 | 450 | 185 | 55 | 350 | 590 | Maximum mess with special duties may add £80 extra. |
| Rear-admiral | 200 | 80 to 400 | 963 | 1243 to 1563 | 250 | 80 to 400 | 963 | 1293 to 1613 | 300 | 80 to 400 | 1200 | 1580 to 1900 | If not in command of a fleet the allowance is less. |
| Vice-admiral | 265 | 400 | 963 | 1628 | 330 | 400 | 963 | 1693 | 385 | 400 | 1200 | 1985 | |
| Admiral | 355 | ... | 963 | ... | 440 | ... | ... | ... | 500 | ... | 1200 | ... | May be considerably more. |
| Civil Branch. | | | | | | | | | | | | | |
| Junior { Doctor / Engineer } | 51 | 19 | ? | ... | 65 | 19 | ? | ... | 84 | 19 | ? | ... | Engineers eligible for torpedo officers, double ordinary pay. |
| Assistant Senior Engineer | 58 | 19 | 60 | 137 | 76 | 19 | 60 | 155 | 91 | 19 | 90 | 200 | Staff Commanders with extra allowances received this pay. There are few now. |
| Senior { Doctor / Engineer } | 91 | 37 | 180 | 308 | 112 | 37 | 180 | 329 | 145 | 37 | 250 | 432 | |
| Fleet { Surgeon / Engineer } | 110 | 55 | 250 | 415 | 145 | 55 | 250 | 450 | 185 | 55 | ? | ... | |
| Inspector { of Hospitals / of Machinery } | 200 | 80 | 400 | 480 | 250 | 80 | 400 | 730 | 300 | 80 | 500 | 880 | |

## RATE OF PAY PER ANNUM OF RUSSIAN NAVAL SEAMEN

| Rank. | Baltic and Black Sea. | | | | Caspian. | | | | Mediterranean or Siberian. | | | | Remarks. |
|---|---|---|---|---|---|---|---|---|---|---|---|---|---|
| | Ordinary Pay. | Mess Allowance. | Extra Sea Pay. | Total. | Ordinary Pay. | Mess Allowance. | Extra. Sea Pay. | Total. | Ordinary Pay. | Mess Allowance. | Extra Sea Pay. | Total. | |
| | £ | Rations. About £2 per annum in lieu of spirit if desired. 1½d. to 2d. a day extra allowance. | £ | £ | £ | Rations and savings; also about 2d. a day. | £ | £ | £ | Rations and savings; also 4d. a day extra. | £ | £ | |
| Sailors, 2nd class | ... | | ... | ... | ... | | ... | ... | ... | | ... | ... | |
| Sailors, 1st class | 16s. | | 1 | 2 | 1 | | 1 5s. | 2 5s. | 1 | | 1 5s. | 2 5s. | Extra duties increase his pay to £4 per annum. |
| Divers | 2 | | 4 | 6 | 2 5s. | | 4 | 6 5s. | 2 5s. | | 5 | 7 5s. | Some of these seem to be additional pay. |
| Captain of guns, Bandsmen, etc. | 16 | | 10 | 26 | 16 | | 10 | 26 | 16 | | 10 | ... | |
| Boatswains | 7 10s. | | 15 | ... | 7 10s. | | 20 and extras | ... | 9 10s. | | 24 and extras | ... | Bo'suns' mates get about half the pay of Bo'suns, but it may total to £35 per annum. |
| Petty Officers (Corporals) | 12 to 25 | | ... | ... | ... | | ... | ... | ... | | ... | ... | |
| C.P.O. | 40 | | ... | ... | 50 | | ... | ... | 50 | | ... | ... | |
| 1st class Stoker | 1 5s. | | 5 | 6 5s. | 1 5s. | | 5 | ... | 1 5s. | | 6 | ... | Writers get £5 per annum. |
| Artificers, E.R. | 6 to 18 | | ... | ... | ... | | ... | ... | ... | | ... | ... | |

to 60 per cent. may be added. It should be borne in mind, too, that Russian officers, being always in uniform, have no expenses for plain clothes, and that uniform, in the junior ranks at anyrate, is relatively cheaper than it is in our service.

In home waters, sea pay is only to be earned about four months out of the twelve. The pay here tabulated is in most cases the average; there are various small duties that increase it.

Men receive pay at the rates as on page 473, the amounts given being *per annum*, unless definitely stated otherwise.

*Where the Russian Admiralty is superior to ours.*

The additional daily allowance varies according to the station and the market price of commodities there. It is given for the purchase of additional food if required. We have much the same thing in practice in the British service, where a bluejacket is practically bound to spend at least 2d. to 3d. or more per diem for ordinary necessaries. His pay, in fine, is nominally higher than it actually is, while the Russian's is nominally lower than the actual. Further, absolutely no difference is made in the British service as to whether the station is a cheap or a very dear one—the Russian Admiralty are more generous than ours over this matter of sailors' pay. The exact minimum daily pay of a Russian bluejacket, *i.e.* ordinary pay, plus the additional mess allowance, and *not including* sea pay and other sources of additional revenue, is as follows with different home ports.

| Port. | Mess. Pence. | Daily Pay. Pence. | Total minimum Pence. |
|---|---|---|---|
| Vladivostok . . . | 3¼ | ¾ | 4 |
| Kronstadt, Petersburg, and Revel | 1¾ | ½ | 2¼ |
| Sveaborg, etc. | just over 1¼ (5½ kopeek) | ½ | 2 (nearly 1⅞) |
| Caspian . . . . | 1½ | ¾ | 2¼ |
| Nikolaiff . . . | 1¼ | ½ | 1¾ |
| Sevastôpol . | just over 1½ (6½ kopeek) | ½ | 2¼ (nearly 2⅛) |
| Archangel . . . | 2 | ½ | 2½ |

This is for seamen of the first class (A.B.'s), and, as noted above, does not include the sea pay, which varies from 6½d. per diem in home waters to 10d. a day on foreign service. A bluejacket on the Pacific Station thus gets a minimum of 1s. 2d. a day, of which 10¼d. to 11d. is clear profit, while grog savings will give him a clear shilling a day. A shilling a day is the pay of Japanese sailors in home waters (they get treble that, *i.e.* 3s. a day, in English ports). An English bluejacket gets a nominal pay of 1s. 7d. a day; he clears perhaps 1s. 4d. or less. This obtains in whatever station he may be. Small as some of the Russian bluejacket's pay looks, it must be borne in mind that with his board and lodging he is better off in his navy than in his previous civilian condition on shore. A penny goes a long way in provincial Russia.

*Shore-going extras.*

Shore pay often exceeds the minimum, as men employed in fitting out ships and about the offices get from ½d. to ¾d. a day extra. So far as I can make out, second-class sailors or stokers get only board and lodging; while first-class sailors get a minimum wage in order to induce them to specialise in something. The number of things in which they can do this is too great to tabulate, nor do I know the exact extra amounts thus earned in many cases.

*Food.*

The men are fed pretty well;[1] all Russians have healthy appetites. On Wednesdays and Fridays they get no meat; but butter is a service ration. Vodka is served out at the rate of about $\frac{1}{4}$ pint per diem. One-third of this is taken up for breakfast or supper; two-thirds for the midday meal. Men who prefer it can receive $4\frac{1}{2}$ kopeek (a fraction over 1d.) per diem in lieu of spirit.

*Spirit ration.*

*Savings.*

Tea (stakán tchi), which is to the Russian what beer is to the British workman, is supplied very liberally, but the sailor buys his own sugar. Being an economical person, his habit is to put a lump of sugar in his mouth, and holding it there, make it do duty for several glasses of tea. Occasionally the knob is passed round to his friends.

*Tea.*

A sailor draws 7 lbs. of tobacco per annum, in a daily ration of about $\frac{5}{16}$ of an ounce. He is also supplied with a small piece of soap daily, which (according to the legend circulating amongst British bluejackets) he is believed to *eat*.

*Tobacco.*

*Soap.*

[1] In 1720 Peter the Great made an inspection of sailors' food, and hung three pursers because the food was bad. He recognised the absolute necessity of feeding his men well, and left explicit directions about it. The word of Peter the Great is still law in the Russian Navy.

The daily meals are :—

| | |
|---|---|
| Breakfast . . | Tea, with biscuit or bread and butter. |
| Dinner (midday) . | Two-thirds of the daily spirit ration. Fresh or salt meat, with vegetables or gruel. Pease and butter only on Wednesdays and Fridays. |
| Supper . . . | Tea, with gruel and butter. |

Tallow, upon which the Russian bluejacket is in this country popularly supposed to be fed, is not served out in any Russian warship.

# XXVII

## RETIREMENT, PENSIONS, ETC.

LIKE all matters connected with pay in the Russian Navy, pensions, retiring allowances, and so forth, are complicated by innumerable side-issues.

In the ordinary course a lieutenant or commander is, as with us, promoted on retirement and draws the full shore pay (not a very large amount) for that rank.[1] This, however, is not all. If married, a certain amount of sea service entitles him to draw money for the education of his children; while in any case, if he has served twenty-five years with credit, he gets a pension varying from £23 to £75 a year, according to his rank; and if he has served thirty-five years, he draws double this.

*Good Service Pension Fund.*

In addition there is a species of deferred pay for all ranks, known as the Good Service Pension Fund. The money is raised by deducting 6 per cent. from the shore pay of all ranks. This brings in nearly as much as the Government pension.

*Gratuities.*

In addition, again, there are gratuities which may mount to a very large sum, according to who the retiring officer is.

[1] There is no half-pay, shore pay is tantamount to that.

Engineers, doctors, etc., receive exactly the same as the corresponding executive rank, *i.e.* as follows :—

| BRANCH. | RANK. | | | | |
|---|---|---|---|---|---|
| EXECUTIVE | Mitchman | Lieutenant | Kapitan II | Kapitan I | Rear-admiral |
| ENGINEERS | Junior Engineer | Asst. Senior Engineer | Senior Engineer | Fleet Engineer | Inspector of Machinery |
| SURGEONS | Junior Surgeon | Asst. Senior Surgeon | Senior Surgeon | Fleet Surgeon | Inspector of Hospitals |
| NAVIGATION (Expiring) | Lieutenant | Staff Captain | | | |
| CONSTRUCTORS | Junior Asst. Naval Constructor | Senior Asst. Naval Constructor | Junior Naval Constructor | Senior Naval Constructor | Inspector of Naval Construction |
| NAVAL WORKS | ... | Junior Constructor | Senior Constructor | Chief Constructor | Inspector of Construction |
| NAVAL ORDNANCE (Expiring) | Lieutenant | Captain | Lieutenant-colonel | Colonel | Major-general [1] |

[1] Lieut.-general ranking with Vice-admiral; General with Admiral.

# XXVIII

## WATCHES

THE Russian Navy is peculiar in its watch-keeping, watches for officers and men being differently arranged, and in neither case as in all other navies.

The "day" begins in both cases at 8 a.m., and the twenty-four hours are arranged into five officers' and four men's watches.

For Officers

| | |
|---|---|
| Forenoon watch . . . . | 8–1 p.m. |
| Afternoon ,, . . . . | 1–7 ,, |
| Evening ,, . . . . | 7–12 midnight. |
| Midnight ,, . . . . | 12–4 a.m. |
| Morning ,, . . . . | 4–8 ,, |

For Men

| | |
|---|---|
| 1st watch . . . . . . | 8–12 noon. |
| 2nd ,, . . . . . . | 12–6 p.m. |
| 3rd ,, . . . . . . | 6–12 midnight. |
| 4th ,, . . . . . . | 12–8 a.m. |

There are no "dog-watches," and the ship's company are divided into the usual two watches, known as the first and second. But as they are subdivided into halves and quarters, some equivalent to the dog-watch is workable.

# XXIX

## RUSSIAN NAVAL FLAGS

THE Russian naval ensign is a long white flag with a blue St. Andrew's cross. The Jack has the same blue cross but a red ground, and a very narrow white cross quartering it; white lines also separate the blue cross from the white ground. The pennant is white, with the naval ensign in the corner, and a slightly peaked tail.

Admirals' flags are square adaptions of the ensign. *Admirals' flags.* Vice-admirals carry a blue band at the bottom, rear-admirals a red band. A general-admiral wears the ordinary admiral's flag,[1] unless he happens to be a Grand Duke; then the Imperial Arms (the black *Grand Dukes.* double-headed eagle on a yellow ground) are borne in a small circle in the centre of the flag. If an admiral is in command of a port he flies the ordinary ensign with a rectangle containing a couple of blue crossed anchors in the middle of the flag.

The Jack is also the national flag of Russia, and it is worn afloat by all the Imperial Family except the

[1] The old custom. About 1723 the general-admiral (Aprăksin) wore a Jack at the main for the first time, an innovation copied for the British admirals of the fleet.—*The Russian Navy under Peter the Great*, p. 121.

Tsar, who, of course flies the Imperial Standard, the

*Jacks.*

double-headed Byzantine eagle upon a yellow ground, so familiar to us because so many books on Russia carry it on the covers under the impression that it is the Russian flag! A Grand Duke's Jack carries a rectangle in the middle with a small Imperial Standard, unless he be the Tsarvitch, in which case there is a circle for the Imperial Arms instead of a rectangle. These same standards are worn in the head of their

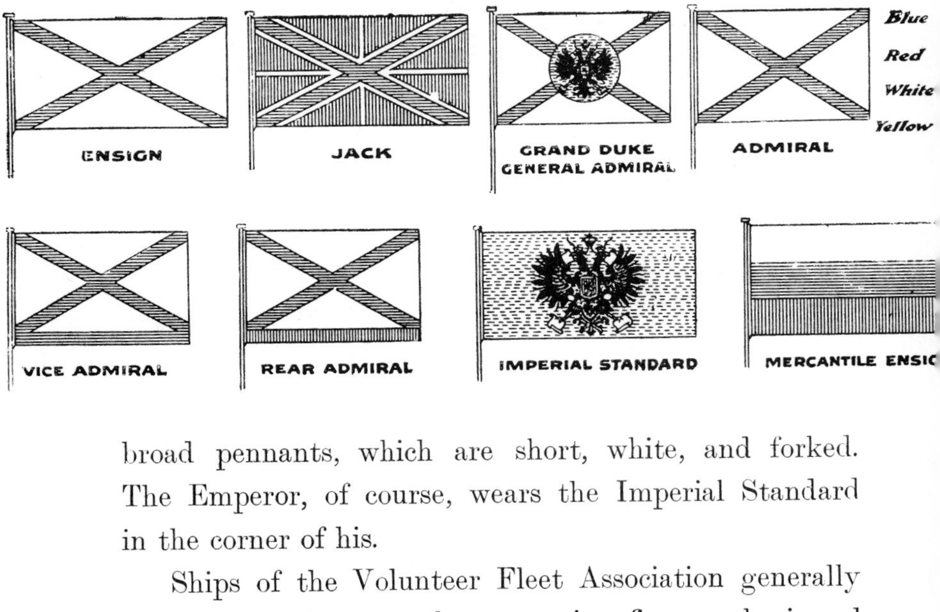


broad pennants, which are short, white, and forked. The Emperor, of course, wears the Imperial Standard in the corner of his.

Ships of the Volunteer Fleet Association generally fly the Russian merchant service flag—a horizonal tricolor, white on top, then blue, and at the bottom red.

The most-used service flag—used, that is, for a variety of purposes, like the Church-pennant in the British Navy—is the Pilot Jack, a flag much like our naval signal " D " and Pilot flag, a white flag with the Jack in a rectangle filling its middle.

Russian flags are, of course, descended from Peter the Great. The present mercantile marine flag (more or less copied from the Dutch) is the oldest, then came the Jack (a copy of the English Jack of that period), then the naval ensign proper. The Imperial Standard, as before remarked, is of much older date, but it is in no sense a naval flag.

# XXX

## ORGANISATION

THE navy personnel[1] for 1904 is thus organised :—

1 General-admiral.

10 Admirals ; 28 Vice-admirals ; 37 Rear-admirals.

354 Staff (*i.e.* Senior) Officers (102 Kapitans I. and 252 Kapitans II.).

1542 Junior Officers (750 Lieutenants and 420 Mitchmen,—the rest reserve, etc.).

503 Engineer Officers of all ranks.

702 Medical and other civil branches.[2]

162 Navy Yard Officers.

58,000 (about) Petty Officers, Seamen, Stockers, etc.

In connection with the personnel, ships are rated as follows :—

1*st Rate.*—All battleships of any importance—armoured cruisers and imperial yachts.

2*nd Rate.*—Small monitors, ironclad gunboats, small cruisers, torpedo gunboats, training ships, miscellaneous steamers, and transports.

3*rd Rate.*—" Flat iron " gunboats, first-class torpedo boats and destroyers, coastguard ships and light-ships.

4*th Rate.*—Second-class torpedo boats and other small craft.

[1] All ranks are being increased in numbers.

[2] Including 160 navigating and 70 ordnance officers (marine artillery) of corps now allowed to die out ; also naval constructors, etc.

This rating has nothing whatever to do with the fighting value of the ships, but depends upon their crews. Practically, every ship with a complement over 200 is first rate; all carrying between 200 and 100 men are second rate; and from 100 to 25, third rate. This offers conveniences for specifying a command, but it is also of use in arranging the "equipages"—a series of corps into which the entire naval force is divided. These are units like small army corps—each containing its own ships, equipage commander, and officers and men of all ranks and ratings, including a treasurer and an adjutant. Equipages are subdivided into companies under lieutenants, and each averages 150 men, but there is no exact number. Neither is there any exact number of companies necessary to form an equipage; there may be only seven, or as many as twelve, or even more in a few cases. The first four companies make up the complement of the first-class ships attached to the equipage, and the commander of the equipage has command of the chief ship. The remainder form the crews of the inferior vessels in the same group.

*Equipages.*

*Companies.*

Equipages are grouped at times, three to nine forming a "division" under an admiral.

When fleets are formed, all the ships of an equipage never get together, of course, but, as has been remarked before, only one-third of the year is spent at sea except on foreign stations, and even there "wintering" is usually done. On shore the equipage commander is a species of commodore or brigadier,[1] and all other kapitans in the equipage are responsible to him. He, on his part, is subject to the admiral of his "division."

*Equipage commander.*

Each admiral of division has a rear-admiral as second in command, a flag-captain (chief of staff), a flag-lieutenant, gunnery lieutenant, torpedo officer, an engineer, a navigating officer, and a doctor.

The equipages are normally grouped thus :—

| | | | |
|---|---|---|---|
| Two Divisions Baltic Fleet . (Mostly serving in the Pacific.) | Kronstadt . | 20 | equipages. |
| | Petersburg . | 1 | ,, (Imperial Guard). |
| | Revel . | ½ | ,, |
| | Sveaborg . | 1 | company. |
| Black Sea . . | Sevastôpol . | 4 | equipages. |
| | Nikolaieff . | 5 | ,, |
| Caspian Fleet . | Baku . . | 1 | ,, |
| Siberian Fleet . | Vladivostok | 1 | ,, |
| | Port Arthur | 1 | ,, |

On pages 488 *et seq.* is the division of ships amongst the equipages. Names in heavier type (thus **Poltāva**) indicate sea-going armoured vessels.

When a ship is to be commissioned her commanding officer is appointed by the Admiralty from the eligible officers in the equipage to which the ship belongs.

*Captains select their own officers.*

This captain selects his own officers, and these are able in a general way to decline with thanks if they like. Thus I met an officer who had been offered a billet in a ship when she went to the Pacific, and who had left the matter open for a time—pending

[6] In the historical portions these titles will be found. See Commodore Greig, Brigadier Dennison, etc.

consideration. Of course, this only applies in cases where the commission is arranged a long way ahead. Another officer I know had just been appointed captain of a ship at Kronstadt. He went down to her, but finding no old shipmates available or any officers that he "knew much about," he requested the Admiralty to appoint officers for him, giving them some idea of the particular sort he would soonest have.

Unofficially, of course, there is something of this kind in the British Navy, but to nothing like the same extent. It is a very good system, and it means, generally speaking, that if a captain gets any "duffers" amongst his officers it is entirely his own fault. Consequently the efficiency of the average Russian warship can be pretty well estimated from her captain —a good captain is practically certain to have a good crew.

[TABLES.

| Name or Number of Equipage. | Ships of 1st Rate. | Ships of 2nd Rate. | Ships of 3rd Rate. |
|---|---|---|---|
| Imperial Guard | **Aprăksin**<br>Polar Star (yacht)<br>Marevo (yacht)<br>Alexandria (yacht)<br>Striela (yacht) | Rȳnda | ... |
| FIRST DIVISION.—Baltic Fleet. | | | |
| I. | **Petropavlovsk**<br>**General-Admiral** | Opritchnik<br>Brononosetz | Grad<br>12 torpedo boats |
| II. | **Senjavin**<br>**Minin** | **Khrabry**<br>Kreisser<br>Edinorog | Abrek<br>Possilni (harbour ship) |
| III. | **Peter Veliki**<br>**Gromovoi** | Voin<br>Smertch | Snieg<br>10 torpedo boats |
| IV. (Grand Duke Alexei's) | **Nahimoff**<br>Korniloff | Tchitchagoff<br>**Otvajny** | Neva<br>Condor (t.b.d.) |
| V. | Sthandart<br>**Nikolai I**<br>Svietlana | Djidjit<br>Peroon | Jorsh<br>Dneiper |
| VI. | **Peresviet**<br>Pallada | Tcharadeika<br>Voivoda<br>Vestchun | Boroon |
| VII. | **Poltăva** | Gilyak<br>Najesdnik<br>Koldoun | Krasna Gorka (survey) |
| VIII. | **Retvizan** | A transport ship<br>Afrika | Sokol (t.b.d.)<br>Vriz (t.b.)<br>Mina |
| IX. | **Navărin**<br>**Vladimir Monomakh** | **Gremiastchy** | Korshun (t.b.d.) |
| SECOND DIVISION.—Baltic Fleet. | | | |
| X. | **Rossia**<br>**G. Edinburgski** | Lieut. Ilyn<br>Latnik<br>Viernii (t.s.) | 1 light-ship<br>1 harbour ship<br>1 steamer |
| XI. | **Oushakoff**<br>**D. Donskoi** | Moriak (t.s.)<br>Tiphun | ... |
| XII. (King of Greece's) | **Pămiat Azova** | Spiridoff<br>Streletz | Vichr<br>Toucha<br>2 steamers<br>1 harbour ship |
| XIII. | **Sissoi Veliky**<br>**K. Pojarski** | Plastoun<br>Lava<br>Ouragan | 12 torpedo boots |
| XIV. | **Alexander II.**<br>Aurora | **Groziastchy**<br>Strelok | Bouria |
| XV. | **Sevastôpol** | Asia<br>Lazareff | Kretset (t.b.d.) |
| XVI. | Pervenetz<br>Kreml<br>Netromenia | Greig | Groza and 2 destroyers |

| Ships of 4th Rate. | Also personnel for. | Normal Total of all Ranks and Ratings. |
|---|---|---|
| ... | ... | 2097 |
| ... | ... | 1438 |
| ... | ... | 1438 |
| ... | Telegraph corps and depôt at Kronstadt | 1438 |
| ... | Steam Reserve | 1438 |
| ... | Bandsmen | 1438 |
| ... | ... | *circa* 1200 |
| ... | ... | ... |
| ... | Men of depôts and schools | 702 |
| 5 small craft | Depôts and shore service | ... |
| ... | Steam reserve | *circa* 1500 |
| ... | Bandsmen and telegraph corps | ... |
| ... | Bandsmen | .. |
| 2 Customs cruisers<br>1 harbour craft | ... | ... |
| 1 harbour craft | Bandsmen and Steam reserve | .. |
| ... | Coastguardsmen | ... |
| ... | ... | ... |

| Name or Number of Equipage. | Ships of 1st Rate. | Ships of 2nd Rate. | Ships of 3rd Rate. |
|---|---|---|---|
| XVII. | **Retvizan**<br>**Rurik** | Viestnik<br>Tsarena (yacht) | ... |
| XVIII. | **Osliabia**<br>Diana | Rasboinik<br>Possadnik | Dodje<br>1 harbour and<br>2 light-ships |
| Revel half equipage. | ... | ... | 3 harbour ships<br>5 transports<br>5 Revenue cruisers<br>2 light-ships |
| Sveaborg Company. | ... | ... | 1 light-ship |
| XIX. | **Pobieda**<br>Bogatyr<br>Novik | Okean | t.b. Vnoushitelniy |
| XX. | **Tsarevitch**<br>Boyarin | Kreisser | New destroyers<br>t.b. Grozovoi |
| XXI.–XXVII., left for future ships, some in process of forming | | | |
| BLACK SEA DIVISION. | | | |
| XXVIII. | **Georgi Pobiedonosetz** | Kubanetz | 12 torpedo boats |
| XXIX.<br>Duke of Edinburgh's) | **Ekaterina II.** | Zaporetz<br>Kapitan Sāken | 10 torpedo boats<br>1 light-ship |
| XXX. | **Tri Svititelia** | Teretz<br>Dneister<br>1 transport | ... |
| XXXI. | **Sinôp** | Uraletz<br>Beresan (t.s.) | ... |
| XXXII.<br>Nikolaiff. | **Efstafi**<br>Pāmiat Merkuria | Donetz<br>Griden | 1 steamer<br>3 transports |
| XXXIII. | **Tchesme** | Tchernomoretz<br>Kasarski | 1 steamer<br>1 harbour ship<br>1 light-ship |
| XXXIV. | **D. Apostoloff** | ... | 3 transports |
| XXXV. | **Rostislav** | Prut | ... |
| XXXVI. | **K. Potemkin Tavritchesky**<br>**John Zlatoust** | 1 transport | 1 harbour ship<br>3 light-ships |
| Caspian equipage. | ... | Stakira<br>Pistchal | 4 steamers<br>1 harbour ship<br>1 light-ship |
| Siberian equipage. | ... | Zabiaka<br>Koreetz<br>Bobr<br>Mandschur<br>Sivoutch<br>Vsadnik<br>Gaidamak | 5 transports<br>2 harbour ships<br>11 torpedo boats |

| Ships of 4th Rate. | Also personnel for. | Normal Total of all Ranks and Ratings. |
|---|---|---|
| ... | Kronstadt depôt men | ... |
| ... | ... | ... |
| ... | ... | 795 |
| 2 harbour steamers | ... | 146 |
| ... | ... | ... |
| ... | ... | ... |
| 9 torpedo craft | ... | ... |
| 1 cutter<br>1 harbour craft | ... | 1438 |
| ... | ... | ... |
| ... | Band<br>Torpedo depôt<br>Harbour service<br>Mining craft | ... |
| ... | Crew of an Imperial cutter | ... |
| ... | Reserve men | ... |
| ... | Swimming school staff; non-effectives | 1200 |
| ... | ... | ... |
| ... | Non-combatants; harbour, signal, and torpedo school | 617 |
| ... | ... | ... |
| 7 torpedo boats | Band; personnel of hospital, swimming schools, harbour service, signal staff, torpedo, and mining | 3087 |

## Fleets in Commission

Russia maintains permanent squadrons in the Mediterranean and Pacific, two "Practice Squadrons" (for four months yearly), and training-ships.

For 1904 the distribution was as follows :—

### Pacific [1]

*Battleships.*—Tsarevitch, Retvizan, Poltāva, Petropavlovsk, Sevastôpol, Peresviet, Osliabia,[1] Pobieda, Navārin.[1]

*Cruisers.*—Bayan, Gromovoi, Rossia, Rurik, Variag, Bogatyr, Askold, Pallada, Diana, Aurora,[1] Dmitri Donskoi,[1] Admiral Nakimoff.[1]

*Small cruisers.*—Novik, Boyarin, Almaz.[1]

*Torpedo gunboats.*—Gaidamak, Vsadnik.

*Armoured gunboats.*—Gremiastchy, Otvajny.

*Destroyers and Torpedo boats.*—Fifty-four (others on way out).

*Mining vessels.*—Amur, Yenesi.

*Miscellaneous.*—Okean, 3 old vessels, 8 gun vessels.

### Mediterranean

*Old battleship.*—Imperator Nikolai I.[1]

*Armoured gunboat.*—Khrabri.

*Torpedo gunboat.*—Abrek.

*Torpedo boats.*—Two.

### Baltic

(*Practice Squadron*)

*Battleships.*—Alexander II., Aprāksin, Oushakoff, Senjavin.

*Cruisers.*—Svietlana, Korniloff.

*Destroyers and Torpedo boats.*—Five.

### Training

*Ships.*—General-Admiral (stokers), Djidjit, Gerzog Edinburgski, Rȳnda, Vernii, Moriak, Kniaz Pojarski.

[1] On passage out to Pacific.

EUXINE

*Battleships.*—Tri Svititelia, Rostislav, Georgi Pobiedonosetz, Sinôp.
*Torpedo gunboat.*—Saken.
*Destroyers and Torpedo boats.*—Four.
*Submarine.*—One.

PREPARING FOR COMMISSION

Borodino, Alexander III. (for Pacific).

# XXXI

## DISCIPLINE

### 1. Control of Admirals

THE case of the British Admiral Byng who, hampered by Admiralty instructions, was compelled to fight an action that he was opposed to attempting, and subsequently shot for his failure to win a victory, is one of the most well-known cases in history of that trouble which in all navies may now and again arise between the opinions of the director at home and those of the admiral on the spot.

There have been similar cases in the Russian Navy ; that of Kruyis (Cruys) being the most flagrant.[1] In this case the Russians had a heavy majority, and Kruyis's failure was due to the general inability of the admiral and everyone else concerned. For this Peter condemned him to death, and though eventually he was pardoned and restored to his rank, Peter at the same time issued an order that no admiral was to attack the Swedes unless he found himself in a majority of at least half as many ships again as the Swedes had.

*An equal force of Swedes not to be attacked.*

[1] See p. 57 and Appendix.

At a later period, off Gangoot 1743, as we have seen,[1] this order was used to cover and excuse a failure far greater than that which cost Byng his life; nor does Peter's law seem to have been questioned till in 1770 Spiridoff immolated himself against a superior force of Turks.

*Result at Tweermunde.*

*Spiridoff.*

In theory Peter's order was absolutely sound. The object of war is to defeat the enemy, not to fight "glorious actions." It is rare indeed that battles between equal, or anything like equal, forces have led to any decisive result—when they have done so, a little investigation will show that it has only been because through great tactical ability the whole of one force has been concentrated upon a portion of the other. No Russian admiral in Peter's time possessed this ability, and it is to Peter's credit that he was able to recognise the fact. He saw that the Swedish unit was superior to the Russian unit, and acted accordingly: it was his ability to recognise this that made Peter a great man.

*Remarks on Peter's order—pro.*

On the other hand, in warfare conditions must arise similar to those that happen so often on the chess-board, where a simple exchange of pieces may have the farthest reaching issues. The mental attitude of Russians to war has a great trend in this direction—"There is the enemy, go for him," has always been their mental substitute for Nelson's famous "England expects every man to do his duty" aphorism. A higher perception of what may be termed the

*Remarks on Peter's order—con.*

[1] P. 75.

chivalrous side of war than of its scientific side has hampered them more than once. To this day the dominant Russian idea of a fleet action is to concentrate upon the *strongest* hostile unit, in contradistinction to that of most other nations, where to destroy upward from the *weakest* is the ideal.

*Modern Russian naval tactics.*

This is not a work on naval tactics, so it will suffice here to merely point out that the destruction of the weakest is necessarily the better policy, not only because some result is thereby more quickly achieved, but because of the moral effect upon the enemy of seeing any one of its units lost. The amount of power needed to destroy or disable the strongest unit is sufficient to destroy two, or perhaps three, of the weaker ones.

*Punishment of admirals.*

At the present day should any punishment be inflicted upon an admiral, an Imperial Edict would be necessary. In the event of such punishment being administered, degradation to an inferior rank would be the one probably selected.

## 2. Officers and Men

The system of discipline generally in the Imperial Russian Navy is exceedingly simple in its broad application. Every officer and petty officer can inflict punishment on those below him in rank.

*Right to punish all inferiors.*

Such a system without safeguards might well lend itself to abuses, but the punishments that may be inflicted by minor officers are very small and slight;

the higher his rank the greater is the gamut of punishments allowed to an officer.

Engineers and their grievances.

To a certain extent this "executiveness of all ranks" may appear to be a solution of the problem raised nowadays by the engineers in every navy, but it is questionable whether it is so. In any case the engineers in the Russian service have their "grievance" as much as those in any other navy. In all cases this agitation is at bottom governed by a misapprehension of, and undue appreciation of, the importance of machinery. Machinery has grown so much in importance of late years that those who have to do with it forget that even machinery has its limits, and that war actual is not really a mere matter of machinery pure and simple. Absolute control of everything on shipboard or connected with ships is the *ultima thule* of naval engineer ambition all over the world, and any lesser claims put forward are merely temporary, or representative of a conservatism of the moment.

The mere fact that engineer agitations should exist at the present moment in four such very different services as the Russian, American, English, and Japanese, is an indication of the universal application of the forces at work. In every State there is a party of the Haves and a party of the Have-nots, the party of conservatism and the party of advance. Machinery on shipboard has produced a like result, and like conditions exist and must go on existing. The engineers represent that party of advance to be found in every State, and like that party they range from a species of Anarchist

No solution likely.

to the "moderate Liberal." No panacea or "sop to Cerberus"[1] can do more than temporarily alleviate this condition, and the attempted American solution of amalgamating the executive and engineer is a remedy so drastic and democratic that no nation is very likely to attempt an imitation until at least the working of the American system has been tested in a tough war. The "Jack of all trades" rock looms too big in these days, when the training for any single branch is a matter of at least five years.

*Ubiquity of the agitation.*

That the engineering problem should be common to the most autocratic and the most democratic countries in the world is a matter worthy of note, hence the foregoing remarks, the applicability of which to the subject of this book might not otherwise at first sight be fully apparent.

To return to the question of punishments. Discipline is rigid and rigidly enforced in most Russian warships. There is a well-known legend at sea that it is quite common for Russian officers to knock men down upon the quarter-deck, but though one or more such instances may have actually occurred, they can scarcely be regarded as representative. Speaking generally, one may say that the enforcement of discipline is no heavier in Russian ships than in British, or that such difference as may exist is racial and on the surface rather than an actual contrast.

*Knocking men down.*

*Scale of punishments.*

The scale of punishments at the disposal of com-

[1] The Japanese gave their engineers executive rank some time since, but it completely failed to solve the problem.

manding officers is greater than in the British or American services. A Russian captain can order a man a flogging if he likes, while a commander or first lieutenant is able to order a junior officer not to enter the wardroom. This is a favourite minor punishment, and probably a very effective engine.

*Under arrest.*

"Arrest" is divided into three sections: "light arrest," "middle arrest," and "strict arrest." "Light arrest" may be operative for a week, but one of the most inferior officers, a corporal for instance, can only inflict a single day's imprisonment, or a single day's other punishment. A sub-lieutenant may give a man four days' stoppage of leave if he chooses, or three days' extra work, or one day's light arrest. Lieutenants are empowered to imprison a man for a week, four days' "black list," or two days' light arrest. Commanders can run to inflicting a month's imprisonment, or, as alternatives for lesser offences, eight days' black list, up to five days' light or medium arrest, or two days' strict arrest, or not exceeding fifteen lashes if the offender is a seaman.

*Punishments different officers may award.*

A captain of the first rank may award ten days' ordinary arrest or four days' strict arrest, or twenty-five lashes.

*Fifty lashes.*

An *équipage* captain may order fifty lashes, and from one month's light arrest to a week's strict arrest. He has also the power to degrade any officer.

All punishment is broadly divided into two classes, correction punishment and criminal punishment.

There is a good deal to be said for this system. An

officer is as it were systematically trained in inflicting punishments, the surest safeguard against abuse of those powers. Only the more serious offences come before the captain, or even before the commander; minor ones are dealt with as they occur by the junior officers.

*An entire crew sent to Siberia.*

In connection with the administration of discipline on shipboard, one cannot but refer to a tale that was very generally published a few years since: that the entire crew of a flagship—both officers and men—had been sent to the Siberian mines for mutiny. This has been much cited as an instance of a good many things. The matter being one the real truth about which is known probably to none save those immediately concerned, it is idle to cite it as proving anything. So far as can be made out, some political plot was at the bottom of the affair, which removes it altogether from being a question of naval discipline. Another version, and perhaps the true one, is that the whole affair is one of those innumerable *canards* that fly around about Russia and the Russians.

# XXXII

## DRESS

### 1. Officers' Uniform

RUSSIAN officers' uniform is the usual blue, and consists of the frock-coat, the ordinary "reefer" jacket worn buttoned, and the "monkey jacket." For the summer these are white. *Officer's coat.*

The cap is that peculiar to the Russians, rather high and full—a somewhat difficult article to describe, but the various illustrations of it will serve to make it clear to anyone not already familiar with its shape. It is blue or white according to the uniform, and more often than not is seen with a red band to it. For full parade dress all officers wear cocked hats. Under the coat a rather high buttoning white waistcoat is worn. The necktie is black, tied in the usual knot. There is no "proper linen collar" to wear with uniform,—individual fancy may be consulted. In the British Navy that with turned down points is authorised, and no other is "uniform." The overcoat is blue, but light grey can be worn. Blue is the regulation, and at Kronstadt only blue is seen; in St. Petersburg, however, the light grey military coat, with a heavy *Cap.* *Waistcoat.* *Necktie.* *Collar.* *Overcoats.*

cape—a sort of semi-mantle—is frequently affected. In either case, the officer's overcoat reaches to the ground, and the grey caped one is a particularly picturesque coat. Amidst the sombre clothing usually affected by women as well as men in the capital, it gives a certain touch of brightness to the streets. In the majority of cases no visible fur collar is worn with this coat—fur cuffs are never seen on it. It is lined and quilted with some sort of red flannel, underneath which there is fur.

OFFICER'S OVERCOAT.

*Winter head-gear.*

Officers and men also, during the winter, wear over the shoulders and down the back a sort of wool cape, of a light buff or brown colour, with long ends over the chest. This, should the weather be extremely cold, is worn peaked over the head and covering the ears. Usually, however, it is not worn thus; during the whole of the time I was in Russia I never saw this head-covering in actual use, and only on two occasions did I notice officers with their coat collars turned up, though a thaw in the morning, followed an hour or two later by a nip of twenty to thirty degrees of frost,—a favourite climatic condition in Russia,—might well seem to necessitate some such precaution occasionally.

During the winter months every Russian is, of

course, wearing goloshes over his boots. The service golosh is quite a plain shiny one. Inside his socks the Russian usually wears some dry mustard, a certain cure for, and precaution against, influenza. *Goloshes.*

The Russian officer, like the German, is always in uniform from the first thing in the morning till the last thing at night, wherever he may be. *Always in uniform.*

There is no "dress" uniform such as there is in the British Navy; any ordinary uniform being correct for any hour. It is a curious item, by the way, that a Russian expects an Englishman to dress for any function or anything after six in the evening, taking it as the correct thing and a compliment that the Englishman should do so, and feeling hurt if he does not. A German, on the other hand, is prone to take an Englishman in evening dress as an insult to himself. *No "dress."*

Meals are taken in the following order :— *Meals.*

*Café au lait*, breakfast on rising.

*Déjeûner*, about 11.30 a.m. to 1 p.m.

Dinner, about 6 p.m.

Supper, any time after 10 p.m.

In an ordinary mess it is customary to smoke between the courses at dinner and supper the little Russian cigarettes, which have not much taste and very little smell. This is never done nowadays at any meal at which ladies are present. Cigarettes only "come round" with the coffee in all cases; previous smokings are matters of individual taste. There are a good many officers who do not smoke at all; with the majority, however, smoking is very much of an institution. *Smoking.*

There are in the Russian Navy none of those regulations about smoking which obtain in the English Navy. In English warships smoking in the wardroom at all, except possibly with the coffee after dinner, is forbidden; it is only in port-guardships and harbour-service vessels that the rule is not adhered to. In some English ships also, smoking is confined to certain hours, though this barbarous regulation is now dying out. There is nothing of that in the Russian Navy, and an officer may light up a cigarette anywhere, where, and whenever he chooses. Even in the dockyards smoking is permissible; in an English dockyard it is, of course, stringently and absolutely forbidden.

*Chaplains.*

Priests are carried as chaplains in nearly all Russian warships. Like the *padrés* in the British Navy, they have no special naval uniform, but wear the ordinary clerical costume.

A CORPORAL.

## 2 Men's Uniform

All over the world the sailor wears pretty much the same uniform. The Russian sailor has a cap that is a cross between those worn by the British and the United States sailors, and this cap has very long ribbon-tails to it, otherwise he is much like any other sailor to look at. In common with all non-British Navy sailors, he wears a moustache.[1] *Cap.*

Corporals wear the sailor's uniform, but have peaked caps instead of the ordinary sailor's cap. *Corporal's cap.*

Russian sailors wear a grey overcoat, not reaching below the knees, and belted around the waist. Under the ordinary sea-service jumper or jacket they wear a jersey, blue and white striped. There are blue and white stripes upon the collar, while in the case of white summer clothing there are also blue stripes upon the cuff. *Overcoats.* *Summer clothing.*

On ship duty, sentry, etc., the cutlass is worn attached to a waist-belt, and the ammunition pouch upon another strap slung over the left shoulder. *Sentry.*

For shore-going duty in marching order the pouch is slung to the waist-belt. On these occasions the sailor usually wears a sort of long military tunic—military except that it has a small turn-down collar. There are shoulder-straps then to indicate the equipage, *Shore duty.*

[1] A recent edict of the Kaiser has abolished the moustache in the German Navy.

also cuffs of a military sort. High leggings are worn with this rig.

*Naval cadets.* Naval cadets have an almost identical uniform to this.

MARCHING UNIFORM OF BLUEJACKETS.

A RUSSIAN BLUEJACKET.

# XXXIII

## DISTINGUISHING MARKS FOR RANK

### 1. Officers

TO those used to the simple stripe distinction of rank used in the British Navy, the Russian method of differentiation is rather confusing, there being as many varieties in the Russian executive uniform as there are amongst all the branches of the British service combined.

A MITCHMAN.

Yet in essence the Russian system is very simple, and there is none of that chance of muddle between a "two and a half striper" and a commander which so puzzles the semi-initiated in a British man-of-war. It is the different equipages and fleets which produce the trouble when the foreigner tries to discover the rank of a Russian officer.

*Grade shoulder-straps.*

The Russian wears no stripes on his sleeves, but is differentiated instead by shoulder-straps. These are marked as follows :—

| | |
|---|---|
| Mitchman (*i.e.* sub-lieutenant) . | One star and one band. |
| Lieutenant . . . . | Three stars and one band. |
| Kapitan II. rank (commander) . | Three stars and two bands. |
| Kapitan I. rank (captain) . . | Two bands without stars. |
| Rear-admiral . . . . | One eagle. |
| Vice-admiral . . . . | Two eagles. |
| Admiral . . . . . | Three eagles. |

The band for executive officers is blue-black on a yellow strap, with silver stars. The corresponding full dress epaulettes are without any bands, but have the stars as usual. Those of lieutenants and mitchmen have no fringe—a commander's epaulette is practically a lieutenant's one with a fringe to it. A captain has a quite plain epaulette; admirals have one, two, or three eagles, according to rank, on theirs, and heavier fringes, each pendant being about half an inch or more in diameter.

*Epaulettes of executive officers.*

All executive officers have gold epaulettes.

Doctors and engineers have silver epaulettes and shoulder-straps; some red in the engineers' marks, the doctors having black.

Both engineers and doctors are divided into two main grades only, junior and senior.

*Engineers.*

The junior engineer has three stars on a red stripe

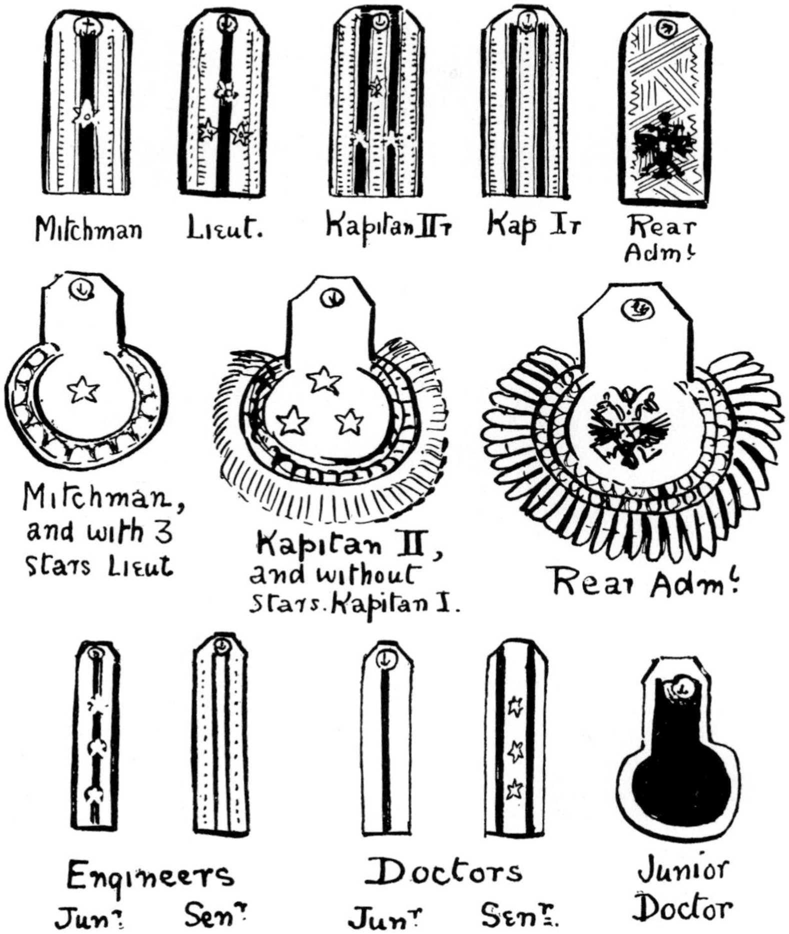


SHOULDER-STRAPS AND EPAULETTES.

on his shoulder-strap, the senior two red stripes without stars.

The junior doctor has a single black stripe without stars, the senior doctor two black stripes and three stars between the band.

*Doctors.*

In the case of both doctors and engineers the shoulder-strap is much narrower than that of an executive officer.

*Engineers' epaulettes.*

The junior engineer has a plain silver epaulette with three stars placed as a lieutenant's stars; the senior's is very like a captain's, save that it is silver instead of gold.

*Doctors' epaulettes.*

The junior doctor has an epaulette exactly like the junior engineer, save that there are no stars and all the interior is black. A senior doctor also has this plain black interior, otherwise his epaulette is almost identical with that of a senior engineer.

In all cases both straps and epaulettes have a naval anchor upon the upper or inner corner.

So far this is fairly simple. But we now come to the complicating features, which, however, are of minor import.

*Aides-de-camp.*

If an officer is an aide-de-camp to any of the Imperial family, he wears a bright red collar to a military looking tunic, and with the military moustache so favoured by Russian officers[1] looks far more like a soldier than a sailor.

[1] No Russian (except a few of the lower orders) is ever clean shaved, he either wears a moustache, or else beard, moustache, and whiskers. In the

Then again, gunnery specialisation turns the executives' black stripes to red; while the different equipages have each their own sign manual. Thus the first fleet equipage entails a *K* with a crown and one broad stripe; the Caspian has a *K* of slightly simpler pattern, no crown, and two narrow stripes. The second fleet equipage is indicated by an *O* with a crown above it, and three stripes above that. Other equipages have the number only, except the Siberian, indicated by the letter *C* (the Russian *S*), and the Sveaboorg, which has *C b* (the Russian *S v*).

*Gunnery.*

*Equipage marks.*

Every sailor has this equipage indication on his shoulder when in shore-going marching order.

*Sailors.*

One of the Black Sea equipages has a good deal of gold about it. This regiment distinguished itself in the past, and its men now wear gold around the caps and gold ribbons as a mark of Imperial distinction.

*A famous equipage.*

Boatswains and corporals in marching order wear a flat gold shoulder-strap; the boatswain's has seven narrow lines on it, the corporal's has the lines a little differently placed, and four of them are merely dotted.

*Bo'suns and corporals.*

British Navy, of course, the clean shaved officer is common,—he is, indeed, the rule rather than the exception; everything, or else a clean shaved face with, at discretion, very small side whiskers, is the regulation. To a Russian the clean shaved man is a curio—"Why don't you grow hair on your face?" or "Why do you English wear your faces like women's?" is a question I several times heard in Russia, where to be clean shaved is an Englishman's hall-mark. So much is this the case that our "bagmen" who do not want to be taken for Germans are either clean shaved or fully bearded;—and the English commercial traveller is a person who normally loves to grow a moustache.

Usually they wear ordinary sailor dress, but a peaked instead of an ordinary round cap with tails.

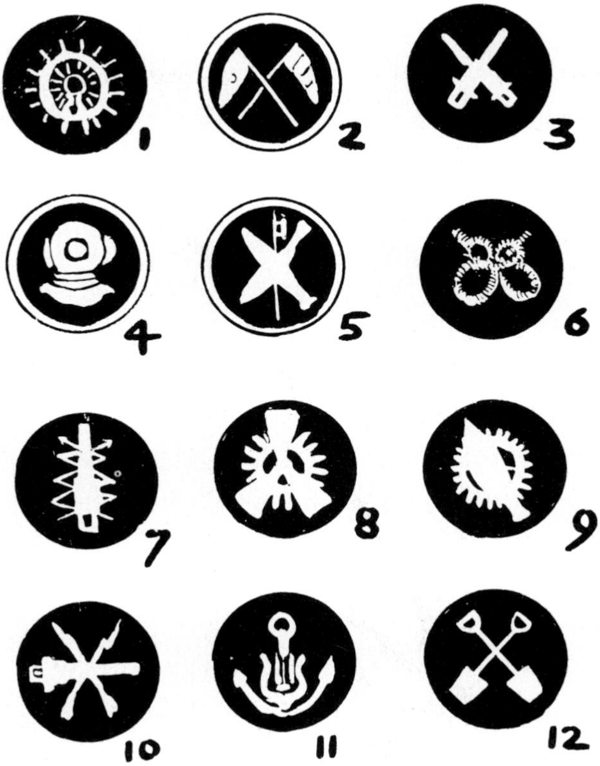

1. Quartermaster. 2. Chief Signalman. 3. Artillery Quartermaster. 4. Diver. 5. Chief Torpedo Q.T.M. 6. Topman. 7. Electrician. 8. Chief Torpedo Mechanic. 9. Engine-Room Artificer. 10. Armourer. 11. Bandsman. 12. Stoker. (In all these ratings the addition of an outer circle indicates a "chief.")

*Men's distinguishing marks.*

The distinguishing marks for the different classes of men can be made out best from the appended illustrations of the circles worn upon the sleeves.

# XXXIV

## PERSONAL CHARACTERISTICS OF RUSSIAN OFFICERS AND MEN

### Officers

MY own exceedingly favourable impression of Russian officers leaks out in a good many places in this book. It will, perhaps, be urged against me that my view was necessarily *couleur de rose*, and that I saw them "best side out." Possibly I did. Certainly the Russian executives struck me as differing from their English brethren chiefly in that some of them wore moustaches; otherwise there was a wonderful similarity. That was in their personalities, and does not, of course, necessarily prove that their efficiency is equal. Again, it may be said that I did not see them all. Altogether, however, I met in Russia over a hundred, ranging in rank from admiral to sub-lieutenant. Intimacy (which is the only sure guide) varied, of course: with some of this odd hundred my intimacy was slight, while with others it was the reverse. In our own harbours and elsewhere, I have come across a few dozen more; altogether, therefore, so far as numbers go, there are presumably enough to sample from, and my impression is that, taking them in the lump, they compare very well with our officers. This is, I hope, an unbiassed opinion, so far as I may be held qualified to deliver one, and is at least based on opportunities that have not, so far as I know, come in the way of any other Englishman. And I do not think that the Russian in me (one-eighth part) can be held enough to bias my judgment. Hence I put on record that the Russian naval officer struck me as more than a skin-deep "jolly good fellow" (a Russian ideal), and further, as a man thinking a good deal about and having a considerable mastery of the theory of his profession. Of the more important practical side I cannot speak so freely,—I have not seen enough of that side to make my opinion of much value.

*Tot homines, tot sententiæ*: I have heard opinions upon Russian officers that are dead against these of mine, and in some cases at anyrate they are opinions not to be discarded as of no weight. For instance, the following on the whole most unfavourable opinion is more or less current in St. Petersburg and other parts of Russia:—

"With the exception of Grand Duke Alexander Mihailovitch and a few of his lot, there's not a captain or commander who is any good at all. They are all after snug billets on shore, and if they do go to sea never do anything except make a muddle. The Germans would beat them easily."

This might be a paraphrase of the opinion of the

contemporary Englishman in Peter the Great's day;[1] possibly its roots may lie there. I have reason to think that it is a fairly general belief in Russia, but the fact of its being fairly general is no proof of its accuracy. Nor can one altogether forget that identical opinions were about in Japan concerning the fleet when the Chino-Japanese War broke out. In that case popular opinion proved singularly incorrect.

In our service I have heard some scathing comments on Russian efficiency much after the pattern of the one quoted *in extenso* above, but on tracing it, its origin proved to be a muddle in striking top-gallant masts in a fourth-rate gunboat! Generally speaking, our people who have seen much of them incline to a good deal more favourable a view, though it may or may not be warped by personal fondness for Russian "opposite numbers."

This fondness is a reciprocal affair, though Russians have always told me that their first impression of English officers was not quite after the pattern. "The English officers don't make friends easily," they say; "it's not till you get to know them that you begin to get so fond of them." When the fondness comes about relations are generally very cordial, even if there was nothing save a pretty politeness in the speech of the officers of a Russian which lay in a harbour with a British and a French warship, when the Franco-Russian alliance was at fever heat. The Russians called first upon the Frenchman, then came

[1] See Appendix.

to the English ship and stayed there, with a—"Duty first, pleasure afterwards."

In such shore-going drill as I saw, the officers appeared fully efficient. I incline to fancy that they are less bellicose than our people. I do not mean by this to imply that the average British naval officer is thirsting for war, but he would undoubtedly accept it easily if it came, and not put himself out to avert it. The feeling is, that a war would tend to better our efficiency. They have not got this feeling in Russia, and would, I fancy, accept war more with a dogged determination to do their best than with a conviction of certain success. At least, this latter sentiment would not be the dominant one. So far as we are concerned, there would not be any attempt to try conclusions with us on the water if it could be avoided.

So far as personal appearance goes, there is little or nothing of the dandy in the Russian naval officer. Here and there one may encounter an officer who has done time in the French Navy, and he will probably stand out as smarter than his fellows. Generally the Russian is less particular about his linen than an English officer, and one who would be regarded as untidy in our service would not be conspicuous in theirs. A wandering Englishman that I met in Russia remarked to me that "Russian naval officers always wore dirty and crumpled collars," but as he pointed out a *Customs* officer to prove his contention, this (more or less generally accepted belief here) cannot be accepted as conclusive! Our naval officers as a class are not dandies; the Russians are rather less so, but they are certainly not slovens—and there the matter ends.

Finally, they are one and all imbued with a patriotism of a distinctive sort, something on a par with our *Civis Britanniæ sum*: they are proud of being Russians. There is enough of this to go a very long way. Loyalty to the Imperial Family is a marked characteristic in them also: with our naval officers the same sort of thing obtains, but while with us the reverence is for the *institution*, with Russian officers it is more directly personal.

## Men

The Russian bluejacket bears no likeness to the British article, nor will the British "blue" fraternise with him. "'E ain't clean enough" is the verdict of our lower deck, and there is no denying that from our standpoint the verdict is justified. Ivan is not over clean. In point of fact, he stands much where our men stood a hundred years or more ago. He comes, too, from a different and lower class; the young British bluejacket has to be a very respectable youth. He is a sailor, too, from boyhood: the Russian joins as a man of twenty-one, and joins because he is told to, not because he wants to. Fraternising between our men and the Russian sailors has never yet taken place, and is never likely to. Yet our men do not altogether despise the Russian blues; with the sort of contempt that they have for them, they have also a species of respect, which takes the form of "we'd like to fight them"—a British bluejacket's antithesis to contempt. Still, Jack has the contempt also;—he believes that every Russian sailor lives chiefly on tallow-candles varied with bear's grease, decayed fish, and soap. He believes that Ivan fears but one thing—cold water. He further believes that Ivan is a person of no spirit at all in the ordinary way,—that it has "all been flogged out of him." He doubts whether Ivan would "like to fight because a proper modern sea-fight must be the most interesting thing a man could see in this world or the next."

Very funny is this British bluejacket's notion of Ivan at sea; but when due allowance is made for exaggeration and so forth, it is not altogether incorrect.

Ivan is a big, strong, burly fellow with a sluggish good temper—like a big Newfoundland dog. He is simple and childish, and his intelligence is not high. He is amenable and willing, anxious to do his best and to find fun in his profession in his own melancholy way. I doubt whether seeing a sheep killed 'tween decks has such charms for him as it has for British tars, who regard watching such an operation as valuable professional training. It would not mean anything more than "something to eat" to Ivan: its finer ethics would be lost on him. This particular trait of the British bluejacket may strike some of our good shore-going folk as very dreadful, but it is an exceedingly good trait practically—the man who is trained to kill and to be killed does not require to be taught to give a virtuous shudder at the sight of blood. Hereabouts lies one main difference: Ivan realises that he exists to *be shot at*; Jack, that he exists *to shoot at others*, and this psychological difference is as heavy a one as can well be:—it is all the difference in the world.

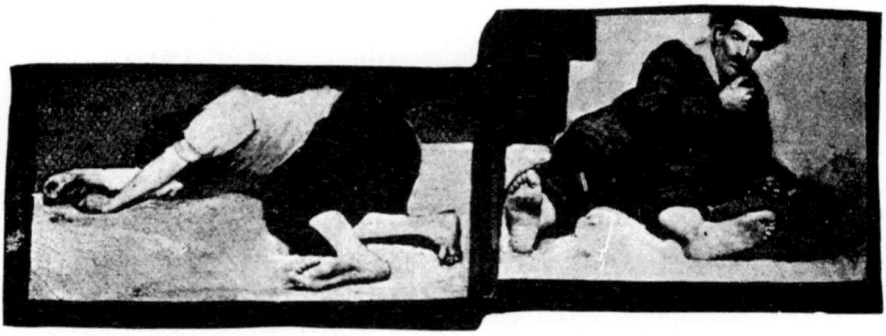

IVAN IN REPOSE.

# XXXV

## THE ARMAMENT AND EQUIPMENT OF THE FLEET

### Guns

THE majority of guns in the Russian service are manufactured at Obukoff Works — the balance come from Canet.

*Obukoff.*

The Obukoff Works on the Neva are a State establishment, and under the control of the Navy. They were first started in 1863, and have grown steadily ever since. At the present time they have a capacity for some 800 guns in hand at once, in addition to torpedoes, armour, and machinery. About 3000 men are employed here,—pay ranging from 1s. to 8s. per diem.

Obukoff guns are generally noticeable in that their energy per ton is relatively a little less than that of foreign pieces: they are made very strong, and the Russians are proud of the fact that none have ever burst.[1]

*Breech mechanism.*

The breech mechanism is an adaption of the Canet, —the Obukoff gun is altogether more or less after the Canet pattern. The newest 6-in. (Russians use the

[1] The Sissoi Veliky disaster was not a matter of a burst gun, though it is usually loosely spoken of as having been so.

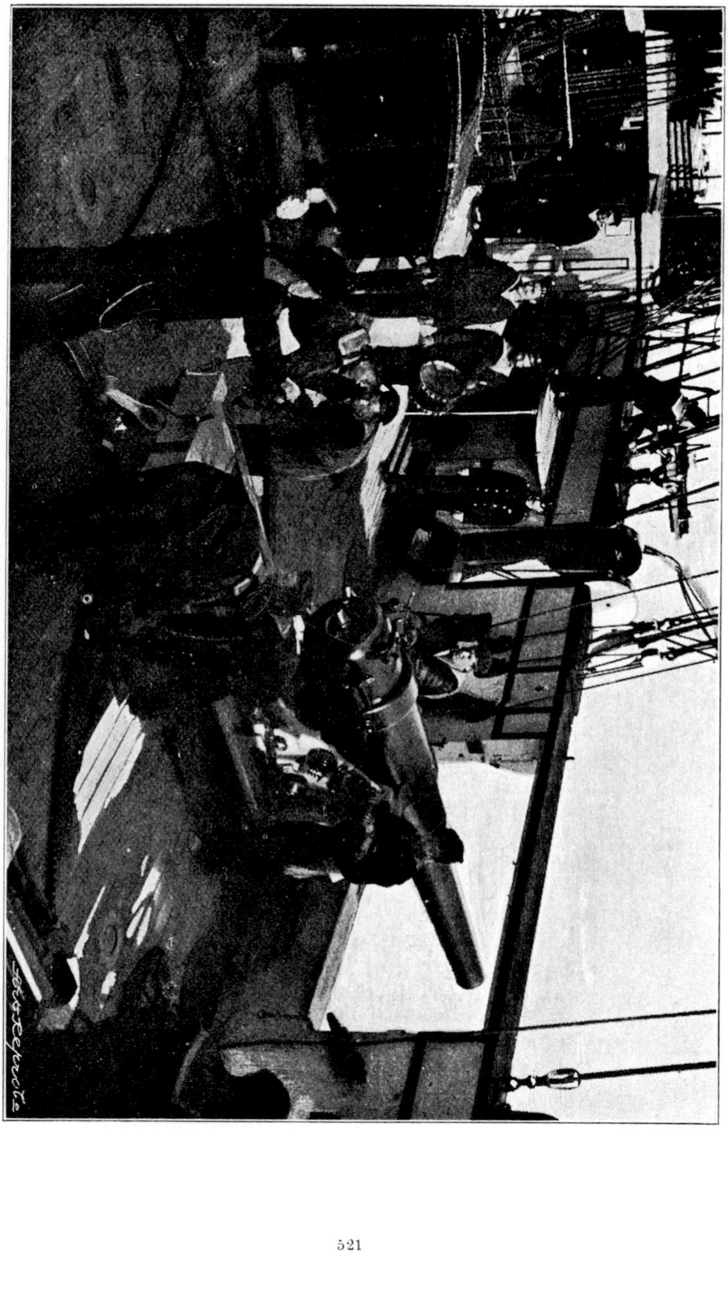

6-IN. GUN DRILL ON BOARD THE DJIDJIT.

inch and not the centimetre for designating their artillery calibre) is practically a simplified 15-cm. Canet. This simplicity is essential, as the Russian bluejacket is not easily able to master intricacies of mechanism. It is a singularly workable piece, heavy for its size (it is 45 cal. long), with a single-action self-locking breech. It is doubly impossible to fire the gun unless the breech be locked.

On the following page are the details of Russian guns[1] now mounted afloat. The alphabetical Naval War Game notation, which is generally used in the plans of ships throughout this book, is appended, and for reference and explanation the armour-notation system adopted to suit rapid comparisons.

The guns being mounted in ships now completing and building are:—

| | | | | |
|---|---|---|---|---|
| A | 12-in. | of | 40 | cal. long. |
| C | 8 | ,, | 45 | ,, |
| D | 6 | ,, | 45 | ,, |
| E | 4·7 | ,, | 45 | ,, |
| F | 3 | ,, | 45 | ,, |

The Baronovski, 3·4-in., from what I have seen of them, are very unsatisfactory in rapidity. They, though short, fire very accurately indeed.

The 40 calibre 12-in. first appears in the Poltāva class; the 10-in. 45 calibre was mounted first of all in the Aprāksin. It is also in the Peresviets and the Rostislav.

[1] These details are taken from *All the World's Fighting Ships*.

## NAVAL GUNS

| Notation. | Nominal Calibre. | Weight. | Length. | Initial Velocity. | Muzzle Energy. *circa.* | Projectile: Common Shell. | Maximum Penetration of Krupp cemented armour, with capped A.P. at 3000 yards. | |
|---|---|---|---|---|---|---|---|---|
| | in. | | Cals. | ft.-secs. | ft.-tons. | lbs. | in. | |
| A | 12 | 56-ton | 35 | 1,942 | 25,000 | 732 | 10 | *a* |
| $A^3$ | 12 | 59-ton | 40 | 2,500 | 30,000 | 732 | 15½ | *aaaa* |
| $A^3$ | 12·4 *or* 12 | 64-ton | 40 | 2,500 | 35,000 | 1,200 | 16½ | „ |
| B | 10 | 32-ton | 45 | 2,500 | 17,000 | ... | 13 | *aaa* |
| B | 12 | 50-ton | 30 | 1,942 | 19,300 | 732 | 9¼ | *aa* |
| B | 9·4 *or* 9 | ... | 40 | 2,500 | 15,000 | ... | 9 | „ |
| C | 12 | (M. 1877) 40-ton | 17 | 1,705 | 10,000 | 990 | 7 | *a* |
| C | 9 | ... | ... | ... | 10,500 | ... | 9 | *aa* |
| C | 8 | ... | 35 | 1,922 | ... | 192 | 6 | *a* |
| C* | 8 | ... | 45 | 2,500 | ... | 200 | 8¼ | „ |
| D* | 6 | ... | 45 | 2,460 | 4,000 | 88 | 6 | „ |
| D* | 6 | ... | 35 | 2,080 | 3,300 | (?) | 3½ | *de* |
| $E^{d}$* | 4·7 | ... | 45 | 2,460 | 2,212 | 46·3 | 3 | „ |
| F* | 3·4 | ... | 20 | ... | ... | ... | ... | ... |
| F* | 3 | ... | 40 | 2,658 | 648 | 13·2 | ... | ... |
| F* | 2·4 | ... | 20 | 1,246 | ... | 6 | ... | ... |

Notes.—All modern Obuchoff guns have Canet breech rifling system and mounting, and are practically equivalent to, and identical with, Schneider-Canet guns.

There are still a few old guns afloat in one or two obsolete ships of other and inferior models to the above, but practically all Russian ships have been re-armed with the above guns. An old 9-inch still exists in the Nikolai, value D, and the Tchesma has, or had, an old 12-inch, value C.

The 12·4 is a doubtful piece, perhaps projected only.

Russian guns use smokeless powder.

The last ship to have the 9·4 was the Seniavin, while the non-Q.F. 8-in. makes its last appearance in the Rossia.

*Projectiles.* The projectiles fired are armour-piercing shell and common shell. Solid shot has been abandoned, as on the testing-ground the "magnetic" capped A.P. shell got through as much armour as solid A.P. shot. High explosives have not yet been adopted, and probably will not be until their success has been more fully demonstrated abroad. Experiments are, however, being conducted with a new explosive of fairly high power and singular safety.

The newer guns fire a smokeless powder.

*Smaller Q.F.*

In Q.F. of smaller calibre than the 3-in. 12-pounder, Hotchkiss, Maxim, and the Russian Baronovski Works are called upon. The calibres are the 57-mm. (6-pounder), 47-mm. (3-pounder), and 37-mm. (1-pounder). There are also Nordenfelts and the ordinary Maxim guns. The Baronovski Q.F. is a 63-mm. (2·5 in.) gun, 17 calibres long, firing a 5½ lb. shell with a muzzle velocity of 1220 ft.-seconds. It is a purely Russian gun. The 37-mm. (1-pounder) are usually revolver guns. The 1-pounder is the smallest shell allowed by the Geneva Convention, and measures only 3¾ in. in height. Some while ago one of these 37-mm. shells, bursting on board a French warship, killed or wounded five men: their utility in action is likely, however, to be limited.

Revolver cannons are also in favour in the Russian Service.

## Small-Arms

The Russian naval rifle is the Mouzin, model 1891, details of which[1] are as follows :—

Calibre, ·3 in. Number of rounds in magazine, 5. Weight of bullet, 208 grains. Charge, 33 grains. Initial velocity, 2001 ft.-seconds.

This weapon is to be eventually replaced by the Lee straight pull, probably the best rifle going. The 1893 model of this arm is used in the United States Navy; it is remarkable for its high initial velocity—2550 ft.-seconds.[2] This is 100 ft. better than the Mannlicher, the next best. Its bore is the smallest known—·236 only, which is rather less than the Mannlicher's.

Revolver. The service revolver is the Smith-Wesson.

Sword. There is nothing particular to say about the swords. The dress sword usually worn by officers is a little thing, a species of midshipman's dirk.

[1] From *The Naval Pocket Book* for 1899.

[2] The Lee-Metford's initial velocity is 2200; calibre, ·303.

## Torpedo

The Russian service torpedo is of the Whitehead type, and is made at Obukoff and at the Loesner Factory, St. Petersburg. Between them these two establishments turn out about 50 torpedoes yearly. There are several models: those of 15 and 17·7 in. being the most common. The latter is 19·68 ft. in length, and of about 30 knots speed. The charge is said to be the enormous one of 300 lbs. of gun-cotton,—half as much again as our 18-in. ones carry.

Russia purchased the right to manufacture gyroscope torpedoes. A "business" description of the gyroscope or Obry apparatus (so called after its Austrian inventor) is as follows:— *Gyroscopes.*

"By the use of this apparatus any deflection of the torpedo out of its original line of fire is prevented, such deflection being produced either by the method of discharge or by some defect appertaining to the torpedo itself. The apparatus consists of a gyroscope, which is set in action at the moment of discharge of the torpedo. The action depends on a rapidly revolving wheel, suspended in gimbal rings in such a manner that all sources of friction are absent, and the axis of the wheel tends to maintain itself in the original direction in which the rotary motion was communicated to it; thus the initial direction of the torpedo is maintained throughout the run. The gyroscope acts on the slide valve of a steering engine, and, on any angular movement of the torpedo from the initial *Description.*

direction, the slide valve is acted on, working a piston connected to vertical rudders pivoted in the tail, and so immediately steers the torpedo back again in the original direction of the line of fire. The higher the rate of revolution of the wheel, the greater the tendency for the apparatus to remain in correct adjustment. Motion is given to the wheel at the moment of discharge by the rapid unwinding of a torsional spring, which spring has to be so held every time before the torpedo is fired. The apparatus weighs between 8 and 9 lbs., is placed in the buoyancy chamber of the torpedo, and is so arranged that it can readily be abstracted for examination or adjustment. It can be taken from one torpedo and readily placed in another. The course of the torpedo with the apparatus in action is of a lateral wave form, with ordinates at the maximum of about 2 metres in length. To obtain good results, careful adjustment, which is done on a special table, is needed. By the use of the Obry gyroscope, torpedoes can be set to run accurately up to 2000 yards, though at lower rates of speed. The accuracy of a torpedo is so enormously increased by this apparatus that the well-known difficulty and delay in preparing torpedoes for service, viz., their adjustment at a range, is obviated. The present cost of these instruments is £50, including royalties."

*Remarks.*

A gun will carry somewhere about 25,000 yards, but the odds are heavy against its hitting at even 5000. In the same way, the 2000-yard range of the Obry-fitted torpedo is more of the possible than the probable. Without the apparatus, about 500 yards is the very maximum distance at which a torpedo is expected to hit the target, and the *war chances* are about 3 to 1 against it then. With the gyroscope there are chances of hitting up to 2000 yards. The apparatus needs considerable care and skill in its use, and plenty of "looking after" at times when it is not in use, else it may prove a boomerang. Still, there is no question but that it is a great improvement on previous methods.

The Russians have not yet discarded torpedo nets. *Nets.* They have still the old pattern, but will probably be introducing the Gromet with its finer mesh ere long. Russian ships invariably stow their torpedo booms the reverse way to the usual,—the booms lying forward instead of aft. This is noticeable in all the illustrations of their modern warships.

Russian torpedo officers, it may be observed, are mostly very efficient. Curiously enough, though Russia did more than any nation to introduce the torpedo, she is nearly always assumed to be behindhand in this matter.

Submerged tubes in the Russian Navy are more or less of the Schneider Canet design, and in the majority of ships bear 20° abaft the beam. It is rumoured that in some of the new ships they are fixed 20° before the beam, but this requires confirmation. The bow tube in the Kniaz Potemkin Tavritchesky is a new Elswick design.

Above-water tubes (training) are being removed, but those fixed at the bow and stern are retained in the very latest types.

It is worthy of note that, as remarked on a previous page, most above-water tubes are placed outside the redoubt without armour protection. The tubes that have been or are being removed are those behind armour. Presumably some recent experiments in the Baltic are the cause of this.

### Gunnery Matters

A short while ago the Russian gunnery practice squadron fired before the Kaiser and German officers. They hit the target every time, both at fixed and moving targets at long ranges, a feat that made a remarkable impression upon the Germans. Probably these were special gun crews, and the gunnery average cannot be assumed equal to this result, but the old theory that "Russians cannot shoot" is a dangerous one to hold.

Gunnery returns are impossible to obtain, and Russian officers are absolutely reticent about their shooting. But it is clear that immense efforts are made to secure efficiency in this direction, and from what is not said rather than from what is, I am inclined to fancy that Russia is behind no nation in gunnery at present. Whether her guns will hit as well in war as in peace, war alone can show, but her men are very unlikely to get excited in battle, and she has an immense advantage in the fact that officers will aim the guns in battle. So many officers are carried that this is possible.

Speculations on the matter are idle, but the general air of confidence characteristic of Russian naval officers when gunnery is on the *tapis*, may well afford matter for serious thought.

### Armour

Till recently Russian armour came from Carnegie's works in America and from the Creusot firm. Of late it has been "made in Russia," but actually Krupp at Essen did much of the making at first. Now there are well established works at Ijoia, where 5000 men are employed, at the Obukoff gun factory. Works also is done at the Putiloff and Alexandrovsky steel works; there is plant, too, at the Baltic works.

Five years ago (1899), I saw men on board the completing Sevastopol filling up cracks in armour joints with wood and putty—the imported armour had got strained in transport and the plates would not meet properly. Ten years ago somebody stole some of the money, and many of the armour plates were imitations made of wood.[1]

To-day (1904) Russian armour appears quite well constructed, well put on, and I have sought in vain for putty filled cracks and imitation plates. The Pobieda, the latest Russian built armour ship, is of excellent workmanship throughout, and so far as inspection can prove the armour was put on with equal excellence.[2]

[1] It was also, however, the practice of Russian officers in unarmoured ships to fit a certain amount of dummy armour over guns to impress British officers visiting them. This was done on the Rossia so late as 1897.

[2] The Peresviet class appear so relatively feeble on paper that only those who have been aboard them have any idea what splendid ships they are from all those points of view which, though they do not show up on paper, go to make a really efficient warship. Everything about them is designed for *war*.

### Engineering Matters

Until comparatively recently the machinery for Russian warships was chiefly supplied by English firms —Maudslay, Sons, & Field; Humphrys & Tennant; and Hawthorn Leslie having been much employed in the past. Now all this is changed; not by reason of any dissatisfaction with the material supplied, but for a variety of other causes. One of them is a patriotic idea about "everything made in Russia,"[1] though the making in Russia often means the employment of French or Belgian firms established there; the normal Russian is no Archimedes. The ubiquitous German, too, is of course inevitable—but mostly Belgians are to the fore. These enterprising people have, on the whole, drawn more advantage from the Franco-Russian alliance than their neighbour: people in Russia take them for French, and contracts are apt to fall their way in return for what the alliance has brought to Russia. At the same time nothing is more remarkable than the really excellent workmanship of all "made in Russia" machinery. Few people have any conception of the strides that Russia has made in this direction.

Russian contracts are peculiar: they invariably cost more than any other, because the slightest superficial and harmless flaw voids the contract for anything ordered by Russia. The same causes, however, that prevented Russian ships being built in England

[1] The "made in Russia" armour plates of the Peresviet were actually constructed by Herr Krupp at Essen, Germany.

prevented engines being constructed in this country. I was told in Russia, not once but a dozen times, that the "Strike Clause" was the stumbling-block, Russia insisting on its absence and British firms (knowing all too well what its absence might mean in these days of agitation) insisting on its maintenance. The agitator helped the British mechanic to kill his goose so far as Russia is concerned.

The water-tube boiler found an early champion in *Boilers.* Russia, which quickly adopted the Belleville, and subsequently the Belleville fitted with economisers. One objection to the water-tube boiler is or was that it smokes unless carefully handled. Russian fuel, however, always gives much smoke, so the matter is of less consequence.

Welsh coal is stored in Russia; this, of course, is *Fuel.* smokeless, but its presence is not always to be relied upon given certain eventualities. In addition, much liquid fuel is used, especially in the Black Sea, and with this there is plenty of smoke as a rule; but, latterly, this has been greatly reduced, and I do not think that Russian ships can be considered particularly smoky now-a-days compared to other foreigners.

With liquid fuel the Russians appear to have *Liquid fuel.* obtained more success than any other nation; the Rostislav, burning it, made 18 knots easily on trial. A new system of using liquid fuel was tested in 1899 in the Baltic on board the torpedo boat Moonsund, fitted with locomotive boilers, and on board the Pernou, which has water-tube boilers. The fuel is *mazut* or *astatki* (a heavy residual oil of Russian petroleum). The system consists in forcing the oil through spiral tubes. At the orifice each tube is fitted with a perforated disc that forms the oil into a very fine spray. The system is the invention of an engineer officer named Shensnovitch, and has so far proved very

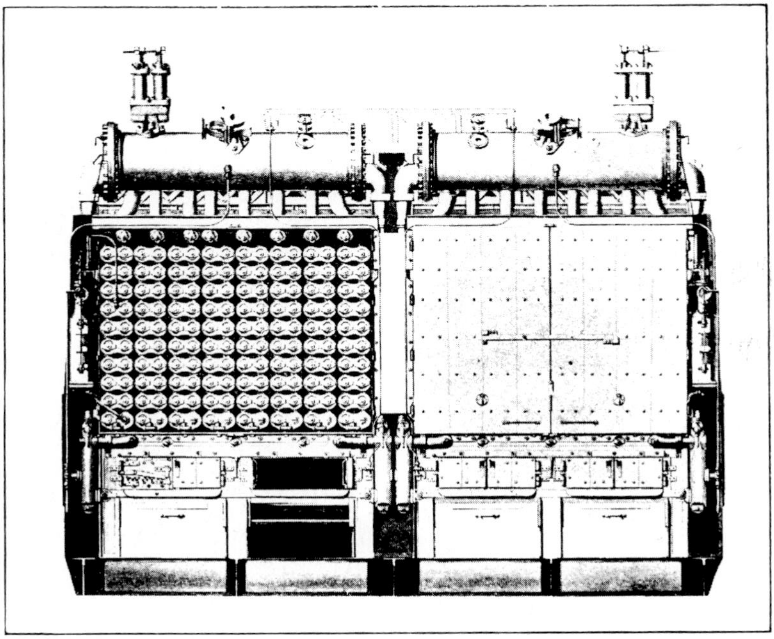

BELLEVILLE BOILERS.

successful. It is an adaption of an Italian idea. The main objection to the Russian fuel is that it has a particularly offensive and all pervading odour. The distinctive smell of it permeates the ship.

*Machinery.*

I have already mentioned the excellence of modern Russian machinery—that is to say, all constructed

# Arrangement of Belleville Boilers with Economisers

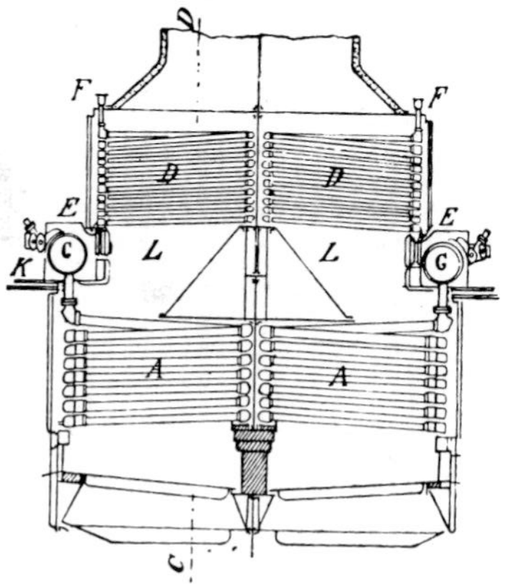

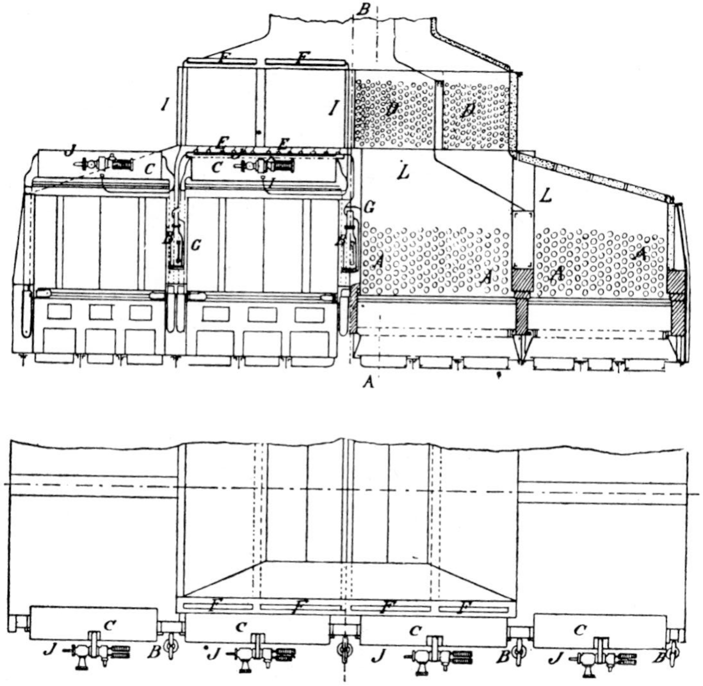

A Boiler, Tube Sections
B Feed Regulators
C Steam drums
D Economiser tube sections
E Cold water collector
F Hot water collector
G Feed connection to regulator
H Connection from feed regulator to cold water collector
I Connection between hot water collector & feed check valve
J Steam stop valves
K Platforms
L Combustion chambers

since the year 1900 or thereabouts. It is usually relatively heavy for the work that it will be called upon to do, and constructed to last.

All the engine-rooms of new ships that I have seen are very roomy, quite different to the cramped spaces in British ships. There is plenty of room to get at everything—everything also is well kept. I have not noticed any signs of slovenliness, such as were plentiful only half-a-dozen years ago: between 1899 and 1903 there is a great gulf in this respect.

In the boiler rooms the same great space is accorded, and there is a marked cleanliness here where one would least expect to find it. One very cardinal error is embodied—the boilers are put fore and aft instead of athwartships as is the usual custom with water-tubes. In consequence, when the ship is rolling (and a ship rolls a great deal more than she pitches), there would look to be considerable risk of the water running out of tubes. Such at least is the usual opinion. It is only fair to state that a Russian engineer with whom I discussed this point was in no way disposed to admit it as counterbalancing the other advantages that it gave. He pointed out also that the Belleville (the only water-tube so carried), being fitted with check valves, and so forth, may be used with perfect safety in this fashion. As Russian ships undoubtedly roll a great deal, and as they have also had no troubles with any of these ships with fore and aft boilers, his contention would look to be correct. Curiously enough, the existence of these safety devices to make it impossible for the circulation to go the wrong way is the chief objection raised by those who object to the Belleville boiler. Theoretically, perhaps, it is disadvantageous, but in practice it appears as wise as the fitting of safety valves. This particular type has, however, come in for so much abuse at the hands of those who uphold the obsolete cylindrical boiler that probably few, if any of the objections, are worth attention. At any rate, they secure none in Russia.

For the manufacture of Belleville boilers there are now four establishments. They are made at Kronstadt both by the Société Anonyme Franco-Russe and by the Chantiers de la Baltique, and at Nikolaieff by the Chantiers Navale de Nikolaieff and another firm. All these hold patents for manufacture. I imagine that the Belleville Company are represented by a supervisor from the French headquarters of that firm, but it is not possible to obtain information upon this point, though I have endeavoured to do so. The matter is of very great importance, because there seems to be little question but that the original failure of the Belleville in the British Navy, though attributed to the general inefficiency of manufacture due to the great engineers' strike, was actually caused by the introduction of "improvements" by those who were at that period naturally without any practical knowledge of the water-tube system. The steaming efficiency of the Russian fleet depends on whether or no the same kind of thing goes on in Russia. If it does, we may probably assume that Russian ships are unable to make their speeds for long; if, on the other hand, the boilers are constructed strictly according to specifications, the odds are that Russian warship speed cannot be neglected in the future as it has been possible to neglect it in the past.

So much has been written against the Belleville boiler that it is extremely difficult to assign its exact value as a war factor. If practical naval opinion be taken, then it is apparently the best type in existence; if, however, the opinion of civilian theorists is allowed weight, it embodies almost every possible defect. Presumably the naval engineer, as the practical man, is the best judge; but the matter, in this country at least, is so complicated by side issues that it is difficult to arrive at the true facts of its worth.

The history of the Belleville in the British Navy is approximately as follows:—

Innumerable troubles were being experienced with cylindrical boilers owing to the increased pressure that naval practice was demanding. Matters were so acute that Admiral Sir John Fisher, the then Controller of the Navy, and Sir John Durston, the Engineer in Chief, despatched a number of naval engineer officers to inspect the working of various water-tube boilers in the French Navy and elsewhere. After studying the evidence, they finally, with the concurrence of the chief constructor, Sir William White,[1] decided to experiment with the Belleville, and a gunboat was

[1] Sir William White's address to the Society of Mechanical Engineers, 1903.

fitted with this type. The experiment was so successful that the boiler was appropriated for all new ships. It appears to have been specified that it was essential for the efficiency of the British fleet to adopt one type only, lest multiplicity of types should cause disaster in war time by rendering it impossible to interchange engine-room complements.

This decision in favour of water-tubes was a blow to all industries manufacturing the old "tank" type of boiler, and the representatives of the old type found a champion in Sir William Allan, the head of a great cylindrical boiler-making concern. The old fight for the retention of the muzzle-loader was repeated in a fight for the retention of the old type boiler. A side issue of considerable importance is the unpleasant fact that Admiral Sir John Fisher and Sir William White, being at the top of their professions, had powerful enemies who did not hesitate to make capital out of the proceedings.

The Bellevilles of early British ships were of an elementary type, badly constructed on account of the engineers' strike, "improved" by amateurs, and handled by unskilled men. The inevitable happened—breakdowns occurred. No doubt many of these were exaggerated, and some perhaps never happened; but there is no question but that trouble was experienced for at least a year. Every one remembers the historical case of the Europa.

Finally a Boiler Committee of merchantile marine experts, with one naval engineer member, was appointed to inquire into things.[1] These, except the naval officer, quickly condemned both the Belleville and the cylindrical. The naval engineer signed a minority report in favour of the Belleville. The majority verdict found favour with the nation as the best way out of an awkward situation, and if, as is possible, all water-tube boilers are about equal, it may be commended accordingly, and the protests of naval engineers written down as mere professional jealousy.

Meanwhile, however, ships fitted with the improved Belleville were completed for sea, and in all these a uniform success was secured. This gave rise to a counter agitation, which at the moment of writing (end of 1903) has just assumed an acute stage. Speeds greatly over the contract were attained by ships in service like the Drake, Spartiate, Vengeance, Good Hope, and Andromeda. Finally, the Europa was sent on a 25,000 miles cruise. The Civilian Boiler Committee said she could not accomplish it; the naval party in the service claimed that she could. The latter proved correct—this one time failure, the Europa, doing the whole trip without a single defect, and—though she proved inferior to other Belleville ships in economy of coal—she beat easily every record of any other type of boiler.

[1] The favourite argument of the reactionaries against the New Scheme in the British Navy is that Admiral Sir John Fisher, having made a mess of boilering the fleet, is sure to have done the same with the New Scheme. The argument is now beginning to recoil on the heads of the reactionaries, but a year ago it had undoubted potency. Time has shown that Admiral Fisher was right, though the absence of any official admission still gives the argument some weight with the general public.

The inference of political intrigue in the battle of the boilers is unpleasantly suggestive; however, the subject need not be pursued here further than is necessary to point out that in Russia no such problem arose, and consequently the serious situation of a whole navy given over to experiments with nearly every type of water-tube boiler as the British fleet now is, has been avoided.[1] To take one boiler type only may, despite the increased efficiency of such a course, embody risks; to fit a fleet recklessly with half-a-dozen different types is, however, as nearly fatal as anything can be.

Russia, like us (and other nations), sent out engineer officers to inspect various types of boilers; unlike us, she was content to allow the Navy to have the final voice in the matter. We left it to politicians and laymen.

No difficulty in working the Belleville appears to have been experienced by the Russian engine-room complements. The reason of this lies mostly in the extremely methodical way in which the Russian Admiralty braced itself to change from the old style to the new.

In the first place a large number of engineer officers

[1] Water-tube boilers adopted by the other chief naval Powers are:—

| | |
|---|---|
| France . . . | Belleville and Niclausse. |
| Germany . . . | Thornycroft-Schulz. |
| Italy . . | Belleville. |
| Japan . . . | Belleville. |
| Russia . . . | Belleville. |
| United States . . | Babcock & Wilcox and Niclausse. |

Though in all one or two isolated ships may be fitted with other types, experiment is carefully kept to them. In the British fleet now completing, every ship of a class has a different type of boiler.

were sent to France to undergo a practical course while the boilers for their ships were being constructed by the Belleville firm. They thus acquired a technical knowledge of the why and wherefore of things that else they would never have possessed probably.

Secondly, a new rating of mechanics—on a par with our E. R. A.'s—was introduced. These men have special pay, get leave when other men do not, and are allowed various other privileges. They prove of great value on board.

Thirdly, stokers were carefully instructed in the art of stoking water-tube boilers. It is a decided art, it being necessary to distribute the coal evenly and moderately a little at a time upon the fires, with only half the doors open at a time. Quantity is the fatal error, too much coal being as bad as too little. With the old type boilers, the more coal that was thrown on the better in reason was the result. Hence the need of training. In the British Navy the raw stoker is first trained on the old type of boiler, then put to unlearn it all for the water-tube. Russia teaches the scientific method to start with.

As every type of water-tube boiler needs a different kind of knowledge and working, Russia has built the transport Okean, fitted with Belleville, Niclausse, Yarrow, and some other type boilers, and men are, so far as possible, drafted according to the boiler that they have been trained on.

In one or two Russian ships the Niclausse boiler has been adopted, the two American built ships being so fitted by Cramp's, who are the U.S. Agents of the Niclausse. A disastrous explosion in one of these ships, the Retvizan, brought the Niclausse type into some disfavour, though it was subsequently shown that the type was not to blame for the occurrence. It was also alleged that the boilers having been constructed in America some error had been made in following the specifications. The American Maine is so fitted by the same firm, however, and she on some rather extensive trials did very well, so the question as to whether American innovations on the construction were in any way responsible in the case of the Retvizan is not clear.

Personally I am not disposed to credit the dissatisfaction statements, and gather that the set back to the Niclausse in Russia is not the result of any defects, real or imaginary, but due to Russian desire not to multiply types.

Water-tube boiler types in the Russian Navy for ships (other than torpedo-boats and destroyers), built, building, and reconstructed, or to be reconstructed, are approximately as follows :—

| | | | |
|---|---|---|---|
| Belleville | in | 40 | ships |
| Niclausse | ,, | 3 | ,, |
| Thornycroft | ,, | 2 | ,, |
| Normand | ,, | 1 | ,, |
| Yarrow | ,, | 1 | ,, |

So much re-boilering has gone on of late that there may be a few more ships with Bellevilles.

The Normand and Thornycroft boilers are somewhat

similar in many ways, except that the Normand has small tubes only. These are objected to on the score of difficulty in sweeping. They are in the Bogatyr. The Novik has the Thornycroft, as also Askold. The Niclausse ships are the Retvizan, Variag, Khraby, and the Alexander III. building is also reported to be so fitted. Of these the Variag did very well indeed on trials. The Belleville is in every other ship from and including the Rossia onward, also in all the re-boilered ships.

The cylindrical boiler is practically extinct. Save for the three Poltāvas and three Aprāksins, no ships of importance in the Russian fleet now carry it, and in the course of a few years it is likely to disappear from these.

In concluding this sketch of engineering in 1903–04 in the Russian fleet, mention should be made of a recent instance of the great improvements in steaming.

The Sissoi Veliky, which was only designed for 16 knots after a three years' commission in the Far East, made 15·3 knots on her paying off trial. The Navarin, a ship nearly fifteen years old, designed for a 16 knots that she never made, reached 14·9, or, according to some accounts, 15·1 knots, and the old cruiser Korniloff about 17 knots. These figures, more than anything else, go to show how immensely Russian naval engineering has improved during the last few years. Five years ago none of the ships could get within a knot of these more recent speeds. The matter demands earnest attention.

# XXXVI

## THE INFLUENCE OF PETER THE GREAT ON THE RUSSIAN NAVY TO-DAY

MOST things in the Russian Navy have a more or less direct connection with Peter the Great, and the entry of officers is no exception to the rule. Until 1885, when there was a reorganisation, everything remained almost exactly as Peter had founded it,—the addition of engineer officers and ratings being the only *Personnel.* differences worth noting.

In Peter the Great's time the *guarde-marines* were entered much as they are at the present day. The system was copied from France, where, in the seventeenth and eighteenth centuries, the ranks of naval officers were stocked by young men about sixteen to twenty years old, and with the clause about nobility as the only one.[1] In Peter's time an examination was necessary for the guarde-marine to become a mitchman, and it more or less covered the ground covered to-day, allowing for progress in modern science.

In Peter's day, too, the supplementaries — then called *Reformados*—existed, and were entered much as they are still. The English system of "cabin-boys,"

[1] "La seule condition a remlir pour l'admission etait d'appartenir à la noblesse."—*La Marine Française*, M. Loir.

"volunteers," etc., was probably the first cause. This system was used at the outset, and the changes in it have only been such as the altered condition of affairs nowadays has rendered necessary.

The corps of marine artillery or ordnance officers, which was not abolished till 1885, and some few of whose members still exist in service, was founded by Peter, out of officers that he sent to Germany to learn gunnery.[1] These were at first known as Bombardiers.

*Matériel.*

In *matériel* Peter again has been the prime guide. The fast ships of the Peresviet type—the Rossia, Rurik, Pāmiat Azova, the idea underlying all these craft is an idea that Peter the Great had and built on. Russia evolved the armoured cruiser, and in evolving it she followed Peter's aim to have ships beyond all other things swift.

*Naval politics.*

In naval politics, of course, the hand of the Great Tsar is visible. The Russian Mediterranean Fleet, which when re-instituted a few years since caused so great a commotion, was something more than a copy of Ekaterina's idea. She, indeed, was the first to carry it out, but long before Ekaterina, Peter had the idea in his head.[2]

[1] A "GUNNERY" NOTE.—In 1714 Peter the Great had tubes for squirting liquid fire (Greek-fire ?) fitted to two of his ships, but nothing seems to have come of its use. At the same time he introduced the quick-firing gun of the period, adopting a device of carrying powder in reeds to facilitate loading.—*The Russian Fleet under Peter the Great.* Vol. XVI. Naval Records Society.

[2] "Just upon the conclusion of the late peace (of 1721) it was hotly talked that the Tsar would send a squadron of men-of-war through the

Again, the making of Libau into a first-class naval port was more or less one of Peter the Great's designs. And though the famous will of Peter the Great has been proved to be a spurious thing concocted by Napoleon, the springs of nearly every Russian action will be found in what Peter did. Some of the things had been vaguely attempted by his predecessors, but only vaguely. They hoped: Peter acted. Many Lives of Peter have been written, many appreciations; but none of them do full justice to his sense of perspective, to his power of attending to details and to grand affairs at one and the same moment. He is always spoken of as a man of great personal courage, and in the historical text that legend has been adhered to. Still, he may have lacked this courage, and indications, such as his behaviour at Narva, and other things, such as the possibility that he did not actually fight at Gangoot; the absence of *direct evidence* as to his fighting anywhere; his hysterical adulation of the gallant Ehrenskiöld; his pardoning after a time of many officers who had been guilty of cowardice,[1]—all these things tend to contradict the idea that Peter was personally brave. It is possible that he was an arrant coward. If so, of course, the greater his greatness.

***Peter may have been a coward.***

There is not the slightest doubt that when he

Sound and British Channel up the Straits into the Mediterranean."—*The Russian Fleet under Peter the Great.* Vol. XVI. Navy Records Society.

[1] Rather strong evidence in the case of a man like Peter the Great. He was singularly disposed in other instances to pardon failings that were his own, while to any failing that was not his own he was merciless. (See Appendix.)

and Charles XII. (another but more erratic genius) embarked on war, Sweden had the balance of courage on her side. The Russian showed dogged perseverance, but all the wild, rash, dare-devil bravery was shown by the Swedes. It is stretching the point to say that Russia was an army of sheep led by a lion, and Sweden, to finish the proverb, an army of lions led by a sheep—but strategically this is pretty true. The Russians had no Löschern,[1] no Ehrenskiöld:[2] they had instead to lead them men like Kruyis,[3] Gordon, Rays, Scheltigna, Little — incompetents, or worse, both in courage and ability. Besides himself, Peter had no one save Aprāksin,[3] and possibly Sievers,[3] and so far as his lower rank would allow, the Englishman Deane: it was the Tsar's personal force that led him to victory. He blundered often; but he knew how to extricate himself and how to learn from his blunders. It is little wonder that, though over a hundred and fifty years have passed since then, Peter the Great is still a living force in the Russian Navy to-day: and for good or evil, he will probably be so till the end of time.

[1] P. 48. [2] P. 61. [3] See biographies of these in Appendix.

# XXXVII

## ANGLO-RUSSIAN RELATIONS

THE future of the Russian Navy is in great measure allied to Russia's relations with that Power which has been nurse, doctor, schoolmaster, and foster-parent to the Russian Navy. On whether England and Russia are friends or enemies much of the map-making of the future must depend. Anglo-Russian relations must, therefore, be viewed from more than one standpoint, and the more or less Russian one is perhaps the best to begin with.

Probably there is no country and no people in the world of whom the British know so little as Russia and the Russians. The Russia of the minor novelist who has secured a little local colour from some Nihilist refugee, is the Russia of the ordinary British citizen, and, one cannot help thinking, also more or less Russia in the eyes of certain of our rulers. Hence it comes about that everything likely to produce ill-feeling against the land of the Tsar grows lustily in England, and in the great Northern Empire something of a return spirit is sedulously cultivated. It is a canon in England that one day, sooner or later, Russia will force war upon us; in Russia exactly the same idea is prevalent with regard to England.

*Russian naval officers.*

Russian naval officers are the men of whom, time after time, one reads in English newspapers that they, beyond all others, are thirsting for a war with England —a statement, by the way, usually published in close connection with the Tsar's Peace proposals. Now, owing to circumstances connected with my visit to Russia, I was thrown into a position of peculiar and considerable intimacy with these men, and the relations of Russia and England were discussed freely and often. Nothing could be more striking than the differentiation between their sentiment to the English as a nation and the English as individuals. Just as in our navy one finds that of all foreigners the Russian is the one for whom there is most respect and regard, so with the Russians the feeling is reciprocated. The naval officers of the two countries know each other ; the other sections of the community do not.

So far as " public opinion " may be said to exist in Russia, it exists in, and only in, the class from which their officers are taken ; there, and there alone, is any " opinion " to be found. Of longing for war there is not the slightest trace. Beyond all men the Russian is essentially prone to be a man of peace—the Tsar's ideals on that subject are no more the copyright of the Emperor than of the meanest moujik in his empire. Verestchagin is no anomaly, no freak ; he merely put on canvas what every Russian feels in his heart,—the voice of the Tsar or the hand of the artist Verestchagin speaks a national, rather than an individual, sentiment.

But—and here we verge on that part of the matter

which we as a nation fail utterly to grasp—the matter is not one of "sentiment," as we understand the word. Were there any "sentiment" in the matter, the Tsar's proposals would not have been worth the paper they were written on—events made them of little more value—but that is a side issue. The Tsar himself, or Verestchagin the painter, may be filled with personal antipathy to the "horrors of war," but that is not the root-feeling in the fighting class of the Russian Empire. Indeed, I doubt whether any men view the awful side of war so calmly as the Russians. There are ships in the Imperial Navy with a great number of guns quite unprotected, and in action the carnage around these guns is sure to be something frightful. I have stood in those batteries and discussed the matter with the men who would have to stand there in action. In every case there was the one single sentiment; no enthusiasm, no fear, merely a simple recognition of the fact that to stand there in action will be almost certain death, but that, if duty necessitates that standing, it will have to be done. And done it will be, without flinching, so long as a man is left to stand. There is only one place where I have noticed this sentiment paralleled—in the British Navy. "The rest must carry on."

That is the whole sentiment—no *la gloire*, no special protection from Heaven promised by a Kaiser, no "for my country" or other sentiment such as will bring down the gallery—merely a bald "duty." But it is that bald duty which carries a man further than anything else in this world. *La gloire* is all very well;

but it runs out when blood begins to flow—duty does not.

This, then, is war as seen by the Russian fighting man, somewhat as the British fighting man sees it. As with the officers, so with the men, sailors or soldiers. A moujik is told to march, and march he does, and on he will go, nothing but death able to stop him, though all the time he had rather not be fighting.

Since the Anglo-Japanese alliance was made England and Russia have been ranged more definitely on opposite sides, but the virulent hatred of the Japanese which characterises Russians is not extended to the British. To the British, Russians have politically a strong antipathy at the present time (1904), but I question whether it is really greater than it was in 1899. What they have not got is the race antipathy which is so marked between them and Japan. The matter is best expressed as follows. Russians hate Japanese because they are Japanese, Germans because they are Germans, but British only because they come from England. This delicate differentiation means a great deal. Between England and Russia racial differences are not enough to create racial antipathies; the Russian is very like the Englishman in his way of looking at many things. A Russian gentleman and an English gentleman have in common certain codes, certain ideas, that the upper classes of other nations have not got in exactly the same way.

*English and Russian naval officers.*

"Your officers, you see, are gentlemen," a Russian will say, and that is exactly the specific characterisation of a Russian officer that one hears in any British man-of-war's wardroom. For example, a German officer is recruited from exactly the same class as an English or a Russian one, and by all canons of birth is just as much a gentleman; but there is a difference. There is just that difference which makes the others feel he is not the same as themselves, and *vice versâ*. And what obtains with one class obtains, more or less, with all others. That peculiar, invisible racial bar between the Englishman and the usual foreigner does not exist so markedly between the Englishman and the Russian as it exists between the Englishman and the German.

Much, of course, is, and often has been, said about the "peculiar charm of the Russians," just as Russians who have come across them may talk of the peculiar individual charm of Englishmen. It is all nonsense; there is no such thing. The "peculiar charm" is nothing save the unrecognised existence of certain common instincts sufficiently strong to outweigh other natural racial divergencies. The two nations, regarded racially, are natural allies, with no conflicting feelings other than those (momentous enough, it is true) which have been artificially created.

It is a theory, little short of a belief, in this country that the Peace Rescript was a purely personal ideal of the Tsar's, in which his people had neither place nor part. We have heard a good deal about "the Book that moved the Tsar," and about his personal antipathy to war. On the other hand, various newspapers at the time of the Rescript gave currency to statements that *Peace Rescript.*

no one else in Russia was peaceably disposed, and one of our leading newspapers stated that there was "feverish activity in the Russian dockyards."

One can emphatically deny this "feverish activity." As an instance, I may cite the New Admiralty Works, where the slip from which the Osliabia was launched was still vacant months later, "waiting to see the result of the Peace Conference."[1] Men were, of course, at work upon the ships under construction, but everything was as normal as possible.

*Railways.*

Railway works are being pushed forward with as much expedition as possible,[2] but railways are as essential in peace as in war, and the colonisation of Greater Russia can only be effected by these means. In the Russian view it is to us "a 'menace' to British interests for Russia to construct a railway anywhere in her dominions," so this particular sword is not yet turned into a ploughshare.

*Canals.*

A further thing that is being pressed forward in Russia is a system of canals. This was lately officially inaugurated by the Grand Duke Alexander Mihailovitch, and will no doubt become another "military design" in due course to England. For myself, I opine that neither these railways nor canals have anything to do with war preparations beyond the fact that it would be possible to transport troops by them.

The fact of the matter is that all these railways

[1] The Borodino was laid down here after the Conference failed.

[2] Russian expenditure on railways, 1899, was greater than that on the navy and army combined.

and canals are absolutely essential to the great Empire of the North. Russia, unlike all other countries, has not enough people to fill her borders: she needs peace to grow people, and railways and people to develop all her latent resources. To properly understand Russia, one has to picture Elizabethan England, with two or three railways and electric light in the towns. Russian towns are modern, but they are only so many islands in a sea of undeveloped country. There is a railway here and there, there is the telegraph, but communication is well-nigh limited to these. Roads such as we are accustomed to do not exist in Russia, where there are hundreds of square miles of virgin forest. Everywhere are the things that will make a most prosperous country a hundred or two hundred years hence, but at present all these things are latent, because there are not enough people to fill the place. Simply, from the most practical everyday point of view, anything tending to check the growth of population in Russia is the one *bête noire* of Russian statesmen. Hence to avoid war is a canon of their statesmanship.

It is true that Russia made war against Turkey in 1877; but that war was a religious war, and in Russia religion is a power that has no similar existence anywhere else in Europe. It is not possible to conceive of any other cause for which Russian statesmen would willingly embark in war, for the simple reason that the whole needs and interests of the country, and of everybody in the country, are antagonistic to such a course.

*Russia and other Powers.*

Turkey, Austria, Germany, Japan, and England—these five are the countries with which Russia stands to be possibly involved in war. In no case can the antagonist do any real harm to her, while England and Japan are the only two that would not run a certain chance of such injury to themselves that they will do everything possible to avoid war. England alone could by war put a heavy drain on Russia, not only in money, but in the waste of human life, more precious to her than money. And England alone out of the five has no real conflict of interest with Russia, though she has fancy ones by the score.

I would not say that the Peace Rescript was aimed at England and England only, but there was behind it, surely, some hope that out of the discussion something might come to put a stop to the constant "verge of war" condition between Russia and England? Russia knows perfectly well that England could do her no vital hurt, the possible offensive is very slight—it is England that would stand to lose most and gain least in a conflict with her. She knows this perfectly well; but there is a large section of the English Press which appears lamentably ignorant of it. Were the Russians a people like the French, England would have been at war with them long ago: it is their natural tendency to peace, and the important fact that peace is more to their interests, that has so far averted that war of which the thoughtless speak so lightly. So, some two thousand odd years ago, may Darius have done. So did Napoleon. Not till we have flying machines will Russia be vulnerable.

*Flying machines.*

To-day the flying machine is regarded as little better than a dream, yet not only is it almost bound to come in time, but already it may be nearer than many folk wot of. In a museum at St. Petersburg may be seen an explosive bullet invented long before the explosive bullet that was barred by the Geneva Convention. This bullet and its secret were bought up and possessed by Russia many years ago. She bought it, and laid it aside in a museum, making no use of the terrible weapon.[1] Is there any other nation in Europe that has done the like, or which would do so? Russia *has.* It is true that there has recently been a serving out of Dum-dum bullets to the Russian troops in Central Asia. Russia had this bullet, or its equivalent, quite as soon as we had, but she did not adopt it till she found that we intended to stick to it. Now it is adopted, but its adoption is confined to those troops which, in the event of war with England, would have to face the Dum-dum. There was, therefore, nothing out of the way, so far as Russia is concerned, in the Tsar's appeal that some stop shall be put to the further development of "killing devices."[2]

*Explosive bullets.*

In that clause there are two things of far more moment than is at first sight apparent. First, there

[1] It should be stated, however, that this bullet may have been used by Russian troops towards the end of the Crimean War. At least, certain wounds gave colour to that idea.

[2] Written before the Dum-dum bullet question was raised at the Hague.

is a reference to flying machines, or, at least, to balloons filling that *métier*. The Russians suppressed the explosive bullet; how much flying machine are they suppressing at present? The submarine boat was also barred. At the present moment Russia possesses (or claims to possess) designs for a submarine boat superior to any other, and fifty of these craft are projected. They are not yet commenced, but there is the design. It is said that goes a great deal further towards a practical solution of the problem than anything yet boasted about in the French newspapers.

Altogether, so far as improved slaughtering machines are concerned, Russia is in a position to be ahead of every other nation—if she chooses, and if, assuming possession, she is able to use them (a thing not to be overlooked altogether). We may put her present situation as regards a desire for peace down to humanity or natural instinct, or we may put it to Russia's credit that, unlike certain other nations, she recognises that no new invention can be kept a secret once it is put into use, and that a Russian flying machine this decade would be her possible enemy's most serious weapon in the next. The abolition of flying machines of any sort as implements of war is to Russia's ultimate interest more than any nation's—even more than to ours. There is no opening to accuse her of claptrap sentiment in this matter.

Point two is even more important. Should this clause limiting means of killing to those at present in use ever be adopted, universal peace will be practically a *fait accompli.* And for this reason. Given no further advances to reckon with, the construction of invulnerable, or nearly invulnerable, warships will soon come about. On land, too, if the bullet is limited, armoured troops will quickly appear. They do not yet do so because it is so easy to conceive of inventions to do away with its advantages; but once check invention of offence, and armour will come in. At present the major portion of a fighting man's time, particularly of a naval one's, is taken up with unlearning the facts of yesterday. But given finality, war must come rapidly to the level of chess, or at anyrate of war games. A level of medium excellence will be fairly quickly reached. The disparities between the armaments of the different countries are such that the issue of a war could be calculated down to two possible results—the certain defeat of one belligerent, or else possibly, but not so probably, something very like mutual annihilation. War, in fine, would become one of the most exact sciences, and it is the chances of war and the fortunes of war which render fighting possible. We are not likely to accept Homeric conditions in these days.

*Finality in war.*

It remains to be seen whether or no Europe will follow the lead offered by Russia, principally with an eye to her own interests. At present the world appears too conscious of the sentimental side of the question. That it should be so is unfortunate, in part because the world is prone to disbelieve in other people's sentiment, in part because sentiment is so apt to remain sentiment and nothing more. A feeling that war is a wicked, awful, and atrocious thing may be all very well in its way, but where the achievement of actual permanent results is concerned the profit-and-loss question is bound to bulk largely in men's minds, even though it be absent from their tongues. And an agreement which will make it a matter of calculable certainty as to whether a nation will win or lose is (presumably at least) better than the present condition of "almost certain." "Eliminate chance, and you will nigh eliminate war," is a pretty true proverb.

*Possible inutility of Universal Peace.*

Whether the world will be a better or more comfortable place when the military element has been abolished, and the company promoter, the shopkeeper, and the business man put to sit in the seats of the mighty, is too deep a question to enter into here. Personally, I incline to fancy that Universal Peace, when it does come, will eventually bring about a reign of the Jew Capitalist, and a mighty premium be put upon fraud, lying, deceit, and kindred qualities: a reign no easier than the military one, and culminating in some frightful upheaval of society in which civilisation and most other things will perish.

Still, "Blessed are the peace-makers": the bother is that no one seems to take the trouble to realise that war can be carried on without sailors and soldiers, and that commercial war, just because it is stripped of the pomp and glory, the chivalry and codes of honour of war proper, is none the less deadly and cruel. The cruelty comes in a different way, that is all. Practically it is the old savage warfare with different weapons, but every whit as exterminating and as merciless. And if Universal Peace is to increase the field for commercial wars, we are better off without it. It is better to perish on the field, with such dramatic accompaniments as patriotism and glory can afford, than to starve in helpless misery in a garret in order that another Jew or two may build himself a palace in Park Lane.[1]

[1] These last two paragraphs have been added since the publication of this article in serial form in the *Daily Chronicle*.

# XXXVIII

## SOME CONCLUSIONS

"WHAT does Russia want with a navy at all? She has hardly any coast and practically no trade." This is a common question in England, where we are apt to regard the Imperial Navy as a direct "menace" to us. Indeed, all our big cruisers are "replies" to Russian ones; even the French have only recently earned a "reply"—the new "mighty cruisers" destined to match the Jeanne d'Arc. Yet actually, Russia in her naval plans no more contemplates meeting us at sea than we contemplate meeting the United States. It is a possibility, it might happen, but the naval programme is not governed by it in any way: if Russia wars with us, her warring will be on the land as much as possible.

*Russia's sea rivals.*

It happens, however, that there are other nations who have navies against which the Russian fleet would be on a numerical equality, and there is no more real occasion to ask why Russia should have a fleet, than to ask why Germany should, or Sweden.

Further, of course, Russia has always in view the possibility of eventualities in which her ships would be acting against us in connection with one or two other

Powers. But this, though a bogey we well know in England, is quite a secondary *raison d'être* of the Russian Navy. For the Russians, with a reasoning ability not possessed by some of our politicians, recognise that, unless given an overwhelming majority, such a combination would have but a poor chance. And for this reason. In a combination an immense variety of different types must necessarily be included; and the difficulties of handling a big fleet so composed —each admiral with his own views on tactics, each side with its ships fitted for different tactics—are more immense than any civilian can possibly grasp. Our eight Majestics would "walk through" a fleet of a dozen hostile vessels of different nationalities, and if there were eighteen the "walking through" would probably be little harder. Every sailor understands why; the landsman must perforce accept it on faith. In addition to all this we have a strategical advantage in position.

*Unlikelihood of a successful combination against England.*

However, let us briefly sum up the Russian Navy itself, without further regard to this particular issue. The Russian Navy is spoken of as created by Peter the Great; actually, however, the early Russians had a reputation as sailors a thousand years ago. Still, Peter was practically the King Alfred of the Russian Navy, and he performed his task with English aid: the Russian Navy is, in fine, a child of the British one. Scotsmen in particular had a kink for the Russian service, and there is a Russian ship called after one of them to this day.

It is usual to reckon up navies by the ships and tonnage, by a judicious manipulation of which anything whatever can be proved. It has the disadvantage of being at the best a worthless system of comparison, and the total energy of fire in ten minutes is little better. For what it is worth, these comparisons have already been made *ad nauseam*; I propose to confine myself to the *personnel*, which is of far more account than the ships themselves. In action, so far as *matériel* is concerned, one battleship will prove pretty much like another; *the* difference lies with the men who do the handling. And in this handling the ability of the officers and the amenability to discipline of the men are the two chief things.

It is customary nowadays to assert that "the battle of the future will be fought in the engine-room," but this catch-phrase of a present agitation is chiefly nonsense—at any rate where ironclads are concerned. The engine-room takes first place only when one side wants to run away; and the run-away side is beaten by the mere fact of its electing to try and "evade," and for the same reason the pursuer is victor.

*Russian bluejackets.*

Till recently Finlanders and Courlanders constituted the bulk of the men in the Russian service. Now, however, men from all over the empire get made into sailors. The true Slav is said to have certain privileges that are denied to the less Russian sailors, matters of leave and so forth. On the other hand, if he is given leave in a foreign port he is a good deal more likely to come back to the ship; but this is a thing upon which opinions as to cause and effect vary. On the whole, I fancy it is the genuine Russ who thinks being a sailor is more "fun." Boyish creatures are these big Russian sailors, more so even than our own "blues." In the drill shed at Kronstadt[1] I noticed that the mere taking off of their overcoats seemed a joke to them; and when they marched past in fours nearly every man of them strutted a bit as he passed the "Anglisk," and then smiled broadly to his fellow. One sees children do the same when a stranger is present.

*Boyishness of Russian bluejackets.*

Now this to the lay reader may seem a very trivial thing to relate, but it has a very high nautical importance. Every naval officer knows that the "boyish" sailor is the man to do things with—a sailor does his best work when he treats the whole thing as a joke.

"I like those chaps," an English naval officer watching some Russian bluejackets once said. "They chuckle like children. That means they're good stuff."

Russia, however, gets her share of what we call "King's bad bargains." Still, the captain of the training-ship Vernii told me that he was fully prepared to take the worst of them, and not a bit afraid of failing to make good stuff of them. "If I'm sure of my officers," he said, "I don't trouble about the men."

He never had any difficulty about licking his men into shape, he told me; though of course it is hard work in the case of men who had never seen the sea. Exactly how the licking into shape was done

*Licking sailors into shape.*

[1] P. 385.

I did not hear, save that it was not by a series of violent and harsh measures. I mention this because there is an impression that "Russian officers are awful brutes to their men." My own experience has been quite the reverse, and I kept my eyes open on this matter.

*Russian officers.*

In 1903, I met him again on board the Bayan, of which he was captain. His men called him "Russia's Nelson," and I do not think that they were wrong.

All details were studied. Every two men had a teapot between them, food was given on an extremely liberal scale. Every man of the crew had been taught to feel "for the honour of the ship," and the most dearly prized reward was to be in the captain's galley. This boat was as smart or smarter than any in our Navy and—as well rowed. Its main *raison d'être* was to make the men feel that they were the equals of any sailors in the world. Eighty of the crew were given leave to go shopping on a day when, as it chanced, only the public houses were open. Not a single man got drunk, nor were there any leave-breakers—every man thought of the "honour of the Bayan." There is food for thought in all this for those who remember Russian ships some ten years ago.

I would not call the Bayan a typical Russian ship—she was too good to be typical of any navy—but I have recently come across other Russian ships that are within measurable distance of her, and if there be others worse there may be others equal. In any case, the Russian Navy is a dangerous one to underrate. And yet it is hard to estimate it at its right value. I may claim, I think, to know it better than most men outside it—but I would not care to try and fix its value in relation to other fleets. If one takes a dozen Japanese, one is a sample of all, but of a dozen Russians three will be useless, two good men, six mediocrities of various grades, and one a genius out-and-out. The next dozen will, however, be differently assorted; and so on. But Russia is as likely a nation as any to produce the Nelson of the future, and I, for one, am inclined to think that she has got him. As I write these words Russia and Japan are on the verge of war. If the Fates are favourable, that man will emerge, if the destinies of men are truly written in their faces. If so, it will be a bad day for Japan.

*Drawbacks to the Russian sailor.*

The drawbacks to the Russian sailor are three: his service is short; owing to the climate his "sea time" is very curtailed; and, finally, he is not very intelligent: but this last is one of those defects which, properly treated, are the best of virtues in a sailor.

In the drills I watched at Kronstadt I was particularly struck by the steadiness of the men. The drills were, of course, more or less military ones; still, if men are good at one thing they are pretty sure to be good at others. And the drills I watched were particularly good.

*Russian naval officers socially considered.*

The profession of naval officer is a very aristocratic one in Russia. The head of the navy, after the Tsar, is the Grand Duke Alexis. He is the Russian First Lord; but a professional one. The Grand Duke Alexander is also in the service. He is much younger, and holds at present a captain's rank. To him beyond all others is due the extraordinary progress of the Russian fleet in efficiency. There are also a good many counts and princes holding commissions in the Navy. It is perhaps rather too fashionable, because the invariable defect of a fashionable profession enters. That is to say, every officer does not become one for love of a sea life, and in consequence is very anxious to secure a shore-going billet. As there are many such, foreign service, especially in the Siberian Fleet, comes to be looked upon as a sort of exile to be avoided as much as possible. This feeling is passing now, the best men seek service in the Far East. A high proportion of officers, too, are married; and of two officers otherwise equal the celibate is always the most effective. That we know in our service.

*Dislike of foreign service.*

*Too many married officers.*

An item of interest is that the Russians make torpedo —and for that matter gunnery and navigation—more a matter of specialism than we do. Our "gunnery Jacks," though they are not called upon for watch-keeping duties, are not much differentiated from other lieutenants; and staff-commander is an expiring rank; whereas in Russia gunnery, torpedo, and navigating officers are as distinct a branch as staff-commanders used to be in our service.

Gunnery and navigating officers are selected from the executive only, and engineer officers have absolutely nothing whatever to do with the care of any machinery connected with the guns. A "torpedo officer" may, however, be either executive or engineer, so long as he has been through the necessary course,—a fairly exhaustive one As a

*Torpedo officers.*

matter of fact very few engineers serve as "torpedo officers," there being a variety of difficulties in the way. To begin with, whereas the executive are allowed a twelve months' course in which to qualify as "second-class specialists," the engineer only goes through a six months' one. It is true some of the necessary subjects, such as physics, are part of an engineer officer's ordinary curriculum; also—again as part of his curriculum—every engineer does a short course (four weeks) in the torpedo school, whether intending to specialise in torpedo or not. Hence the difference between the six months' course for engineer officers, and the twelve months' one for executives, may be more apparent than real.

*Social status of naval engineers.*

There are other difficulties. Socially in the Russian Navy an engineer officer occupies much such a position as he did in our navy forty years ago; and as a general rule he is selected from the same class as locomotive engine-drivers on shore. This is not invariably the case, as I met one engineer officer, a senior engineer, who spoke French and English; but the junior engineers speak nothing but their native tongue, which, in such a linguistic country as Russia, is the sure mark of the mechanic class.

*Naval engineers' agitation in the Russian Navy.*

There is in the Russian Navy an Engineers' agitation exactly as there is in ours or in the United States Navy. I spent a good deal of time trying to probe this question, being especially anxious to find whether it was of home growth or imported. I was able to get very little indeed of the engineer side of the question; and as to the executive side, many of my questions may not have been fully understood. But, so far as I could make out, the trouble arose from a desire on the part of the engineer officers to be eligible for gunnery as they are for torpedo. The Administration apparently solved the problem by taking their engineer officers after that from a different class; the junior engineers in the Russian service in 1899 seemed to be on a par with the engine-room artificers in our navy, and to hold an equivalent rank. Nominally they rank with, but after, mitchmen (sub-lieutenants); while a senior engineer ranks, nominally with, but after, a kapitan II. class (commander). Actually, however, only senior engineers now appear to hold rank with the executives in any way.

*Efficiency of Russian naval engineers.*

As a class the Russian junior engineer officers were in 1899 inefficient. From what I saw of them, they appeared interested enough in their profession, but lacking intelligence, and to have little or no knowledge of anything outside their own immediate concern. Many of them—so the Russian executives said—were continually causing minor accidents through ignorance; they have a weakness for turning taps off and on in a casual way. Executive here means gunnery officers, who hate the engineers very bitterly. Probably the engineer side of the question would tell the story somewhat differently. Since then they have improved wonderfully.

*Executive control.*

The question of executive control of their own men by engineer officers is not heard of in Russia; nor is there any friction between them and the ordinary lieutenants except on the score of intelligence. Everyone in the Russian Navy has executive rank over his subordinates or anyone below him, and a junior engineer may punish a stoker as much as he chooses according to the limit of punishment allowed to his rank. He can flog him, to the extent of three or four lashes, or give him two days' imprisonment.

The gunnery question is, however, acute. The first solution, the abolition of the old-type engineer officer and the substitution of mechanics, is admitted to be a failure, and a new scheme was on foot in 1899. Under it no more mechanics were to be entered as engineer officers, and possibly those in the service rated at a rank equivalent to our artificer-engineer; while cadets from the executive were all to go through an engineering course (elementary), subsequently as sub-lieutenants to be eligible to specialise in engineering in exactly the same way as they now can for gunnery or torpedo. This scheme (which closely resembles Admiral Fisher's "New scheme of Entry" in the British Navy) was yet in embryo, and still is; for there is a difficulty in the way, and that is that the supply of cadets barely suffices for the demand. The Russian regulation is that every executive naval officer must be a nobleman, or the son of an officer who fulfils the original requirements. Nobles are pretty plentiful in Russia, but 100 cadets a year are required in the ordinary course: the engineer change, if made, will make at least 150 per annum required (there are comparatively few engineer officers borne in the Russian Navy, certainly less than half our proportion).

*Scheme to defeat present difficulties.*

The theoretical technical training of Russian naval

Theoretical training.

officers is on a scale altogether beyond anything we have in our navy. They study tactics and strategy regularly, not as an exotic. I came across a curious instance of this. Some while ago there was a good deal written about tactics in the *United Service Institution Journal* by Admiral, then Captain H. J. May, R.N. But if any officer in our service is familiar with these writings, he is so of his own volition only, not because of our powers that be. In Russia, where they study the *United Service Institution Journal*, this theory of tactics is part of the recognised curriculum; it is actually better known in a foreign navy than to the navy for whom it was originally propounded! I could cite a dozen similar instances.

"War game" is a recognised naval institution in the Russian Navy. All through the winter, two days a week, at the Naval Academy, the officers, as part of their regular training, play a strategical game invented some while since by the Grand Duke Alexander. This game covers all those minute but vital questions of coal endurance, supplies, and so forth; and every possible contingency that the Russian Navy might be called on to face is worked out. In the event of any meeting of hostile forces, the ensuing tactical problems are then carefully worked out by the tactical Kriegspiel associated with my own name. I feel here that I am on a little awkward ground; but the game being more or less officially used in most navies, it is in a way beyond my own private concern, so perhaps I may be forgiven for mentioning it. The Russians play this tactical game with full rules,—a state

SET OF NAVAL WAR GAME PIECES, SPECIALLY MADE FOR H.I.H. GRAND DUKE ALEXANDER.

*(The row of models in front is the Russian fleet.)*

of things that renders the word "game" very inappropriate. Admirals play frequently, and for an admiral to be beaten at his own business by a junior officer is an awkward *contretemps*, to say the least; but it is bound to happen occasionally: while with admirals new to the game it is likely to be frequent. There are certain orthodox formations that good and intelligent gunnery must render fatal, though on paper they look unassailable. I saw a Russian admiral so beaten, and badly beaten, by an officer much his junior, with an inferior force better handled. When it was over, the admiral laughed: "I should have adopted that formation in a real battle," he said, "and it's better to be beaten in a sham fight than in a real one." In a real fight bad gunnery on the enemy's part might have made a difference—it might not; in any case, tactics built on the chances of an enemy's faults are bad. Subsequently that admiral played the same action again, adopting other tactics and winning.

If this were all, it would not necessarily amount to much. These games were some of many that we played nightly at the Xenia Palace—from seven-thirty to one o'clock in the morning. From twelve to fifteen officers usually participated, and subsequently every move was discussed and argued out at the Naval Academy. It is this discussion that does the teaching, and for good or evil there it is as the characteristic of the Russian naval officer of to-day.

It is not unique: the French, for instance, to some extent, the Japanese to a great extent, are after the same pattern, but the Russian carries it further. Of course there are plenty of officers in our service who "think things out," but they have to do it more or less individually, they are not encouraged to do so officially.

Altogether, I fancy these pretty little future war-pictures we read about, where the Russians are always beaten because they blunder at tactics, might bear a little editing. If it came to a war, there are more of us, we have infinitely better opportunities for practical training, and in the case of the sailors longer service: we are fully practical and versed in practice. In all these things we have a great pull. But let us make no mistake, there would be not merely brave men against us, but also able men, who think of other things than "spit and polish," and on the whole very well.

In conclusion, I have elsewhere[1] made comparison between Russian and British officers as men, so not much more need be added. Before all things the Russian is a *sailor*, in which he differs mightily from the German naval officer, who is "a soldier at sea," as the Russians say. Otherwise, beyond the racial differences, concerning which I have elsewhere written, all naval officers are much of a pattern,—the sea air produces a certain well-known type. The Russian officer, from some strong racial similarity, possibly also from things inherited from those Britishers who helped to found his navy, is

[1] See pp. 516 and 550.

more like the English officer than any other. A lovable fellow he is—one cannot help liking him whether one wills to or no.

And if ever we do go to war with Russia, whatever may happen on land, at sea, if there is a battle, when it is over and the best man has won, there will be a good deal of friendly handshaking as the smoke blows away over the water. War may be very horrible and wicked, but in its modern form it has at least certain virtues, that the act of fighting (on the sea at any rate) engenders regard and cements it. Even the Japanese and Chinamen, who had an hereditary racial feud, grew fond of each other after the Homeric contests at Yaloo and Wei-hai-wei.

# XXXIX

## RUSSIA IN THE FAR EAST, 1899 AND 1904.

"WE took Port Arthur to keep the Germans out of it"—so runs the Russian statement.

"Germany," a Russian would go on to say, "fixed her eye on Kiao Chao a good ten years ago, and waited her opportunity. England? No, we really never thought about England in the matter; we never expected England to *do* anything about it, only for her to do some dog-in-the-manger *talk*. Ever since Germany began to cast eyes on China, Russian movements towards Manchooria have been perfectly plain and obvious. And there were never any English interests in Manchooria till she woke to the fact that Russia was there."

And if you go on to mention Wei-hai-wei he may politely refrain from quoting back numbers of ministerial speeches about "the integrity of China," but he will lay his finger upon Wei-hai-wei on a map, and after that upon the land behind it, and the great bulk of Imperial Russia behind it again.

"A place where soldiers can march," he will say; and to his mind no more needs saying after that.

From the Russian's point of view, England being

at Wei-hai-wei is in no way undesirable. If England were not there, some other nation would be. Russia herself does not want the place: she prefers to have her own territory at the back of her outposts. "Always in the mass" is the Russian watchword of imperial expansion. *Wei-hai-wei.*

In the event of war, Russia knows perfectly well that she can go across China to Wei-hai-wei and overwhelm that place by sheer force of numbers; this isolated base is more a source of weakness than of strength to England. Leu-kun-tau is of course an island, but an army on the shore would soon make it an uncomfortable place. This, coupled with the difficulty of satisfactorily defending the place, is probably why we have so far made no attempt to do anything with Wei-hai-wei.

The thing, however, that puzzles all Russians is why England saw her commercial rival Germany take Kiao Chao without a murmur, while she gnashed her teeth and hinted at war directly Russia was mentioned in connection with Manchooria and Port Arthur. One would really think our merchants believed the German traders they feel the pinch of to be Russians. In the British mercantile marine every foreigner is "a Dutchman"—for all that Holland is the least represented nation in our forecastles. Some similar process would seem to make our trading people use a Russ in much the same way.

It was clear—quite clear even at the time when we were fulminating so finely about the integrity of China

—that Wei-hai-wei and the parts adjacent must eventually fall to England, Germany, or Russia. Russia would not have the place unless the having entailed possession of all the territory between there and her own borders—a large order, and one for which she was not prepared to fight us, as assuredly she would have had to in such case. Germany had Kiao Chao, a place that she selected in preference to Wei-hai-wei many years ago. Japan had a temporary hold upon the place, but she had no desire to retain it. We may disguise it as we will, but in taking Wei-hai-wei we more or less took "leavings." It was a cheap way of "standing up to Russia"; and from that point of view was an advantageous step to the Government, if not to the country.

Now supposing, instead of taking a place that we shall be unable to hold in war if Russia means to have it, we had had the wisdom of Japan and left the place alone. Japan is bent on being a second England and a trading nation, and it is with China that much of her future trade will be, with China that most of her present trade is. Japan was in a particularly advantageous position had she wished to "lease" Wei-hai-wei, but she refrained from any such action. None of the Powers interested would have made war upon her for it if she had, and Japan was perfectly well aware of that. She refrained for other reasons. From this we come to the question, "Why, if Japan does not consider a slice of China necessary for her trade, is it necessary for us?"

Suppose, therefore, we had done like Japan and left China alone, and instead boldly suggested that Russia should take her fill? The territory would have become Russian, the Chinese capital would have had to be moved elsewhere, and the country would have been opened up. The Russians are not traders;[1] some other nation would have had to do the trading. It is a canon with us that Russia is hostile to British trade and "the open door"; but as she cannot progress without outside trade, she must be some nation's market sooner or later. We might once, perhaps, have traded Manchooria for a market, as Russia's fixed policy is to try and trade chiefly with her friends.

*Russia the oldest European Power in the Far East.*

All this is the *pro* Russian side; indeed, it treats on the matter as Russia sees it. She began operations in the Far East in the seventeenth century, and coast-line thereabouts is her coast-line just as much as the shores of the Black Sea or the Baltic.[2] After a long interval we, as a Power owning all the waters of the world (that was our root-idea in those days), set up at Hong Kong—a long way distant from Russian shores. Then, finally, Germany came along, erecting an outpost in territory more or less within the sphere of what would have been ultimately Russian expansion.

*German cleverness at Kiao Chao.*

The moment was cleverly chosen: it suited both England and Russia to have Germany as a counter-poise, and no doubt Germany took good care that that

[1] They have just at present a legend that they are a commercial nation, but they are not, and never will be for a great many years.

[2] Kamskatcha was Russian coast-line *before* either the Baltic or the Black Sea! It was formally annexed in 1697-

view was uppermost to both. But when all is said and done, we should remember that Germany's position in the Far East to-day was ours of yesterday, and that Russia is as much justified in regarding us as intruders there as we are in so looking upon her when her supposed designs in the Persian Gulf come upon the tapis.

This Russian side of the question we not only ignore in England, but are probably three parts ignorant of. Our crime is rather the ignorance than the ignoring.

When all is said and done, however, it is exceedingly doubtful whether Russia really objects much to what we may do or say in China. There was, it is true, a temporary wave of fierce indignation when a few years ago Lord Charles Beresford, in the character of travelling Member of Parliament and investigator of commercial interests, was fulminating about Russia in the Far East. But this indignation was not at Lord Charles as an individual, but because he held a commission in the British Navy, and so his words were supposed to be inspired by the British Government. No Russian admiral would dream of saying anything publicly against another nation, unless directly inspired to do so. However, these bellicose speeches of Lord Charles' were probably potent factors in such understandings with Russia as we arrived at just afterwards, and for the reason stated. A general agreement with us in China is probably not what Russia wants, except at a price we are not yet

*The crusade of Lord Charles Beresford.*

prepared to pay, though the Beaconsfield legend is dying. Russia wants Constantinople, and every bit of tussle with us in the Far East has or had the city on the Bosphorus as its axis. In China they can (or think they can, which comes to the same thing) turn us out from all inland places, just as we can control the seaboard; and there is very little doubt but that they would give up almost anything in China (easily to be retaken) for a free hand at Constantinople. It is over a thousand years since the first Russian tried to capture Constantinople; and it is a good many hundred since that Grand Duke Ivan of Muscovy, who married Sophia Paleologus, and since Byzantium falling to the Turk, the ruler of Russia held himself to be legitimate heir to the throne, for which reason he called himself Cæsar (Tsar) and took the double-headed eagle to himself.

Russia is not the nation to let the labours of a thousand years slip by because Lord Beaconsfield and others had theories as to the necessity of the Turk in Europe. If anything in this world is sure, it is certain that Russia will eventually obtain Constantinople, and the recent evidences that the Emperor of Germany may have designs are more likely to hasten than delay it.

This, then, is the situation, as it was when Japan, robbed of the fruits of her victory over China, rested and prepared for the struggle that she anticipated with Russia. In 1899 both nations had that struggle well in view: it was obvious to them from the moment that the Russian flag floated at Port Arthur.

The reason is as follows: Port Arthur is a greatly overrated place. It is too small for the Russian fleet, it is incapable of proper expansion. It is to be starved out quite easily by any Power that is able to command the sea enough to land troops in its rear and keep them there. It can also be shelled at long range from many of the bays round about it. To mend this Russia worked also at Dalmy and Talienwan; but in a very little while she realised that she had made a fatal error in not discovering the ideal harbour of Masampho on the Korean coast. Having Port Arthur she began that conquest of Manchooria of which so much has been heard, but her real objective was Masampho or some other Korean harbour—preferably Masampho. This Japan swiftly recognised, and did what she could by fortifying and making a strong base of Tsushima in the island of Takashiki seventy miles away. Here she might have rested content, perhaps, but a corresponding situation that might occur nearer home will show why as a nation she will not so rest.

At the present day Germany is credited with designs upon the Netherlands, which face us much as Korea faces Japan. We have only to imagine Germany about to seize the Netherlands to be able to view the question as Japan views the Korean situation.

We face France just as nearly as Germany would face us were she to obtain possession of the Netherlands, but that argument would go for nothing were Germany to act up to her supposed designs on the Low Countries. So is it with Japan—she feels about Korea as we would feel about the Netherlands. In addition much of her trade is with Korea—this trade would die once the Russian flag flew in the Hermit Kingdom.

Let us glance now at the other side. Once let Japan be admitted to Korea, Russian expansion would be at an end without a long and costly war, and there is every probability that did she oust Japan the Powers would refuse to allow her the fruits of victory. Her minimum is, therefore, that Japan must obtain no footing in Korea.

On a basis of an independent Korea it would look as though peace were easily to be assured; but as Japan has not the slightest faith in any Russian promises, the crux of the present friction (January, 1904), is obvious: so, too, the certainty of war in the long run, either next week, next year or some time. Any permanent agreement is practically impossible unless Russia is prepared to sacrifice all expansion in this direction. Such a sacrifice would mean loss of all prestige with China, and the loss of such prestige would be unquestionably serious.

Russia, in fine, cannot withdraw (or at the most can only do so temporarily), while any yielding on the part of Japan seems incompatible with every ambition that she possesses. More, it seems to render certain her ultimate extinction by the mass of Russia.

There are only two Powers that have any real prospect of owning China in the hereafter—Russia and Japan. They alone understand China. To reason with a Chinaman on Western methods is purely wasted labour, to fight them on such methods is to court disaster. Those who went to the relief of the Pekin Legations know well that they came back alive only because Russians and Japanese went with them. As one of our officers told me: "When I went up it was all I could do to keep myself from killing some of the Russians for their brutality—on the return I knew that their action alone saved us."

The Russian method was to kill all Chinese indiscriminately. They would fire big guns at individual Chinamen—the programme was general terror. They succeeded in inspiring it, the Chinese understood this, the only argument with them, and the expedition returned alive. Those wholesale massacres on the Siberian frontier, about which such shrieks were made, saved the Legations. Of course it was horrible, but it was necessary. In that relief of the Legations there was much that was more horrible still—for instance, Japan's contribution to the salvation of the expedition consisted in tying every captured Chinaman to a dead one, face to face, and leaving them thus! This sounds atrocious; but like the wholesale Russian massacres it did what none of the ordinary fighting did, frightened the Chinese. War to them on European lines is a mere bagatelle—on their own lines it frightens them into submission. The only alternative is not to fight them at all.

When Russia and Japan go to war it will be Greek meeting Greek with a vengeance. No Russian officer

It is no good laughing at the absurdity of these assertions, for their effect is too great.

Their existence shows how Russia may be compelled to fight, so as to back up her words with deeds. The so-called war party are those who see this, who realise that Russia must be ready to fight if need be. And they have laboured and spared not against such a day.

# XL

## OUR MISTAKE IN DEALING WITH RUSSIA

FROM beginning to end the whole of our trouble with Russia has been due to our official terror at anything like saying "Come on." Indeed, it is probably only due to a series of small actions on the part of our naval officers at different times on the China Station that war between England and Russia has not taken place long ago. When a few years since Admiral Sir Vesey Hamilton casually took his fleet into Vladivostok in a fog,[1] he did more to further the cause of peace than half a dozen diplomatic agreements, or, for that matter, half a dozen Tsar's Rescripts. In England the incident never had much publicity; it has long since been forgotten. There were no "strained relations" at that particular moment; it was merely a casual call. Yet nothing before or since has made such an impression upon the Russians: and because of Admiral Hamilton there are deeper reasons than our numerical superiority why they will not seek to contend with us for the mastery of the sea for many a day yet if they can avoid it. If, however, the incident frightened them, it also did more than that. The

[1] P. 398.

Russian is no coward; individually he is quite as brave as any Englishman. What Admiral Sir Vesey Hamilton's call chiefly did was to evoke an intense admiration, and a feeling that a nation which could do a thing of this sort was a better friend than foe. Behind it, swelling and increasing it, there have been a hundred little incidents, few of which have ever even found their way into print at all in this country, but in Russia they are known. British cruisers during periods of strained relations, with cold shot laid ready to heave into any boat coming alongside; solitary British gunboats calmly steaming into harbours where two or three large Russian ships, possible enemies, were lying; —incidents of this sort by dozens and by scores, and most or all of them due to the mere individual initiative of British captains and commanders. It is not Trafalgars in the past, but things like these in the nearer living present, that have made and built *prestige.* Trafalgar is dead, Nelson is dead: it is the incidents of *to-day* and the day before that now bear fruit.

In all these things our Governments have never had part or parcel; if they heard of the incidents they probably reproved the makers of them.

Far inland ships cannot go. Far inland they matter nothing. Far inland has Russia been moving. Inasmuch as she has had few or no signs of objection from us save verbal ones, which, no matter how violent, count for nothing, she scarcely believes in the reality of our caring about it. To Russia our protests are election cries, catch-votes, padding, — anything meaningless.[1]

For the British Army the Russians have none of the feeling that they have for the British Navy. Our army means very little to them; they are (or were) ready enough to face it if necessary, expecting to force it back should any unforeseen series of circumstances bring about a conflict. Apart from the question of the individual soldier against the individual soldier, Russia sees on her side numbers, and a possible Indian mutiny behind our troops.

But—and here we come upon the most extraordinary part of the situation—the Russian soldier would far sooner face a German or any other foreigner than an English Tommy. And why? The impressionable gentleman who started the story about the massacre of the wounded in the Soudan is the cause of the whole thing. The tale was given a good deal of publicity to in Russia, and was accepted there as fact. Every denial merely served firmly to convince them that the tale is true; and nothing will ever make them believe the contrary.

Then Mr. W. T. Stead came upon the scene, and he had a good deal to say about the digging up of the Mahdi's body. Every educated Russian has in one way or another heard of W. T. Stead, and in all cases he stands to them as something more than a cipher. A good many of those that I came across

[1] This statement is not a mere "opinion" of my own, but an authoritative Russian view.

regarded him as a huge joke; others held him to be a sort of feeler, with the British Government at the other end of the string,—some of the Grand Dukes had that idea.

But whether they regarded him as a kind of Punch, or as the emissary of a timid Government, or as an omnipotent Kleon—all Russians are at one in believing him to be a man who knows. Everything Mr. Stead said at his Peace Meetings about the Mahdi's body was believed in Russia, and the name of Kitchener would be as good as an army corps against them.

What wounded Russians underwent at the hands of Bashi-Basouks and camp-followers in the last Turco-Russian war is not forgotten in Russia; it left a very painful memory. But in the British Tommy the Russian sees a worse enemy still—a horrible, disciplined savage, armed with explosive bullets, who will, if he catches a wounded Russian, either prop him up in the sun and leave him waterless to die by inches, or else do bayonet practice on his helpless body! The incarnation of merciless devilry,—that is the Russian ideal of a British soldier. Russia was full of such stories at the time of the South African war.

The Russian himself can be "brutal" enough at times, but brutality in his case seldom or never amounts to more than treating men just like men, in the more or less ordinary way, treat animals. Prisoners of war they have always treated well;[1] and the sluggish, good-tempered moujik can hardly com-

[1] As a rule; isolated exceptions can of course be named.

prehend hot blood and passion on the battlefield. He fights as he ploughs—because he is told to. The wild tales of how British soldiers treated the Soudanese are all the more terrible to him because he cannot understand, and in reaching him they grow to more and more horrible proportions. Put into circulation in Russia at a time when strained relations with this country rendered desirable a showing up in the newspapers of the extreme wickedness of the Ingliski, the effects have exceeded all calculations.

So far as we are concerned, it is all right all round; the detraction of the British Tommy has encircled him with a halo of prestige. Not on a par, indeed, with the sailor's prestige; still its practical results are the same: Russia doesn't want to fight us just yet.

The moujik as a warrior is not at all brave in our sense of the word: the lower class Russians as a whole are a timid nation, despite individual instances of high physical courage. They are "sheep led by a lion" more or less. This does not mean that they are cowards in any sense, but rather the reverse, since they have that moral courage which enables them to go forward when they want to run back. Our bluejackets and Tommies go forward without appreciating the danger. It should be added that the Russian soldier is the hardiest in the world, able to live on next to nothing, indifferent to temperature, and an excellent marcher.

Numerically the Russian army is weaker than it appears to be. There is, of course, plenty of it, but that plenty is only a fraction of the "paper" force,—

the soldiers are left working on the land. Tyrannical, and all that, as the Russian Government is accused of being, it somehow or other has about it a good deal of that "grandmotherly legislation" that our most progressive and enlightened Radicals so loudly shriek for here. It is a little unfortunate that the *bête noir* of advanced friends of freedom should practise what these advanced ones who hold it up as a foul tyranny preach, still the fact remains.[1] Behind all the outward show of autocracy there is plenty of communism and socialism in the Russian methods of government, and there is a good deal in the saying that "Russia is in many ways the freest country in the world." It is—so long as a man does not meddle with politics. If he interests himself too much in them, he is likely to be missing one fine morning, and that is the end of his politics. A little arbitrary, of course, yet one has to confess to points in it. There are a good many demagogues in this country who could be similarly "missed" without much general discomfort to the nation.

To resume: we make a fatal mistake in failing to realise the two real Russias; we are so prone to put up instead a totally imaginary Russia. Actually there is first of all the more or less Arcadian State, slow, primitive, and peaceful—about as dangerous as a tame elephant. With these is the other Russia, made up of the descendants and followers of Peter the Great,

[1] Our assumption that "Russia is internally rotten and likely to tumble to pieces" is, I fancy, a grave error. It appears so to political refugees in this country, but these folk have often very distorted visions. Any revolutionary will tell the same tale of the country he has fled from.

holding steadfastly and generally blindly to the ideals of the Great Tzar. A good deal of Russian duplicity and bad faith may be explained by the fact that this party knows little more than the rest of the world what it really wants. Now and then there arises a leader like the Grand Duke Alexander, who realises how essential it is to secure efficiency, but generally the mainspring is a dim preparation for the coming of another Peter the Great. I have never met a Russian "Jingo" who would admit this; but I have never spoken to one who did not obviously have this faith in his heart—that a great Tzar will come some day. Every recent Emperor has had his ideals of how he may be that Tzar; Nikolai II. has his dreams of being the Prince of Peace. Other men have other ideals. Thus is Russia a mystery, but we shall understand her better if we can realise that in many ways she is a gigantic replica of the late South African Republic—and quite as strange a mixture.

It is a little foreign to the subject, at first sight, but I cannot forbear quoting here a conversation I had with a *uyezdnyi nachalnik* (marshal of nobility) of a remote district—J.P. and county court judge rolled into one would be our nearest equivalent to him. He was talking about the Jews—a pretty serious problem in Russia. "We are allowed a certain amount of individual discretion," he said. "We don't have 'Law' like you English have. But we have to give justice. So if a case comes before me of a Jew and a moulik, if I find the Jew has charged more than fifty per cent. interest, I have that Jew knouted!"

This is "grandmotherly legislation" again, good for everybody except the local Isaac Gordons. In this country, unless the gentle Hebrew so far forgets himself as to add insult to usury, he can charge several hundred per cent., and the Law will help him to vindicate the sacred rights of contract. Yet I have no doubt whatever but that my marshal of nobility is one of those wicked Russians who so "cruelly and fiendishly ill-treated the poor harmless and innocent Jew."

So be it. Probably also he is one of the instruments for founding and weaning an empire of the future greater than any the world has yet seen, because he and his fellows, and the Government behind him, are wise enough to take the bull boldly by the horns and see to it that their nation shall not exist for the Jew usurer to grow fat on.

In one way and another, therefore, there is a good deal that is "grandmotherly" in the Russian system of government. And this is our particular concern in this way. The Russian Government seek to follow the line of least resistance in managing for their immense and poverty-stricken population. They do not take more men than they can help for military purposes, and they are by no means anxious to lose such as they do take. War would mean that all present problems would assume a tenfold import; the loss of bread-winners by death or by service with the colours would have a heavy meaning. Russia has not population enough as it is; she wants to increase, not diminish it. Nor are there any men in Russia anxious to go hunting *la gloire* on a battlefield.

Yet Russia expands; she is always expanding those borders that already she cannot fill. The reason is simple enough; she is building not for to-day, but for a hundred years hence,—for that great Slav empire of which so many Russians dream.

Building in this way, and expanding as she always does in the mass, with nearly all Asia to choose from, it is not a matter of the first importance to her in which particular direction she grows. For the reasons stated she is not desirous of a conflict with us, and certainly not expanding for the express purpose of annoying us—as so many people here seem to believe. But—so Russians say—if they colonised the North Pole the British Government would lodge a protest to the effect that British trade interests were imperilled.

Were this all, it would not immediately concern the British Empire—at anyrate not at present. The unfortunate part of this dog-in-the-manger system—for it is often no better—is that, having decided to adopt such a rôle the Government do not strictly abide by it. In the fable the dog sat tight, and the ox had to go without the hay. Our principle is to jump on the hay and do the snarling, but directly the ox seeking other hay comes near, to jump off in fright. It is not a very dignified spectacle, and the point or object of it is not quite easy to see.

What we ought to do should, however, be fairly patent, and it is certainly simple enough. There is nothing on earth to prevent our clearly telling Russia what we want and what we do not want. We can lay it down publicly that because of our vital trade interests such and such a part of China is not to be taken. We are fully able to stipulate that, if other parts where our interests are less are "leased," no fortifications are to be erected on the coast, and that if any such are started our ships will blow them down. Our ships can. We can and also ought to state what parts do *not* concern us. There is then an absolutely clear course.

If we laid down such a statement honestly, claiming no fancy interests, but only real and actual ones, it is to the last degree improbable that Russia would trouble about those districts. Why should she? To do so in face of such a declaration would mean an asking for war—the last thing Russia wants. There is room for both of us—plenty of room.

The advantages of such a course would not end with the absence of Russian war scares. Admiral Sir Richard Vesey Hamilton, at Vladivostok, taught the Russians not merely to fear but to respect and esteem the British sailor. By the display of a little "backbone" the British Government could do the same thing for the nation as a whole. An Ingliski would then no longer be synonymous with a person who politically promises what he never means to perform.

The Englishman *per se* is defined and differentiated by the Russian as a man who always does what he says he will do—that is *the* trait of an Englishman in

Russian eyes, the thing that marks him out from all other foreigners. The antithesis, in fine, of all those successive Governments of ours for which the Russians have as much contempt as they have respect for the individual Briton.

If ever we have an alliance or real understanding with Russia it will be upon this "say what you mean and do what you say you will" principle. Every compromise, every graceful concession, simply paves the way for further demands from a Power in whose eyes the British Government is merely a Western edition of the Tsung-li Yamên.

# XLI

## OTHER NAVIES AS SEEN BY THE RUSSIANS

THE following are a few notes upon such opinions as I gleaned from Russian naval officers concerning other navies. I do not pretend that they are necessarily *representative*; however, they come in each case from men who have had opportunities of forming opinions, and, speaking generally, naval opinions are apt to run in grooves. It does not necessarily follow, either, that the opinions are correct; our British opinion upon the Japanese Navy, for instance, is very different to the Russian one here given! It is only fair to say that the Japanese one upon the Russian Navy is very little better; indeed, in a great many cases all through, what the Russian seems to think of any particular foreigner is strangely akin to what that particular foreigner thinks of him. There are exceptions; still the rule largely obtains.

AUSTRIA-HUNGARY.—"Very good officers, very good navy—what there is of it."

ENGLAND.—Detailed views upon the British Navy *personnel* have been quoted *in extenso* elsewhere. More generally and broadly, its characterisation runs:

"The English Navy is very strong and powerful, and never lets slip a single opportunity of impressing that upon the world, without any regard to the rest of the world's feelings. In actual war it would very possibly be much less efficient than we suspect, because every politician in the country would try and have supreme control of it. If England had a single ruler, her navy would be much more dangerous than it is." [1]

FRANCE.—"A lot of us laugh at the French Navy and believe it is no good at all, and so did I till I served in it for a while. Now I think the same as all other officers of ours who have seen inside it do. The French are very good, and manage things very well; the French is a very good navy indeed. They think out tactics and strategy that your English admirals never dream of."

GERMANY.—"Soldiers at sea! But they are very good soldiers, and they manage all their little things very well. Perhaps they wouldn't manage big things so well: a little thing and a big thing are equally important to a German, and they might fuss

[1] The following from the *Novoe Vremya* may also be quoted,—though of course it is more of an official "feeler" than much else:—

"It would be fruitless, in view of the very striking facts before our eyes, to try to hide the fact that England by the strength of its fleet holds all Western Europe in a state of fear. Without any effort England has obtained Central Africa from France, and it now looks as if it will succeed in obtaining similar concessions from Germany in the Samoan Archipelago, and perhaps also in the Far East. Thus the time has now fully arrived for all Powers whose colonial interests are menaced by the pretensions of England, to put an end to this state of things once and for all by concerted action. However, no one in Western Europe seems to think of such united action."

about little things that didn't matter, to the detriment of big things that did. And then they have the German Emperor!"

Italy.—"No good—the French could beat them."

Japan.—"We do not like the Japanese. I know some Japanese that I like much; but taking them as a nation—no. Their navy is good—too good; but they would never fight Russia fairly. They would invite us to a dinner, and poison us, or something like that![1] Treacherous: you can't trust them."

Spain.—"Brave and stupid, but nothing like as inefficient as is made out. They would have beaten the Yankees had they had half a fair chance."

Sweden.—"An exceedingly smart and good little navy: the most efficient in the world, perhaps."

United States.—"Bounce! They have never been tried yet, and are all talk, talk, talk—so far. You fill your English newspapers with talk of how brave they are, and what good gunners they are! And at Santiago they made two per cent. of hits! Some of your newspaper men ought to have been put into lunatic asylums. You English are getting nervous, and think that by flattering America you'll get her to help you. Tut! she will be your worst enemy—your

[1] This is a common belief in Russia, not merely a naval sentiment. As for Japanese naval opinion of Russians—well, "brutal savages" is merely part of it. Japanese in Russia are treated—well, they are treated quite differently to the way they are in England. How the two navies would sort together in the event of a general war in the Far East (the probability being that Russian and Japanese ships would have to act together) is a pretty problem, but outside the scope of this book. Japan is to Russia to-day what Turkey was in the last century.

very worst enemy. We could always get her to help us against you. . . . Her officers are good; but her men are bad, as they have next to no discipline: winning so easily in that war with Spain has done them all a lot of harm."

# XLII

## ANGLO-SAXON *VERSUS* SLAV

FINALLY, perhaps, I may add to Russian opinion of others their opinion of themselves as a navy.

"We are not like your English Navy. We have to get lots of our poor fellows from the centre of Russia, where they have never seen the sea in their lives. You can't expect them to be very good all at once. But we all try to do our best; and if we were fighting your English ships or any other navy, you would find us all try."

Possibly this opinion of themselves is as faithful a one as can be got. But it is not quite all. "We shall be" is in every Russian's heart, if it does not often come to his lips. Every Russian feels himself a member of the empire that will be the world-empire of the future. And that empire will be a great sea-empire, since the sea is now what the land once was in the matter of communications. At some future date that great struggle between the British Empire and the Russian, between the Anglo-Saxon and the Slav, that so many prophesy, may come off. The day is probably yet far distant ere this new Punic War comes about. When it comes and all, it does not do to too hastily assume that England is its Carthage and Russia its Rome. With the sea its highway, the British Empire is the really homogeneous one. Russian homogeneity is deceptive: no lines of railway can act like the sea highway. Land and sea have changed places since the Punic War, and, on the whole, the Russian Empire may be more like Carthage than the British. But it does not do to attempt to push the analogy too far: neither nation is likely to crush the other as Rome crushed Carthage. Yet the war of the future, when it comes, is none the less likely to be absolutely decisive, for one mighty empire or the other will in all human probability split into fragments. Either *may* do so before the day that sees this war arrives. Failing this, it is likely to be a fight between peoples, rather than one between their fleets and armies—and in the people themselves will be the seeds of defeat or victory.

Discussing this, our writers tell us how superior the Anglo-Saxon is to the Slav. It is a comfortable assurance; but granting that it is correct to-day, will it always be so? Is not the Anglo-Saxon already showing signs of decay? Egyptians, Athenians, Romans—where is their superiority to-day? Athens had her Kleon and his friends; from the Augustan age the history of Rome is a history of decline. We in our empire to-day have our "Little Englanders," while Russia has her Nihilists (the supposed death of Nihilism is mostly fictitious). The Little Englander and the Nihilist are not to be put on a par: the latter, to use a paradox, is better in that he is far worse. He is illogical, and demonstrably so, while the Little Englander is not. Mr. Morley is quite logical—ethically. We may call Mr. Labouchere a buffoon, but when he characterised Imperialism as calling South African German Jews "British patriots," we know in our hearts that he was logical, and no liar. If we are not ruled by the democracy and the counting of noses, as we pose to be, and call it the highest product of civilisation in our posing, we are ruled by a plutocracy, which is worse. To spread empire for the benefit of the Stock Exchange, or to combat its spread by looking at our neighbour's corns through the wrong end of the telescope, and by a hypersensitive regard for feelings that the nation sympathised for does not probably possess, neither one nor other of these things makes for empire. The course of empire, like most practical everyday things, is ethically all wrong. What is nowadays contemptuously spoken of as being "insular," a brutal disregard for the rights of any country save our own—these are the ways by which empire is made. The Slav has these things—"Holy Russia" is the beginning and end of the argument with him; he cares not a rap for the ethics and superficial morality of the question. We were pirates when we made our name upon the sea; while we held it firmly, neutrals had no rights, and the foreign warship that declined to dip its ensign to us was sent to Davy Jones, with the approving smile of God. That was our substitute for ethics in those days. We were not "Jingoes" then: we simply had the very useful notion that a foreigner was a person whom we let live on sufferance, an inferior creature altogether.

Russians possess that idea now. They do not put it into words: putting such ideas into words puzzles them, as witness its practice in China. But they have the idea, while we have educated ourselves out of it.

Russia also has Religion, a power that we cannot understand. Religion to us means little or nothing save going to church. The only Religion of a potential nature existing amongst us is the Salvation Army, and that is nowhere compared to the Greek Church. It was not a factor in the South African War—indeed, religion was used in some cases against it. The Church in Russia can wield a power like Mahomedanism in Turkey. We have nothing to put against "Holy Russia," which is God and the big battalions both.

It is not likely that this generation will see it, nor perhaps will the next, but in end those two words are likely to be our undoing as an empire. No race or empire can last forever, and with the benefits of ultra-civilisation it must accept the evils of decline.

These views are pessimistic, and I do not suppose that they will be palatable. But, as the Russians say, "You cannot be everything, always."

Here, as elsewhere in this book, I may seem to have wandered from the subject of the Imperial Russian Navy. But the wandering is more apparent than real: these things are bound up with the Navy whose white flag with the blue S. Andrew cross Russians dream shall one day rule the seas, as the white flag with the red cross of S. George now rules it. "Holy Russia," "We *shall* be," and, finally, "We will try," are phrases which we cannot afford to ignore or neglect; and most meaning of all to us should be that "We will try."

THE END

[APPENDICES.

# APPENDICES

# APPENDIX A

## PERIOD 1645–1726

PETER THE GREAT'S first galleys for use in the Sea of Azov were constructed at Vorōnege on the Don, where there existed a dockyard. In the course of two years 170 of various sizes were built.[1] *1696.*

When larger ships were required the galley-builders were ordered to construct them, and this led to many early failures.[2] The cost of early shipbuilding was defrayed by a species of Ship Money tax on the Boyars and other landholders, who were divided into companies for this purpose,[3] and it was calculated that 48 vessels could be provided by this means. A number of the vessels, about 100, first built, intended for merchant and internal service, were never launched, and a good many more were soon laid up.[4] Upon the Caspian small craft, *evers* (a type used in the Lower Elbe) and *snows* (a Fleming craft having no connection with the British type of that name), were built at Kazan, previous to Peter's foreign tour. At this time Graf

[1] Prince Louis of Battenberg, *Men-of-War Names.*

[2] Russian Imperial Records.

[3] Brückner, *Peter der Grosse.*

[4] *Russian Fleet under Peter the Great*, ed. Admiral Bridge.

Golovin was admiral,[1] and Aprāksin chief of the Navy Staff.

Admiral Kruyis [2] was one of the first, if not the first, foreigner brought over by Peter. He joined in 1697 as a shipbuilder,[3] and many Dutch and Danes came with him.

"The Tsar . . . fixing the following persons at Taveroff (on the Don) and Voronezh (Vorōnege), Messrs. Joseph Ney, Richard Cosens, and John Deane, Master Builders: Davenport, Hadley, Johnston, Gardiner, and Webb, Assistant Builders: Baggs, a Master Block maker: and Wright, a Master Mast maker; all Englishmen." (From *The Russian Fleet under Peter the Great.*)

*One of the earliest Russo-Swedish encounters.*

In 1703 (or 1702) the Swedes despatched a snow of 12 guns and a long-boat of 4 guns to reconnoitre at Kronstadt. Peter ordered his *lodtkys* to attack, and the Swedes running aground were captured — most of the crews having been killed. Van Werden, the captain of the snow, survived, and was made a captain in the Russian Navy.[4] Other attacks are spoken of,[5] but do not seem to have been more important.[6]

[1] *Russian Fleet under Peter the Great*, ed. Admiral Bridge.

[2] "Cruys" is another spelling, and later "Kruse" was adopted. He was a Norwegian, but came from Holland. See General Appendix.

[3] *Dict. National Biography.* (See also General Appendix.)

[4] *Russian Fleet under Peter the Great.*

[5] Russian Records.

[6] Swedish attacks by land were made on St. Petersburg, and frustrated by strategy. Bogus orders for mobilising troops were sent out, which, the Swedes capturing, threw them into an apprehension of a large covering force.—*Russian Fleet under Peter the Great*, ed. Admiral Bridge.

The first ships upon Lake Ladoga were built by Messrs. Bent and Browne, Englishmen.

## 1705

Swedes destroyed stores at Kronstadt (then called Kronslot) in this year, but were beaten off by the fortifications.

The first fight upon the Gulf of Finland was an attack of 7 Russian galleys on the Swedish frigate Revel.

The Swedes also sent a fleet to bombard Kronstadt, but ran aground on the shallows, and lost 78 killed and 48 wounded in the main attack, and 560 killed and 114 wounded in soldiers sent to flank the island (Swedish official report). The Russians had very poor fortifications, and but for the Swedes running aground the place would have been taken (Russian statement).

About the year 1707 the Swedes began to build a galley fleet to oppose the Russians: their ordinary *1710.*
ships having proved useless to operate against Kronstadt with.

## Engagement off Gogland, 1713

The Russian fleet was :— *1713.*

| | | | |
|---|---|---|---|
| Riga, | 52 guns.— | Captain | De Ruyter (Admiral Kruyis). |
| Viborg, | 52 ,, | ,, | Blorey (Commodore Scheltinga). |
| Poltāva, | 54 ,, | ,, | Turnhoud (Commodore Rays). |
| Ekaterina, | 60 ,, | ,, | Gosler. |

| | | | |
|---|---|---|---|
| Pernau, | 52 | guns.—Captain | Besemacher. |
| Sampson,[1] | 32 | ,, ,, | Edwards. |
| S. Paul, | 30 | ,, ,, | Wersel. |
| S. Peter, | 30 | ,, ,, | Brant. |
| Sthandart, | 24 | ,, ,, | Papagoy. |
| S. Jacob, | 16 | ,, Kapitan-lieut. | Falkenberg. |
| Lesela, | 14 | ,, ,, | Trane. |

The three senior officers were court-martialled and condemned to death for this affair. Kruyis and Scheltinga were eventually pardoned. Rays was sent to Siberia, and died there. A Captain Nelson of the Strafford sat on this court-martial.[2]

The Bolingbroke, 52, contract-built in England, was captured by the Swedes on her way out in 1713.

### Battle of Gangoot

Swedish official accounts say that Aprāksin himself was shut up inside the bay at Gangoot, and that he ran the blockade in a fog with the loss of only one galley. In Admiral Bridge's edition of *The Russian Fleet under Peter the Great*, Peter's message runs, that if Ehrenskiöld would surrender he should be well treated, but that if he fought he would when taken be treated as a common prisoner of war.

Ehrenskiöld's answer is reported without the insinuation about Russian bad faith : possibly this part was suppressed by the officer who took it back to the Tsar.

[1] The Sampson was a rasée. Originally a 40-gun ship purchased in Holland, 1711. She was provided for the Navy by Prince Mentchikoff.

[2] *The Russian Fleet under Peter the Great*, ed. Admiral Bridge.

The same account distinctly states that the Tsar himself did not fight, but watched the affair from a distance. Every other account speaks of his participation, including official accounts, both Russian and Swedish. These are followed in the text.

A facsimile of the letter sent by Peter the Great to the King of Sweden when Admiral Ehrenskiöld, of Gangoot fame, was set at liberty, in which only the first line, "My well-beloved brother," and the signature are in Peter's own hand,[1] appears on p. 65.

The following German letter (a translation signed by Peter the Great himself) accompanied his autograph letter to the King of Sweden concerning Admiral Ehrenskiöld :—

"Translat. von Jhro Czarischen May$^{tt}$ Schreiben an Jhro Konigl. May$^{tt}$. Datiret Petersb. d. 24. Octob. A$^{o}$ 1721. Upl. for K. M$^{tt}$ i Raolet d. 2. Nov. 1721.

"GELIEBSTER HERR BRUDER,—Aldie weihlen, nunmehro zwischen unss und Ew. Königl. May$^{tt}$ die freundtschafft glücklich befastiget worden, und Ew. May$_{tt}$ vice Admirall Ehrnschilt, nach inhalt des Friedensschluss, sich nun mehro zu Rück nach seinen Fatterlandt begiebet; alss haben wier durch Ihm, dieses unser schreiben, an Ew. Königl. May$^{tt}$ abgefertiget, und Euch, unsere wahre zu Ew. May$^{tt}$

[1] This letter is preserved in the State Archives at Stockholm.

tragende freundtschafft zu versichern, und danebst oberwehnten vice Admiraln Ehrnschildt zu Ew. Königl May$^{tt}$ hohe gnade, auff dass höchste, under bester massen zu recomendiren, aldieweihlen wier veranlasset Sein, Ihm eine treue und wahre gezeugnis zu geben, dass er bey der Ocasion da Er gefangen worden, Sich so Ritterlich und Manhafftich verhalten wie solches müchlichst von Jemandt kan vermuhten, und verlanget werden; Wodurch Er dan unsern æstim in der that verdisnat;

"Selliger vice Admiral wirdt die Ehre haben, mündlich mit mehren unsere zu Ew. Königl. May$^{tt}$ tragende gute und wahre vorhaben zu versichern. Und wier verbleiben umb alle gute gefällichkeit zu Erweissen.

"Ew. May$^{tt}$,

"Getreuer Bruder,

"PETR.

"ST. PETERSBURG,
"d. 24 *Octob.* 1721."

### BRITISH FLEET IN THE BALTIC, 1719

(2) 80 guns. Cumberland (flag, Admiral Norris), Dorsetshire (flag, Rear-Admiral Hobson).

(3) 70 guns. Prince Frederick (flag, Rear-admiral Roper), Hampton Court, Monmouth, Suffolk.

(5) 60 guns. Plymouth, York, Monk, Medway, Defiance.

(5) 50 guns. Assistance, Dartmouth, Worcester, Falmouth, St. Albans.

(2) 40 guns. Leinster, Gosport. (1) 20 guns. Port Mahon.

2 Fire-ships. Bedford Galley and the Pool.

1 Small craft. Le Marchand de Lisbon, Royal George.

British Fleet in the Baltic, 1720

(1) 90 guns. Sandwich (flag, Admiral Norris).
(1) 80 guns. Dorsetshire (flag, Rear-admiral Hobson).
(6) 70 guns. Prince Frederick (flag, Rear-admiral Hosier), Suffolk, Buckingham, Revenge, Elizabeth, Bedford.
(5) 60 guns. Medway, York, Nottingham, Kingston, Defiance.
(6) 50 guns. Warwick, Dartmouth, Gloucester, Monk, Falmouth, Worcester.
(1) 40 guns. Gosport. (3) 20 guns. Greyhound, Port Mahon, Blandford.
2 Fire-ships. Bedford Galley, Pool.
2 Bombs. Speedwell, Furnace.

The Swedish fleet that joined this one was as follows:—

(2) 70 guns. Prins Fredrik Carl (flag, Admiral of the Fleet Count Sparre), Carlskrona (flag, Admiral Baron Wachtmeister).
(3) 64 guns. Stockholm (flag, Vice-admiral Count Wachtmeister), Pommern (flag, Vice-admiral Baron Sjöblad), Bremen.
(3) 60 guns. Wenden, Götha, Skåne.
(1) 56 guns. Werden. (1) 50 guns. Öland.
8 Frigates. Revel, Svarte Örn, Jarramas, Ebenezer, Kisken, Anclam, Danska Örn, Stora Phœnix.
7 Armed merchantmen, 5 brigantines, 4 bombs, 2 fire-ships, 11 galleys, and 1 hospital ship.

This combined "fleet in being" lay inactive at Söderarm, while an inferior Russian fleet, under Brigadier Von Mengden (a Dane), raided the Swedish coast.

As before stated, neither Norris nor Count Sparre would waive precedence. Sparre, of course, being a general-admiral, was senior officer *de jure.*

The orders of Admiral Norris[1] were as follows :—

"To protect the Swedish coast, but to avoid fighting the Russians."

In 1721 the same thing happened again, Lascy being in supreme command of the Russian expedition, which destroyed everything that had not already been raided on the previous occasion, and carried away several hundred prisoners.

Letter from the King of Sweden to Admiral Norris, 22nd May.

(*Translation.*)

"As in the Council of yesterday, held in my presence, it was unanimously agreed that the best place for establishing the combined fleet with a view of insuring the safety of our coasts would be Söderarm, where the harbour is just as safe as convenient to watch and check the enemy's galleys, and also offers great facilities for putting to sea in case the enemy should venture to run out with his grand fleet, I have ordered my general-admiral, Count Sparre, to join my squadron, and by the first favourable wind proceed from Elgsnabben to Söderarm. He will furnish the ships of your squadron with able pilots, in order that nothing may prevent your acting in accordance with the decisions of yesterday.

[1] Norris and Peter the Great were and had been personal friends for a long while. Peter tried to imitate Norris in his nautical bearing.

MAP OF THE BALTIC.

"When the combined fleet has taken up the said station, I trust to your circumspection and wide-known experience for taking such measures against the enemy as the protection and safety of our coasts demand, and I have no doubt that if he ventures out of port with his grand fleet or his galleys, you will use the fine opportunity for a decisive battle, and gain for yourself all the esteem a successfully performed act of this kind will insure.—I remain, etc."

Norris had the same fleet as on the previous year (1720). The Swedish force was :—

(2) 92 guns. Enigheten, Götha Lejon (flag of Admiral Count Wachtmeister).
(1) 84 guns. Ulrika Eleonora (flag, Admiral of the Fleet Count Sparre).
(1) 70 guns. Prins Fredrik Carl.
(2) 64 guns. Stockholm, Bremen.
(3) 60 guns. Fredrika Amalia, Vestmanland, Skåne.
(1) 56 guns. Werden.
(1) 50 guns. Öland.
4 Frigates. Svarta Örn, 30; Jarramas, 30; Ebenezer, 36; Örnens Pris, 30.
2 bombs, 2 avisos, and 1 hospital-ship.

It is by no means impossible (in view of what used to happen at a later date to Denmark) that the inactivity of the British fleet was due to its having some ulterior object that did not "come off."

## APPENDIX TO CHAPTER V

SUBJOINED is the Crown Prince Carl, Duke of Sudermania's official report of the battle of Gogland, from the Gustavian Collection, Upsala. This report has never before been published or ever referred to in any shape or form; its existence was not known to many people, and it was only found after some considerable search.[1] *1788.*

The librarian's warranty follows the report.

### No. 159

### Tres Humble Relation

*De la Bataille Navales entre les Flottes Suédoises et Russes auprès du Banc de Kalkboden dans le golphe de Finlande, donnée le* 17 *Juillet* 1788.

La flotte Suédoise, forte de 15 vaisseaux de ligne et de 5 fregattes étoit parvenuë dans le cours de sa croisière à la hauteur de Kalhboden dans le détroit que forment le bas-fond et d'Isle d'Ekholmen dans le golphe de Finlande, lorsque le vent étant à l'Est et la brume épaisse, on entendit plusieurs coups de cannon au vent, quoique les avis les plus reçents portassent que la flotte Russe étoit encore à l'ancre à Sé-Skãr. Les

[1] The spelling of Prince Carl's original is strictly preserved.

ordres furent donnés en conséquence à la Flotte, à 3 heures et demi du matin, de se ranger en ordre de bataille Tribord, ordre naturel ; mais l'avant-garde fut empechée par le calme et les courrants, sous l'Isle d'Ekholmen, ce qui m'obligea dans les manœuvres, qu'on faisoit pour gagner le vent à 6 heures de faire ranger la Flotte en Ligne de bataille Tribord, ordre renversé, et de faire signal qu'elle se preparât au combat. Bientôt l'on commença à distinguer à travers la brume quelques vaisseaux de guerre Russes, et l'on réçut en même tems [1] des informations contradictoires sur leur force. Neaumoines et malgré l'éspace étroit pour un combat naval, je donnai le Signal à la Flotte de virer de bord et courir en échiquier pour aller à la rencontre de l'Ennemi qui parût en plein à 10 heures, rangé sur la perpendicule du vent et portant sur nous avec toutes voiles dehors. Notre bût étoit de prendre l'avantage du vent. Nous assurâmes en même tems [1] le pavillon de Suède. Le grand nombre de vaisseaux et la brume ne permittoient pas encore de distinguer lesquels dans cette Flotte étoient des vaisseaux de guerre ; mais l'on découvrit enfin qu'elle consistoit de 33 voiles, dont un vaisseaux à 3 ponts, 8 de 74, 8 de 66 cannons, et 7 grandes frégattes. Quand les deux flottes furent à deux portées de cannon l'une de l'autre et l'Avant-garde de la Flotte Russe vis-à-vis de notre centre ; je donnai ordre à 11 heures à la flotte de V. M. : de virer de bord et de se mettre en ligne de bataille tribord ; mais voyant que la Flotte Russe con-

[1] The spelling of Prince Carl's original is strictly preserved.

tinuoit de se porter avec toute sa forçe sur la queue de l'Arrière-garde, faisant alors l'Avant-garde, ee qi ne rendoit pas la bataille assez décisive, et que d'ailleurs la proximité des bas-fonds auroit bientôt mis notre Flotte dans la nécessité de former, sous le feu de l'ennemi, un nouvel ordre, j'ordonnois à la Flotte à une heure et demie de virer de bord et de former sa ligne babord amur, ordre naturel, qui me donna encore l'espérance d'oter à l'ennemie l'avantage du vent en prolongeant notre lignes sur son aile gauche et pour profiter aussi de la faute que leur Flotte paroissoit avoir faite, en ce que par des mouvements contraires, elle s'étoit ouvert vers le centre ; mais l'amiral Greigh ne tarda pas à changer cette disposition. Il laissa son arrière-garde revirer et arriver sur la Flotte Suédoise à petites voiles, cherchant á se placer lui-même, vis-à-vis du vaisseau amiral. Son Chef de file s'étant approché jusqu à la portée du fusil, je donnois à 4 heures le signal de commençer le combat qui devint bientôt general tout le long de la ligne et avec une telle vivanté que ce même vaisseau après une heure de combat, fut obligé de sortir de la ligne à l'autre bord étant couvert dans sa rétraite par d'autres vaisseaux. Notre fumée et celle des ennemis que le vent chassoit de notre coté nous empêchoit de voir les signeaux et aucune partie de la ligne. Des pellatons de vaisseaux ennemis dirigeoient leur feu sur la hanche de mon vaisseau et se remplaceaient succesivement ; l'attaque paroissant conduite de même sur notre avant-garde. La fumée s'étant un peu dissipée l'on distingua plusieurs vaisseaux ennemis très endommagés dans leurs greemants, et conduits à la rémorque au vent de la ligne. Tandis que les ennemis continuvient de ce porter en force sur l'avant-garde, L'Amiral Greigh lui-même y étant passé, le vent baissa entierement pour nous par l'effêt de la fumée et notre flotte se retrouva dans le même courrant que nous avions déja éprouvés le matin sous l'Isle d'Ekholm, de manière que les vaisseaux ne pouvaient plus gouverner ni se tenir dans la ligne malgré les échalouppes que nous mêmes pour rémorquer. Dans une position aussi critique, durant laquelle le feu des ennemis enfiloit nous vaisseaux de l'avant à l'arrière, le vaisseau Vasa ayant dans cette occasion couvert de son feu le vaisseau Amiral, j'envoyai l'Enseigne Ekholm vers l'avant-garde pour lui donner à connoitre que la Flotte vireroit vent en arrière tribord amur, le courrant ne permettant aux vaisseaux de venir au vent que de ce côté-là. Le combat recommença à 8 heures du soir avec la même chaleur et un nouvel avantage pour la Flotte de V. M. car l'ennemi fut obligé de virer de bord sous notre feu pour appuier son arrière-garde et couvrir ses vaisseaux desemparés qui s'etoient réfugiés en arrière de la Flotte ; mais malgré leurs forçes réunies, nous nous emparâmes du vaisseau Uladislaff[1] doublé en cuivre de 74 cannons, parmi lesquels ceux de la batterie inférieure sont de 32 et 42 livres de balle, et de 783 hommes d'equipage. À 10 hs. du soir le feu cessa de part d'autre.

Pour éviter le basfond de Kalkboden, et dans la

[1] *I.e.* Vladimir.

double intention de conserver notre prise qui approchait de la queuë de Notre ligne et de reprendre le vaisseau Prince Gustave qui parvissoit desemparé et sans pavillon, je fis virer de bord à tante la flotte et se former amur babord ; Mais l'Amiral Russe et toute sa flotte ont fait le même mouvement pour le conserver. Dans la nuit la Flotte ennemie parut tenir le vent et s'éloigner du champ de bataille, tandis que la Flotte de V. M. a eu ses feux allumés et a répété tonte la nuit des signeaux à coups de cannon. Pendant ce tems arrivèrent de plusieurs vaisseaux les informations qu'ils manquoient d'ammunition et qu'ils avoient reçu plusieurs boulets à fleur d'eau. Après leur avoir donné l'ordre de réparer leurs greemants et de remplir leurs gargousses à poudre, la Flotte se rangea malgré le calme, sur la ligne de bataille tribord. La flotte russe avoit de son coté rémorqué les vaisseaux desemparés et conserva sa position de manière qu'aucune attaque sous le vent pendant le calme ne pouvoit avoir lieu, ce qui me fit prendre la résolution de diriger notre course vers la rade de Helsingfors, pour y réparer les vaisseaux qui avoient le plus soufferts, et les fournir d'ammunition, la plupart ayant durant l'action tiré jusqu'à 60 coups et au-délà sur chaque cannon.

Le vaisseau pris donne à juger que la Flotte Russe étoit d'un tiers plus forte que la Nôtre en équipages et ammunition, sa destination pour la Méditerrannée ayant rendu ces précautions nécessaires. Notre perte est de deux Chefs de Vaisseaux, et un Capitaine tués, et de 5 Officiers blessés.

Le nombre de vaisseaux ennemis qui furent desemparés, les indices certains qu'un d'entre eux a été coulé a fond, et enfin les efforts de l'ennemi pour se mettre hors de la portée de notre cannon, tout prouve jusqu'à quel point le feu de la Flotte Suédoise a été soutenu et bien dirigé. Tous les Chefs out aussi avec beaucoup de zêle et de bravoure manœuvré, conservé leur poste dans la Ligne et allé à la rencontre de l'Ennemi. D'une autre part la Flotte russe nous attaqua avec l'andace que devoient lui donner tous les avantages qu'elle avoit du nombre et de la forçde e ses vaisseaux, du vente et de l'endroit même. Cette fermeté qui ne se dementit pas un instant malgré la durée d'un combat vif et opiniatre, et le courage, l'ardeur même des èquipages, animée et soutenue par l'example des Chefs, sout dignes de tous les éloges et méritent d'être détaillées dans une relation particulière sur chaque vaisseau. La Liste cè-jointe montre l'etat actuel de la Flotte. A bord du Vaisseau Amiral, Le Roi Gustave III. à l'ancre sur la rade de Helsingfors le 20 juillet 1788.

(Étant signé) CHARLES.

Afskrift ur Gustavianiks Samlingu: Upsala Universitetsbibliotek T. xi. in 4to, innehållande bref frañ hertig Carl till Kon. Gustaf. III. (Ienne handling dork ej original.)—Rätteligen afskrifsen, betygar

L. BYGDÉN,
*Vice-Bibliotekáne.*

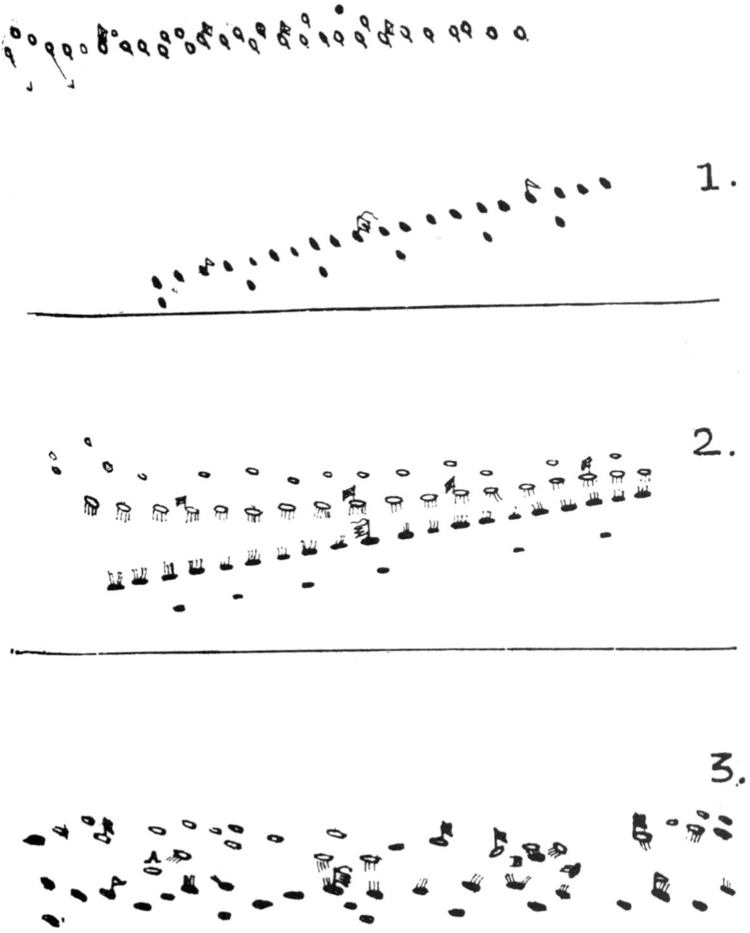


BATTLE OF GOGLAND (KALKBODEN), 17TH JULY 1788.
(Russians, *white* ; Swedes, *black.*)

1. Russians coming down before the wind.
2. Fleets engaged on port tack. 3. End of battle.

A. Vladimir captured by the Swedes.
B. Prince Gustav captured by the Russians.

### Alleged use of Fire-shell by the Russians

*(Condensed Translation of a Swedish Statement.)*

"In the battle off Högland (Gogland) of the 17th July 1788, the Russians used shells filled with combustibles, of which the Swedish flagship bore unmistakable marks."

Prince Carl (Duke of Sudermania), writing to Admiral Greig, said, after stating the evidence—

"I must remind you that projectiles of such a kind are not used by civilised nations."

Reply of Admiral Greig.

*(Copy of Letter as preserved in the Swedish Royal Archives.)*

"Sire,—Colonel Christiernin[1] has informed me that Your Royal Highness has shown me the honour of writing to me a letter which, however, I have not as yet received, purporting that in the last battle some of our ships should have used combustible shells.

"I use this opportunity to assure Your Royal Highness that I have issued the strictest orders that no ship under my command should make the least use of combustibles against the Swedish fleet; and I have no doubt that Y.R.H. has given out similar orders to the officers commanded by Him.

"I take the liberty, however, to inform Your

[1] An officer in the Swedish Navy sent on special mission to the Russian headquarters.

Royal Highness that the sail of the mizzen mast of my own ship twice during the action caught fire through combustibles, but was fortunately again extinguished. A burning fire-ball was likewise thrown on to the ship of Admiral van Dessen, and fastened on a rope by means of an iron hook, which Colonel Christiernin forwards with this. Admiral van Dessen owns that he, after that fire-ball, which was put out, fired a few such ones, 15 in all, concerning which I have been fortunate enough to be informed that they had had no effect, and I have good reason to think that they were the only fire-balls that have been fired from our fleet, because I have not permitted any to be fired from my own ship, although our sails were set fire to twice.

"Your Royal Highness will graciously consider that the fleet under my command was fitted out against the Turks, and that this war service being of a desperate nature, there must be some excuse for carrying desperate arms never intended to be used against a civilised nation. If, then, Y.R.H. should be disposed to promise me that such destructive arms will not hereafter be used by the Swedish fleet, I in my turn hereby plight my honour that neither shall the Russian fleet make use of them, it being my earnest desire to reduce the cruelties of war to such an extent as the nature of the service will allow. I have the honour to be, etc.,

"GREIG.

"On board Rostislav, 27 *July* 1788."

(*Translation from the Swedish of Copy of Prince Carl's Reply.*)

"Sir,—I have received your letter of the 27th of July. Surprised at its contention that combustibles should have been fired from any of the ships under my command, I hereby assure you on my honour that no such fire-balls with hooks as that which you have sent me are to be found in any ship under Swedish flag, as you even might have ascertained in the Prins Gustaf you captured in the last battle. I have, on the contrary, found such ones in the Russian ship Wladislaw that was captured in the same battle, as also in both the frigates which were captured a fortnight ago. You understand then how convinced I may feel that the fire-balls found in your own and Admiral van Dessen's ships have been fired by your own ships, a mishap caused perhaps through the smoke. Several ships under my command have—through red-hot missiles, of which I send you a sample—been set on fire, which, however, was fortunately got under. I rely on your word of honour that hereafter no such things be used against a nation which from times of yore has been known for her generous warfare, and you will for that very reason all the more readily please accept my declaration that I have never been using arms against you which not only humanity and my very presence would forbid, but which also in later times no longer form part of the Swedish ammunition outfit. In conclusion,

I beg to assure you of the esteem with which I remain,—Yours very benignly,

"CARL
DUKE OF SUDERMANIA."

(Date and place unknown.)

In reply to this, Admiral Greig wrote a second and more specific letter.

Reply from Admiral Greig to H.R.H. Prince Carl of Sweden.

(*Copy of Letter as preserved in the Swedish Royal Archives.*)

"MONSEIGNEUR,—J'ai pris la liberté de m'adresser à vôtre Altesse Royale en langue Anglaise dans ma dernière lettre, par les assurances que m'a donné Monsieur le Colonel Christernin que c'est une langue à Elle bien connûe, cependant je voudrois bien attribuer quelques expressions dans la Reponse qu'elle a bien voulu me faire au manque à habitude en cette langue.

"Permittez, Monseigneur, de vous assurer que je'aurai jamais hazardé, d'avancer un propos, ou il y aurait ces le moindre doute à la Veracité. Sur le Vaisseau le Prince Gustave, nous avons trouvé des Carcasses chargées des Combustibles, dans des Cartouches de Velain, dont Monsieur le Comte de Wachtmeister peut rendre temoignage à votre Altesse Royale. Il n'y a pas de doute que les Voiles de mon Vaisseau furent embrazées par cette même espece de Combustibles tiré par un des Vaisseaux Suedois.

"Dans ma lettre j'ai fait observer à Votre Altesse Royale que la Flotte que j'ai l'honneur de Commander etait destiné contre les Turcs, ou la Nature de Service peut justifier l'usage de pareilles Armes, et ou un homme determiné vis-à-vis d'un Ennemie peu humain, vent plutot perir que de se rendre.—La Flatte sous les Ordres de Votre Altesse Royale étant armée expressement pour faire la Guèrre contre la Russie, il n'existaient pas le mêmes raisons, et je me flatte que tous les Offiçiers Suedois que le sort de la Guèrre a fait tomber en mon pouvoir, n'auraient jamais le moindre sujet de plainte contre la Conducte que j'ai eu vis-à-vis d'eux.

"Au reste d'après les assurances que Votre Altesse Royale mà bien voulu donner, J'espere que ni d' une ni d' autre part pareille façon detruisante de faire la Guèrre ne sera plus à Craindre.

"J'ai l'honneur d'etre très Respectueusement,

Monseigneur!
De Vôtre Altesse Royale
le très humble et le
très obeissant Serviteur,
"SAM$^{L}$. GREIG.

"*Le* 31*r Juillet, V.S.*
*l' an* 1788."

With this letter this particular correspondence appears to have terminated.

I have unfortunately been unable to secure any Russian documentary evidence other than Greig's letters directly bearing upon this matter.

As regards the fire-shell, Greig's remark that his fleet had been intended to operate against the Turks was perfectly true. These shell were undoubtedly used by the Russians in defiance of the custom of the period.

In view of the recent discussions about the Dum-dum bullet at the Peace Conference, the above correspondence about the fire-shell has a special interest apart from its connection with Russians and Swedes, since the sentiments expressed in Greig's second letter are almost exactly akin to what has been said and written in 1899 about the Dum-dum bullet! *À propos* of this in the twelfth century, much the same thing was said about the cross-bows.

In connection with the correspondence the following contemporary Swedish account of how one of the letters was delivered is worthy of note :—

(*Translation.*)

"Lieutenants Klint and Brelin were despatched in the despatch - vessel Makrissen (a little vessel of 4 guns), which flew a flag of truce, to Revel with this letter. In the harbour the Russian frigate Pallada of 32 guns (Captain Bilau)[1] was stationed as watchship. Such was the dread a Swedish man-of-war inspired in those days, that on arriving in the harbour the Makrissen was fired upon by the frigate, which weighed anchor at once and cleared the decks for action, and when the Swedish officers came in a pinnace to the frigate,

[1] Bilau was a Dane.

Captain Bilau, sword in hand, demanded their purpose.

"In the frigate's pinnace, and accompanied by a Russian officer, the messengers, after much parleying, were sent to Revel, where the Governor, just as ignorant of the customs of war as Captain Bilau himself, announced that he 'would detain them pending the pleasure of the Empress.'

"The letter was received, however, and forwarded to Kronstadt, where a Russian captain, who had served in the Anglo-American War and knew something of how negotiations should be treated on such occasions, was able to instruct the Governor accordingly; and, after having been detained four days, the Swedish officers were at last released, and returned to their vessel."

The value of this as a side-light upon the condition of the Russian Navy in 1788, depends upon how much of it the reader is inclined to accept. The Russians of course deny the story *in toto*, and point out that there are plenty of earlier instances of communications under the flag of truce.[1] It may be observed that Greig's fleet was hastily and secretly refitting at this time for a surprise dash upon the Swedes, and this could account for the whole incident.

[1] References to such can be found on pp. 61, 97, and 616.

## The Relations between British and Russian Officers in the Russian Navy *tempus* Admiral Greig

(*Translation of a Letter, dated Copenhagen, 6th November* 1788.)

"The news of the death of Admiral Greig is accompanied by such circumstances as will make the loss of this excellent sailor still more serious to Russia and remarkable to the enemies of that realm. It is asserted that the principal cause of the said admiral's death was chagrin over the jealousy and persecution to which both he and the other English officers were exposed from the Russians; and it is believed that if the Empress (Ekaterina II.) omits to put a stop to the intrigues in a decided (*éclatant*) manner and satisfy the English, they (the English) will desert her service in a body."

I have been unable to procure any other direct evidence bearing upon this interesting question.[1]

Indirectly there is no doubt whatever that some of the Russian captains failed to support Greig at Gogland as they ought to have done. In the text[2] this remissness was attributed to the influence of that old order of Peter the Great's which laid down the

[1] See, however, biographies of British officers in Russian service, p. 714.

[2] See p. 93.

proper proportion of Russians to Swedes, but, of course, it is equally to be put down to the jealousy complained of in this letter.[1]

As a matter of fact, British officers to the number of sixty or more did resign in 1788 when the notorious Paul Jones was made a Russian admiral, and a number of others followed a little later. But this was apparently more as a mark of personal British hostility to Paul Jones than anything else.

### Reports, etc., *in re* Ships captured at the Battle of Gogland

Count Wachtmeister, captain of the Swedish ship Prins Gustaf, taken by the Russians at the battle of Gogland (Högland), seems to have been very anxious to remove every doubt as to his having honourably done his duty, and for that reason obtained a statement from Admiral Greig to the following effect:—

"Je certifie par le present à tous ceux à qui il appartient, que j'ai visité moi même le vaisseau de querre Suèdois le Prince Gustave après qu'il à été pris par la Flotte sous mes ordres, et j'ai trouvé le corps du vaisseau, mais particulièrement les mâtures et les agrîts tant delabrés, qu'il êtait impossible pour le dit vaisseau de se défendre plus longtems ou se rétirer de Notre flotte, et je avois un dévoir de rendre justice au mérite de M. le Comte de Wachtmeister Commandant

[1] The apparent absence of any jealousy at Tchesme, 1770 (p. 82), should be borne in mind before a conclusion is arrived at.

l'avant garde de la flotte Suedoise, et des officiers sous ses ordres, qu'ils ont fait la plus brave défense, et ne ses sont rendres que par la necessité de leur situation actuelle. En foi de quoi j'ai signé le present et y ai fait apposes le cachet de mes armes, à bord du Rostislaff ce 9 Juillet 1788. SAML. GREIG.

"Amiral Commandant en chef la flotte de Sa Majesté imperiale de toutes les Russies, Chevalier des ordres de St. Alexandre Nevsky, de St. George de la seconde classe, de St. Vladimir de la première et de Ste. Anne."

(From the Gustavian Collection in the University library of Upsala. Greig's spelling is preserved in the copy.)

The following report, found in the State Archives at Stockholm, is by Captain L. Berch of the Russian ship-of-the-line Vladimir, captured by the Swedes at Gogland (Högland), 1788, and was intercepted on its way to Russia. Captain Berch was a German, and apparently a military officer, but his officers and crew were Russian, and the report may be taken as an interesting indication of the amount of punishment a Russian ship would take in those days; it may possibly serve also as some gauge for these and the future; while to present-day idea both this and the Swedish report may possess certain unintentional bits of humour.

"AU COMTE DE CZERNICHEFF

"TRES ILLUSTRE COMTE,

"MONSEIGNEUR,—Mon cœur plein de reconnoissance est incapable d'exprimer à V.E. le trouble dont il est agité dans ce moment. Dieu m'a conservé la vie, il est vrai ; aussi je lui en rends mille graces : mais cette même vie me serot plutôt à charge, sans la consolation et le soutien que me porte votre gracieuse lettre, Monseigneur, qui remplie de bonté daigne m'assurer da la bienveuillance, que V.E. vent bien me continuër. L'homme est toujours le même, mais les idées et les pensées qui l'occupent fort souvent se contredisent ; C'est ce qui m'est arrivé aussi à moi, dans l'heure funebre, qui j'ai été forcé de me rendre ; tantôt je me flatois, de n'avoir pas mal fait, tantôt je craignois le contraire, puis je crois, que, peut-être il auroit mieux valeî faire de tolle ou d'une autre façon. Cette collision des idées si opposées me ravit toute ma tranquilité. Voici, Monseigneur, la fatal détail du combat soutenû par le Vladislaw, vaisseau confié par S. M. à mes ordres ; Te l'ai tiré, hélas ! de mon triste journal. Plût à Dieu, que je puisse marquer en place à V.E. une complête victoire !

"Le signal pour la bataille donné à—

"5. *heures* du matin ; je gardois clos la ligne du vaisseau Admiral, et dès qu'il out gagné le vent, d'après son premier coup de canon, je començois d'abord la cañonade, aussi de mon côté. Il fésoit un brouillard si épais, qu'il m'étoit impossible de remarquer les manœuvres de notre flotte. Bientôt le

Mitchman de la Caïoute et deux matelots furent tués ; nous perdimes le pavillon du *Besanroon* (bow-sprit),[1] et la *Kreutz-Cramstenga* (mizzen top-gallant mast) fut fricassée. Après une heure : (nos *sables, timaglasen* (hour-glass) étant deja cassés, il falloit nous rêgler d'après nos montre de poche :) c'est à dire à

"6. *heures* du matin les boulets de l'ennemi firent tomber notre *Flora Marsegel* (main topsail) et la verge, *Stenga* (the yards) en resta tellement endommagée qu'elle ne seroit plus—Dans ses entrefaits il crêva un canon à prouë, sur l'Overdecke (upper deck) qui tua tous les hommes qui etoient auprès. Des douze hommes qui s'étoient tenus, sur le *Stor Marsegel* (main topsail) dix perdirent la vie.

"À 7. *heures.* nous perdimes le *formarsegel* (foresail) qui tomba sur *l'Eselhofd* (the cap of the mast). Alors il me parut observer, quoiqu' avec peine, que notre Flotte avoit haussé tous ses *Marsegel* (main sails) et je vis, que je me trouvois dernié de la ligne ; je tâchois de m'éloigner sous vent et en arriere et durant cette évolution le *Kreutzsegel* (cross-jack) tomba aussi sur *l'eselhofd* (the cap) et bien que nous tâchames d'attacher une autre voile et de remêttre notre timon à l'obeissance, c'étoit en vain, et étant tombé trop sous vent, il me fut même impossible de faire tourner la prouë vers l'ennemi, et la cañonade des deux bords devint infructueuse. Nous perdimes vingt cinq hommes sur le *Schantz* (poop), et tous les gens qui étoient autour d'un canon dans le *second deché*, qui avoit crêvé ;

[1] The technical terms, in italics, are as often as not *Swedish.*

nous perdimes encore quatre autres hom̃es et peu après cinq autres. À

"8. *heures.* Ayant enfin après tous les éfforts possibles reussi, à reduire le vaisseau à l'obéissance, je recom̃ençois de nouveau la cañonade par le bord gauche, et j'ajoutois aux boulêts des *Cartesches,* ainsi que l'avoit fait l'ennemi.[1] Je fis signe à notre flotte, que j'avois besoin de l'assistance ; le Grot avoit pris feu, lequel cependant fut éteint. Le vaisseau se mit à pencher considerablement sous vent et trainoit droit à l'arriere garde ennemie. Le cable d'un des gros ancres rompit, et l'ancre tombe en mer. J'apperçus alors le *Victor* qui passoit près de nous, et puis dans quelque distance aussi le *Dercis,* tous deux sur le hals gauche (port tack), et dans le moment je fis la même manœuvre à

"9. *heures* pour m'abboucher avec le *Victor* et lui demander du secours ; Il m'aida en consequence à tenir *lag* (broadside) contre l'ennemi, par le moyens de ses chaloupes, les miennes ayant été dispersées pendant la bataille. Il m'envoya encore un *Cutter.* Le brouillard continuant toujours, nous empêcha de voir distinctement les mouvemens de notre Flotte ; je remarquais seulement dans la distance d'un cable les susdits deux vaisseaux *Victor* et *Dercis by de vind* et dans la distance de cinq cables à peu près le *Bogoslow* en pleins *Mar* (maintop) et *Bramsegel* (top-gallant). Penché à toute force sur mon *hals*

[1] Inflammable shell ; see correspondence between Prince Carl and Admiral Greig, p. 630.

(tack), et ayant perdû encore plus de trente hommes, je tâchois à l'aide du *Cutter* du *Victor* faire tourner mon vaisseau sur le *hals* gauche et puis sur le *droit*, mais n'y ayant absolument pas moyen de me tenir, le vent porta mon vaisseau directement à l'arriere garde de la flotte ennemie. Dans les entrefaits de ces manœuvres il se fit entre l'ennemi et moi un terrible feu de canons et cartêches. Mais à

"10. *heures* dans l'impossibilité de sauver le vaisseau, etabbandoñé par le *Victor*,*Dercis* et *Bogoslow*, j'éxpediois le dit *Cutter* avec trois Mitschman (sub-lieutenants) et trois gardes marine (midshipmen), pour faire avertir la Flotte de ma malheureuse situation. Je perdis encore 45. homes ; mon vaisseau souffrit en plusieurs endroits, tellement que je ne pus me servir d'avantage de mon artillerie, et me voyant dans l'espace d'un quart d'heure entourré de cinq vaisseaux, et toute l'arriere garde de l'ennemi s'approchant ; pour sauver la vie de cinq cent hoñes, je saisis enfin la derniere triste ressource dans cette occasion de crier à l'ennemi, qu'il arrêtat le feu, et je me rendis.

"Au commencement du combat le vaisseau ne fésoit que 17. et à la fin 70. pouces d'eau. J'ai tiré au delà de 2035. coups de canons. Je comptai 227. morts et 30. blessés, dont 15. étoient sans esperance de recouvrir. Du nombre des morts, des officiers, il y a le lieutenant Leantovitsch et le lieutenant d'artillerie Tioucharin.

"Tout l'équipage generalement, sans exception a rempli son devoir, avec intrepidité jusqu' au dernier moment, et ce qui plus m'a touché, c'étoit de voir deux de mes officiers, agé chacun 17. ans, l'un nommé Mordvinoff et l'autre Rimschneider, qui ne me quittoient pas une minute, et qui plusieurs fois me repetoient, qu'à présent ils ne connoissoient ni père ni mère ; 'La Souveraine,' me dirent ils : (d'un ton plein de courage :) 'est notre Mère, et tu es notre père, pour le moment ; c'est avec toi que nous voulons vivre ou mourir.' La seule peine qui m'accable, est le malheur de n'avoir pû réussir à cueillir des lauriers des gloire et de victoire. Daignés, Monseigneur, nous accorder votre pitié, et exciter la genereuse compassion de l'auguste Monarque à notre égard. Au reste dans l'état, où le destin nous a reduit, nous avons tout lieu, autant qu'un pareille sort le permêt, d'être satisfaits du gracieux traitement du Monarque Suedois, et sa bonté envers nous s'étend même jusqu' à ses sujêts. Le 15. d'Août, j'ai en la permission, sur ma parole, de me rendre dans cette Capitale, où je me trouve depuis le 1er de ce mois. J'ai avec moi le capitaine lieutenant Kousmitzeff et les Lieutenants Flit et Bontschenskoy ; Les autres de notre vaisseau, qui sont restés à Sveabourg seront aussi conduits ici. Le comandeur des Fregates Bardoukoff, ses officiers et les gardesmarine ont été envoyés à Upsal, ou l'on en a un soin particulier. Les soldats et les matelots se trouvent dans un endroit pas loin de cette Residence ; on les traite bien, el ils sont payés de leur travail.

"Je suis avec respect Mons, Votre Seur,

"LUDVIG BERCH.

"STOCKHOLM, *ce* $\frac{12}{23}$ *Settbre* 1788."

Following is the captain of the Swedish ship's report of the action and his surrender:[1]—

"SIRE!—J'ai été pris, malheureusement pour moi, au premier combat de la guerre, mais je me flotte qu'on ne m'a pris pour rien et j'appelle aux Juges les plus Severes du monde de visiter mon battiment et de voir si j'aurrai pu me defendre un quart d'heur davantage sans avoir eu la honte de voir tuer mon pauvre Equipage sans pouvoir faire de mal à mon Ennemie; L'Amiral Gregge m'a du moins assuré qu'il n'a pas vu un vaisseau de ma force se soutenir plus long tems contre autant des Ennemis Superieurs; Au commencement du combat j'aurrais pu echaper d'etre pris, mais le moyen aurrait été de me tenir eloigné de l'Ennemi, mais n'attendant pas un calme parfait je le croyais indigne d'un Svedois et aussi de la route que m'ont traies mes Ancetres; Si le vent aurrait duré je me serais necessairement sauvé à l'Armée et m'aurrait plutot fait couler au fonde qui de me rendre, mais il fut si calme qui mon vaisseau à la fin ne pouvait se remuer, et dans cette position entre quatre vaisseaux pendant cinq quart d'heures tous les coups de canon et mitraille porterent aisement à bord sans garder un boulet, touttes esperances pour me sauver furent malheureusement finies; Ma partie etait toujours prise de ne jamais laisser mon vaisseau à l'Ennemi en etat de servir, et voila sur quel point je

[1] From the Gustavian Collection in the University Library at Upsala.

peus avoir l'honneur dans la plus profonde soumission d'assurer Votre Majesté que le Vaisseau ne put jamais sortir du port sans une radouble comme à neuve ; J'ai cru que le certificat de l'Amiral pourrait produire l'heureux effet d'assurer Votre Majesté de ma conduite, qui pourrait etre noircie, mais j'aurrait donné ma vie d'avoir pus me sauver dans l'etat que je me sois rendu, et je sois sur qu'au moins ma famille et mon nom aurrait été sans tache ; l'Amiral et tous les Officiers Generaux sont venus me complimenter et m'ont montres toutes les distinctions possibles ; On n'a pas voulu m'oter mon epé ni celui de mes Officiers à cause de notre conduite, ils m'ont tous donnes des lettres pour les premiers Seigneurs de la Cour et l'Amiral Gregge m'a fait la grace de me parler de son rapport à l'Impératrice et aux Ministres qui etait trop flateux pour un homme qui n'a fait que son devoir ; J'ose me jetter aux piés de Votre Majesté et dans la plus grande soumission presenter ce compte rendu de mon combat, non pas pour ma personne, mais pour Sauve Guarde de ma Famille de mes Officiers et de mon Equipage, dont je ne puisse asses rendre justice ; Monsieur Stjevusparre et tons ces Messieurs Officiers de terre m'ont étés de la plus grande utilité ; Mon Equipage a été tres bien traité et tous me blesses mises à l'hopital, où ils font aussi superieurement bien traites ; — Je sois un peu malade d'inquietude, d'une forte contusion et d'une blessure au bras droit, que j'espere n'aurras pas de Sorte ; Je ne sais pas où on m'enverrat ni mes Officiers, mais meme au fond de la Siberie, je n'oublierais jamais touttes les bontes dont Votre Majesté a daigné de m'honnorer et j'espere que l'avenir justifiera ma conduite presente et passée. J'espere que Votre Majesté excusera que j'ose prendre l'hardiesse de presenter la relation du combat et la liste de blesses à la Sacrée Personne de Votre Majesté ne sachant pas si le Prince Charles soit en Croissé ou non.

"J'attends les ordres de Votre Majesté par rapport de mes pauvres Officiers, combien et de quelle façon Votre Majesté ordonne pour leur soutien, pendant qu'ils sont prisonniers; Votre Majesté daignera bien par sa bonté ordinaire m'en faire donner des ordres.

"C'est avec la plus grande soumission que j'ose me dire encore, Sire, de Votre Majesté, Le plus humble et le plus devoué Sujet,

"Clar Wachtmeister.

"À bord de Prince Gustave,
*ce* 22. *Juillet* 1788 à Cronstad."

Here there follows a detailed list of killed and wounded; 148 altogether.

(*Found in the Library at Upsala.*)

Extract from an enclosure in a letter from the Prussian envoy at Stockholm, Baron von Borcke, to H.M. the King (Gustavus III.), dated "St. Petersburg, le 17 Juillet, 1788":—

"Les affaires de Finlande donnent actuellement le coup de chagrin à la Cour. Tous les jours il arrive des Couriers qui annoncent ou dès échecs nos des mesintelligences qui regnent parmi les trouppes autant sur terre que sur mer. Le soi disant Pr. de Nassau en a envoyé sur mer pour fair Savoir à S.M.T. la triste élate de sa flotille. Après avoir renvoyé deja plusieurs galères qui n'ont pù terier la mer, il s'est vu forcé dénremoyer encor 5. pour leur délabrement et faute de matelots et de soldats, en ayant 1700 de malades. Aussi seur facon de manœuvrer de ce coté là prouve bien l'état de foiblesse où l'ou se trouve. Non seulement le Roi de Suide sontient sa position au dela du Kimene, mais songe seneusement à s'emparer de Fredrickshamn qu'il fait aussi examiner par mer. Il a pour cet effet 10 à 12 batimens dans le Gulfe du surdit endroit, le reste de sa flotille est range sur les cotes. Celle des Russes se tient à 5 ou 6 miles en arriere de Pyltis sans songer à forcer l'autre à quittes sa position. . . . D'ailleurs on pretend que tandisque les Suédois sont toujours fort bien instruits, les Russes ne savant jamais a qui se passe chéz l'ennemi. Cela prouveroit bien qui le Roi de Suède n'est pas aussi generalement detesté chéz lui qu'on voudroit le faire croire ici. . . ."

(*Translation of the Duke of Sudermania's (Prince Carl's) Official Report of the Battle of Öland, now deposited in University Library at Upsala.*)

"His Royal Highness the Grand Admiral's most humble report to His Majesty the King of Sweden on the battle between the Swedish and the Russian fleets on the 26th July 1789, 12 German miles E.S.E. of the south point of Öland.

"Your Majesty's fleet had, after staying in Kjögebugt, been cruising between the Swedish, German, and Öland shores, and was on the 24th July about to fetch fresh crew, water, and munitions from Carlskrona, for which purpose the frigates Illerim, Jarramas, and Jarislawitz were gone thither with the sick of the fleet, when it was reported that the Russian fleet commanded by Admiral Tchetschakoff, counting some 24 to 30 battleships, with many frigates and fire-ships, had been seen off Gotland. I decided at once rather to go and meet than wait for the enemy, though 4 frigates, with the frigate Camilla and a cutter, were absent. In the course of the day the fleet arrived off Öland by a smart westerly wind, where the frigate Illerim joined, returning from its expedition.

"On the 25th Your Majesty's fleet steered S.E. with the then westerly wind with a view to cut the enemy's way, when the frigate Minerva signalled the enemy. I at once pressed with all sails set, and got the sight of him at 2 o'clock p.m., ranged the fleet in *ordre de bataille* while bearing away, and gave signal to close on the enemy's rear. The enemy too formed. At 6 o'clock in the evening the fleets were only separated at a few shots distance, when the wind growing strong, which prevented my own and several other ships from using the lower battery, made me put off the battle. Your Majesty's fleet lay by during the night, as did the enemy. The strength of the enemy now appeared to be between 20 to 24 ships-of-the-line with 3 three-deckers, but afterwards 21 ships got into line.

"On the 26th at dawn Your Majesty's fleet anew bore down on the enemy. The division commanders were invested with full powers to manage their divisions, in order that every chance should be taken advantage of. The wind was brisk, afterwards slackening with slow speed. The enemy bore away in *ordre de bataille* and plied alternately with the van and the rear. Repeated signals were therefore made to increase force and press with sails, attack at half a gunshot's distance, and during the firing close on the enemy, and concentrate all strength on his rear and double on the ships most rearward, and to the leader to make for the enemy's leader. Fearing to lose this chance, because the second division, forming the rear, was straggling aft and to windward, I collected five of the nearest ships, viz. Ömheten, Prins Carl, Galathea, Försigtigheten, and Wladislaw, but accompanied by King Adolf Frederik only, and bore down on the enemy's line. A three-decker of the rear being the nearest, began to fire at long range, but soon plied with the other ships under the guns of our ships, which returned the fire with such effect that the second ship ahead of the three-decker was obliged to leave the line, although our ships on account of the sailing order could not use the broadside. Half an hour later, at 2.30 p.m., the third division came in action, and two hours later the enemy's leader appeared to have been disabled; and soon after two other ships, probably because of

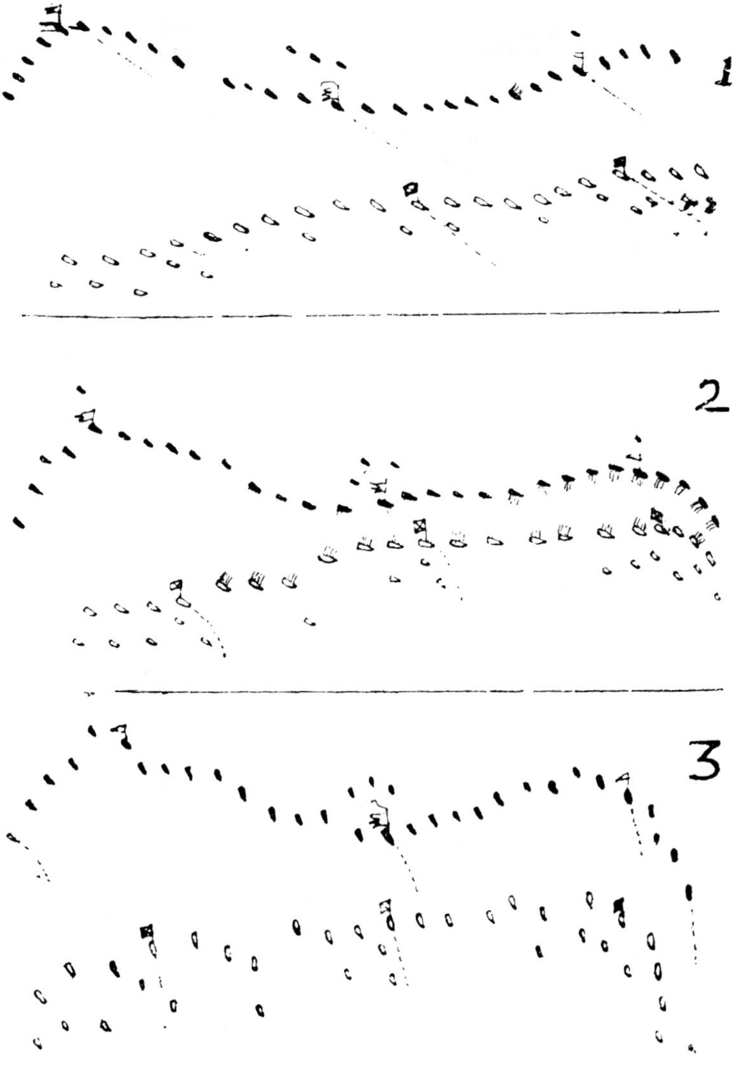


BATTLE OF ÖLAND, 26TH JULY 1789.
(Russians, *white* ; Swedes, *black.*)

1. Russian fleet bearing away from Swedish.
2. Van and main body of both fleets in action.
3. Russians again bearing away.

damage between wind and water, were seen to drop out of the line.

"During all this time I had only with me my second seconding ship, and in the evening the Fädernislandet; but the entire second division under Rear-admiral Liljehorn did not the least sign of obeying my orders, except Colonel and Knight Leijonankar, Major and Knight Whitlock,[1] Major and Knight Grubb, and Lieutenant-colonel and Knight Wagenfeldt, who all pressed down on the enemy, but were obliged to resume their stations in the division, because the centre admiral would not support them. The firing being very heavy about the third division, I hastened to its assistance, but the enemy's *corps de bataille* had in the meanwhile had time to get away, that the shots had no great effect, for which reason firing ceased in this part of the line, and at 8 o'clock in the evening in the van. The enemy continued bearing away as long as he was visible. Against 19 of the enemy's ships we had had only 17 ships and frigates, viz. the third division and a part of the main.

"The wind turned on the south in the night, and Your Majesty's fleet keeping in the wind in order to have the luff, the enemy had the audacity early in the morning to the 27th to press on our tack. But as soon as Your Majesty's fleet was somewhat ranged *en echiquier*, I bore down in line of battle on the enemy, and gave signal to cut off the enemy's leader. But the

[1] This Whitlock was the descendant of a ship-carpenter (British) who was employed at the Royal Dockyards about 1670.

whole Russian fleet made haste to turn, and bore away with all sails set, and could not be brought to action, despite all my endeavours. In the evening both the fleets were in line, the Swedish to windward and astern, for which reason I gave Colonel and Knight Modée order to advance in the night with 5 ships of the *queu*, and at dawn attack and double the enemy. The wind fell calm during the night.

"On the 28th in the morning the enemy was distant only a couple of gunshots and had large openings in his *tête* when Your Majesty's fleet employed its smaller ships to get at him. The van got order to break through on purpose to bring about a decisive action, the leader using his bonnets and tow. The wind turning on east gave the enemy the luff at 8 o'clock in the morning. He closed his order and kept by the wind. I ranged Your Majesty's fleet in line and offered him battle, but as he turned again, and my rear through the change in the wind was much a-lee, the order was changed *en echiquier* in purpose to get the luff. At 11 o'clock in the morning the enemy turned southwards, formed his line on the larboard tack, and spread a quantity of canvas. I therefore let Your Majesty's fleet go about and form into line on purpose to attack his rear on the opposite tack. The wind slackened and the enemy's rear bore away fast with all sails set. I was obliged then once more to turn *en echiquier*, in order to keep the Swedish fleet athwart the enemy. Yet he did not evince the least inclination to attack, however advantageous was the position I left him for doing so; he on the contrary pressed with all sail to get away. The wind increased and seemed to steady. By this I lost all hope to bring to action an enemy who in guns and large ships was much superior to Your Majesty's fleet, but whose only object seemed to be to gain time, from which I concluded that he waited in these parts for the squadron from the Sound; but as I was so near the German shore that no other fleet could be present in these waters, I gave order to change tack in the wakes of each other, which the enemy had done two hours before, and as he steered northwards I took for granted that his object was either to keep on this latitude or return to the Bay of Finland. I decided then to make for the Sound squadron at once, if it had got under way with westerly wind, or attack it at anchor if the Kronstadt fleet went off to cover the ships stationed in the Bay of Finland; as also to put the enemy in doubt, if not the object of the Swedish fleet was to head for the Bay of Finland.

"On the 29th at 10 o'clock in the morning the Utklipporna[1] were seen. The frigates stationed there reported that the Sound squadron had been in its place on the 27th and that it had not been seen off Bornholm. I therefore ranged Your Majesty's fleet in line of battle, and went about and steered for Bornholm in order to wait for the Kronstadt

[1] A group of rocks about three English miles south of Carlskrona.

fleet, and as long as the wind, now in the east, not permitted the Sound squadron to run out, make a further attempt to bring the Kronstadt fleet to action.

"On the 30th in the morning our advanced frigates signalled the approach of the Kronstadt fleet, who, barely sighting us, hauled to the wind southwards. The wind falling calm I waited what chance a new wind might bring for an attack; it began to blow from the north and gave the enemy the luff. This wind giving him the chance of placing himself between Carlskrona and Your Majesty's fleet, and because of his strength and smart-sailing ships for some time avoid other engagement than such as would be all advantageous to himself until the Sound squadron put in sight, which would give him a decided superiority, I manœuvred so as to frustrate any such purpose, used the chances the wind gave me for taking the luff, and went to meet him, he again bearing away. The wind now turned on N.W. and became steady. I kept the Swedish fleet all night athwart the enemy, and steered southwards in the morning to the 1st of August, the enemy heading in the same direction when he got sight of Your Majesty's fleet. As the pursuit of him would have brought Your Majesty's fleet on the other side of Bornholm, and the wind was favourable for the Sound squadron to effect a junction, I have not considered myself justified to tempt the fortune of the Swedish naval power against such odds, but anchored in the Carlskrona roads at 5 o'clock in the evening, having made all possible efforts to bring a superior enemy to defensive action.

"Flagship Gustaf III., at anchor on the Carlskrona roads, 1st of August 1789.

"CARL SUNDVALL."

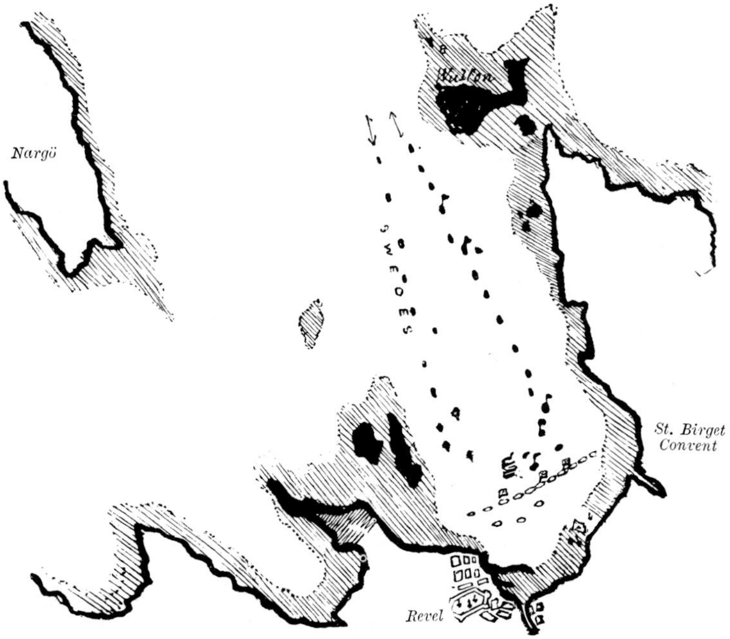


PRINCE CARL'S REPULSE BY THE RUSSIAN FLEET AT REVEL, 14TH MAY 1790. (*See p.* 101.)

*B.* Swedish ship aground.

# SWEDEN'S ÆGOSPOTAMI

THE following are the details of the fleets engaged in the battle of Viborg. As before, the names of commanding officers said to have been British are indicated with asterisks. 1790.

## RUSSIAN GRAND FLEET

### SHIPS-OF-THE-LINE

| *Name.* | *Guns.* | *Commander.* |
|---|---|---|
| Rostislav . . . | 108 | Captain Tchitchagoff. (Admiral Tchitchagoff.) |
| Ivan Christil . . . | 108 | Captain James Preston.* (Vice-admiral Kruse.) |
| Dvenadsat Apostoloff . | 108 | Major-general Fedoroff. (Vice-admiral Sogatin.) |
| Saratov . . . . | 108 | Captain Bark.* (Vice-admiral Guschkin.) |
| Trechievarkoff . . . | 108 | Captain Abalaninoff. (Rear-admiral Povalitchin.) |
| Prince Vladimir . . | 108 | Captain Kierewski. (Rear-admiral Spiridoff.) |
| St. Nikolai . . . | 108 | Captain Pekin* (?). |
| Ezekiel . . . . | 78 | ,, Curananaolejff. |
| St. Helena . . . | 74 | ,, Brayer.* (Rear-admiral Chanekoff.) |
| Sissoi Veliki . . . | 74 | Captain Chakoff. (Rear-admiral Adinosoff.) |
| Ivan Bogisloff . . . | 74 | Major-general Adinosoff. |
| Constantine . . . | 74 | Captain Skoratoff. |
| Pobiedoslav . . . | 74 | ,, Jimanieff. |

## RUSSIAN GRAND FLEET—*continued*

### SHIPS-OF-THE-LINE—*continued*

| *Name.* | *Guns.* | | *Commander.* |
|---|---|---|---|
| Peter Veliky . . . . | 74 | Captain | Chamatoff. |
| Seislaff . . . . . | 74 | ,, | Baristoff. |
| Tsar Ivan . . . . | 74 | ,, | Test.* |
| Mistisloff . . . . | 74 | ,, | Bilow. |
| Yaroslav . . . . | 74 | ,, | Telepnoff. |
| Prince Gustavus (*ex* Swede) | 70 | ,, | Treveyer * (Tregenna ?) |
| Netro Menia . . . . | 68 | ,, | Trevennen.* |
| Jannarii . . . . | 66 | ,, | Kleboff. |
| America . . . . | 66 | ,, | Sorin. |
| Pautolemov . . . . | 66 | ,, | Lateraff. |
| Georgi Pobiedonosetz . | 66 | ,, | Tunaschoff. |
| Boroun . . . . | 66 | ,, | Skorbo (Skorboff). |
| Bogatyr . . . . | 66 | ,, | Tchitchusoff. |
| Tchesma . . . . | 66 | ,, | Van Sievers (*d*). |
| Prince Charles . . . | 66 | ,, | Van Grevens (*d*). |
| Khrabry . . . . | 66 | ,, | Kilemin. |
| Svetlana . . . . | 66 | ,, | Batchinunoff. |

### FRIGATES-OF-THE-LINE

| | | | |
|---|---|---|---|
| Streletz . . . . | 44 | Captain | Palitchin. |
| Gabriel . . . . | 44 | ,, | Pustanchin. |
| Braschislav . . . . | 44 | ,, | Loman * (*or Lomax*). |
| Pumaschvan . . . . | 44 | ,, | Prince Vesenski. |
| Venus . . . . | 40 | Brigadier | Crown.* |
| Posadnik . . . . | 36 | Captain | Palitchin. |
| Peresviet . . . . | 36 | ,, | Stanisloff. |
| Tootcha . . . . | 36 | ,, | Tane. |
| Cape of Good Hope . . | 36 | ,, | Badiskoff. |
| Marie . . . . | 36 | ,, | ? |
| Alexander . . . . | 36 | ,, | ? |
| Alexandra . . . . | 36 | ,, | (?) Switen (*g*). |
| St. Helena . . . . | 36 | ,, | ? |

(*d*) Probably Dutch.
(*g*) Probably German—name doubtful.

### RUSSIAN GRAND FLEET—*continued*

FRIGATES-OF-THE-LINE—*continued*

| *Name.* | *Guns.* | *Commander.* |
|---|---|---|
| St. Paul . . . . | 36 | Captain ? |
| St. Nikolai . . . | 36 | ,, Ismailoff. |
| Diana . . . . | 36 | ,, ? |
| Constantine . . . | 36 | ,, ? |
| Patria . . . . | 40 | Sir F. Thessiger.* |

3060 guns and about 25,000 officers and men.

### SWEDISH GRAND FLEET

| *Name.* | *Guns.* | *Commander.* |
|---|---|---|
| Dristigheten . . . | 64 | Lieutenant-colonel Puke. |
| Tapperheten . . . | 64 | ,, ,, Wagenfeldt. |
| Finland . . . . | 60 | Captain Treutiger. |
| Dygden . . . . | 64 | Lieutenant-colonel Billing. |
| Adolf Frederik . . | 70 | Rear-admiral Modée. |
| Göta . . . . | 70 | Colonel Hysingskjöld. |
| Ävan . . . . | 64 | Lieutenant-colonel Holst. |
| Frederik Adolf . . . | 62 | Major Ekenman. |
| Hedwig Elisabeth Charlotte | 64 | Lieutenant-colonel Nanckhoff. |
| Fädernislandet . . . | 64 | Major Tingvall. |
| Vladimir (*ex* Russian) . | 74 | Colonel Fust. |
| Gustaf III. . . . . | ... | Rear-admiral Nordenskjöld. (Admiral of the Fleet, Prince Carl, Duke of Sudermania.) Sir Sidney Smith.* |
| Försigtigheten . . . | 64 | Colonel Fahlstedt. |
| Louisa Ulkika . . . | 70 | Lieutenant-colonel Ameén. |
| Prins Ferdinand . . | 60 | Captain Ramborg. |
| Manligheten . . . | 64 | Major Pley. |
| Omheten . . . . | 64 | Major Grubbe * (?). |
| Sophia Magdalena . . | 70 | Colonel Leijonanker. |
| Rettvisan . . . . | 64 | Lieutenant-colonel Wollyn. |
| Vasa . . . . | 62 | Major Hellman. |
| Enigheten . . . | 70 | Major Feiff. |

## SWEDISH GRAND FLEET—*continued*

### FRIGATES-OF-THE-LINE

| *Name.* | *Guns.* | *Commander.* |
|---|---|---|
| Fröja | 42 | Captain Count Wrangel. |
| Gripen | 44 | ,, Söderwan. |
| Camilla | 42 | Major Baron Cederström. |
| Zemire | 42 | Captain Neyendorff. |
| Thetis | 42 | ,, Petterson. |
| Upland | 44 | Major Rahm. |
| Euridice | 42 | Captain Feiff. |
| Galatea | 42 | ,, Count Wallden. |

### OTHER FRIGATES

| | | |
|---|---|---|
| Illerim | 32 | Captain Ankarloo. |
| Ulla Feren | 18 | ,, Blom. |
| Jarislawitz | 32 | ,, Gahn. |
| Jarramas | 32 | ,, Lagerstrale. |
| Hector | 26 | ,, ? |
| Dragon (brig) | 16 | ,, ? |
| Disa (schooner) | 12 | ,, ? |
| Höök (cutter) | ? | ,, ? |
| Postiljon—fire-ship | ... | ,, ? |

1900 guns and 12,000 men.

## THE "GALLEY FLEET"

Royal Yacht Amphion.
,, ,, Amadis.

| | | | |
|---|---|---|---|
| 1 | out of | 8 | turumas. |
| 1 | ,, | 3 | hemmemas. |
| 2 | ,, | 3 | udemas. |
| 10 | ,, | 15 | gun barges. |
| 20 | ,, | 27 | galleys. |
| 80 | ,, | 127 | gun sloops. |
| 50 | ,, | 87 | gun yawls. |
| 10 | ,, | 15 | bomb barges. |

| | | | |
|---|---|---|---|
| 8 | out of | 8 | small bomb vessels. |
| 1 | ,, | ? | brig. |
| 1 | ,, | ? | cutter. |
| ? | ,, | 11 | "Admiralty ships" (flagships). |
| ? | ,, | 6 | ammunition ships |
| ? | ,, | 33 | provision ships |
| ? | ,, | 4 | hospital ships |
| Transports | | | for horses, guns, provender, forage, etc. |

3048 guns and 18,000 men.

The first set of figures is the number of ships shut in, the second, the number of the force when the campaign began.

Total Swedish force blockaded at Viborg was 30,000 men and 4948 guns. The Russians outside had, as stated, 3060 guns and 25,000 men in big ships, as well as an indefinite and continually increasing force of coast-ships.

The following is a detailed Swedish account of the Viborg affair, and events immediately preceding and following it, from a history by Admiral C. A. Gyllengranat, late of the Swedish Navy,[1] compiled from official records.

"The object of the Swedish fleet sailing for Kronstadt had been to cover the attack on Fredriksham. This business over, both the fleets moved westward, the grand fleet keeping under sail, the coast-flotilla on the 2nd of June anchoring off Björkösund on the road leading to St. Petersburg.

"On the 3rd of June the Russian Kronstadt fleet

[1] I am indebted to the kindness of Mr. C. G. Björkman of Stockholm for this translation.— F. T. J.

appeared. It consisted of 17 ships (of which 5 were three-deckers of 108 guns) and 13 frigates, besides some smaller vessels, under the command of Vice-admiral Kruse on board the 108-gun ship Ivan Christel, Vice-admiral Sogatin in Dvenadzat Apostolov of 108 guns, and Rear-admiral Povalitchin in Trechievarkow of 108 guns. The Swedish fleet counted in the line, 23 ships of 70 and 40 guns, and a reserve of 6 frigates ; but although it was superior in ships, it was considerably inferior in guns, the Russians counting more than 1950 guns against 1828 Swedish. The van was commanded by Rear-admiral Modée, and the rear by Lieutenant-colonel Leijonankar, the main led by H.R.H. Prince Carl. At 3 o'clock in the morning the enemy having, the wind turning, got to windward, made a dash at the Swedish van, and a heavy cannonade took place, lasting from 4.45 to 8 a.m., Kruse engaging the ships of Prince Carl broadside to broadside, but without any result except some damage to the rigging on both sides, and the wind falling out, the Russian fleet withdrew out of range about 11 o'clock p.m. The following day the fleets encountered each other afresh, but the enemy fell back as soon as we made an attempt to close. The tactics of Kruse were evidently to draw the Swedish farther into the bay, so as to permit the Revel squadron to run out of port and put the Swedish fleet between two fires.

"And about 9 o'clock in the evening a scouting vessel signalled the news that the Revel squadron, now

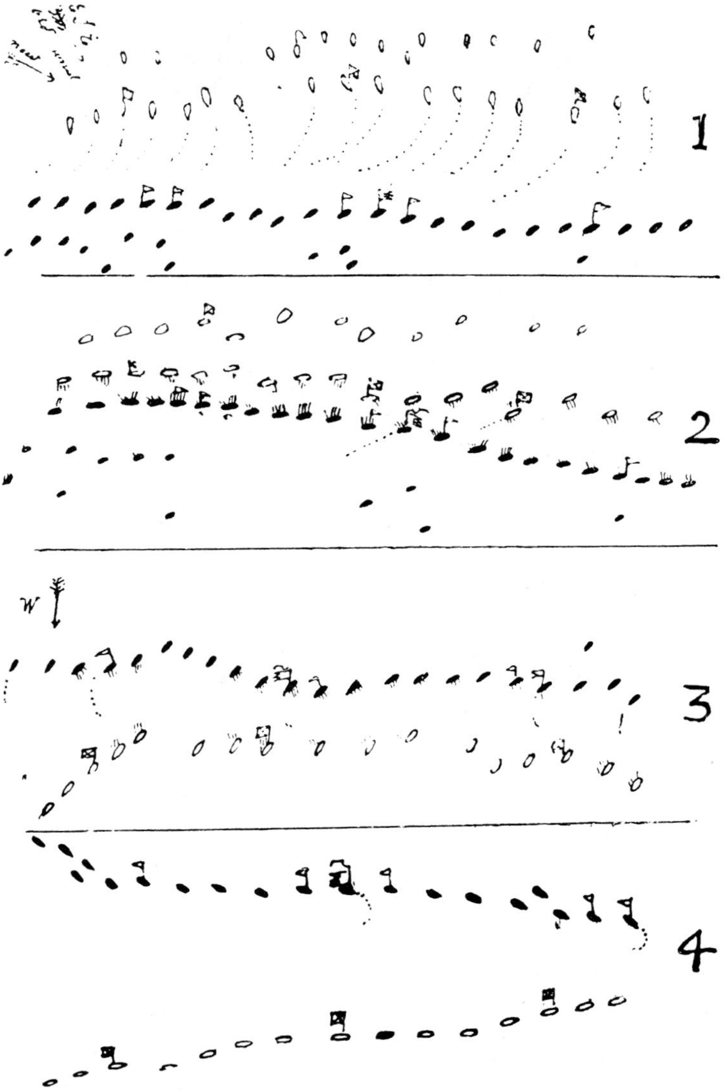


BATTLE OFF REVEL, 3RD JUNE 1790.
(Russians, *white*; Swedes, *black.*)

1. Russian fleet making a dash for the Swedish.
2. 6 a.m., fleets engaged.
3. 3.30 p.m., Swedes following retreating Russians.
4. June 4th, 8.30 a.m., Swedes retreating on approach of the Revel fleet.

counting 10 ships and 8 frigates, had slipped out and was coming up behind the Swedish. Now the Swedish fleet found it necessary to give up following Kruse and face the newcomers, but on nearing the Revel squadron the latter fell back, evading battle, while the Kronstadt squadron, which had turned, pressed, all sails set, on the Swedish rear. In the night to the 6th of June, Sir Sidney Smith (the Englishman) arrived with order from the king that the fleet should go into the Bay of Viborg in order to protect the coast flotilla there assembled, which it did, and anchored in the Viborg roads at 6.30 in the morning. This most unfortunate order, given out by the king, who had no idea of naval tactics, occasioned the disaster of Viborg.

"On the 7th of June the combined Russian fleet-of-the-line arrived off Viborg, and anchored in a line across the bay.

"The fleets remained in their positions up till the 18th, when the Russians weighed anchor and approached the Swedish to a distance of half a nautical mile, where it again anchored. It had now been reinforced by 1 ship, 4 frigates, 2 cutter-brigs, 3 yachts, and some 50 other vessels. The fleets remained inactive up to the 29th of June, when a further reinforcement of a great number of frigates and coast-vessels under the Prince of Nassau joined the Russian fleet, attacked the Swedish squadron lying at Björkö, and forced it to fall back.

"It had now become a vital necessity for the Swedish fleet to attack the blockading enemy, and it was decided that it should get under weigh on the 3rd of July. Preparing for this, the transports hitherto stationed at Björkö Sound were sent up in the bay north of the fleet. In order to cover this movement, 3 divisions gun sloops and bomb vessels were sent to attack the Russian ships-of-the-line stationed east of Wasikasari. The attack began at 2 o'clock in the morning, and the firing continued to 5 o'clock, when the purpose had been won, and the party returned to join the fleet. Everything now being ready, the whole fleet set sail and, ranged in convoy order, proceeded on its perilous voyage, led by the ship Dristigheten, to break through the Russian line at Krosserort.

"The Russian line was so closely drawn that there was hardly room for a ship to pass between the poop of one and the bowsprit of another. Dristigheten passing the Russian line between the third and fourth ship of its left wing at 8 o'clock a.m., was received with a continuous broadside fire, to which she at first could answer only with her bow guns. But passing the enemy she in return poured a raking fire into the Russian line, and, admirably supported by the ships following in her wake, she silenced the nearest adversaries, some of which hauled down the flag, having only 40 to 60 men left out of a crew of 700. Abreast of Dristigheten sailed hemmema Styrbjörn, leading the coast-fleet, followed by a sloop in which the king had embarked. A shot cut off the arms of one of the oarsmen, and another cut down the flag. The king then went on board the yacht Colding and got safely off to

Svensksund (Rotchensalm) though pursued by the Russian frigate Venus. The fleet meanwhile proceeded steadily under a heavy fire on both sides, and there is no doubt but that the fleet had got off unscathed if an accident had not occurred.

"The Swedish fleet had only one fire-ship (the Postiljonen). This vessel sailed abreast of the ship Enigheten. When about passing the Russian line it prepared to attack the enemy, but the master handled the ship so badly that all ablaze it sheered down on the Enigheten. This ship fell away in order to avoid the fire-ship, but collided with the frigate Zemire, which sailed on her port quarter. Both the ships were set fire to. Major Feiff, all surrounded by flames, called out to the gun sloops and transports to keep out of the way, 'as he was likely to be blown up in a minute.' About 9 o'clock a.m. the ship was blown in the air, and immediately after, the frigate, whose captain, however, saved himself by jumping overboard. The air, darkened before by smoke, now became almost black, and the consequence was some disorder in the rear, several ships losing their bearings and running aground. Thus the ship Ömheten, the schooner Kosacken, and three galleys ran aground on the Pensar shoal, and the Hedvig Elisabeth Charlotte on another farther to the south. On the Passalolo shoals the same happened to the Louisa Ulrika, and the frigates Upland and Jarislawitz. Also the ship Finland had gone too near the Kmato reef when setting sail, and could not be taken off.

PLAN OF THE BATTLE OF VIBORG.

Covering operations from 6th June to 2nd and 3rd July 1790.

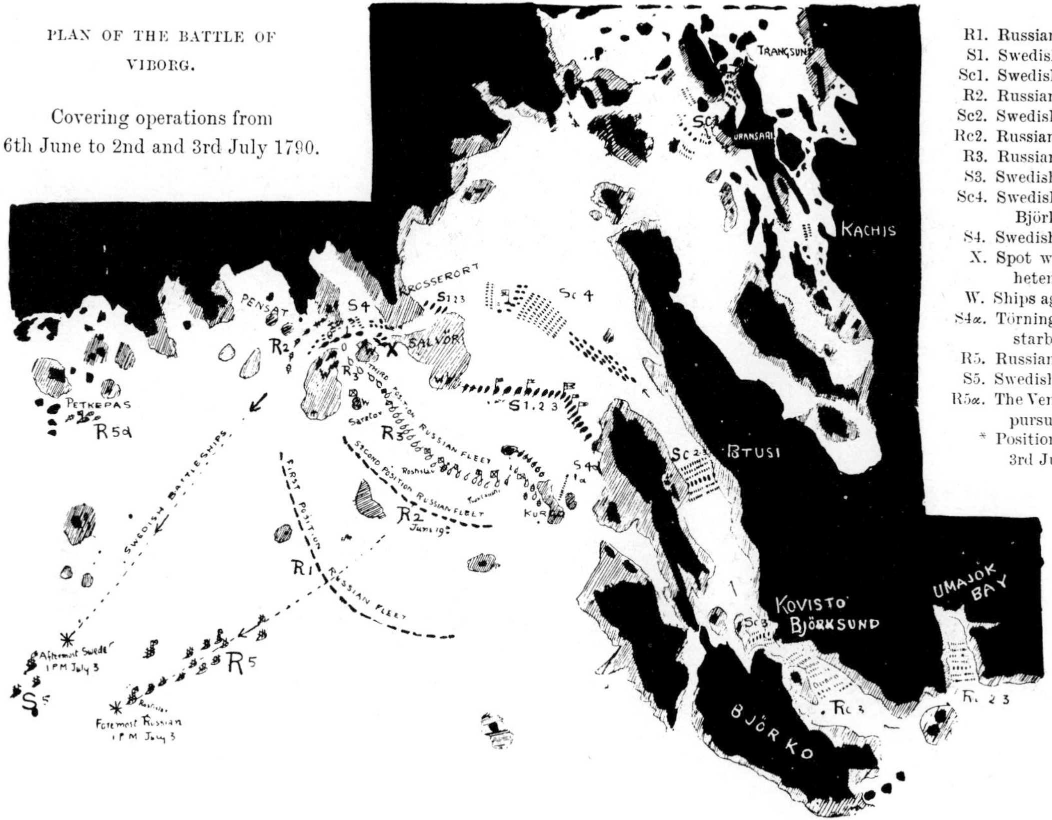


R1. Russian fleet, 7th June.
S1. Swedish fleet, 7th June till 3rd July.
Sc1. Swedish coast-fleet, 20th June.
R2. Russian fleet, 9th–19th June.
Sc2. Swedish coast-fleet, June 20–30.
Rc2. Russian ,, ,,
R3. Russian fleet, 20th June–3rd July.
S3. Swedish ,, ,, ,,
Sc4. Swedish coast-fleet retreating from Björkösünd, 3rd July.
S4. Swedish fleet forcing its way out.
X. Spot where fire-ship set the Enigheten alight.
W. Ships aground.
S4α. Törning attacking the Russian starboard division.
R5. Russian fleet, 1 p.m., 3rd July.
S5. Swedish ,, ,, ,,
R5α. The Venus and other frigates which pursued the Swedish coast-flotilla.
* Positions of foremost ships, 1 p.m., 3rd July.

"About 10 o'clock a.m. the Russian fleet, seeing its prey escape, weighed anchor, but went to work so slowly, that the whole of it was not under sail before 2 o'clock p.m. The Swedish fleet was about that time well ahead, with the exception of some bad sailers, Sophia Magdalena and Rättvisan, which were overtaken and captured, the former about 10 o'clock at night after a desperate battle with 2 three-deckers and a frigate, the latter about 9 o'clock the following morning.

"The yacht Aurora, with Sir Sidney Smith on board, had been sunk off Krosserort; but Smith himself caught hold of a piece of wreck and was saved by the schooner Disa, after being in the water for an hour.

"The Swedish grand fleet, followed by a great part of the coast-fleet with transports, came into Sveaborg harbour on the 4th of July with a loss, as above shown, of 7 ships, 3 frigates, and a schooner. The coast-fleet, which took refuge at Svensksund, lost, besides the three galleys aground at Pensar, 4 galleys, 6 gun sloops, 7 gun yawls, 1 bomb ketch, and 30 transports, of which a part was sunk, the other captured by the Russian squadron, under Brigadier Crown (frigate Venus), stationed at Pitkepas. The total loss of officers and men in killed, wounded, and prisoners amounted to about 6000, including the inmates of sickships and floating hospitals.

"The next object of the Russians was to capture or destroy that part of the Swedish coast-fleet now at Svensksund which had not proceeded to Sveaborg, and on the 8th of July the Prince of Nassau in command of the Russian coast-fleet anchored between the isle Kyrkogărdsön and Aspö, numbering 8 frigates, 6 chebeques, 14 galliots, 10 cutters and bomb ketches, 3 floating batteries, 22 galleys, 8 'demi-galleys' (or tschaijks), and 80 gun sloops, with a crew of 18,500 all counted. The Swedish counted 2 hemmema, 1 turuma, 2 udema, 1 cutter-brig, 16 galleys, 2 demi-galleys, 99 gun sloops, 54 gun yawls, 10 gun barges, and 8 bomb vessels, manned with altogether 14,000 officers and men.

"The Swedish had taken up position as follows:—

"The main, or *corps de bataille*, consisting of 2 hemmema, 2 udema, and 15 galleys, under Lieut.-colonel Stedingk, across the roads N.N.W.—S.S.E., between Krăkskär (south of Kotka) and Sandskär banks, N.W. from Kutsalö. At right angles to the main line, between Krăkskär and the rocks of the Musalu Isle, 40 gun sloops and 15 gun yawls, under Colonel Törning, forming the right wing. The left wing, consisting of 37 gun sloops and 15 gun yawls, under Lieut.-colonel Hjelmstjerna, formed a line between the Kutsalö bank and the Isle of Läckmäsari. The rest was detached to cover the rear and defend the inlets to the position, which on the whole was a very weak one.

"On the 9th of July, being the birthday of the empress, the Prince of Nassau advanced in three columns, the frigates leading, anticipating an easy victory in celebration of the day, and having made preparations on board his own ship for the reception of the Swedish king, whom he meant to take prisoner.

"At 9.30 a.m. the first shot was fired, the enemy ranging himself on a line parallel to the Swedish, and within a quarter of an hour the firing became general. After two hours' cannonade, the enemy's left wing, though very close and strong, was forced to retire. Reinforced, it attempted a new attack, but fell into disorder and suffered greatly under the Swedish fire, and was obliged again to retreat, a part of Swedish reserve now reinforcing the line. Several Russian galleys and 1 chebeque were obliged to strike, and a frigate (the Nicholas) got so many shots between wind and water that she sank. On the Swedish side an udema was so damaged that it was run aground to save the crew. In the afternoon the entire Russian line was broken, but the firing continued till 10 o'clock p.m., when the battle ceased, the enemy trying to get under sail to save himself from further loss in the gale which now was rising,—an attempt, however, in which he did not succeed.

"A dense fog obscured the field of battle the following morning, but dispersed about 9 o'clock. Several Russian vessels tried to avail themselves of the opportunity and escape, and a frigate had beaten up to windward and was nearly giving us the slip, when they were attacked by Swedish gun sloops and had to give in. The fight was at an end about 10 o'clock, and the Russian fleet completely routed. It had cost us

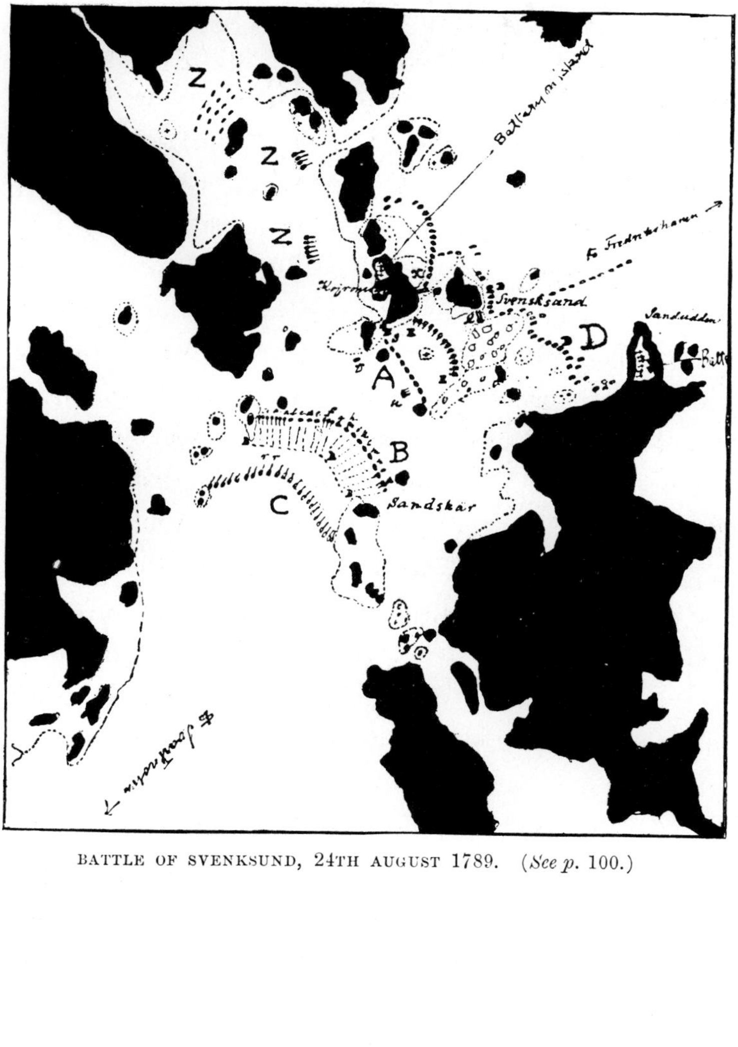


BATTLE OF SVENKSUND, 24TH AUGUST 1789. (*See p.* 100.)

1 udema and 3 gun sloops, 10 officers, 9 petty officers, and 162 men killed; and 12 officers, 7 petty officers, and 104 men wounded. The Russian loss was 3 frigates captured, 2 frigates sunk, 16 galleys (of which 9 were sunk), 1 hemmema, 3 chebeques (of which 2 sunk), 1 brig (sunk), 9 galliots (of which 3 sunk), 1 tchaijk, 2 cutters, 3 bomb vessels (1 sunk), 2 floating batteries, 3 bomb barges (1 sunk), 3 gun sloops, 1 demi-galley, and 3 admiralty yachts; altogether, 53 vessels with 1784 guns. Their loss in killed and wounded is estimated at 3000; 279 officers and 6200 men were taken prisoners. The Prince of Nassau had a narrow escape. His flag-captain was among the prisoners, as was also the Brigadier Denizon (Dennison)."

## Battle of Viborg, 3rd July 1790

The following are extracts from a narrative of the battle written by a Danish officer, who seems to have been present and had free access to the Russian ships, found in the Royal Archives, Stockholm:—

"The Swedish ship Sophia Magdalena, captured by the Russian 74-gun ship Mistisloff, commanded by Captain Bilow (a Dane). . . .

. . . "One of the Russian ships that attacked the Swedish ship Retvisan was commanded by Captain Ziewerts (a German). . . .

. . . "During the action, when the Swedish fleet forced the passage at Salvor, Captain Bilow got order to reinforce Trevenen's (Trevenna's) ship with

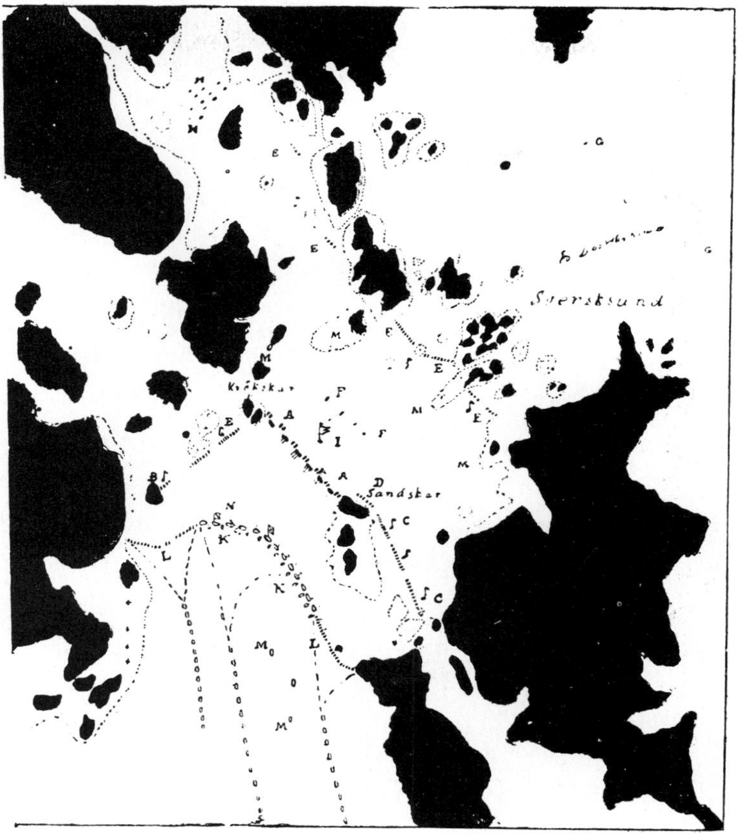


DEFEAT OF THE RUSSIANS AT SVENKSUND, 9–10 JULY 1790.

A A. Swedish main: 2 hemmema, 2 udema, 15 galleys, 1 brig.
B B. ,, right wing: 55 gun sloops, etc., at right angles to A.
C C. ,, left wing: 52 gun sloops, etc.
D. 6 bombs.
E E. Swedish reserve: 1 turuma, 1 galley, 33 gun sloops and yawls.
F F. ,, gun barges.
H H. ,, transports.
I. King of Sweden.
K K. Russian main: 22 frigates, xebecs and floating batteries, and 22 gun vessels.
L L. Russian wings: 26 galleys, 80 gun sloops.
M. ,, sunk.
N. ,, frigate Nikolai sunk.

40 men and 1 officer, and another captain received a similar order. Trevenen is badly wounded, as is also his next in command, Captain Aken (Aitken or Akers ? ), an Englishman.

"Admiral Tchitschagoff has been rewarded with the first degree of the Order of St. George—2400 peasants. His son has been made a colonel, and has received a golden sword with the inscription 'For Bravery.' Admiral Kruse has not got anything.

"The Swedish can congratulate themselves at having got off so cheaply, for it is in reality only 3 able ships that they have lost, the other 5 being old ships which they had only kept floating all along by aid of the pumps.

"KAAS.

"The loggert Larken, 20 *July* 1790."

## DEFEAT OF THE RUSSIANS AT ROTGENSALM (SVENKSUND), 9-7, 1790

Extract from a letter written by a Swedish officer who was present at the battle of Svenksund. (French was the language of the Swedish Court at that time.)

"Le brigadier, Denison, Anglais, qui après une defence vigoreuse fut fait prisonnier, était mortallement blessé à la tête. Il plut donc à S. M. de la renvoyer à Frederiksham pour mieux obtenir les soins que lui étaient necessaires dans cet état. . . . L'on a ensuite appris la mort de ce Brigadier. . . .

"Durant la bataille il fut rapporté au Roi que la p$^{ce}$de Nassau, était blessé au bras, et qu'il c'était refugiée sur un île."

The Russian port admiral at Frederiksham (Svenksund) when the Swedes took it in May 1790 was Brigadier Slissen (said to have been a Dutchman).

## ANGLO-SWEDISH OPERATIONS AGAINST RUSSIA, 1808–9. CONTEMPORARY SWEDISH ACCOUNT

(*Translation—Condensed.*)

THE English fleet which in 1808 was sent to the Swedish waters to co-operate with the Swedish fleet against Russia, arrived at Gothenburg in April, and was commanded by Admiral Saumarez. It counted 16 ships-of-the-line and 20 other vessels. A part of it was despatched to the Baltic, and the rest stationed in the Sound to prevent a French army of 50,000 men under Field-marshal Bernadotte crossing from Denmark to Sweden. Swedish naval power was very weak about that time. The war had broken out in the middle of the winter. The Swedish army went from victory to victory, but was nevertheless obliged to retreat before the overwhelming Russian armies pressing on its flanks, and had no other choice than to burn the parts of the coast-fleet lying ice-bound in the harbours of Warkaus, Christina, and Ăbo. On the 6th of April the commander of the strong fortress Sweaborg settled the terms of surrender with General Suchteben, when it was agreed that the fortress should be given up on the 5th of May, unless relieved before that time by a Swedish squadron of at least 5 ships-of-the-line. We could and would have sent this relief, but the courier despatched to Stockholm with the draft of surrender was detained by the Russians, and arrived in Stockholm only on the very day the fortress was to be handed over, and thus we lost at one blow not less than 110 men-of-war lying in the harbour and included in the surrender. Of our coast-fleet only a third were now left, a sorry lot of 159 old and decayed galleys and gun sloops, with which we had to maintain war with the Russian Empire.

However, the Russian fleets were hardly in better plight than the Swedish; in fact, Russia had neglected her naval defences even in a greater degree than had Sweden. Of xebeques, galleys, and semi-galleys, there was hardly one that would keep afloat, and of other vessels Russia could muster only 11 floating batteries, 60 gun sloops, and 55 gun yawls in the dockyards of Kronstadt, 10 gun sloops in the harbour of Ruotensalmi[1] (a new-built fortress on the Kotka isle at Svensksund), 21 gun sloops at Willmanstrand, and 13 at Ladenoie-Pole. Of the grand fleet, a third was mere rot, another had been sent to the Mediterranean, and the rest consisted of 9 ships and 7 frigates. The Anglo-Swedish fleet then reigned supreme in the Baltic, and the Russians, fearing an invasion over the sea, made haste to put their coast defences in order. Thus 20,000 Russians were stationed in the provinces of Estland, Liffland, and Kurland; another 15,000 in Sugermanland and Wiborgs län; and the fortresses of Kronstadt,

[1] Rotgensalm.

Wiborg, Fredrikshamn, and Ruotensalmi were reinforced by 15,000 more. But we had sufficient to do in keeping the men at bay in Finland, even to think of an invasion; and Russia again began to gather courage. On the 26th of July her fleet, counting 9 ships, 7 frigates, and 13 smaller vessels, under Rear-admiral Chanikoff, ran out from Kronstadt on purpose to observe the Swedish fleet, and if possible cover the south coast of Finland. On the 6th of August he arrived off Hangö, where he lay inactive during two weeks. On the 21st of August he advanced towards Örö, where the Swedish fleet of 10 ships and 6 frigates, under Rear-admiral Nauckhoff, lay at anchor. Just then 2 English ships-of-the-line under Rear-admiral Hood joined the Swedish fleet, which on the 25th weighed anchor and gave chase on the enemy. The Russians at once spread all canvas they could carry, and went away fast enough towards Port Baltic. On the 26th, in the afternoon, the two English ships, which were better sailers than the rest, got up with the enemy's rear and captured the rearmost ship,[1] after a battle which did the Russians all honour. After that the enemy was blockaded at Baltischport. On the 30th Admiral Saumarez joined the Swedish fleet with 4 ships and 1 frigate, and out of the whole force 5 ships and 2 frigates now were detached to blockade Kronstadt. On the 2nd of September an attack on the Russian fleet in Baltischport was discussed, but abstained from because of the strong fortifications of the place. The blockades were given up on the 20th of September.

[1] Svlod. See p. 123.

The Russian fleet at Baltischport left that place on the 2nd of October and arrived at Kronstadt on the 12th, the combined Anglo-Swedish fleet parting and returning each to its own country.

Saumarez returned to Sweden in 1809, arrived in Carlskrona on the 4th of June with 10 ships-of-the-line and 17 other vessels, and in the Bay of Finland in the middle of the month, taking up his station in the Revel Bay between Nargön and Surepudd, whence he despatched detachments, and cruised over the whole Bay of Finland and the Bay of Riga. On the 20th of June one of his detachments made an attempt to seize the Russian battery on Hangö Point (Gangout), but the 10 boats sent from the two English ships were beaten back by the two gun sloops and 6 gun yawls with which the Russians met them. Another attempt was more successful. In the night between the 8th and 9th of July, 270 Englishmen in 20 boats surprised a Russian flotilla of 2 gun sloops and 6 yawls lying at Porkala,[1] and captured all the vessels except 2 yawls, after a severe fight. The Russians lost 150 men killed, wounded, or prisoners; the English, 50.

On the 14th of July Captain Dessen left Kronstadt with 25 gun sloops and 7 transports to reinforce the Abo squadron of the Russian coast-fleet. On the 22nd his rear and transports were attacked by English cruisers, more especially by a ship-of-the-line, which, however, was obliged to make for the open when Dessen turned on it with all his strength. But on the 25th

[1] See p. 124 for Russian version.

the English, with 320 men in 19 boats, renewed the attack, seizing on 4 gun sloops which towed some transports, and captured after a desperate fight 3 sloops and 1 transport. The casualties were 76 men on the English side and 147 on the Russian.

By the end of July the English fleet were stationed as follows :—at Porkala Point, 1 ship and 1 frigate ; at Aspö, 2 ships and 2 frigates ; at Torsari, 1 ship and 1 frigate ; at Monö Sound (between Ösel and the mainland), 1 ship and some smaller men-of-war ; in the Bay of Riga, 1 frigate ; and at Nargön (Bay of Revel), 5 ships-of-the-line.

Peace concluded on the 17th September, the English fleet left the Baltic.

A letter from Admiral Saumarez to the King of Sweden is dated "His Britannic Majesty's Ship The Victory, off Gothenburg, 18th May 1808" :—

"À bord de la Victoire près de Port Rogervik le 30 Aout 1808. J'ai l'honneur de prévenir votre Excellence de mon Arrivée hier au soir à la Hauteur de Hangó Nor, bon 'attendant à m'y réunir avec la Flotte Suèdoise que d'après mes derniers Rapports étoit près de l'Isle d'Orö le Matin de très bonne neau je rencontrai la Frigate Suedoise le Chapman et j'appris de son Commandant le Capitaine Améen que la Flotte Russe fut partie de Hangó le 25 et avoit été poursurvie par l'Escadre de la Majeste Suèdoise avec le deux Vaisseau de Sir Samuel Hood, et que l'Ennemi s'etoit refugiée dans ce Port. J'arrivai ici cet après midi à deux Heures, et jèus la satisfaction de trouver à l'Ancre les Escadres unies que bloquaient l'Ennemi qu'il avoient poursuior le 26 le Vaisseau Implacable par la superiorite de ses Voiles força le Vaisseau Russe le plus en arrière à se battre et a baisser Son Pavillion : mais la Flotte Russe s'etant arretée peur le recouvir, le Capitaine Martin fut dans la Necessité de l'abandonner. Le Centaur[1] l'attaqua en suite et l'aborde de la manière la plus brillante ; mais la Vaisseau ayant touché, en fit oblige d'y mettre le feu et de le detruire après avoir sauvé tons les Prisonniers et les blessés.

"L'Admiral Nauckhoff et toute l'Escadre Suèdoise eut montré le plus grande Zèle à la Poursuite de l'Ennemi : mais n'etant pas si bons Voliers, ils n'ont pu l'attendre.

. . . . . .

"SAUMAREZ."

(Traduction d'un lettre d'Admiral Saumarez à S. M. le Roi de Suède.)

[1] Flag of Rear-admiral Hood.

# THE OPERATIONS OF THE PETTY FLEETS (GALLEY FLEETS) IN THE WAR WITH SWEDEN, 1808–9

SINCE any campaign in the Baltic along or near the Finnish coast would entail the use of coast-flotillas, an account at length of the "petty fleet" operations in 1808–9 is here given. Any modern operations would have to move on more or less similar lines, and the matter is thus invested with an importance that its historical importance would not at first sight seem to warrant.

The following matter is based upon Swedish naval histories, supplemented by official records and memoranda. I am entirely indebted for it to Herr C. G. Björkman of Stockholm.

During the eighteen years that had elapsed between the peace of Werelä and the outbreak of hostilities in 1808, the Swedish Navy, and especially the petty fleet, had been sadly neglected. The petty fleet counted nominally 273 men-of-war, but of the lot no less than 81 were altogether useless. Of the rest, 1 cutter, 1 schooner, 3 royal yachts, 9 galleys, 22 gun sloops, and 2 gun barges were stationed at Stockholm; 12 gun sloops, 12 gun yawls, 2 gun barges, and 1 bomb barge at Gothenburg; 11 gun sloops at Malmo;

9 gun sloops at Landskrona; 2 hemmemas, 1 turuma, 1 cutter-brig, 20 gun sloops, 49 gun yawls, and 1 gun barge at Sveaborg; and 23 gun sloops, 8 gun yawls, and 2 gun barges at Åbo. At Warkaus and Kristina (Finland) were stationed some 20 gun sloops and yawls, but they were all useless.

Sweden was at war with France since 1805, and at the end of February a Russian army marched into Finland without any previous notice, and occupied, among other places, Åland. On the 14th of March, Denmark, ever true to her principles of attacking Sweden when in difficulties, declared war, and Sweden had consequently to contend with three Powers simultaneously. Her fleets were ice-locked in their harbours; she was obliged to burn the squadrons at Åbo, Warkaus, and Kristina, lest they should fall into the hands of the invading Russians; and in May she lost her stronghold in Finland, the fortress of Sveaborg, with 91 vessels of the petty fleet and 19 of the grand fleet, through the treason of Admiral C. O. Cronstedt, a Finlander. On the 1st of April the Russian emperor had issued a manifest in which he proclaimed the annexation of Finland.

The Baltic at last open, a Russian expedition of 9 transports, with 1650 soldiers and 6 guns, under Rear-admiral Bodisco, left Libau and landed on Gotland on the 22nd of April, and marched into Wisby on the 27th. Informed of this somewhat daring exploit, Rear-admiral Baron Cederström, who commanded a Swedish squadron of 3 ships, 2 frigates, and 3 small vessels, took on board 1850 troops with 6 guns, proceeded to Gotland, landed on the 14th of May, and on the 16th Bodisco capitulated.

The labyrinthean archipelago between the Ålands haf and south-western Finland, probably one of the most extensive in the world, may properly be divided into three large groups, as follows :—*the western Åland archipelago, between Ålands haf and Delet*, comprising Aland proper, Eckerö, Lemland, Lumparland, Wårdö, and Foglö ; *the eastern Åland archipelago, between Delet and Skiftet,* comprising Brändo, Kumlinge, Såttunga, and Kökar ; and *the Åbolän archipelago, between Shiftet and the main of Finland,* which, again, may be divided into three smaller groups,—the *northern*, the *central*, and the *southern.* The northern group comprises Töfsala, Sudsalö, and Vartsalö ; by Lypertö it may be entered from the west ; through Grönvikssund from the south. The central group, the largest, comprises Rimito, Inio, Roslax, Korpo, Nagu, and the isles surrounding Pargas. This group is entered through Palvasund, past Korpo Berghamn from the west, and by Pargas port from the south. The southern group comprises the Kimito main and the isles south of it ; this group, which is separated from the central group by the Guldkronafjärden, may be entered from the west through Jungfrusund, and from the east by Hangö. The principal fair - way between Sweden and Finland enters the western Åland archipelago at Ledsund, runs north of Foglö, cuts the eastern Åland ·archipelago at Små - Såttunga, and divides there into two lines—the *Åbo line,* past Korpo Berghamn, north of the Korpo and Nagu mains, across the Erstafjärden and through the Bockholmsund; and the *Hangö line,* through Korpoström and its easterly extension, Billholmssund, across the Guldkronafjärden through Jungfrusund.

The Russians had in the beginning of April sent a Colonel Vuitsch with 700 troops to take possession of Åland. When at the end of the month the ice began to break up, Vuitsch's communication with the mainland and the isles (on which he had distributed his troops) was cut off. He succeeded, however, in collecting some of his detachments, and stood with 470 men at Kumlinge, when, one of the first days of May, a Swedish squadron of 1 schooner and 2 gun barges, under Lieutenant Arrhén, landed 450 seamen and five 2-pounder guns, attacked him on the 10th of May, and after a brilliant fight forced him to surrender. This done, Arrhén proceeded to clear the other isles from Russians, and succeeded so well that in two days the archipelago was again in Swedish hands.

The remnants of the Swedish petty fleet left Stockholm and the other ports during the first part of June, and on the 13th of that month 22 gun sloops, under Lieut.-col. Jönsson, had assembled at Korpo Berghamn.

On the 2nd of June a Russian squadron of 15 gun sloops, under Captain Mistroff, had left Sveaborg going westward, and was followed on the 9th by

7 gun sloops and 6 gun yawls under Lieutenant Grawne. Both divisions were bound for the Åland archipelago, and passed Jungfrusund on or about the 11th.

On the 23rd of June Centre-admiral Hjelmstjema arrived at Korpo Berghamn with a reinforcement of 4 galleys and 4 gun sloops, and took command of the whole Swedish force. He at once despatched Captain Sölfverarm with 8 gun sloops to Jungfrusund, with the object to oppose the passage of the Russian reinforcements expected from Sveaborg, a detachment of the grand fleet, which had arrived off Hangö, having been sent there on the same purpose. The first two Russian divisions had, as before stated, already passed Jungfrusund, and on the 23rd effected a junction at Bockholmssund, where Captain Selivanoff had assumed the command of the combined squadrons, and now erected several land batteries on the flanks of his position on purpose to keep the place as a place of refuge. Thence Selivanoff himself went on a cruise to the Åbo waters, and despatched Lieutenant Mäkinin with 12 gun sloops and 2 yawls to look for the Swedes. As soon as Hjelmstjema got news of this he decided to attack Mäkinin, and on the 28th went in search of him with 4 galleys and 15 gun sloops, and, in order to conceal his approach, he used a brisk N.N.W. to go north of Innamo and close under the south shore of the Hanga main. Mäkinin, however, got the wind of the danger, and took up position in a creek between the point of Kimito Kramp and Krampholmen close under the shore, so that he could rake the entrance

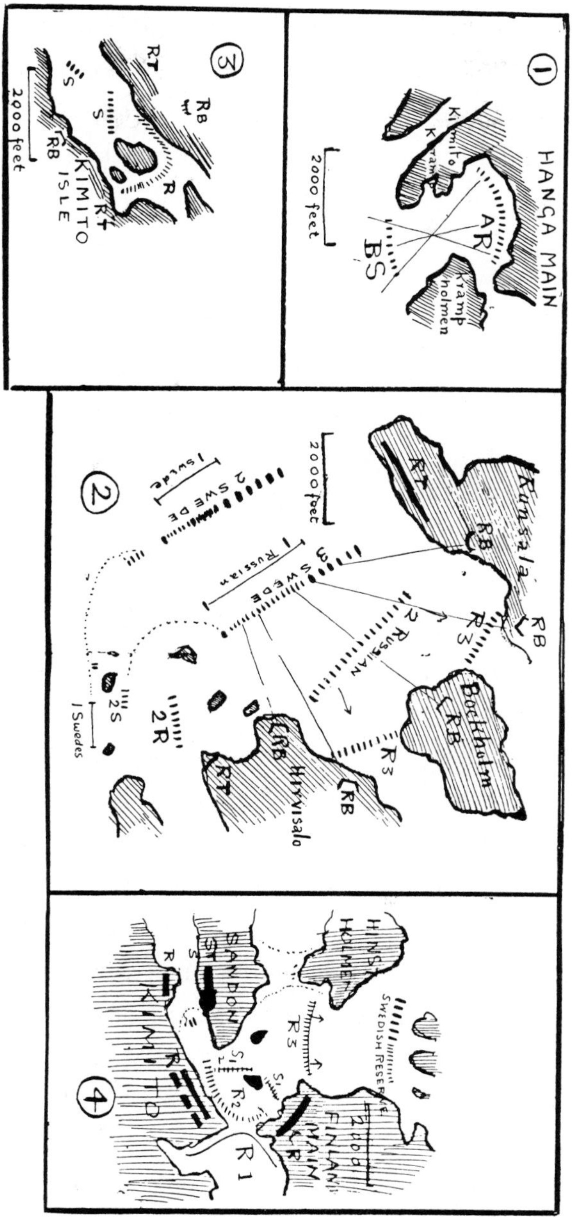

1
HANGA MAIN
Kimito
Kramp
Kramp holmen
AR
BS
2000 feet
2
Runsala
Boekholm
Hirvisalo
Russian
SWEDE
2 SWEDE
1 Swede
1 Swedes
2000 feet
3
KIMITO ISLE
2000 feet
4
HINST HOLMEN
SANDON ST
SWEDISH RESERVE
FINLAND MAIN
KIMITO

with his guns; and when the Swedish squadron, marching close under the Hanga main with 11 gun sloops in platoon columns foremost, 4 galleys in the middle, and 4 gun sloops closing the order,

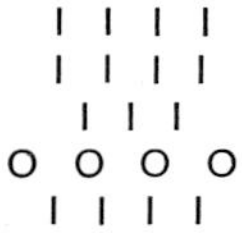

turned Kimito Kramp, it was at 2 o'clock p.m. received with a well-aimed and destructive fire, and suffered great losses. The wind blowing from ahead and becoming gusty, Hjelmstjema, who was with the galleys, could not support the gun sloops effectually, and for that reason ordered the sloops to withdraw under the Skäb-isles till the hurricane was over, and meanwhile prepare for a second attack. Selivanoff, who arrived later in the day with 2 gun sloops and 1 yawl, would not risk a new encounter, however, and retreated in the dark of the night, running out between the Hanga main and Krampholmen, and was far out on the Erstafjärd, making for Bockholmssund, when Hjelmstjema, early in the morning of the 1st of July, went to renew the attack. Hjelmstjema advanced, however, to Fårskinnsholmarne, and anchored opposite the Russian position at Bockholmssund, in order to blockade Selivanoff. Here he was reinforced by 4 galleys from Stockholm.

On the 4th of July, early in the morning, the king (Gustavus Adolphus IV.) arrived in his yacht Amadis, accompanied by the adjutant-general of the fleets, Vice-admiral S. M. von Rajalin, to inspect the

Swedish fleet. He at once gave orders that the enemy's position should be reconnoitred, and Captain Wirsin with 8 gun sloops was in the afternoon despatched to the south of the Jorois (or Jervis) isle on purpose, under cover of some islets, to approach the enemy's left flank, and 10 other gun sloops were despatched to the west point of the Jorois isle to support him. But the Russians were on the alert, and, as soon as the Swedes approached, Selivanoff turned out, 22 gun sloops and 6 yawls strong, showing fight, supported by Major-general Konovnitzin, who arrived from Abo with 150 sharp-shooters, whom he posted on the points of Runsala and Hirvisala. The king now ordered 6 galleys to support the reconnoitring party and close up on the left of the 10 gun sloops, and, at 6 o'clock p.m., the two Swedish divisions advanced, forming a right angle, causing the Russians to form into the same order. The concentrated fire to which the Russians became exposed forced them to fall back, and they retreated under the batteries, the Swedes during the pursuit forming on a line in close order with the flanks drawn back from the shores to avoid the firing of the Russian sharp-shooters. When night came the Russians were safe under their batteries, of which they had one on the Bockholmen, two on Hirvisala, and two on Runsala, and all beginning to play the Swedes were forced to break off the pursuit and withdraw out of range.

On the 25th of June the Russian reinforcement of 1 hemmema, 1 brig, 1 yacht, 2 gun sloops, 40 gun yawls, and 24 transports, under Captain Semikin, expected at Jungfrusund, had left Sveaborg and arrived one of the first days of July off Jungfrusund; but as the passage was obstructed, and it was not considered possible to force it, Captain Hayden, who now took over the command, would try to effect a passage through the sound between the isle of Kimito and the main, which hitherto had been considered impracticable. Leaving the other vessels in the vicinity of Jungfrusund, he proceeded with the sloops and yawls northward, and arrived on the 13th of July at Strömma, where the sound is only 20 feet in width and the passage obstructed by bars laid down in the time of Czar Peter. He cleared the sound in two days, brought his squadron through on the 15th, and on the following days turned the point of the Kimito.

The Swedes stationed at Jungfrusund had seen the Russian vessels arrive and as soon disappear. In order to see what had become of them a reconnoitre was made towards Kimito, when it was found that the Russians had moved north and were about effecting a passage through the Kimito Sound. If their endeavours were crowned with success, the blockading Swedish squadron at Fårskinnsholmarne ran the risk of being attacked in the back, and even if it withdrew in time the enemy would by the junction of his two squadrons become so superior in strength that the Swedes would have little chance of retaining their sovereignty in the archipelago of Abolän. It, therefore, was of great import to prevent the Russians executing their design, and in order to do so Captain Sölfverarm with 8 gun sloops was on the 12th despatched to Sandöström (the eastern mouth of Kimito Sound). An order was at the same time sent to Hjelmstjema to send him some support.

Sölfverarm, arrived at Sandöström, at once set about barring the sound at Tallholmarne. On the 19th of July he was reinforced by Captain de Brunk with 4 gun sloops, but General Buxhöfden, who commanded the Russian Army in Finland, sent several hundred light infantry to disturb the Swedes, in whose back two batteries, one on each shore, were erected, the guns to which had to be pulled by hand across the cliffs. On the 21st of July, at 3 o'clock in the morning, Hayden advanced from Rölax on purpose to force the Swedish position. Sölfverarm had then succeeded in blocking up the two narrow sounds between the Kimito main and the isles of Tallholmarne, and half of the sound between the large isle of Tallholmen and the Finnish main. Hayden approaching, Sölfverarm placed 8 of his 12 gun sloops 1000 feet behind the passage in order to oppose the enemy, but somewhat askew, so that they could use the bow-guns against Hayden's squadron and the stern-guns against the Russian battery and the infantry on the Kimito island; and the other 4 at right angles, so that they could bring their guns to bear on the flank of the said battery. In this position they kept the overwhelming Russian forces at bay for three hours, but the enemy beginning, under cover of their battery on the Finnish main, to squeeze himself through, he was then obliged to retreat, the sloops having suffered a great deal under the cross-fire to which they had been exposed. His loss in killed and wounded, however, was only 46 men. The Russians count their loss to only 20 men, but it must certainly have been much greater, considering the great damage inflicted on their material, which prevented them following up their advantages and caused them to desist from pursuing the Swedes, —Hayden had been wounded.

Sölfverarm, who had retreated only some 5000 feet from Sandöström, was on the 24th of July reinforced by 10 gun sloops, under Lieut.-col. Jönsson, who now assumed the command of the Swedish force. Jönsson placed 12 sloops between the Kimito main and the Röfvarholmen, and 8 others between the latter and the Finnish main, so that the guns of both divisions bore concentrically on the Sandö Sound at a distance of some 600 feet. Two sloops were posted behind this line, in order to prevent Russian infantry passing the narrow ford between Kimito and Sandö, and rake the three Russian batteries on the southern shore. Sixty chasseurs were told off to hold the Sandöw, and on the Röfvarholmen a battery of four 12-pounder guns was erected. But the Russian forces had also been reinforced on all points. On the 6th of July a further division of 9 gun sloops and 4 gun yawls, under Captain Lutochin, had left Sveaborg. It arrived off Strömma on the 22nd, and on the 31st it joined the force at Tallholmarne, and now the combined Russian squadron counted 11 gun sloops and 44 yawls, under Captain Dodt. The infantry on the shores had been increased to 1000 troops, and 5 batteries erected, 3 on Kimito and 2 on the main. Great interest was concentrated on the coming fight. Thus, for instance, the Russian generals, Buxhöfden, Konounitzin, and Suchtelen, were present. At 3 o'clock a.m. on the 2nd of August the whole Russian flotilla advanced. Twice it tried to form into line at the narrowest part of the sound, but was beaten back by the sweeping fire from the Swedish gun sloops, which, however, were exposed to quite as destructive cross-fire from the shores. The heavy cannonade and musketry to which the right flank of the Swedes was exposed made it necessary for them to draw back from the Kimito shore about 5 o'clock a.m., and the Russians taking advantage of it squeezed forward, and caused the Swedish right wing to bend backwards and take up a new position between Sandö and Röfvarholmen. This movement gave the Russians an opportunity to develop their whole strength. The battle raged for three hours, and both parties suffered considerably. On the Swedish side Lieut.-col. Jönsson fell fatally wounded, but Captain Sölfverarm, who again assumed the command, fought obstinately, trusting to receive expected reinforcement. At 8 o'clock a.m., having received no relief, he was obliged to withdraw, and did so in good order, Captain de Brunk covering the retreat with 4 gun sloops. The Russians pursued hotly, routed the small detachment of chasseurs on Sandö, and stormed the battery on Röfvarholmen. The retreat had continued under constant firing for about an hour when Centre-admiral Hjelmstjema, who had been detained by bad weather and a heavy sea, at last arrived with the galleys in the nick of time to save some yawls from being captured, and now the combat revived. After $2\frac{1}{2}$ hours of fighting the Russians were driven back within cover of their batteries. Hjelmstjema left them there, himself falling back to Holmön for repairs. The losses had been on the Swedish side 173 killed and wounded, against 330 Russians. Of the gun sloops, 12 Swedish and 22 Russian were out of fighting condition.

Some days after the Russians effected junction with Selivanoff's squadron, but made no attempt to disturb Hjelmstjema. The Swedish squadron fell back to Korpo Ström, and afterwards proceeded to Små-Såttunga, where it arrived on the 9th of August.

On the 11th of July a fifth Russian squadron, under Captain Novaktschenoff, had left Sveaborg, and on the 3rd August joined the squadron off Jungfrusund. The Russian force at that place now consisted of 2 hemmema, 2 floating batteries, 1 brig, 1 geolette, 3 yachts, 9 gun sloops, and 8 yawls. At Orö a detachment from the Swedish squadron off Hangö was posted.

While Selivanoff and Hayden, who had reassumed his command about the middle of August, watched the northern and the central archipelagoes, Novaktschenoff was on the move in the southern part, where he several times disturbed the Swedish squadron off Jungfrusund. In the night between the 16th and 17th August he

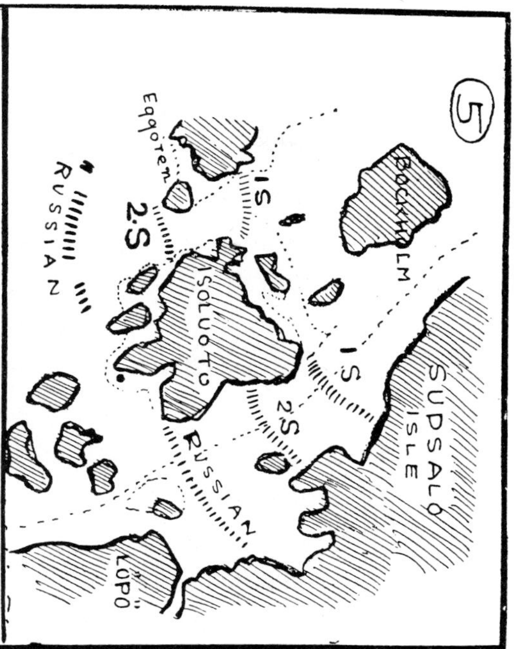
5
BOCKHOLM
SUDSALO ISLE
SOLUOTO
LÖPÖ
Eggoten
RUSSIAN
1S
2S

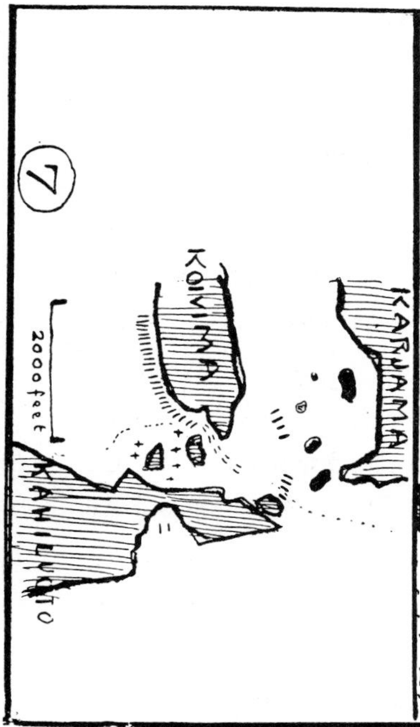
7
KARJAMA
KOIVIMA
KAHILUOTO
2000 feet

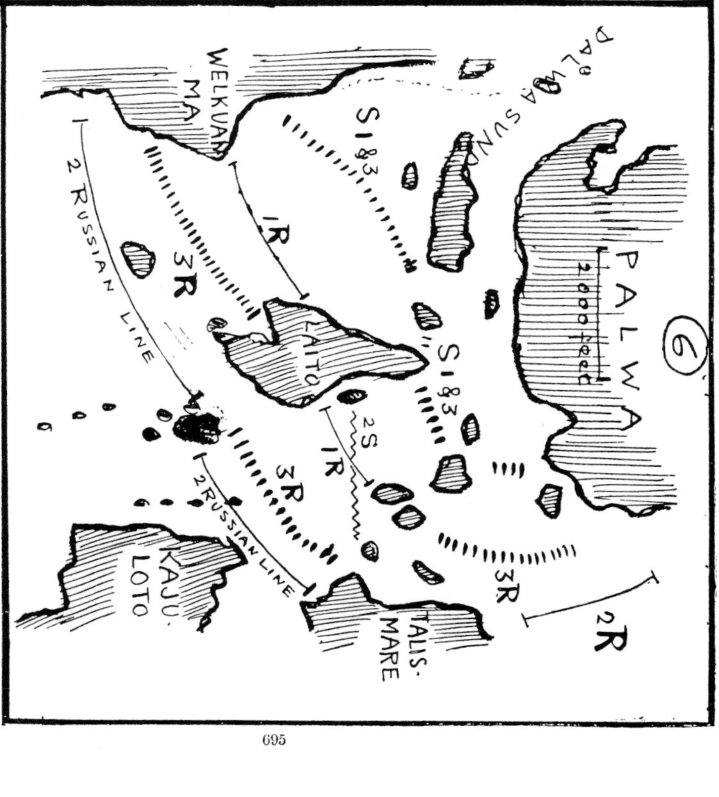
6
PALWA
2000 feet
WELKUAMA
LAITO
KAJULOTO
TALIS-MARE
S1&3
1R
2R
3R
2S
2 RUSSIAN LINE

attacked a Swedish ship-of-the-line with a floating battery and some gun sloops, but was obliged to retreat after some fighting. He renewed the attack the following night with 2 floating batteries, 6 gun sloops, and 6 gun yawls, approaching the Swedish ship by a roundabout way from Jungfrusund. Rear-admiral Nauckhoff, who commanded the Swedish squadron, had, however, somewhat earlier despatched an officer with 132 seamen in 24 small boats to make a similar attack on the Russian squadron at Jungfrusund, and that party boarded and captured 1 hemmema and 1 brig. Novaktschenoff, then on the way, heard the cannonade and returned at once, opened fire on the Swedish boats, and forced the Swedes to relinquish the hemmema. The brig, however, was carried off. In prisoners, killed, and wounded the Russians lost 183 men; the Swedish casualties were 30 killed and wounded.

On the 18th of August Rear-admiral Mäsojedoff arrived from Hangö at Jungfrusund, and assumed command of the whole Russian petty fleet in the Aland archipelago. He brought with him 1 hemmema and 1 corvetto (turuma). The Swedish squadron at Orö having left its station on the 25th, Mäsojedoff proceeded to Omminais, where he combined with Hayden.

Hjelmstjema, after his arrival at Små-Såttunga, had been inactive for several weeks. At the end of the month (August) he received news that the Russians had despatched a part of their strength to Nystad, and he decided to profit by the opportunity and attack the detachment. Of the 39 gun sloops he had brought back from Sandöström, 12 were still under repairs, but he had been reinforced by 8 new gun sloops from Stockholm. He himself remained with the galleys at Såttunga, but despatched Lieut.-col. Brandt with the available 35 gun sloops to Nystad. Brandt passed by Kumlinge, Fiskö, and Jurmo to Lypertö, where he arrived on the morning of 30th August. Here he was informed that the enemy lay at anchor off Löpö, not at Nystad. Although uncertain as to the strength of the Russians, he decided at once to attack them, and steered at forced oars for Grönviks-sund on purpose to take the enemy at unawares. But Selivanoff had nevertheless been warned in time and had placed 28 gun sloops behind the sound between Sudsalo-Isoluto and 16 between Isoluto and Eggören. When the Swedes, at 12 noon, approached the sound of Sudsalo-Isoluto, and would form into line, they were received with fierce firing, which told all the better as the narrow sound did not allow more than half their number to use the guns, and the other half, all eager to get into action, crammed on. It being ascertained that the sound between Isoluto and Eggören, which had been known as impassable, could be passed, 10 of the Swedish sloops tried to get round that way, but were even there met with a destructive fire. The Swedes were determined to force the passage at any cost, and so one of the hottest artillery fights of the war took place. During six consecutive hours of fighting the Swedes were not able to proceed more than some 800–900 feet, and the aspect was not promising. However, about 7 o'clock p.m. the Russians began to fall back, and the retreat soon became general. Brandt pressed hotly on the flying enemy, and pursued him for $1\frac{1}{2}$ hours, stopping at Palva Sound at 8.30 p.m. His losses had been considerable, viz. 242 killed and wounded, the material greatly damaged, 1 sloop blown up and another sunk. The Russians reported their loss as very slight, but it was estimated at one-quarter of the whole force: "*the entire fjord between Grónvik's and Palva Sounds was strewn with wreck*," and it is evident that a fierce battle of more than eight hours' duration must needs cause great losses in people and material.

Having returned to Grönvikssund, Brandt went to Fiskö for repairs. There he received a reinforcement of 7 repaired gun sloops. Selivanoff withdrew to Åbo.

After the battle of Grönvikssund the Swedish contemplated a diversion in the back of the Russian armies in Finland, and a corps of 2600 troops, under Major-general Lantinghausen, had been despatched to Lokalax to carry out that design, and landed at the point of Waranpää on the 17th September. In order to cover the expedition, Admiral Rajalin, who had in the meanwhile taken command of the Swedish power assembled at Grönvikssund (thither Brandt again had returned), had arrived at Palvasund with 34 gun sloops, and occupied, after having driven away the

Russian outposts, a position to prevent the Russian fleet from disturbing Lantinghausen. Mäsojedoff had, however, from Omminais approached Palva, and on the 17th he warped his big vessels into position. The combined strength of the Russian fleet was 2 floating batteries, 1 hemmema, 2 brigs, 1 cutter, and some 90 gun sloops and yawls, thus outnumbering the Swedes by many times. Rajalin had placed his force in front of the sound in such a manner that 24 sloops formed a concave line between Welkuanma and Laito, and 10 sloops formed a convex line between Laito and Palva. Mäsojedoff's plan of attack was this: 20 sloops and yawls should engage the Swedish right wing, between Welkuanma and Laito, and 19 the left wing, after having formed behind the isles of Kajoluto and Talismare; 30 sloops and yawls and the big vessels were to support the attack; 10 sloops to turn the Swedish flank by going round Welkuanma, and 10 sloops to do the same by going round Palva. Early on the morning of the 18th September the Russians advanced in a very ostentatious and overbearing manner, bands playing and drums beating, to crush the little Swedish squadron, but owing to a fog that had come on they fell into disorder, and were engaged in re-forming their line of attack when at 5 o'clock the fog rose. The Swedes had order not to fire before the enemy had come within pistol-range, and when the Russians, about 6 o'clock, arrived at that range they were received with such a shower of bullets that they at once fell back. Now the whole Swedish line advanced upon the enemy, but the Russian reserve coming to the rescue, and the Russian right wing at this moment coming forward from behind the isles of Kajuloto and Talismare, the Swedes had to resume their former position. Now it was the Russians' turn to advance, but they failed in their attempt to warp their big ships into position under the ricochetting fire of the Swedes. But the Russian fire was overpowering as it was, and at 9 o'clock a.m. the Swedish left wing was obliged to fall back. The Swedish right wing now became exposed to a flanking fire, and at 10 o'clock it had to retreat, and immediately after the whole Swedish squadron filed through Palva-sund, without any particular loss. Well through, it again formed into line in order to oppose the passage of the Russians, and kept them thus at bay until the Russian detachments that had been sent round Welkuanma and Palva approached its flanks, when it retreated to Grönvikssund in such good order that the enemy did not venture to pursue. The losses had not, despite the duration and obstinacy of the fight, been very great. Of Swedish casualties there were nearly 100; of Russian, some 200. One Swedish sloop blew up, and 3 Russian sloops were sunk.

On the 26th September a new diversion was made in the back of the enemy, this time at Helsinge, where Lieut.-col. Lagerbring landed with some 3600 troops, and Major Sjoholm was despatched with 18 gun sloops and 1 bomb barge to Kahiluoto Sounds to cover the expedition ; Rajalin, who had received some reinforcements, remaining with 33 gun sloops at Gronvikssund. Sjoholm barred the sounds between Tofsala-Leiluoto and Asamaa-Kahiluoto with tree branches and stones, placed 8 sloops behind the sound between Leiluoto and Asamaa, and 10 sloops and the barge behind the sound between Kahiluoto and Koivima. Sjoholm himself commanded the former party, Captain de Brunk the latter.

The Russians too had received reinforcements, and the fleet now under command of Mäsojedoff counted 100 sloops and yawls, and 7 big vessels. When Mäsojedoff heard the cannonade at Helsinge, where the Swedes were attacked by superior Russian forces and obliged to re-embark, he advanced from Palva, and with 7 big vessels and 60 sloops and yawls took up position off Löpö, detaching 40 sloops and yawls towards Kahiluoto. The latter detachment were received with splendid gallantry by the Swedes. Captain de Brunk had posted his 10 sloops 800 feet behind the narrowest part of the sound, between Koivima and Kahiluoto, where only two or three of the enemy's vessels could advance at a time, and only by presenting their sides to the concentric fire of the Swedes, and thus the Swedish fire could be concentrated on a particular spot. It proved so destructive, too, that those exposed to it had to fall back with battered-in vessels and reduced complements. In this manner De Brunk for a whole week succeeded in preventing the Russians forcing the passage, despite their fourfold superiority and the fire from the troops they had landed on the isles around. In the morning of the 2nd October the enemy, under cover of a snow-storm, made a last attempt to break through, but were even now beaten back. Everything else failing, the Russians then put ashore and began erecting batteries on the isle of Koivima close to the Swedish flank. In order to put a stop to that, Lieutenant Hagelstam with 2 gun sloops turned the north point of Kahiluoto and took up a position in their right flank at a place where he, at a distance of 1200 feet across a low isthmus, could cannonade their gun sloops lying by the shore. This he did, and the result was that the Russians gave up their undertaking, embarked in great haste, and returned to Löpö.

This was the last encounter between the petty fleets of Sweden and Russia during the war. On the 4th October the Russians left Löpö and proceeded to Palva, where they lay inactive for a month, ultimately going into winter quarters at Abo. The Swedish fleet assembled on the 5th of November at Degerby, whence it returned to Sweden.

In June 1809 a part of the Swedish petty fleet, counting some 60 gun sloops and 40 gun yawls, under Vice-admiral Baron Cederström, turned out to fend off a supposed Russian attempt to invade Sweden from over the Baltic. The Russians, fearing quite a similar Swedish attempt, despatched their petty fleet, counting 2 hemmemas, 6 floating batteries, 3 brigs, 5 yachts, 51 gun sloops, 64 gun yawls, and 1 bomb ship, with

5000 men, under Admiral Siadoff, to Åland; but no action ensued.

The Swedish petty fleet had, however, in the winter been rebuilt and was daily increasing in number, so that in August it consisted of 9 galleys, 1 semi-galley, 126 gun sloops, 54 gun yawls, 15 espings,[1] 9 bomb ships, and 6 cutters; total, 220 vessels.

On the 17th of September peace was concluded.

[1] A small vessel 32 × 9 ft., 10 pair of oars, one 18-pounder carronade and two 2-pounder guns.

# APPENDIX B

## CONDENSED BIOGRAPHIES OF SOME DISTINGUISHED OFFICERS IN THE RUSSIAN NAVY, 865–1899 A.D.

[*Note.*—British and American officers will be found tabulated by themselves in Appendix C. Some of the officers in the following list are foreigners; the names of these are indicated by different type—thus *Kruyis.*]

ADINOSOFF.—Major-general (Corps of Ordnance) in Ivan Bogisloff at Viborg, 1790.

ADINOSOFF.—Rear-admiral in Sissoi Veliky at Viborg, 1790.

ALEXANDER.—Grand Duke Alexander Mihailovitch, grandson of the Tsar Nikolai I. Born 1866. Married Grand Duchess Xenia, sister to the present emperor. Kapitan I. rang. Author of several naval works; inventor of the Strategical Naval War Game as played in the Russian Navy. At present serving in the Aprāksin.

ALEXEI.—Grand Duke Alexei Alexandrovitch, third son of the Tsar Alexander II. Born 1850. Unmarried. General-admiral (Commander-in-Chief) of the Russian Navy. Translated Mahan's *Influence of Sea Power on History* into Russian.

APRĀKSIN.—Feodor [1] Matveievitch Gray Aprāksin, born 1671, was the father of Peter the Great's navy. In the account of this navy by a contemporary Englishman (previously

[1] Feodor, or Fedor, is the Russian form of Frederick.

cited) Aprāksin is the only Russian who comes in for praise. He was a scion of the old nobility, and a member or connection of the Romanoff family. In person and habit he was exceedingly dignified and good-tempered, and noted for his sincerity. He was originally a soldier, and did not take up the navy till about 1710, in which year Peter bestowed the rank of Graf (Count) upon him. In 1711 he commanded in the Black Sea, and later in the Baltic, being finally created General-admiral. His naval knowledge was real, not superficial, though no one discovered how he managed to learn it. He was a bit of a radical in his way, and openly expressed uncomplimentary views about the state of the country. On several occasions he is reported to have disagreed with Peter, to whose interests, however, he was devotedly attached, and the Tsar esteemed him always, if he did not love him. His energy was tremendous, and he alone was able to control the disorderly foreign officers in the Russian fleet. With all this he stole the public moneys for his own use; but this combination of theft and efficient performance of duty is easy in the Russian character. He was not entirely popular,—few able men are; but he stands out as one of the greatest Russians who ever lived. Died 20th November 1728.

Aprāksin, Alexander Feodorovitch.—Son of the above, distinguished himself in the war against Sweden, in which he held the rank of kapitan-lieutenant. In 1719 he was in command of the Lansdown.

Arens.—Mitchman. Commanded the Mina torpedo boat, in the war against Turkey, 1877–78.

Askold.—In command of Rurik's fleet which attacked Constantinople in 862. (Name also spelt Oskold.)

Bali.—Mitchman in command of torpedo boat Tzarevna in the attack on the Seifé, 1877.

Basheloff.—1724.

*Behring, Vitus Jonassen.*—A Dane. Born 1681. Sat on the Kruyis court-martial, 1714, as kapitan-lieutenant.

Kapitan in Pearl, 1715. Since famous as a great explorer (Behring Straits, etc.). Died 1741.

*Berch, Ludvig.*—A German. Captain of the Vladimir in 1788, replacing an Englishman, Samuel Gibbs (*q.v.*). Berch fought the Vladimir at Gogland, 1788, and struck to the Swedes.

Bredal.—Admiral in the operations against Turkey, 1736–39.

*Buss, Count de.*—An Italian. In command of the Galley fleet. In 1713, through ignorance of flags, he destroyed five Dutch vessels at Helsingfors, massacring the crews more or less barbarously, under the impression that they were Swedes! He died in 1715.

Chanekoff.—Rear-admiral in the St. Helena, Viborg, 1790.

Constantinoff.—Rear-admiral in Viscislav at Gogland, 1788.

*Cruys* (*see Kruyis*).—Norwegian admiral. Died 1715.

*Deruyter.*—Dutchman. Flag-captain of Viborg, 1712; Riga, 1713. Dismissed the Russian service, 1714, for running the ship aground.

Dir.—In command with Askold against Constantinople in 865.

Dmitri Donksoi.—Grand Duke of Muscovy. Died 1389.

Doubaskoff.—Lieutenant in command of the torpedo-boat flotilla which sank the Seifé, 1877. In command of the Tsarvitch.

*Eckolf, Clays.*—Dane. Director of pilots in the Gulf of Finland, 1724.

George.—Grand Duke George Alexandrovitch, son of the Tsar Alexander III. In 1890 he served in the Pāmiat Azova, and made a tour to India and the Far East, cutting the first sod of the Trans-Siberian railway at Vladivostok. During this tour he was wounded in the head by a Japanese fanatic. A special Tsarvitch medal —a lifebuoy—was given to all officers of the Pāmiat Azova and Korniloff, which accompanied the expedition. Grand Duke George was always in delicate health and resigned his succession. He was known as the Tsarvitch. He was exceedingly popular with the Russian Navy. Died suddenly, July 1899.

GOLOVIN.—Nikolai Feodorovitch Count Golovin, a favourite of Peter the Great's. Joined the service at an early age. In 1719, captain of the new Kronslot (Kronstadt). In 1712, served in the Caspian, not liking the Baltic service. Subsequently became admiral, and refused to attack the Swedes on the ground that their force nearly equalled his own (1743). In 1641, councillor of the Empress Elizabeth. Died 1745.

THE LATE TSARVITCH.

*GOSLER, MARTIN.*—A German. Captain of équipage. Sat on the board that drew up the Articles of War under Peter the Great's orders. Flag-captain to Peter the Great in the Ekaterina (60) in 1714.

GUSCHKIN.—Rear-admiral in the Saratov (108) at Viborg, 1790.

HIRST.—Mitchman in command of the Torpedoist, torpedo boat at Sukhum Kalé, 1877.

IGOR.—Grand Duke of Muscovy, son of Rurik. Personally led a fleet against Constantinople in 947. He tried to overcome the Greek-fire by rushing through it, but his entire fleet was annihilated. He escaped with half a dozen vessels.

ILYIN, DMITRI SERGEIEVITCH.—Born 1734. Entered navy, 1761. Greatly distinguished himself at Tchesma, 1770. Retired as kapitan I. rang, 1777.

ISMAILOVITCH.—In the Galley fleet. On the death of Count de Buss he was put in chief command (rear-admiral). Promoted vice-admiral, 1721, on occasion of the peace with Sweden. The atrocities perpetrated by the Galley fleet upon Swedish towns were so great that the Russian officers in big ships would have no dealings with the galley folk: under Ismailovitch these barbarities were a good deal mitigated.

KAZARSKI, ALEXANDER IVANOVITCH.—Was kapitan-lieut. of the Merkuria, 1829, and in May of that year gallantly fought a superior Turkish force. Died 1833.

KORNILOFF, VLADIMIR ALEXEIVITCH.—Born 1806. He served at Sinope, 1853, and was in naval command at Sevastôpol during the Crimean War. Had his advice been acted on, the invading army would probably have been destroyed at sea. Mortally wounded in the defence of Sevastôpol, 1854.

*KRUYIS (Cruys), CORNELIUS.*—A Danish-Norwegian, who went at an early age to Holland, and thence entered the navy of Peter the Great as vice-admiral about 1700. Stationed at Péterbōurg at its foundation. In 1711 flew his flag in the Viborg, and in the following year met, with his fleet, but failed to capture a Swedish ship, frigate, and snow, to which his fleet rather showed the white feather. In 1713, flying his flag in the Riga (52), and having with him four other ships-of-the-line and six frigates, he met and chased the Swedish Commodore Raab,[1] and again showed a certain amount of white feather and a good deal of incompetence. He was court-martialled for these two affairs, and condemned to death. The sentence was commuted to banishment, but after a while he was pardoned

[1] See p. 57.

by Peter and made vice-president of the Naval Academy. When peace was made, 1721, he was promoted admiral of the Blue. Died 1725.

LAZAREFF, MIHAIL PETROVITCH.—Born 1788. Served in the British Navy, 1803–8, being present at Trafalgar. In 1808, in consequence of the Anglo-Russian War, he left the British service. In 1820, and again in 1822–25, he was engaged in explorations. In 1827 was flag-captain in the Avoz at Navarino. Admiral, 1830. Died 1851.

MAKAROFF. — Flag-captain at Gogland and Viborg in the Vicislav.

MAKAROFF.—A descendant of the above; greatly distinguished himself in the war against Turkey, 1877–78. He is now an admiral, and also famous as designer of the celebrated Ermak, ice-breaker.

MENSHIKOFF, PRINCE ALEXANDER DANIELOVITCH.—Began life as Alexander Menshik, the son of a *bauer* (free peasant). He attracted the notice of Peter the Great, and was renamed Menshikoff, and subsequently ennobled. He joined the navy with the Tsar, and as commodore sat on the court-martial which condemned Kruyis (Cruys) to death. He never appears to have seen active service worth mentioning, but he rendered useful aid in many matters. Flew his flag as rear-admiral in the Alexander, 1718. In 1721 created vice-admiral of the White. A descendant, Prince Loris Menshikoff, commanded in the Crimea, 1854, and refused to allow Korniloff to try to destroy the allied fleet encumbered with transports.

MIHAILOFF, PETER ALEXEIVITCH.—Tsar Peter the Great was always thus known when afloat. Born 1672. Tsar, 1682. Founded the modern Russian Navy. Took part in many battles afloat, details of which will be found in Chapter III. Died 1725.

MISHUKOFF, ZACHARIA.—Sat on the Kruyis court-martial, 1714. Then a lieutenant. Member of the first Admiralty Board. In 1758–59 Admiral Mishukoff cruised with a Russo-Swedish fleet looking for a British fleet to attack. None was forthcoming. He subsequently attacked Colberg, but was beaten: in 1761 he succeeded. Died soon afterwards.

NAHIMOFF, PAUL STEPANOVITCH.—Born 1803. Served under Lazareff in 1822; at Navarino, 1827. Admiral in command of Russian fleet at Sinope, 1853. Killed during the siege of Sevastôpol, 1854.

*NASSAU-SIEGEN, CHARLES HENRY NICHOLAS OTHON, PRINCE OF.*—Born 1745. Entered Russian service 1787, and took command after the death of Admiral Greig, 1788. Left the service after the death of the Empress Ekaterina in 1796, and settled in France, where he in vain courted the favour of Napoleon. Died 1808.

NILOFF.—Mitchman in command of the Toutchka, torpedo boat. Attacked by a Turkish monitor off Nikopolis, 1877 and nearly sunk by her.

OLEG.—Commander of a Russian fleet which operated against Byzantium, 907–12.

ORLOFF, COUNT ALEXIS.—Commander-in-Chief of the first Russian fleet sent to the Mediterranean by Ekaterina the Great. He was surnamed Tchesmesky in commemoration of the battle of Tchesma.

OTO.—Commodore. First commander of the Bombardiers (Marine Artillery). Participated in drawing up the Articles of War ordered by Peter the Great.

OUSHAKOFF, FEODOR FEODOROVITCH.—Born 1735. Entered service 1766. Served against Turkey, 1768–74, in command of a squadron. Vice-admiral, 1790. Served in the Mediterranean, 1793, when Nelson wrote uncomplimentary letters about him. Commander-in-chief in Baltic, 1801. Retired 1807. Died 1817.

PERSIN.—Mitchman. In command of torpedo boat Djidjit in the war, 1877–78.

PIFAREFSKY.—Lieutenant. Commanded the torpedo boat Sinôp in the Sukhum Kalé affair, 1877, when he was wounded.

POPOFF, ANDREI ALEXANDROVITCH.—Born 1821. Entered the navy 1837. Served at Sevastôpol, 1854–55. Admiral in the Baltic, 1860; Pacific, 1867. Designed many warships, including the circular "Popoffkas," and the Tchesma and Sinope class. Full admiral, 1891. Died 1897.

POUTSCHINE.—Lieutenant. Commanded No. 1 torpedo boat in war against Turkey, 1877–78. Killed when his boat was sunk.

POVALITCHIN.—Rear-admiral. Flew flag in the Trechievarkoff.

*RAYS.*—Commodore in Poltāva, 1713. Sent to Siberia for neglect of duty, 1714.

ROJDESTVENSKI.—Lieutenant in command of torpedo boat No. 2 at Sulina, 1877.

RURIK.—Founder of the Russian Empire. In 865 he sent a fleet to attack Constantinople.

SAKEN, CHRISTOPHER IVANOVITCH VON.—An Esthonian in the service of Ekaterina II. In 1788, his galley being surrounded by Turks, he blew himself up.

*SCHELTINGA, WYBRANT.*—A Dutchman. Commodore in the affair with Raab, for which with Kruyis (*q.v.*) he was court-martialled. Subsequently restored. He performed various minor services, and managed to muddle a good deal in the matter of recruiting officers from abroad. In 1716 he became paralytic. In 1718, in the New Year's Day promotions, Peter the Great made him rear-admiral of the Red as a sort of compliment to a dying man. He died three months later.

SENIAVIN, DMITRI NIKOLÆVITCH.—Born 1765. Fought against Turks, 1791. In 1806 was in command at Corfu against the French. In 1807 defeated a Turkish fleet, covering retreat of a British fleet from the Dardenelles. Sides changing, he evacuated the Mediterranean, but was blockaded by the British in the Tagus, and surrendered. Died 1831.

SENIAVIN, IVAN DMITRIEVITCH.—Captain-commodore *tempus* Peter the Great. Chiefly notable for incompetence. Captain of the Revel (60) in 1718.

SENIAVIN, NAHUM DMITRIEVITCH.—Brother (?) of the above, and a very efficient officer. As a captain he commanded, amongst other ships, the Devonshire and Riga. Flew his broad pennant as captain-commodore for the first time in 1719 in the Portsmouth (60), Captain Urquhart, but does not seem to have been on board when that ship was lost. Promoted rear-admiral of the Blue, 1721.

*SIEVERS.*—Dutchman, *tempus* Peter the Great. He was an admiral, and squabbled with the Scotchman, Gordon. Sievers was undoubtedly the better man of the two. (See "Gordon," in the biographies of British officers.)

SOGATIN.—Vice-admiral in Dvenadsat Apostolov at Viborg, 1790.

SPIRIDOFF, GREGOR ANDREIEVITCH.—Born 1710. Fought against Turks, 1736–39; in 1756, at Copenhagen and Stralsund; 1760, port-admiral at Revel; 1765, admiral at Kronstadt. In 1770 in command in the Mediterranean at Tchesma. Retired in 1774. Died 1781.

SPIRIDOFF, ALEXEI GRIGOROVITCH.—Son of above. Rear-admiral on St. Helena at Gogland, 1788, and Prince Vladimir at Viborg, 1790.

TCHESTAKOFF.—Lieutenant in command of the torpedo boat Xenia which sank the Turkish monitor Seifé on the Danube in the war of 1877–78.

TCHITCHAGOFF, VASSILLEI FEDOROVITCH.—Took command of the Russian fleet after the death of Greig in 1788. Admiral in the victory of Viborg, 1790. Defeated at Svensksund the same year.

TCHITCHAGOFF, PAUL VASSILIEVITCH.—Son of the above. Born 1762. Entered navy in 1782; flag-captain to his father at Viborg, 1790; vice-admiral, 1802; admiral, 1807. In 1812 commanded an army corps against Napoleon. Retired 1815. Died 1849.

*TURNHOUD.*—Dutchman. Kapitan in Poltāva, 1713; in the Victory, 1714. Flag-captain to Sievers in Le Firme, 1714; Richmond, 1715.

*VAN HOFFT.*—A Fleming who served under Peter the Great. Kapitan of the St. Anthony in 1714; Pearl, 1715. He invented the Greek-fire tubes[1] which were fitted to certain ships. Rose to be a rear-admiral of the Red.

*VAN OESSEN.*—Probably Dutch. Rear-admiral in the Retvisan, Captain Todd, at Gogland, 1788.

VISHNEVETSKI.—Lieutenant in command of the Navārin, torpedo boat, at Sukhum Kalé, 1877.

VLADIMIR.—In command of the fleet which attacked Constantinople in 1043. He partially defeated the Greek fleet, capturing five ships, but in a second action was totally annihilated.

ZATZAVENNYI.—Lieutenant in the torpedo boat Tchesma. Attacked the Turkish fleet at Sulina in 1877. Also at Sukhum Kalé, where he distinguished himself for bravery.

[1] See p. 546 (footnote)

# APPENDIX C

## BRITISH AND AMERICAN OFFICERS IN OR CONNECTED WITH THE RUSSIAN SERVICE

PETER THE GREAT had a fancy for British officers and shipbuilders in preference to other foreigners, and brought over as many as he could: giving them commissions or posts according to his estimate of their capabilities. After the peace with Sweden the services of many were dispensed with, and in Ekaterina the First's reign comparatively few remained. When, later, Ekaterina the Second (the Great) came to the throne, she, however, imported British officers and men wholesale.

Following are biographical notes upon all whose names I have been able to come across; but merely a fraction are here down. Unless they were in command of ships, no accessible record usually now remains of their names and services.

The details, where given here, have been drawn chiefly from the following sources:—

Russian and Swedish official records; *The Russian Navy under Peter the Great*, ed. Admiral Cyprian Bridge; Vol. XV. Navy Records Society; *The Diction-*

*ary of National Biography*; and a few private sources.

It will be noted that the proportion of Scotchmen in the following biographies is a great deal smaller than popular notions on the subject would have led one to suspect. In a few cases nationality may be wrongly stated; but, generally speaking, the small proportion of Scotch names may be due to the fact that but a small number of those who went over had held commissions in the British Navy, and these would, as a rule, have been rated as lieutenants, and stand not to appear here, or if appearing, leave no record save the name.

ALLAN (or ALLEN), ANDREWS.—Scotchmen, *tempus* Ekaterina II. No details procurable. Probably lieutenants.

ARMITAGE, SAMUEL.—Englishman. Captain of the Marlborough (70) in 1717.

ARSCOTT.—Lieutenant in some ship at battle of Gogland, 1788. Probably in the Rostislav (108).

BAGGS.—A master blockmaker brought from England by Peter the Great.

BAKER, WILLIAM.—Englishman. Joined the Russian service in 1714, bringing the Fortune, which he remained captain of till 1716, when he was in the Arundel (46). Captain of the Varakiel (52) in 1717. He was dismissed the Russian service in 1717.

BARK.—Englishman. Captain of the Saratoff at Gogland, 1788, and Viborg, 1790. No details.

BATTING, WILLIAM.—Captain of the Lesela (114) in 1715. Subsequently captain of St. Paul, which was sent to Archangel, but being very rotten, never got beyond Copenhagen. Flag-captain to Gordon in the Lesnoy, designed by Peter, which sank at Kronstadt that year.

BENT.—Englishman. Master shipbuilder. Came to Russia in 1705, and was employed in building ships on Lake Ladoga—two of 52 guns. Died 1710.

BIGGS, JOHN.—Kapitan, 1788.

BILLING.—Captain (lent from the British Navy), employed *circa* 1780 in command of a Russian expedition which was sent to explore the north coast of Siberia and seek the North-West Passage.

BRAYER (or PLAYER).—Captain of the St. Helen at Viborg, 1790. No other details.

BROWNE (or BROWN), RICHARD.—Englishman. Master shipbuilder from Chatham. Arrived in Russia with Bent (see *ante*) and worked with him. Afterwards designed many of the largest Russian ships, notable for speed. These included the Viborg and Rija (52-gun ships) (1710). He also "razeed" the Dutch-built Sampson; built the Ekaterina (60) (1712), and, in conjunction with Peter the Great, the Poltāva (54) (1712). Chief Constructor at Kronstadt, 1722.

BURN, J.—Scotchman. *Circa* 1780. Lieutenant (?).

COLE: COLES.—No data.

COOPER.—Ex-naval storekeeper at Portsmouth. Brought to Russia about 1721 by Gordon, with whom he soon squabbled, and presently fell into poverty. In 1724 was put in charge of naval stores at a salary of 600 roubles (then £300 English) per annum, with promise of a quadrupled salary if he did any serious work.

COSENS.—Englishman. Shipbuilder *tempus* Peter the Great. Employed at Kronstadt in 1722.

CROWN (or CRONIN).—Irishman. Holding the rank of commodore, and captain of the Venus, frigate, at Gogland and Viborg, 1790. Nearly captured the King of Sweden.

DAGNELL, L.—No data.

DAVENPORT.—Englishman. Shipbuilder on the Don, and later at St. Petersburg, 1700–20. Made a Master Builder 1719. Chief Constructor at Revel, 1722.

DEANE, JOHN.—Son of Sir Antony Deane, of Harwich, England.

He met Peter the Great at Deptford and accompanied him to Russia, where he was made superintendent of Vorōnege dockyard. Subsequently served afloat. Sent to Archangel, 1714, to bring round the Ezekiel in 1715, but she leaked and had to return for repairs. Setting out again, got frozen in at Trondhjem, and lost half his men. Reached the Baltic next year, and made captain of the Samson. In 1719, by flying Swedish colours he captured several merchantmen right under the guns of a fortress at Burgwick in Gotland; and generally distinguished himself at scouting and commerce destruction. Captain of the Devonshire (60) in 1719, when the London and Portsmouth, her consorts, were wrecked. He came in for much censure in consequence, though in no way to blame.

DELAP, JOHN.—Irishman. Lieutenant I.R.N. in 1714 on board Peter the Great's ship Ekaterina. He volunteered to land Peter in a gale of wind that year off Björko. Captain of the Ezekiel, 1719, in the action in which three Swedish ships were captured.

DENE.—No data.

DENISSON, FRANCIS. — Captain at battle of Svenksund, 1790. Mortally wounded, and taken prisoner by the Swedes.

DENNISSON (*another*) (or Tennyson ?).—Captain of the Boteslav at Gogland, 1788. No other details. There is a Tennyson an officer in the Russian Navy at the present time.

DENNY.—No data.

DENT.—No data.

DUFFUS, LORD.—Scotchman. Ex-officer British Navy; became involved in Jacobite plots in 1715, and was subsequently invited to enter the Russian Navy by Peter the Great, who made him rear-admiral, and gave him an important post in the Russian Admiralty. No record of any war service in the Russian Navy; in the British his early record was a brilliant one. Died *circa* 1730.

DUGDALE.—Scotchman. Lieutenant in command of the fire-ships at Tchesma, 1770. Deserted by his Russian crew, he managed to bring the fire-ship alongside a Turk, set fire to her, and so to the whole fleet. Resigned in 1788.

DUNN.—No data.

DUNNING, T.—No data. Probably served 1770–90.

EAST.—Mate *tempus* Ekaterina II.

EDWARDS, BENJAMIN.—Captain of the Pernau (52) in 1712; Sampson (32) in 1713, in action off Högland; L'Esperance (46) in 1714, off Gangoot; flag-captain to Prince Mentchikoff in the Slutelburg (64) in 1715; dismissed the service 1717.

ELPHINSTONE, H.—An officer of the British Navy, who was attached to the Russian service as rear-admiral in 1769. He planned the destruction of the Turkish fleet with fire-ships at Tchesma in 1770, and subsequently tried to induce Orloff to force the Dardanelles. Owing to strained political relations between Russia and England he was recalled about 1778, and re-entering the British Navy, was captain of the Magnificent in the battle off Granada, 1789, and in 1790.

FERGUSSON.—One of the first mathematical, etc., instructors at St. Petersburg Naval Academy, 1717.

FIELD, M.—Lieutenant *tempus* Ekaterina II. No other data.

FITCH.—Englishman. Captain of the Arundel (46), a ship that came to Russia (contract-built in England) in 1714. Served in her off Gangoot in 1715.

FITCHEW.—No data.

FOLEY.—No data.

FUNK.—No data.

FURSDON.—No data.

GARDINER.—Shipbuilder *tempus* Peter the Great, at Vorōnege and Archangel.

GARDNER.—No data. GASCOIGNE.—No data. GAY.—No data.

GIBBS, SAMUEL.—Englishman. Captain of the Vladimir in 1788; replaced by the German Berch.

GREIG, SAMUEL.—Born Scotland, 1736. Formerly in the British Navy, in which he served at Quiberon, 1759. He entered the Russian service as a lieutenant in 1764, and was a commodore in the Rostislav at Tchesma in 1770. Governor of Kronstadt *circa* 1776. In the war with Sweden he was in command of the Russian fleet, flying his flag in the Rostislav, and was wounded in the battle of Gogland, 1788. He died during the subsequent blockade of Sveaborg, 1788.

Greig, Alexei Samuelovitch.—Born 1775; son of Admiral Greig. He was appointed midshipman at birth by the Empress Ekaterina's order. He saw service in the war against Turkey, 1827–29; and subsequently reorganised the Russian Black Sea Fleet. Died *circa* 1840.

Greig, Samuel Alexeievitch.—Born 1810; son of the foregoing. Was an officer in Korniloff's fleet at Sevastôpol, 1854; and distinguished himself during the siege of that place. A son of his subsequently served in the Russian Navy.

Gordon.—Scotch. Jacobite refugee. Brought to Russia by Peter the Great from Holland in 1717. Made rear-admiral of the Red (3rd rank) in 1719, New Year's Day promotions. Jealousy between him and rear-admiral of the Blue (2nd rank) Sievers. Flew his flag in the Lesnoy, Captain Batting (*q.v.*), in 1719. Transferred his flag to the Moscow (64), Captain Hay.

In 1721, on the anniversary of Gangoot, when all were drunk, Gordon told the Tsar his grievances against Sievers, and generally tried to make bad blood between the British and Dutch. Aprāksin took Sievers' part against Peter and Gordon. Subsequently Peter tried to reconcile Gordon and Sievers, but failed, and all foreign officers took one side or the other. The Tsar's esteem for Gordon was considerable; and in 1722 he gave him command of a fleet, in preference to Sievers, on the strength of his having been a British officer. Vice-admiral, 1726, at Kronstadt. Went out to meet the British fleet under Sir C. Wagner; but having told the Empress (Ekaterina I.) that action was hopeless, courtesies were exchanged instead of cannon balls. In command of fleet that brought about the surrender of Dantzig in 1734.

GURNEY, EDWARD.—No data.

GWYN.—Welshman. First mathematical instructor at the Naval Academy, St. Petersburg, 1717.

HACKER, OLIVER.—American, *tempus* Ekaterina II. No data.

HADDON, EDWARD.—No data.

HADLEY.—Shipbuilder *tempus* Peter the Great. Made Master Builder, 1719. At Kazan, 1722.

HAY, WILLIAM.—Arrived in 1717. Flag-captain to Gordon in the Moscow (62) in 1719. Dismissed the service, 1724.

HAYNES, R.—*Circa* 1740.

HEADLEY.—No data.

JACOBS.—No data.

JOHNSTON.—Shipbuilder. Brought from Deptford by Peter the Great.

JONES, PAUL.—The notorious American privateer. Made an admiral in Ekaterina II.'s reign.

JONES (another).—No data.

KANE,<br>KAY. } *Tempus* Ekaterina II. No data.

KEITH, FRANCIS EDWARD JAMES.—Scotchman, born 1696, died 14th October 1758 (killed in action at Hochkirch). Was a "general" *tempus* Peter the Great. In command of the Russian coast-fleet at Korpo Ström, 21 galleys and some gun barges. On 20th May 1743 he was attacked by the Swedes, under Schoutbynacht Falkengen, with 15 galleys and two divisions of gun sloops. After two hours' severe fighting the Swedes were repulsed with heavy loss, being unable to force the position taken up by Keith, with land batteries on his flanks. In 1747, on account of disputes and ill-feeling with his Russian comrades, Keith resigned his commission.

LANE, EDWARD.—Welshman. Designed the Kronstadt forts and docks. Promoted captain of équipage in 1724.

LASCY (LACY), PETER.—Born at Kiltedy, County Limerick, Ireland, in 1678. Went to France owing to political troubles, then into Russian service. He became colonel in 1708, major-general 1712, lieutenant-general 1720, graf (count) and field-marshal 1736. Died 1751. He served in 1719 with the Galley fleet, and signalised himself by his tremendous depredations on the Swedish coast in the operations of that year.

LAUDON.—Scotchman. Imported by Peter the Great. Officer in Russian Navy *circa* 1715. No details.

LAUDON, GIDEON.—Son of the above. In the Russian Navy 1740–46, when he left, and entered the Austrian Army, in which he acquired considerable fame, and became a field-marshal.

LAURENCE, JAMES.—Englishman. Flag-captain to Sievers in the Ekaterina, 1716.

LAURIE.—Scotchman. No data.

LESLIE, JAMES.—Scotchman, *circa* 1717.

LITTLE, ROBERT.—Englishman or American. Relative of Rear-admiral Paddon (*q.v.*); came over with his family in 1718, and was made a captain by the Tsar soon afterwards, and appointed to the London (52). He ran this ship aground the same year while cruising—chiefly through nautical ignorance. Condemned by Peter to six months' imprisonment, degraded to youngest lieutenant in the Galley fleet. Reinstated in 1722, New Year's Day.

LOBB, B.—Probably shipbuilder, *circa* 1715.

LOLGNET (*probably* Longley or Langley, or possibly Lockyer).—Captain of the frigate Penderaklia at Gogland, 1788.

LOMAX (or LEAMAN).—Captain of a frigate at Gogland, 1788, and killed in that action.

LORD.—No data.

MACKENZIE.—Scotchman. Lieutenant with Dugdale at Tchesma (*q.v.*). Killed in action then, or shortly afterwards.

MANN.—No data.

MICHELL.—Medical Inspector-General of the Russian Navy *circa* 1790, or later (date uncertain). Retired owing to difficulty with Russian colleagues. Descendants still living in Russia.

MITCHELL.—Vice-admiral in 1799, flying his flag in the Mistisloff at the blockade and capture of the Dutch fleet in the Texel.

MITCHELL.—Lieutenant *circa* 1799, probably son of the above.

NARLAND, STEPHEN.—Commander, 1788.

NELSON.—Englishman. Captain. Brought out to Russia the Strafford (74), 1713. Sat with Peter the Great in the court-martial upon Admiral Kruyis. Captain of the Elias (28) in 1715. Died 1717.

NEY, JOSEPH.—Master shipbuilder. At Taveroff, 1703. At Kronstadt, 1717–1723.

NIBLETT.—*Tempus* Ekaterina II. No data.

NOBLE.—Captain of the Lansdowne (40) in 1716.

PADDON, GEORGE.—American (New England). Joined 1717, as rear-admiral of the White (1st rank), and hoisted his flag in the Slutelburg. In temporary command of the fleet that year, but the Russian officers refused to obey him. In 1719 his wife and family came to Russia from Copenhagen. In the early winter of that year he died.

PAPAGOY.—American (New Yorker). Captain of the Standard (24) in 1713 in the action off Gogland. Died 1718.

PEEL, JAMES.—No data.

PEKIN (PETERKIN *probably*).—Captain of the St. Nikolia (108) at Viborg, 1790.

PERRY, JOHN.—Captain. Born at Rodborough, Gloucestershire, England, 1670. Entered British Navy. In 1690 was wounded. In 1693 lost the Cygnet fire-ship, and dismissed the English service. Arrived in Russia 1698, when he was engaged as a civil engineer at £300 a year. He superintended the Volga-Don Canal and a great many other works, but in fourteen years only once received his salary. Returned to England in 1712, and in 1716 published *The State of Russia under the present Czar*. Died 1732.

PRESTON, JAMES.—Probably Scotch. Captain of the Ivan Christil at the battle of Viborg, 1790.

PURNELL.—Employed to bring over foreign-built ships, 1714.

Brought Le Firme from England, and narrowly escaped capture by Swedes.

RAMSEY.—Scotchman. Imported by Peter the Great. Made a Master Builder, 1719. Chief Constructor, St. Petersburg, 1722.

RUE (or REW), THOMAS.—Englishman. Came to Russia 1714 as captain of a contract-built English ship, Ormonde (50). Left Russian service in 1717.

SABINE.—*Circa* 1715. No data.

SADLER.—American or English. Served 1788–90.

SALIS (or DE SALIS).—No data.

SAUNDERS.—Probably Scotch. Brought over from Holland with Gordon as équipage captain in 1717. In command at Revel, 1718, whence he was removed in consequence of his quarrels with another captain, Van Hofft, a Dutchman. Flew his broad pennant in the Neptunus (70) in 1719. In the dispute between Gordon and Sievers (*see* Gordon), he joined Sievers' party.

SEELEY, EDWARD.—From New York, 1780. No other data.

SEROCOLD, JOHN.—Kapitan-lieutenant in 1717.

SHANE.—No data.

SIMPSON, ANDREW. — Scotchman. Senior captain of four ships that were sent to Constantinople from Azov after the peace which entailed the destruction and capitulation of the Black Sea Fleet. In 1711 went to Archangel to bring ships to the Baltic. Short of men, he impressed the crews of foreign merchantmen, 1713. A Swedish squadron tried to intercept his ship, the St. Mihail. Left the Russian service 1714.

SIMS.—American. Lieutenant in 1790.

SIMSON.—*Circa* 1790.

SIMSON (another).—No data.

SMITH.—Englishman. Lieutenant I.R.N. in 1710, when he was in command of a *snow*. He was sent into Viborg under a flag of truce, and made prisoner by the Swedes.

SMITH (another).—*Tempus* Ekaterina II. No data.

STUBBS.—Englishman. Captain at Kronstadt, 1722.

Tait, George.—Captain of the Kir Ivan at Gogland and Viborg, 1790. No other details.

Tennyson.—*See* Dennison.

Thesiger, Sir F.—Ex-British naval officer, entered the Russian service in 1788. Captain of the Patria frigate at Gogland, Viborg, and Svenksund, 1790. He distinguished himself in the latter action.

Tillard, P.—No data.

Todd, James (known as Tott).—Scotchman. Captain of the Retvisan at Gogland, 1788. Brother or cousin of Captain Todd, Royal Navy, captain of the Queen Charlotte when she was burned.

Trevennen, Jacob.—Cornishman. Captain of the Netromenia at Viborg, etc., 1790, where he was badly wounded.

Treveyer (*probably* Trevegar). Cornishman. Captain of the Prince Gustaf (a captured Swedish 70-gun ship) at Viborg, 1790.

Tynan, P.—Irishman (?). No data.

Urquhart, Adam.—Scotchman. Kapitan-lieutenant, 1717. Captain of the Portsmouth, 1719. He ran on a sandbank a little west of Kronstadt, and a mast falling on him, he was killed.

Usher.—Englishman. *Tempus* Ekaterina II. No data.

Vaughan.—Englishman. Sent to Holland to bring over the Pearl in 1714. Driven into Pernau by the Swedes. Équipage captain of the Narva (60) in 1714. This ship was struck by lightning and blew up in Kronstadt roads in the following year, when Vaughan and most of the crew perished.

Waldron, John.—England (West). Captain of the Hobet (16) in 1711. Left the service 1713.

Webb.—Shipbuilder. Came from Deptford with Peter the Great.

Wells.—No data.

Wesley (or Worsley).—No data. Probably shipbuilder.

West, Jonas.—American. Lieutenant, 1790.

Wright.—Englishman. Master mastmaker. Came over from Deptford with Peter the Great.

# RELATIONS BETWEEN BRITISH AND RUSSIAN OR OTHER FOREIGN OFFICERS IN THE IMPERIAL RUSSIAN NAVY IN THE EIGHTEENTH CENTURY

IN the body of this work, and also in the foregoing biographical notes, occasional references have been made to "differences" between our countrymen and the Russians. Some further investigation of this matter may be interesting.

Properly to appreciate the matter, it is better to divide British service in the Russian Navy into its two main periods—the reign of Peter the Great and that of Ekaterina the Great, between which periods, so far as the greater number were concerned, two generations passed. In the first period internal evidence on the British side points to the blame lying in that quarter; the second may possibly be in a not-proven condition either way.

In Peter the Great's reign, in nearly every case the British officers were attainted persons—Jacobites and the like. Now the man who "rises" for any cause, be it "freedom," or loyalty to an exiled king, or anything else, is and has been, in nineteen cases out of twenty, a turbulent person, who has acted as he has from natural inclination to disturbance, and the "cause" has merely been a convenient peg. Gordon, on the evidence of his own countrymen,[1] was a turbulent mischief-maker; and in a purely personal dispute between himself and Sievers, did not hesitate to make it a racial matter between the British and the other foreigners in the Russian service.[2] Although Peter was favourable to his foreign officers, the people about the court were not, while naturally patriotism played its part with Russian-born officers. They did not love the foreigners in their midst; and in addition to the fact of this foreigner question there was a strong conservative feeling in Russia against Peter's innovations. The great Tsar did not *lead* Russia: he *drove* it.

The Russian officers, with the exception of Aprāksin and one or two others, were very inefficient, even if the description of them by the contemporary Englishman in Vol. XV. of the Navy Records Society's publication is exaggerated.[3] On

[1] *The Russian Fleet under Peter the Great.*

[2] A precisely similar state of affairs existed in the Chinese Navy prior to the Chino-Japanese War: British and Americans were at daggers-drawn with the Germans.

[3] "There are some men of capacity also amongst the Russians, but as to the generality of these, in the capacity of lieutenants, foreigners ever desire to leave 'em ashore; seeing in good weather their pride is insupportable, taking great state upon them, and arrogating much attendance; but in bad weather, or any extremity, are sick abed, when they should be serviceable . . . thunderstruck with the terror of an approaching engagement . . . Russians, whose known property it is ever to recoil from danger, even when immediate presence of mind is requisite to repel an otherwise unavoidable ruin."

the other hand, it is a regrettable fact that the attainted Jacobites, officers dismissed the British Navy by court-martial, and all the rest of Peter's foreigners, were in exceedingly few cases any better than the Russians.[1] Batting lost his ship at Kronstadt, Lane ran the London aground through ignorance, Urquhart did the same with the Portsmouth, Gordon never distinguished himself save at squabbling, Paddon was unable to keep discipline. Of other foreigners, Kruyis the Norwegian and Scheltinga the Dutchman are two notorious instances of incompetence. Through ignorance and carelessness foreigners were always getting their ships on sandbanks, and Deane, Delap, Lane, and Lacy were the only Britishers who distinguished themselves to any degree. Sievers was the only other foreigner of note. If the Russians failed to appreciate them generally, the foreigners undoubtedly had chiefly themselves to thank: there were not more than half a dozen who would have been suffered to remain had they been in the British Navy at that time. There is another side to the picture. Their pay was uncertain,[2] and the Russian officers'

[1] Again a comparison with the Chinese Navy may be made. Japanese officers have told me that the mass of the "Westerners" in the Chinese service (other than officers of the British Navy lent for service) were more or less the dregs of the West, so far as capacity went. It is certainly not to Japanese interests to exaggerate this incapacity, so it may be taken as a fact were there no other evidence.

[2] "The usage of foreigners in Russia is too notorious for any to go there unless incapacitated to live in other countries; and the want of a due provision for men disabled by age or accidents is still an

attitude[1] in fomenting their disputes between themselves annoyed them. They further claimed to leave when they chose: Peter's great idea was to enlist them permanently. Still there is absolutely no doubt but that the Tsar treated them better than they deserved.

The shipbuilders, engaged under different conditions, do not seem to have had any disagreements.

There is now Ekaterina the Great's period to consider. Here different conditions obtained. The majority of the Britishers were naval officers, supplied and attached by Ekaterina's request to the British Government. They were an infinitely better lot of men professionally than the attainted Jacobites and officers dismissed by court-martial of Peter the Great's day. They agreed no better with the Russians than their predecessors, and the letter printed on page 637 covers a very general complaint. The chief *pros* and

additional discouragement."—*The Russian Fleet under Peter the Great*, ed. Admiral C. Bridge. See also biographies of Cooper and Lane (a notorious case of *mala fides*).

[1] The following incident, from the battle of Narva, is illustrative of the feeling prevalent in Russia against foreigners :—

" . . . When now the remaining Russian troops found that their line of retreat was cut off, the defence was renewed. The Prince of Croy and General Allart tried to arrange a square of waggons, and pulled forward some guns; but at that moment the long-fostered animosity broke forth against the foreigners, to whom the Russians ascribed the war and all misfortunes, several German officers were murdered, and the Prince of Croy, General Allart, the Polish envoy, von Langen, and some foreign officers were obliged to seek refuge in the Swedish camp in order not to be cut down with the others. . . ."

Carl Eugen, Duke of Croy, was prince of the German Empire.

Allart was probably a Frenchman, but may have been Scotch.

*cons*, so far as I have been able to collect them, are as follows :—

| British Side. | Russian Side. |
|---|---|
| Pay was uncertain. | The British officers considered themselves infinitely more able than their Russian colleagues (as they indeed were), and they let their opinion be clearly visible. |
| Russian officers, from inability or dislike to their British colleagues, refused to co-operate properly. | They frequently did not know Russian. |
| Individual Russians tried to steal the credit of work done by Britishers. | They absolutely ignored Russian custom and sentiment. |
| Paul Jones, the notorious American privateer, was made an admiral, whereat the best part of a hundred Britishers resigned *en masse* as a protest. | |

The problem is a very old one : has always existed, and always will. The interests of mercenaries can never be the same as those of the people employing them, and friction between the units is inevitable. And if the mercenaries are abler than their employers, they are bound to look upon their own interests as the only thing worth the employers' consideration. Peter the Great would probably have done better without any foreigners save instructors in his navy. The same cannot be said of Ekaterina's time : Elphinstone, Greig, Dugdale, and Mackenzie won the battle of Tchesma ; and Elphinstone, but for Orloff's hesitation, would have taken Constantinople for Russia. In the Swedish War that followed, Greig saved St. Petersburg from the Swedes, for the

Russians by themselves would never have fought the battle of Gogland. Had Greig lived, no Swedes would have got away from Viborg, and the disaster of Svenksund would never have taken place. But neither this nor any other instance can be held to affect the friction, which had deeper causes than dependence or otherwise upon foreigners.

# INDEX TO SUBJECT-MATTER


Abo, 57, 297, 368, 412.
Abrek, the, 297.
Admiral Aprāksin, the, 270.
—— Greig, 167.
—— Korniloff, 244, 290.
—— Lazareff, 167.
—— Nahimoff, 210, 369.
—— Oushakoff, 270.
—— Seniavin, 270.
—— Spiridoff, 167.
—— Tchitchagoff, 167.
Admirals, 463, 472, 501.
Admiralty, the, 446.
—— New, Dockyard, 341.
Alexander, Grand Duke, 339, 414, 436, 460, 514, 554, 567, Appendix.
—— Nevski, 40.
—— I., 115, 118 *et seq.*
—— II., the, 229, 432.
—— III., the 544.
Alexei, Grand Duke, 41, 294, 447, 463, 567, Appendix.
Alma, battle of the, 144.
American officers in Russian Navy, 714.
—— influence on ship designs, 156, 160.
Amiens, war after Peace of, 118.
Andrei Pervoswanni, the, 422.
Anglo-Russian relations, 549.
Antiquity of Russian fleet, 23.
Aprāksin, General Admiral Graf, 55 *et seq.*, 463.
—— the, 270, 343,
Archangel, 40 *et seq.*, 48.
Armed neutrality, the, 87, 113.
Armoured cruisers, 171, 430.
Artillery corps in 1859, 152.
—— —— founded. *See* also Guns.
Asiatic dockyards, 394.
Askold, the, 332.
Aspe, action at, 124.
Assar-i-Chevket, attack on the, 195.
Astrabad, 412.
Attachés, Russian Naval, 451.
Aurora, the, 349.
Azov, 45, 87.

Baku, 412.
Baltic, the, 44, 56, 78.
—— Euxine Canal, the 415.
Baltic powers and provinces, 47.
—— Works described, 356.
Barbarous outrages by Russian petty fleet, 708.
Baronovski guns, 307.
Battles of Aaland, 97.
—— Aspe, 124.
—— Byzantium, 24 *et seq.*
—— Chios, 82.
—— Colberg, 76.
—— Dorpt, 53.
—— Gangoot, 61.
—— Gogland, 91 (*i.e.* Kalboden), 623.
—— Hangö-ued, 61.
—— Högland, 91.
—— Lemnos, 86.
—— Munderos, 86.
—— Öland, 97.
—— Revel, 101.
—— Sissoi Veliky, 108.
—— Sveaborg, 97.
—— Svenksund, 107, 670.
—— Tchesma, 84.
—— Viborg, 102, 664.
Battleships, new, 417.
Batûm, 189, 199, 412.
Bayan, the, 328.
Belleville boilers, 260, 286, 530
Berdau rifle, 526.
Black Sea, 72, 190.
—— —— dockyards, 403.
—— —— fleet, 492.
—— —— —— equipages of, 490.
—— —— in 1855, 135.
—— —— Steam Navigation Co., 334.
Bluejackets, Russian, 372, 517.
Borodino, the, 412.
Breech system, Canet, 382.
British assistance to Russia, 80, 82.
—— allied with Russia, 120, 126.
—— bluejackets' view on Russian ones, 476.
—— do work at Tchesma, 83.
—— hostilities with, 117, 147.
—— officers and Russian ones, 515, 577.
—— officers in Russian service, 84, 155.
—— ports Russian bases, 87.
—— prestige, 590.
—— workman, 530.

Building slips, 341, 358.
Byzantium, 24, 31, 585.

CANALS, Russian system of, 413, 554.
Canet guns, 382.
Captains, 460.
Carl, Prince, of Sweden, 97.
Caspian, the, 475.
—— equipages of, 511.
—— fleet, 490.
—— naval command of, secured, 133.
Catherine I., 71.
—— II. (the Great) (Ekaterina), 76 *et seq.*
Catherine II., the, 223.
Characteristics of Russian officers, 513.
—— —— men, 517.
Charles XII. of Sweden, 46 *et seq.*
China and Russia, 148, 402, 578.
Circular ironclads, 172, 434.
—— yacht, 244.
Civil branches, 469.
Club, Naval, at Kronstadt, 385.
Coast-defence ships, 167, 270.
—— extension, Russia's weakness, 148.
—— flotillas. *See* Petty Fleets.
Commanders, 460.
Commissioning ships, system of, 487.
Condition of Russian fleet in 1859, 151.
Conductors, 468.
Constantinople, Russian attacks on, 24.
—— —— desire for, 241, 585.
—— —— probabilities of securing, 585.
Corea, 399.
Corporals, 468, 505.
Crimea, 87, 140, 387, 404.
Cronstadt, Cronslot. *See* Kronstadt.
Customs of Russians, 517.

DAMAGE to ships at Sinope, 136.
Danube, operations on, 126, 196.
Dardanelles, British fleet forces, 120, 202.
—— Russia kept out of, by old forts whitewashed, 85, 584.
—— opened to Russia, 87.
Deane, Captain, 716.
Destroyers, 427.
De Tott fortifies Dardanelles, 85.
Diana, the, 349.
Disaster on board Sissoi Veliky, 286.
Discipline, 494.
Djidjit, the, 177, 219, 521.
—— torpedo boat, 187.
Dmitri Donskoi, the, 208, 290.
Dockyards, Imperial Russian, described, 340 *et seq.*
—— —— administration of, 337.
Dockyardsmen, 355.
Drill, Russian, 385.
Dvenadsat Apostolov, the, 236.

EARLIEST Russian Warship, 29.
Eastern Question, the, 23, 584.
Efstafi, the, 423.
Ekaterina I., 71.
—— II. (the Great), 76 *et seq.*
—— II., the, 223.
Elphinstone, British officer in Russian service, 78, 84, Appendix.
Emperor of Germany, the, 45, 51, 585.
Engineers, 179, 334, 542.
—— naval, problem of, 179, 497.
—— pay, 472.
—— qualifications, 530.
—— uniform, 501.
Entry of men, 464.
—— of officers, 457.
Epaulettes, 508.
Equipages, 340, 485, 488, 511.
Ermak, the, 381.
Expansion, Russian, 598.
Explosive bullets, 383.

FALL of the British Empire, 608.
Far Eastern Question, the, 23, 581.
Figureheads, 378.
Finance, 535.
Finland, 101.
Fir-built Russian ships, 133.
Fire-shell used by Russians, 94.
—— correspondence *re*, Appendix, 630.
First ironclads, 154.
—— ship of modern Russian Navy, 42.
Flags, 481.
Fleet, Russian, at Navarino, 127.
—— —— at Sinôp, 136.
—— —— in 1853, 135.
—— —— in 1859, 151.
—— —— in 1877, 178.
—— —— inactive in Crimean War, why, 144.
—— —— organisation of, 484. *See also* Dockyards, etc.
Floating batteries, 154.
Fondness of Russians for English officers, 515.
France, alliance with, 307.
—— hostilities with, 71, 110, 141.
Franco-Russian alliance, 307.
—— —— Works, 346.
French Navy, Russian estimate of, 602.

GALERNII ISLAND (Galernii Ostrov), 346.
Gangoot, the, 239, 374, 437.
—— —— (old ships), 128, Appendix.
—— battle of, 61.
General Admiral, the, 447.
—— —— the (ship), 171.
—— —— Graf Aprăk in, the, 270.
Georgi Pobedonosetz, the, 265, 432.
Germany, 335, 415, 581, 602.
Giliak, the, 324.
Gogland, battle of, 96.

Gollovin, 75.
Good service pension fund, 478.
Gordon (Scotchman in Russian service), 70 *et seq.*
Greek fire, 34.
Greig, Samuel (Scotchman in Russian service), 77 *et seq.*, 364, Appendix.
—— —— death of, 97.
—— —— letters written by, 630.
—— —— reasons alleged as to his death, 637.
—— —— son of, 719.
—— —— grandson of, 719.
—— —— great-grandson of, 719.
—— the, 167.
Gremiastchy, the, 243.
Griden, the, 297.
Gromoboi, the, 359, 430.
Grosiatschy, the, 243, 437.
Guarde-marines, 454, 545.
Gunnery, Russian, officers, 459.
—— —— school, 381.
—— —— theory of, 350.
Guns, 520.
—— in 1859, 153.
—— modern, list of, 524.
Gyroscopes, 527.

HAMILTON, Admiral Sir R. Vesey, 398.
Hassan of Algiers, 80 *et seq.*
Helsingfors taken, 57.
Hemmema, 100.
Hobart Pasha, 181.

ICE-BREAKERS, 381, 397.
Ijora, 412.
Imperator Alexander II., the, 229, 432.
—— —— III, the, .
—— Nikolai I., the, 229, 370.
—— Paul, the, 418.
Inactive list, the, 464.
Intelligence Department, the British, 298, 449.
—— —— the Russian, 448.
Ironclad, first Russian, 154.
Ivan VI., 74.
Ivan (Russian bluejacket), 518.
Izmurud, the, 420.

JANE Naval War Game, the, 264, 385, 523, 572.
Japan, 335, 373, 396, 399, 401, 448, 581, 603.
Jaroslav. *See* Yaroslav.
Jemtchug, the, 420.
John Zlatoust, the, 418.

KAGUL, the, 423.
Kapitan-lieutenant Kazarski, the, 297.
—— Saken, the, 251.
Kapitans, 460.
Kazarski, 130.
Kertch, 86.
Khrabry, the, 286.
Kinburn, 87, 88.
Kniaz Potemkin Tavritchesky, 410.
—— Suvaroff, the, 421.
Korniloff, Admiral, 144.
——, the, 244, 290.
Kronstadt, 331, 332, 366, 459.
—— dockyard described, 366 *et seq.*
Kruse, Admiral, 102.
Kruyis, Admiral, 57.

LEMNOS, Orloff defeated at, 86.
——, Russian victory off, 121.
Letter, Admiral Greig to Prince Carl, 630.
—— Admiral Saumarez to King of Sweden, 680.
—— Peter the Great to King of Sweden, 617.
—— Prince Carl of Sweden to Admiral Greig, 634.
Levant, the Russians in, 118.
Libau, 391.
Lieutenant Ilyin, the, 250.
Lieutenants, 459.
Liljehorn fails to fight at Öland, 99.
Liquid fuel, 293, 532.
"Little Englanders," 607.
Lividia, the, 221.
Lodkys (Lodjas), 48, 49.
Lutfi Djel, the, sunk, 185.

MAGNETIC shell, 383.
Makaroff, 95.
—— the present admiral, 188 *et seq.*
Malta, Russian designs on, 113.
Marines, 152, 178.
Meals, 477.
Mediterranean, Russian ships in, 78.
Memel taken, 75.
Men, entry of, 465.
Mentschikoff, 144 *et seq.*
Minin, the, 168, 203, 370.
Mishukoff waiting to fight the British fleet, 76.
Mistake in dealing with Russia, our, 589.
Mitchmen 458.
—— pay of, 472.
—— uniform, 501.

NAHIMOFF, 135.
—— the, 210, 369.
Napoleon, 23, 117.
Narva, battle of, 46.
Naval Attachés, 451.
—— War Game, 264, 385, 523.
Navārin, the, 252.
Navarino, battle of, 128.
Navigators, 459.
Navy Staff, the, 152, 448.
Nelson and the Russians, 111 *et seq.*
—— a captain (in Russian service), 722.
New Admiralty Dockyard, 341.

Niclausse boilers, 422, 543.
Nikolai I., the, 229, 370.
Norris, Sir John, 62 *et seq.*
Novgorod, 172.
Novik, the, 427.

OBUKHOFF guns, 320, 520, 534.
Odessa, 333.
—— bombarded, 142.
Officers, Russian, 458, 472, 494, 501, 584.
Official Reports, etc.—
On battle of Gogland, 623.
—— —— Kalboden, 623.
—— —— Oland, 648.
—— —— Viborg, 661.
—— surrender of the Prins Gustav, 645.
—— —— —— Vladimir, 637.
Oranienbaum, 379, 45[illegible].
Orel, the, 747.
Organisation, 484.
Orloff, Admiral Count, 79 *et seq.*, 374.
Osliabia, the, 324, 343.
Otchakoff, the, 420.
Otvajny, the, 243.
Oushakoff, 111.
—— the, 270.

PALLADA, the, 349.
Pāmiat Azova, the, 129.
Paul, Tsar, 110.
Pay of Russian Admirals, 472.
—— —— men, 473.
—— —— officers, 472.
—— in lieu of rations, 473.
—— sea, 471.
—— shore, 475.
Peace Conference, 560, 587.
—— Russian desire for, 552, 597.
—— Society, the, 141.
Peculation, Russian, 435, 447.
Peipus, battles on Lake, 41, 48.
Pensions, 478.
Pereseviet, the, 29, 154, 324, 373.
Permit to view Russian dockyards, 345.
Persian Gulf, Russia in the, 335.
Personal characteristics, 513.
Personnel, Russian, 152, 178, 484.
Peter III., 76.
—— Alexeievitch Mihailoff. *See* Peter the Great.
—— the Great, 41, 44 *et seq.*, 70, 545.
Peter Veliky, the, 370.
Petersburg (Péterboorg), 51 *et seq.*
—— dockyards of, 341 *et seq.*
Petropavlovsk, 147.
—— the, 311.
Petty fleets, 100, 124, Appendix.
—— officers, 468.
Polarnia, Sviezda, the, 307.
Police, Russian, 379.
Poltāva, the, 308.
Poltāva, the battle of, 55.
Popieda, the, 531.
Popoffkas, 172, 443.
Port Arthur, 335, 399.
—— Baltic captured, 101.
Portsmouth, Russian fleet at, 79.
Posadnik, the, 297, 367.
Poyema, 100.
Prince Gustav, the, captured, 93.
Punishments, 499.
Putrid Sea, the, crossed dry-shod by Russians, 73.

RAAB chased by Kruyis and Russian fleet, 57.
Rätvesan, the, 96.
Relative rank, 479.
Religion, political value of, 608.
Retvisan, the, 326.
—— disaster, 328, 543.
—— (old), 95, 109.
Revel, 67, 101, 114 *et seq.*, 389.
—— the, 738, 745.
Revolver, Russian, 526.
Rifle, Russian, 526.
Riga, 55.
Rogerswick, 123.
Rossia, the, 263.
Rostislav, the, 154, 286, 293, 408.
—— (old), 82, 93 *et seq.*, 136.
Rotchensalm (Rootensalm) (Svenksund), 100, Appendix.
Rurik, 26.
—— the, 256.
Russian sailors in great demand, 31.
—— warships, early, 29.
"Russian Menace," first appearance of, in England, 89.
Russian weakness in extended coastline, 148.

SAILORS, Russian. *See* Bluejackets.
Saken, 89.
—— the Kapitan, 251.
Scheltinga, 57, 711.
School of gunnery, 381.
Screw ships, 135.
Scythians, 23, 144.
"Sea Power," 144.
Seagoing ships, the first Russian, 52.
Sebastôpol, *See* Sevastôpol.
Seifé, the, sunk by the Xenia, 188.
Seniavin (Senjāvin), 120 *et seq.*
—— the, 270.
Sevastôpol, 31, 134, 403.
—— the, 308.
—— the (old ironclad), 156.
Seven years' war, the, 90 *et seq.*
Shell at Sinôp, 135.
—— guns adopted, 136.
—— illegal use of, alleged, 94, Appendix.
—— in present use, 383, 524.
Shoulder-straps, 508.

Siberia, 147.
Siberian équipage, 487.
—— Fleet, 567.
Sinôp, the, 223.
—— (torpedo boat), 195.
Sinope, battle of, 135.
Sissoi Veliky, battle of, 108.
—— —— the, 286, 454.
—— —— gun accident in, 288.
Slava, the, 417.
Slips, Russian building, 341.
Small-arms, Russian, 526.
Smith, Sir Sidney, 108.
Soap, 476.
Sokol, the (destroyer), 297, 367.
Som, the, 428.
Spies, Russian, 451, 453.
Spiridoff, Admiral, 82 *et seq.*
—— the, 167.
Standart, the (Sthandart), 307.
Steamers, first use of, 134.
Strategy, bad, of allies in Crimean War, 144.
Submarine boats, 368, 428.
Submerged torpedo tubes, 449.
Sudermania (Sundvall). *See* Carl, Prince of Sweden.
Sukum Kalé 192.
Sulina, the, blown up, 197.
Supplementary officers, 429, 545.
Suvoroff, the, 417.
Sveaborg, 97, 147, 412.
Svenksund (*see* also Rotchensalm), 107, Appendix.
Svietlana, the, 293, 349, 372.
Svlod, the, captured by British after a gallant fight, 123.
Sweden, 40, 47–50, 53–70, 74, 76, 88, 91–108, 113, 123–125, 548, 603, 607, Appendix.
Swords, Russian, 526.

TALIENWAN, 337, 402.
Tallow, 477.
Tcharodeika, the, 160
Tchitchagoff, Admiral, 97 *et seq.*
—— the, 167.
Tenedos, Turks captured at, 121.
Torpedo nets 529.
Torpedoes, 183, 298, 468.
Torpedoist, the, 195.
Toulon, Russian fleet at, 307.
Trafalgar, Russian officers at battle of, 128.
Trans-Siberian railway, 334, 395, 399, 587.
Tri Svititelia, the, 279.
Tsar, the, 551.
Tsarvitch, the, 398.
—— (battleship), 423.
Turkey, war with, 44, 55, 73 *et seq.*, 80 *et seq.*, 109, 121, 128, 135, 190, 555, 584, 593.
Turuma, 100.
Types of Russian ships in 1830, 134.

UDEMA, 100.
Uniform, officers', 501.
—— sailors', 505.
United States Navy, 603.
Ushakov. *See* Oushakoff.

VARANGIANS, 26.
Ventilator masts, 323.
Vesey Hamilton, Sir R., 590.
Viborg, 55, 102.
Vice-Admiral Popoff, the, 172.
Views of British bluejackets on Russian ones, 517.
Vitiaz, the, 216.
Vladimir, 34.
—— the, 94.
—— Monomakh, the, 204.
Vladivostok, 148, 333, 335, 394, 590, 599.
Voivoda, the, 297.
Volunteer fleet, 333.
Vsadnik, the, 297.

WACHTMEISTER, the, captured, 64.
Warrant officers, 468.
Wars with Denmark, 71.
—— with England, 117, 141.
—— with France, 71, 110, 141.
—— with Germany, 335.
—— with Japan, 335.
—— with Sweden, 46, 53, 76, 88, 91.
—— with Turkey, 44, 55, 130, 135, 180.
Waryag, the, 424
Watch keeping, 480.
Water-tube boilers, 531.
Wei-hai-wei, 396, 581.
White Sea, the, 147.
Wiborg. *See* Viborg.

XENIA (t. b.), the, 187.

YACHTS, Imperial, 307.
Yarrow, 365.
—— boilers, 297.
Yenikalé, Straits of, 73, 87.

ZENIA, the, sinks the Seifé, 187.